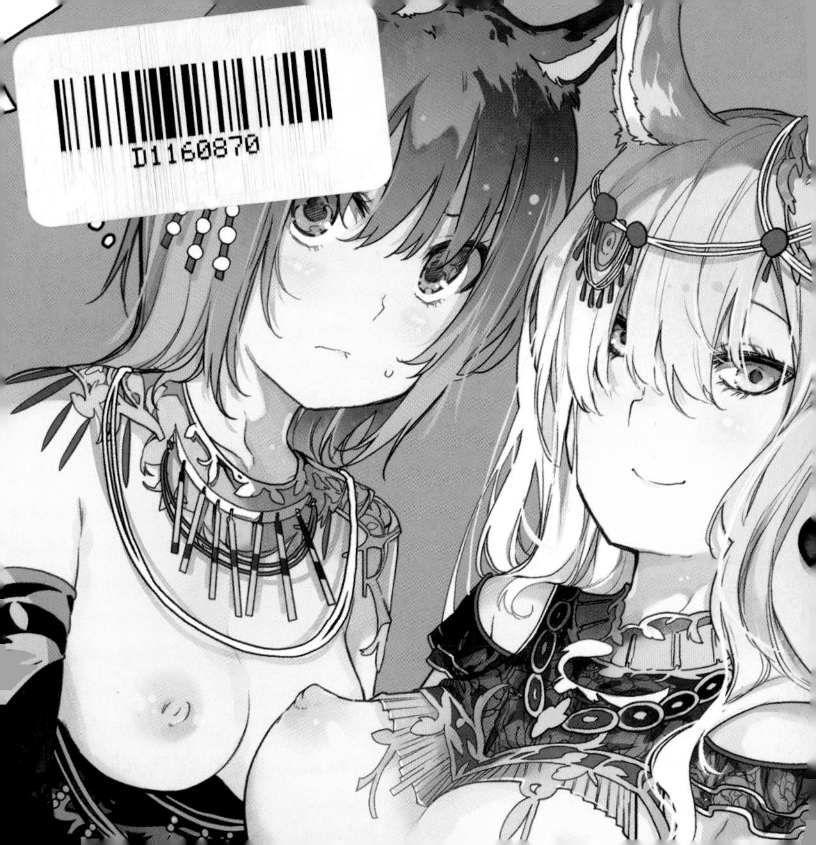

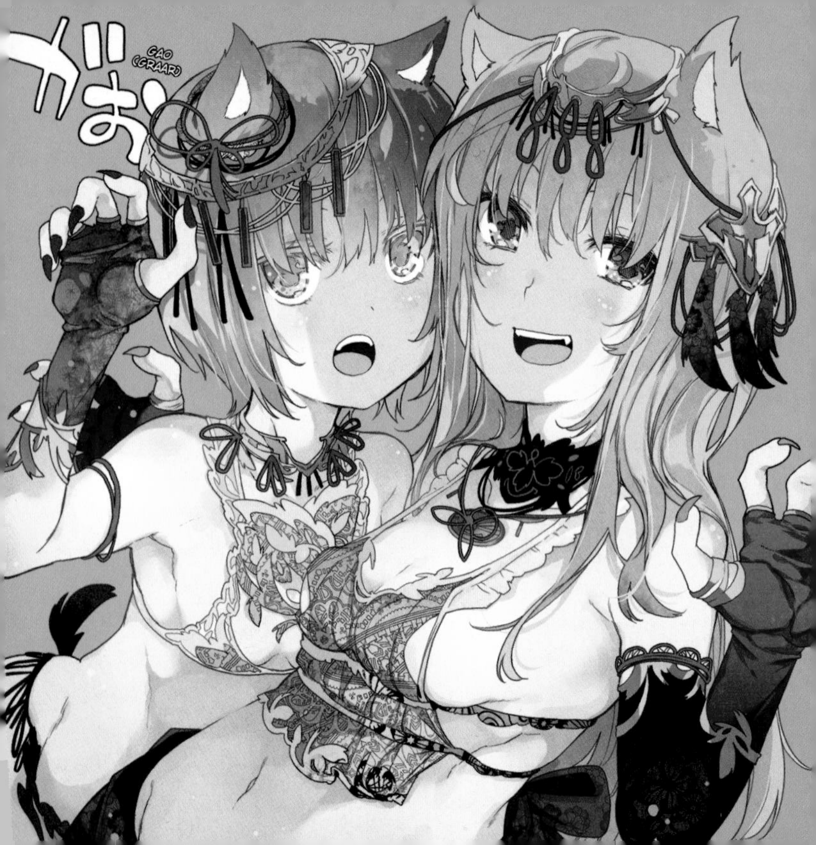
がお
GAO
(GRAAR)

Chapter 61: The Maiden's Family

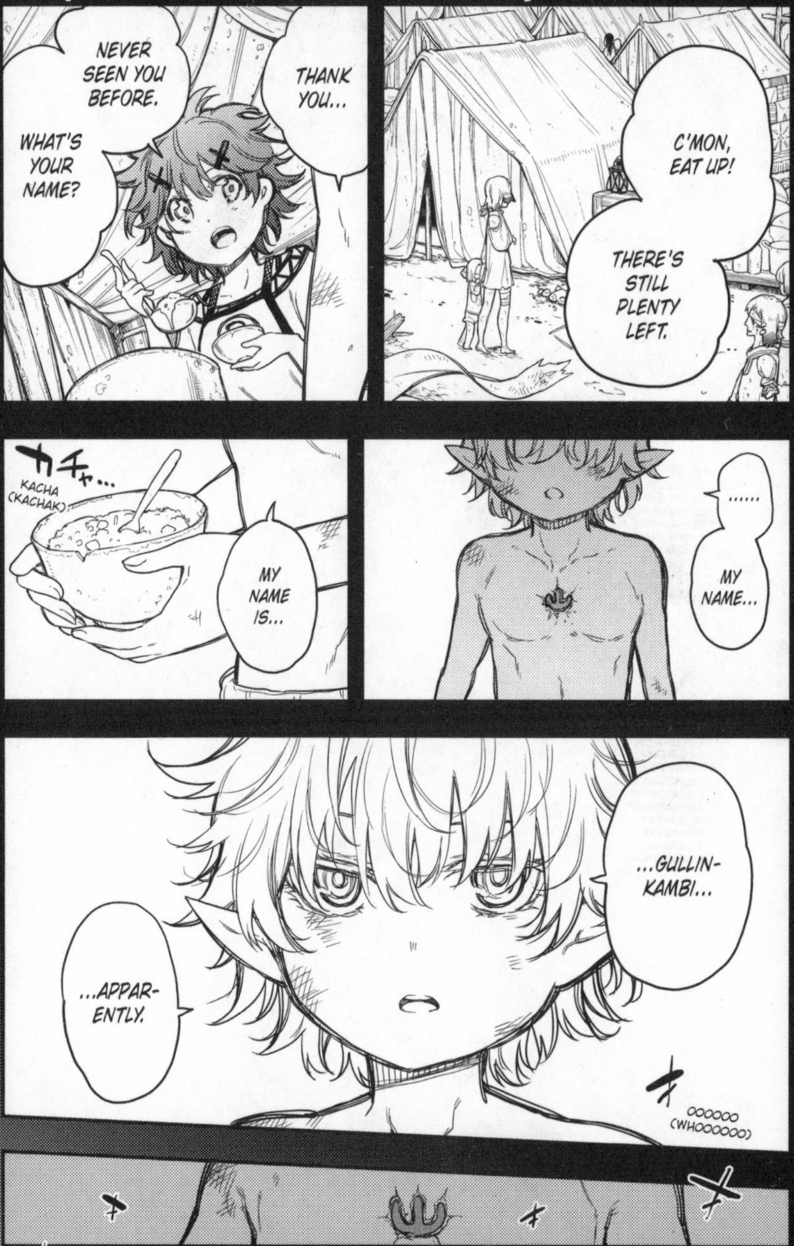
C'MON, EAT UP!
THERE'S STILL PLENTY LEFT.
THANK YOU...
NEVER SEEN YOU BEFORE.
WHAT'S YOUR NAME?
......
MY NAME...
カチャ...
KACHA (KACHAK)
MY NAME IS...
...GULLIN-KAMBI...
...APPAR-ENTLY.
OOOOOO (WHOOOOOO)

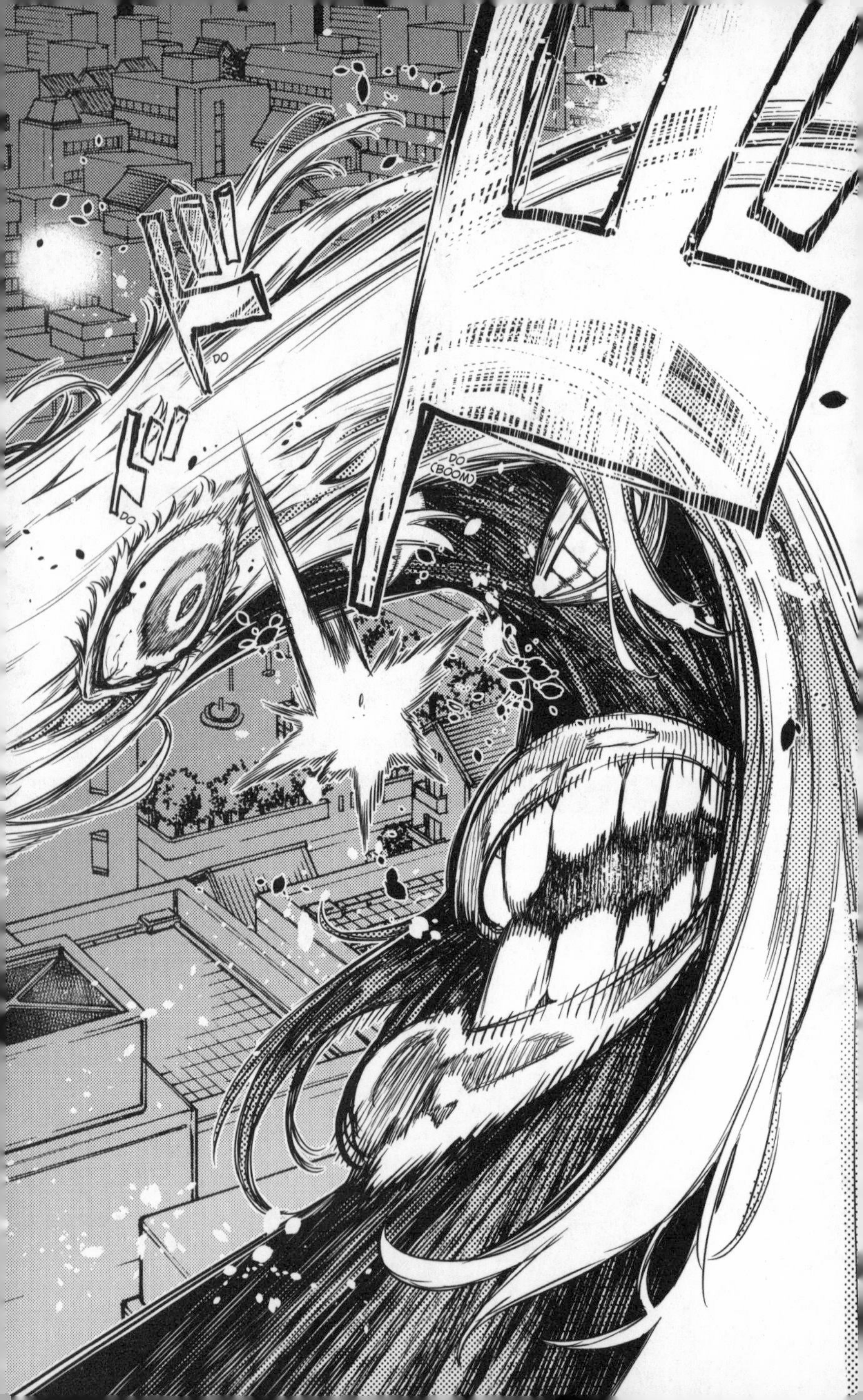
DO (BOOM)
DO
DO

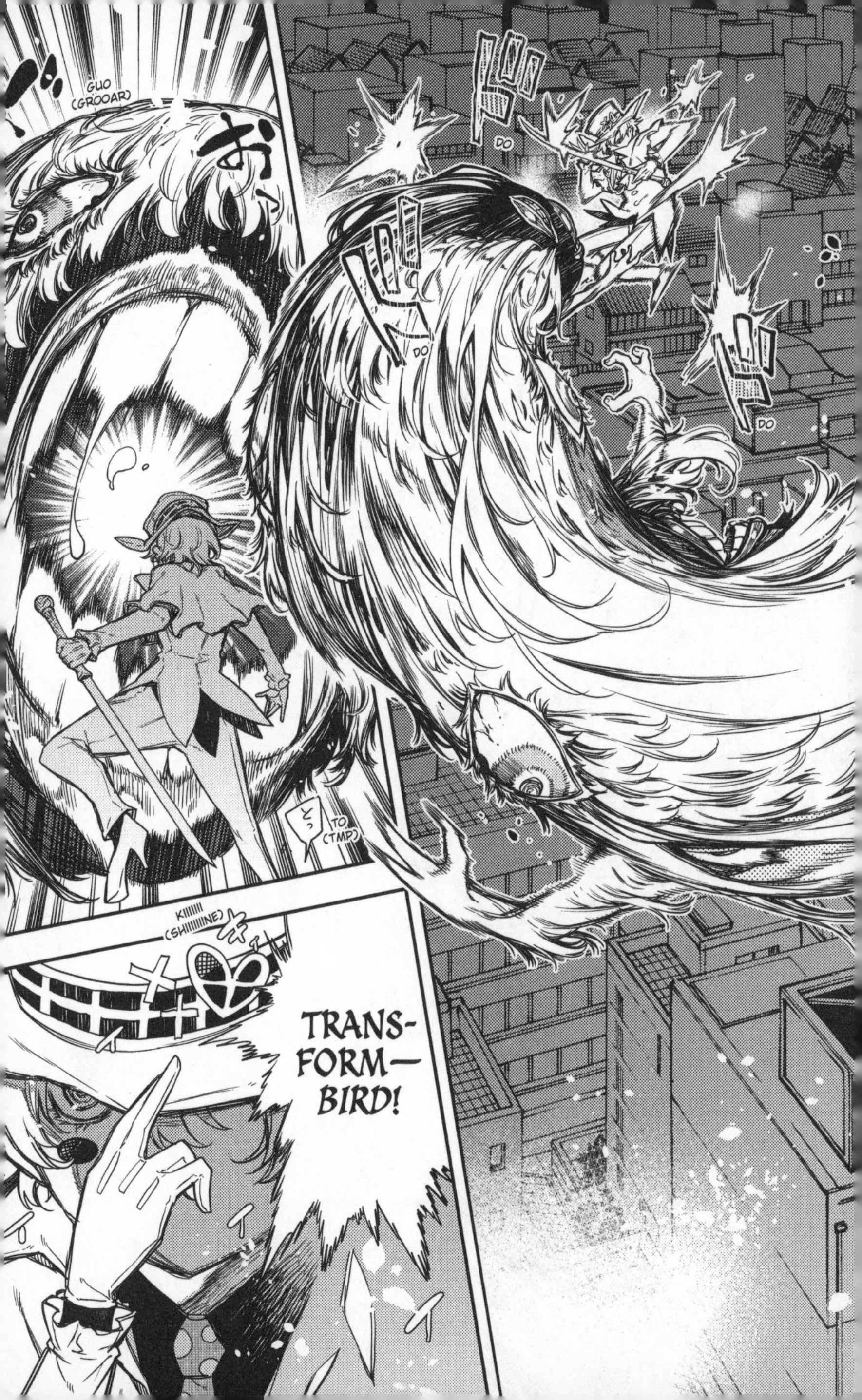
DO
DO
DO
GUO
(GROOAR)
TO
(TMP)
KIIIIIII
(SHIIIIIIIINE)
TRANS-
FORM—
BIRD!

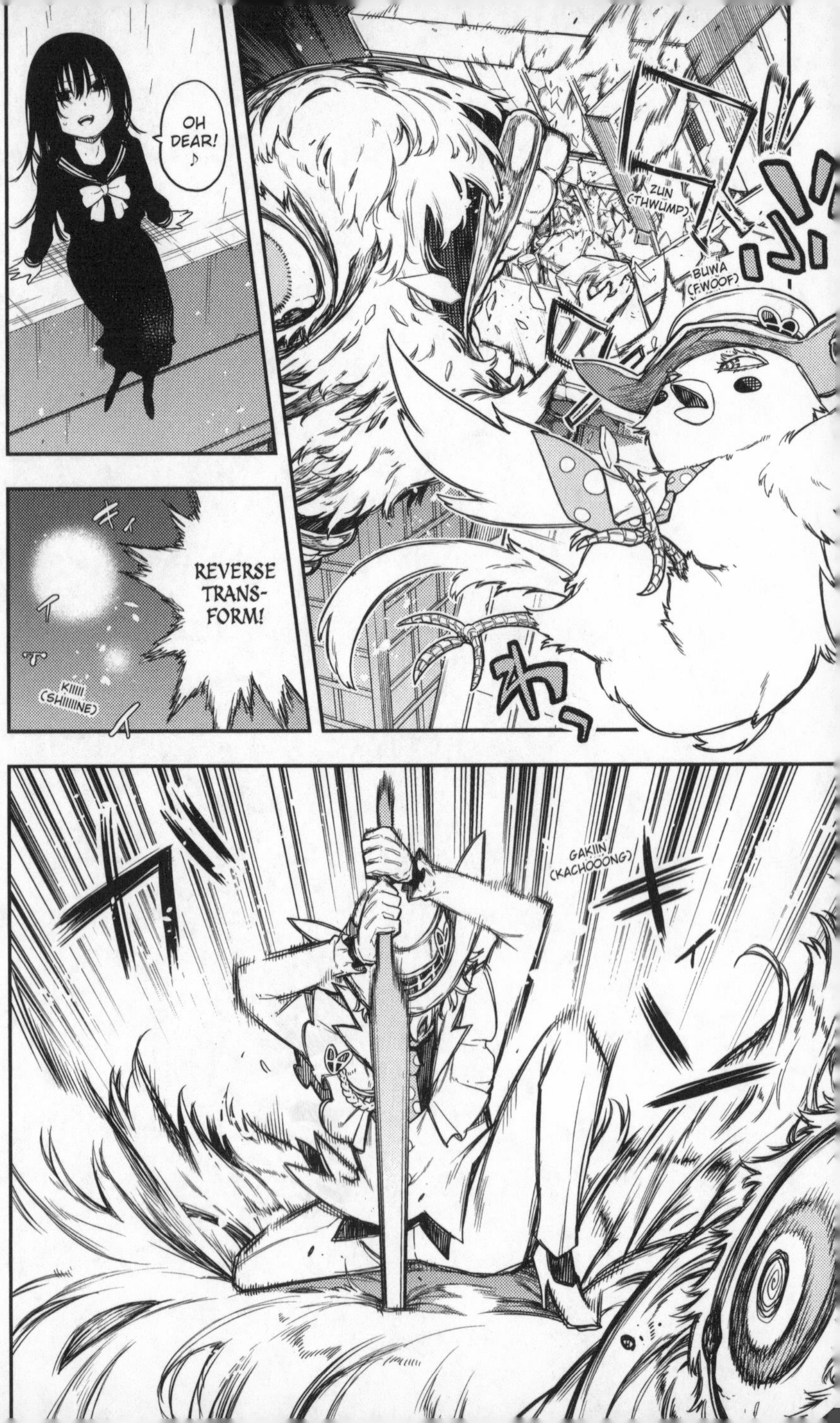
ZUN (THWUMP)
BUWA (F.WOOF)
OH DEAR! ♪
REVERSE TRANS-FORM!
KIIII (SHIIIINE)
GAKIIN (KACHOOONG)

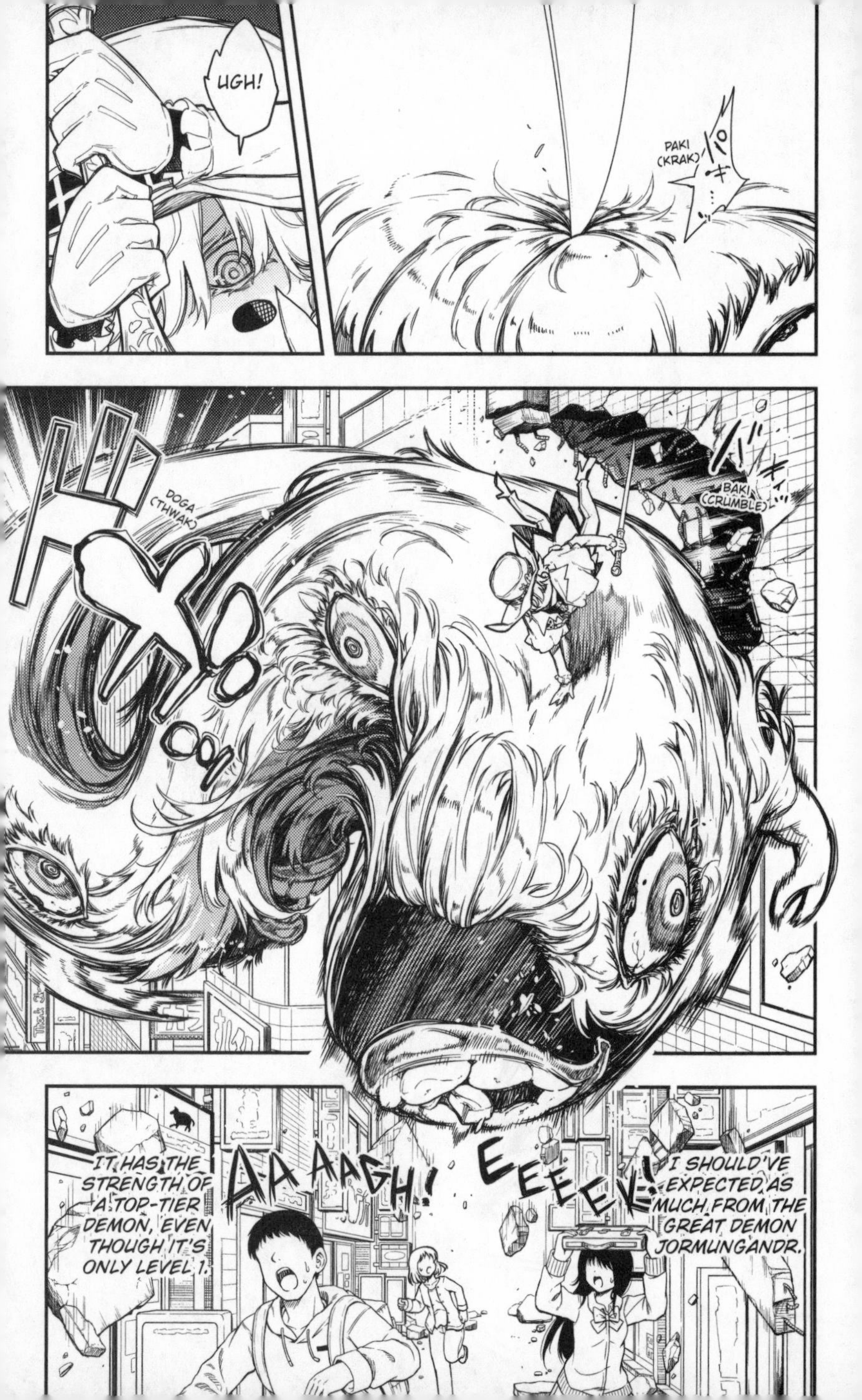
PAKI (KRAK)
UGH!
BAKI (CRUMBLE)
DOGA (THWAK)
I SHOULD'VE EXPECTED AS MUCH FROM THE GREAT DEMON JORMUNGANDR.
EEEEK!
AAAAGH!
IT HAS THE STRENGTH OF A TOP-TIER DEMON, EVEN THOUGH IT'S ONLY LEVEL 1.

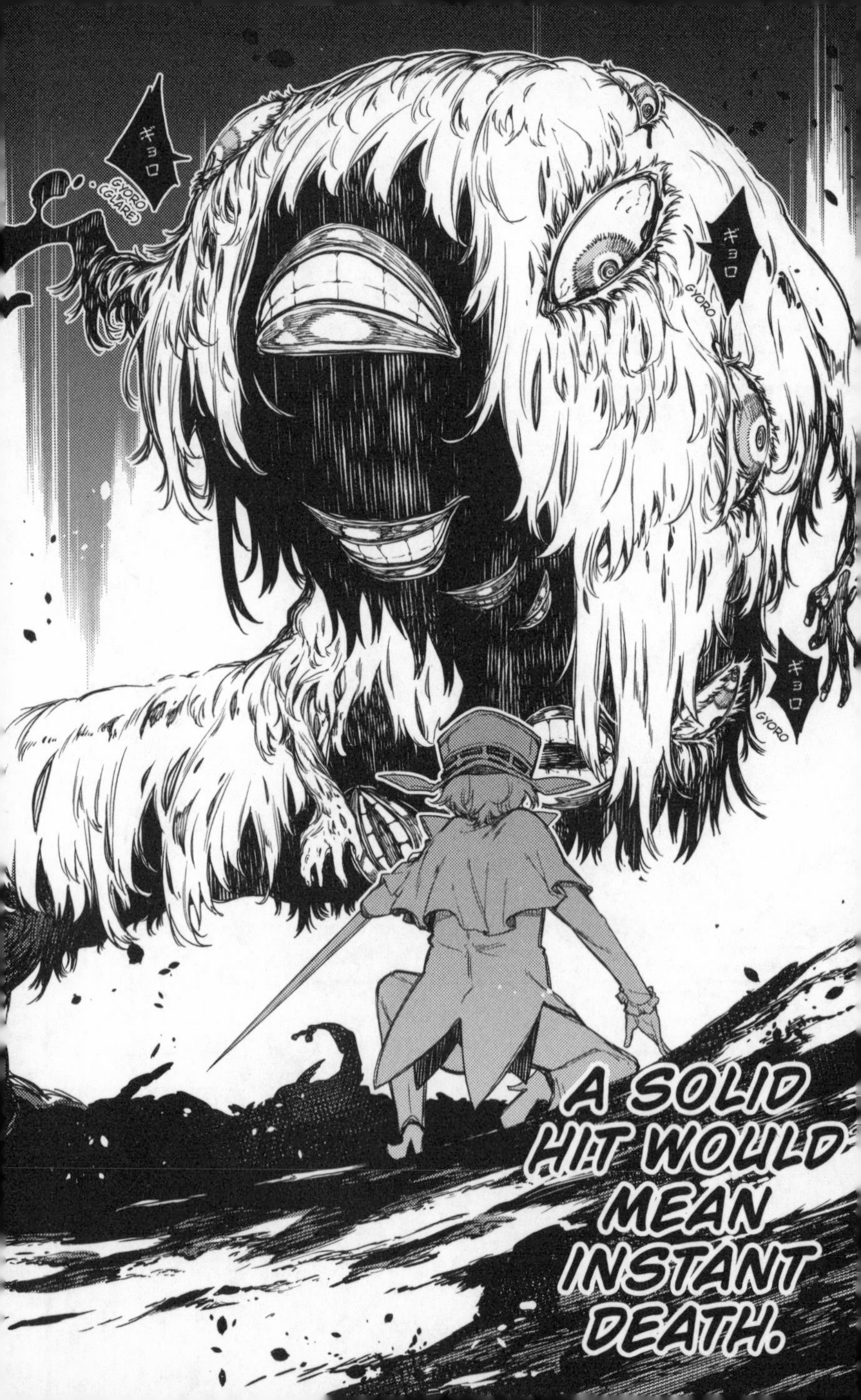
ギョロ
GYORO
ギョロ
GYORO (GLARE)
ギョロ
GYORO
A SOLID HIT WOULD MEAN INSTANT DEATH.

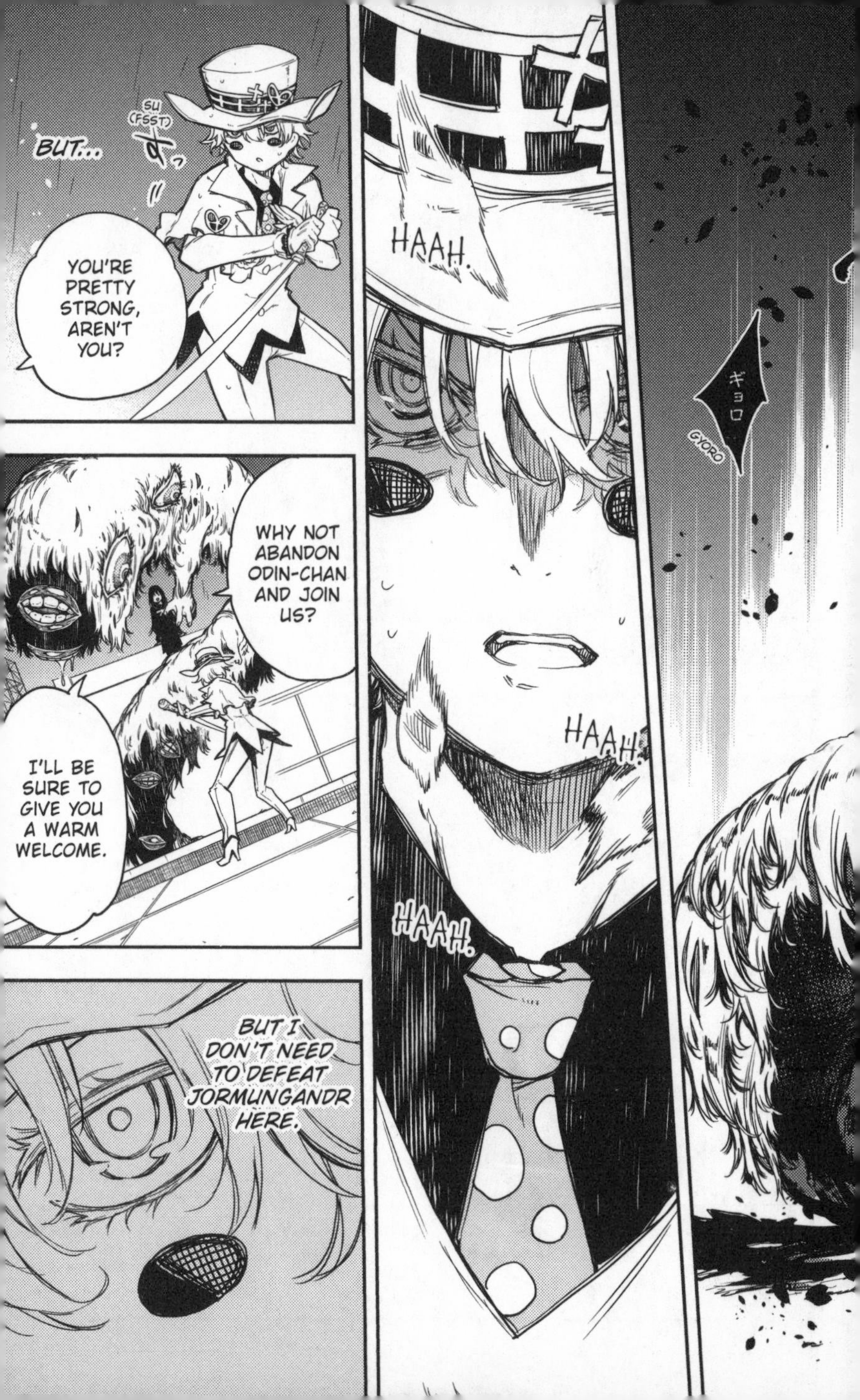
ギョロ
GYORO
HAAH.
HAAH.
HAAH.
BUT...
SU (FSST)
YOU'RE PRETTY STRONG, AREN'T YOU?
WHY NOT ABANDON ODIN-CHAN AND JOIN US?
I'LL BE SURE TO GIVE YOU A WARM WELCOME.
BUT I DON'T NEED TO DEFEAT JORMUNGANDR HERE.

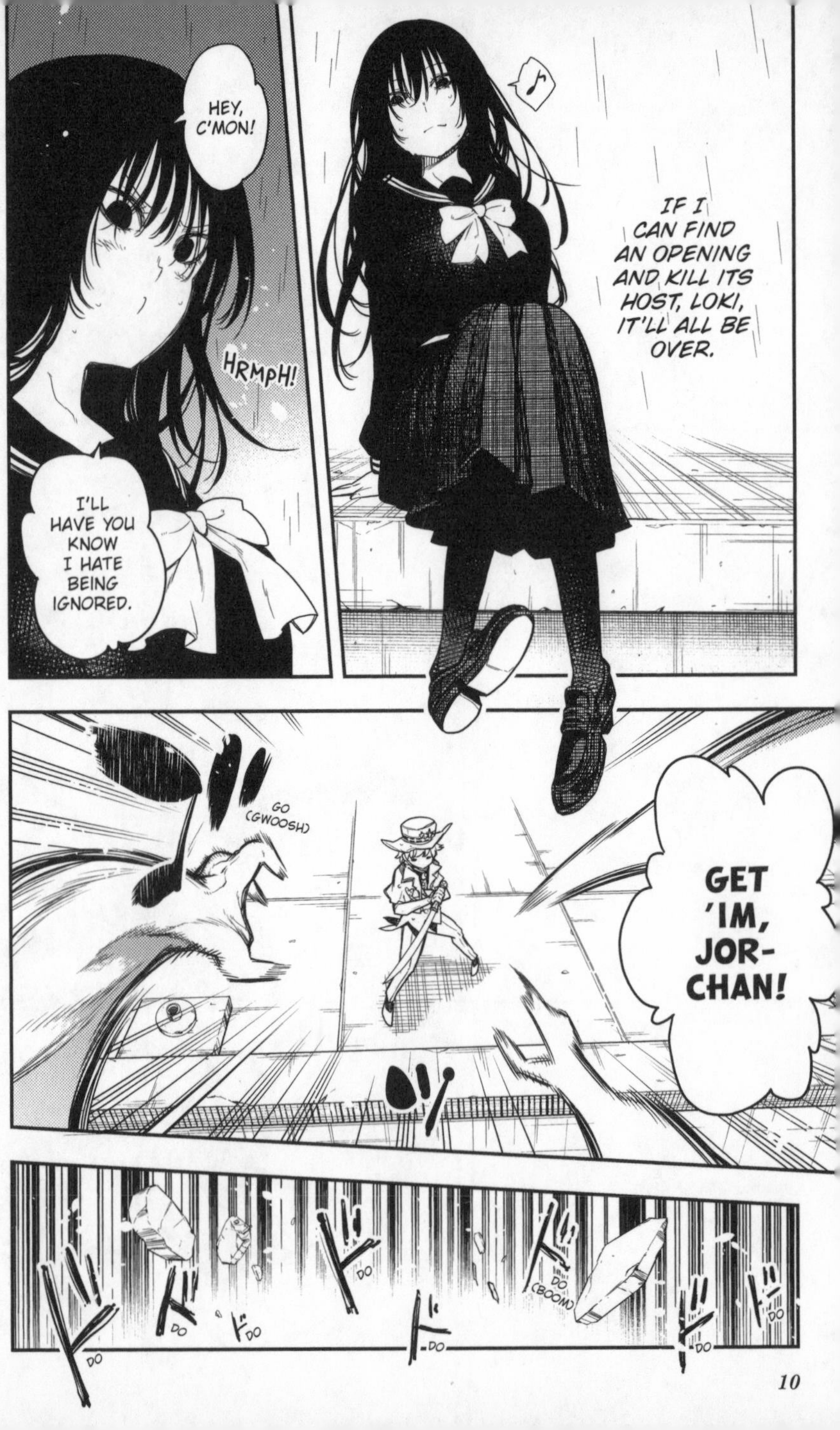
♪
IF I CAN FIND AN OPENING AND KILL ITS HOST, LOKI, IT'LL ALL BE OVER.
HEY, C'MON!
HRMPH!
I'LL HAVE YOU KNOW I HATE BEING IGNORED.
GET 'IM, JOR-CHAN!
GO (GWOOSH)
DO
DO
DO (BOOM)
DO
DO
DO
DO
DO
DO

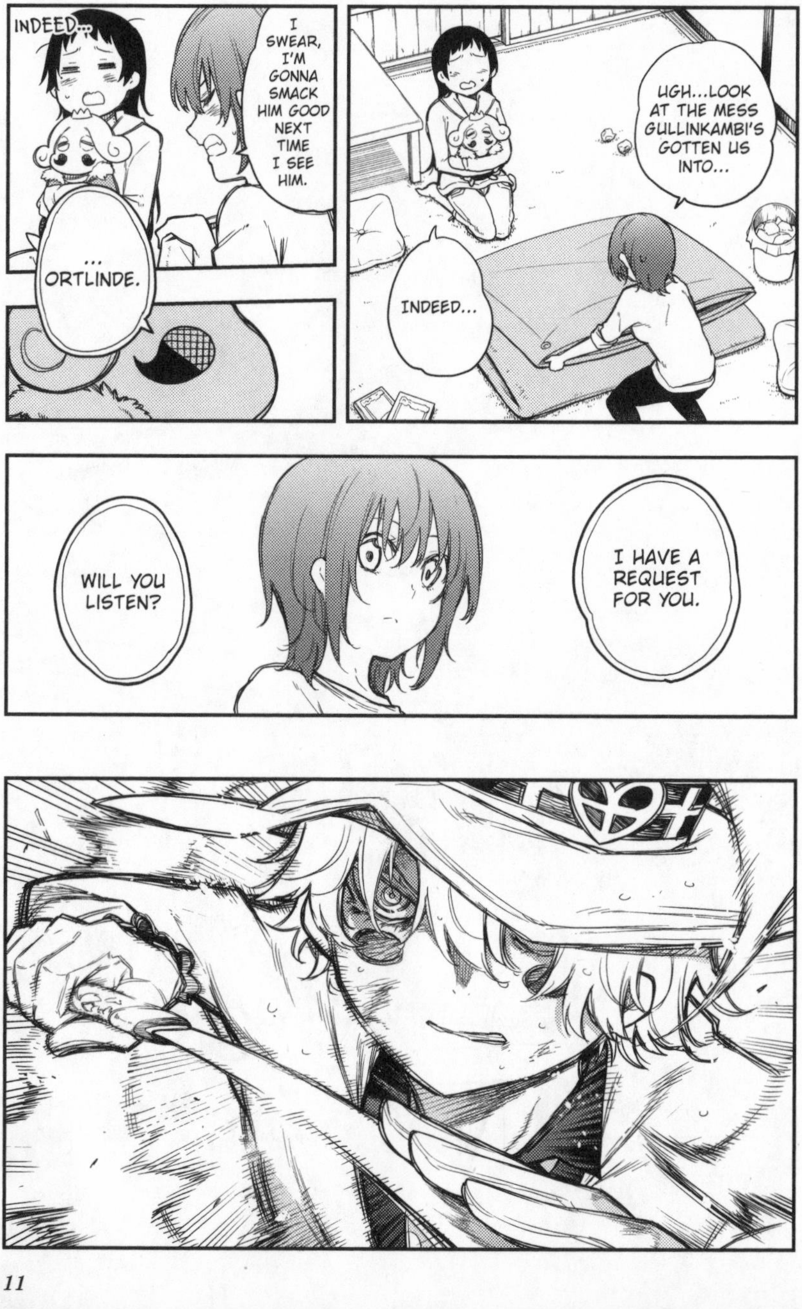
UGH...LOOK AT THE MESS GULLINKAMBI'S GOTTEN US INTO...
INDEED...
I SWEAR, I'M GONNA SMACK HIM GOOD NEXT TIME I SEE HIM.
INDEED...
... ORTLINDE.
I HAVE A REQUEST FOR YOU.
WILL YOU LISTEN?

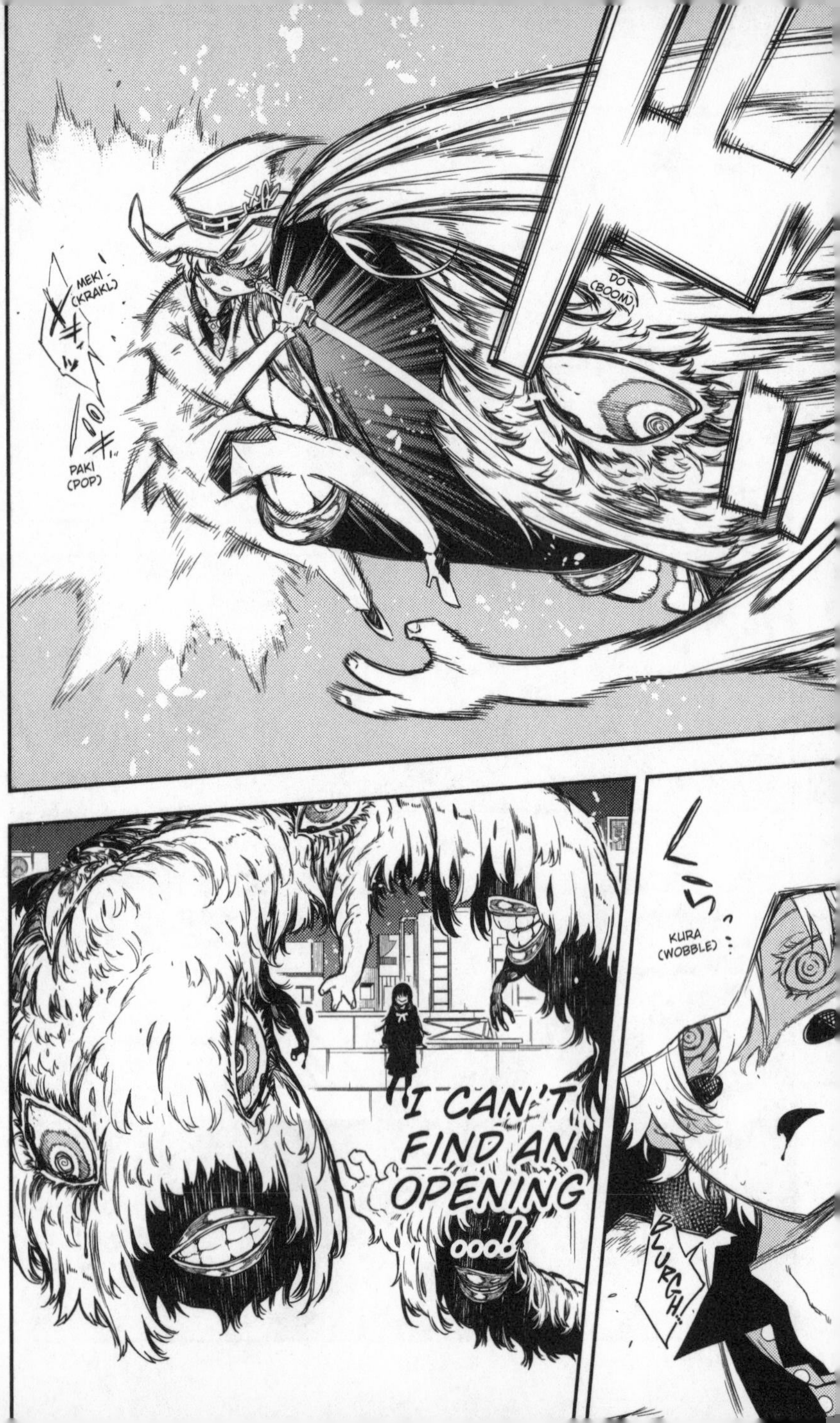
DO (BOOM)
MEKI (KRAKL)
PAKI (POP)
KURA (WOBBLE)
BLURGH!!
I CAN'T FIND AN OPENING OOO!!

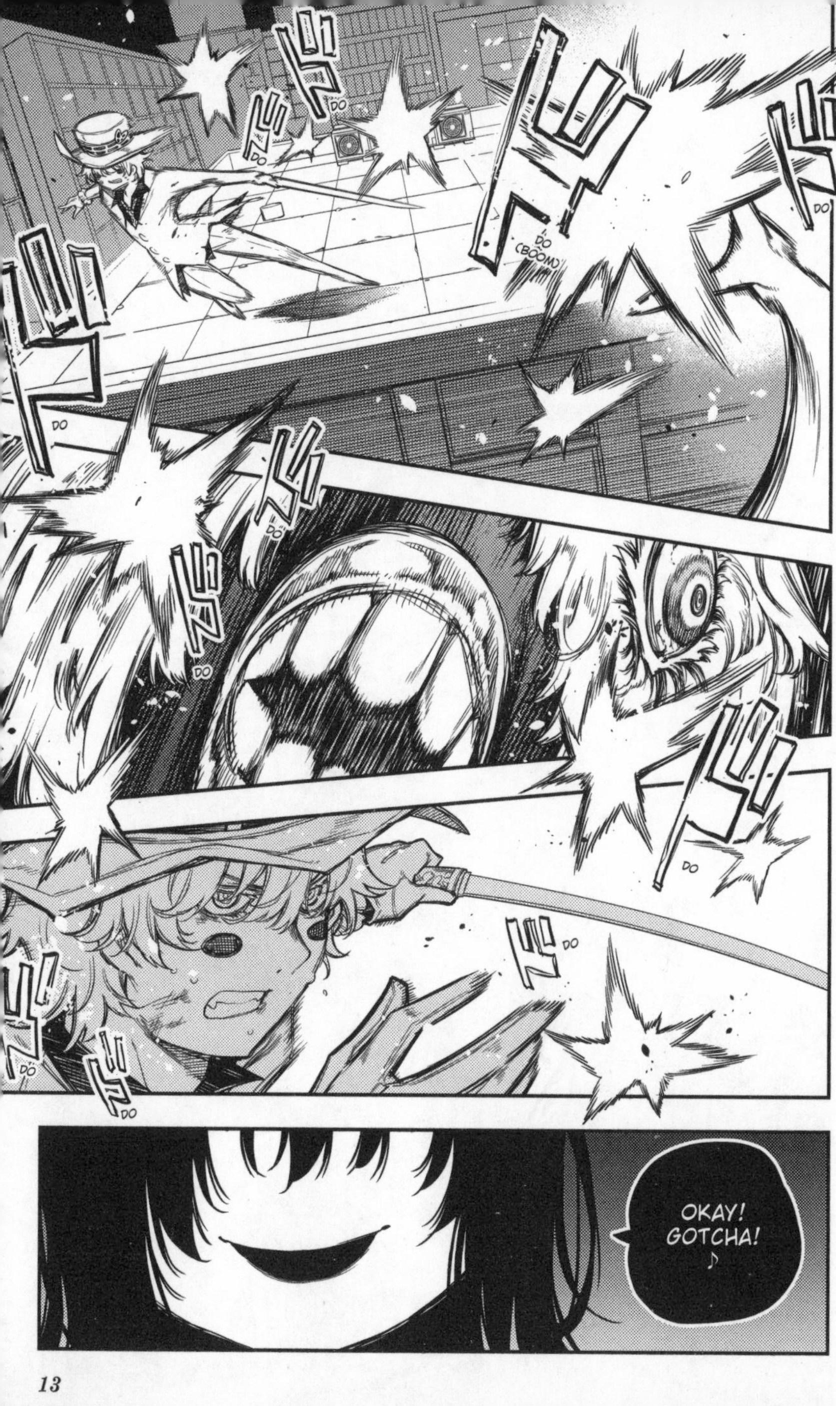
DO
DO (BOOM)
DO
DO
DO
DO
DO
DO
DO
DO
DO
OKAY! GOTCHA! ♪

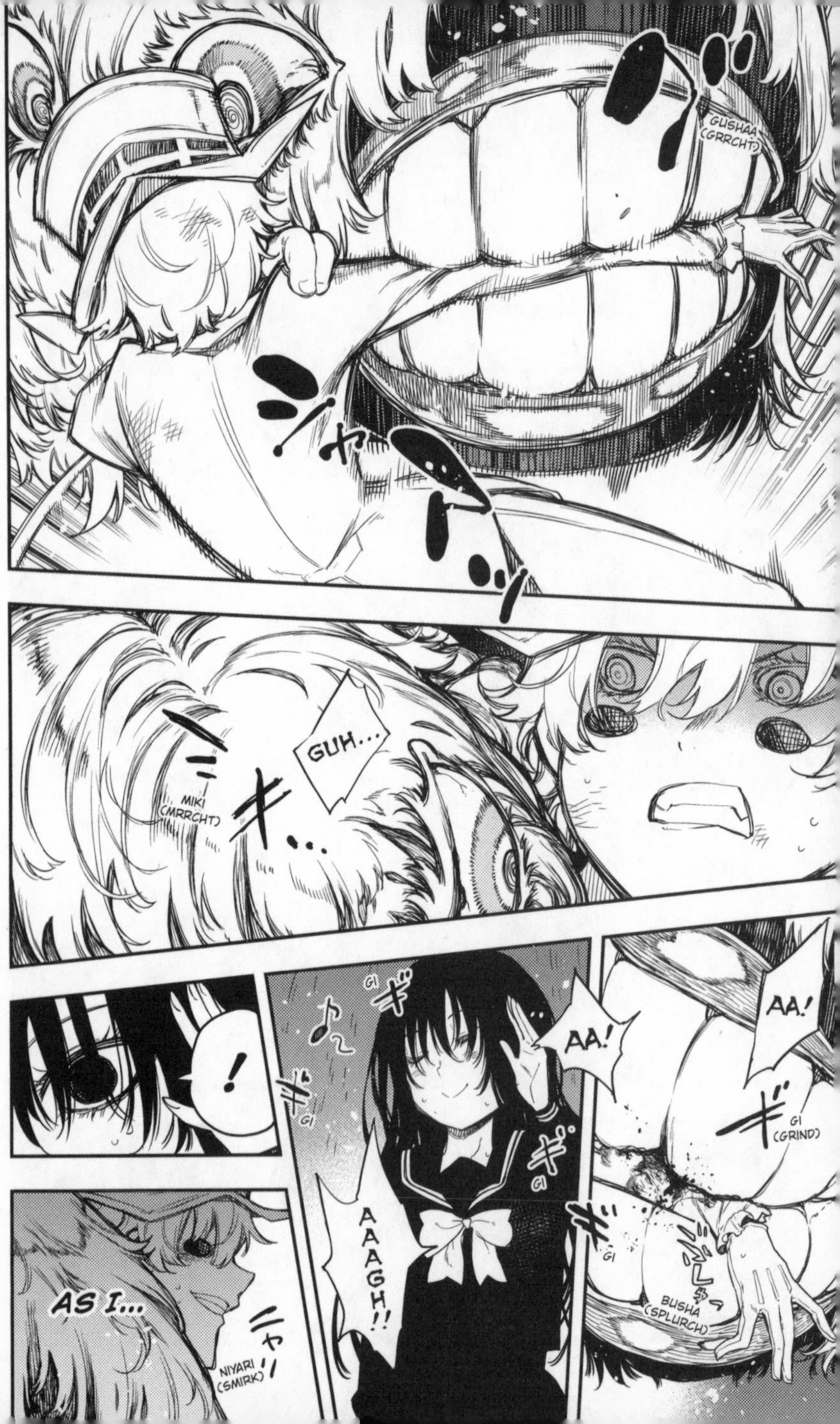
GUSHAA (GRRCHT)
GUH...
MIKI (MRRCHT)
AA!
AA!
GI (GRIND)
GI
BUSHA (SPLURCH)
GI
GI
GI
AAAGH!!
!
AS I...
NIYARI (SMIRK)

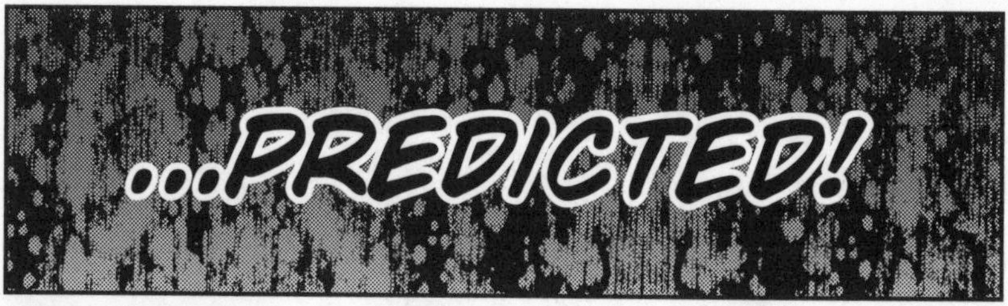
...PREDICTED!
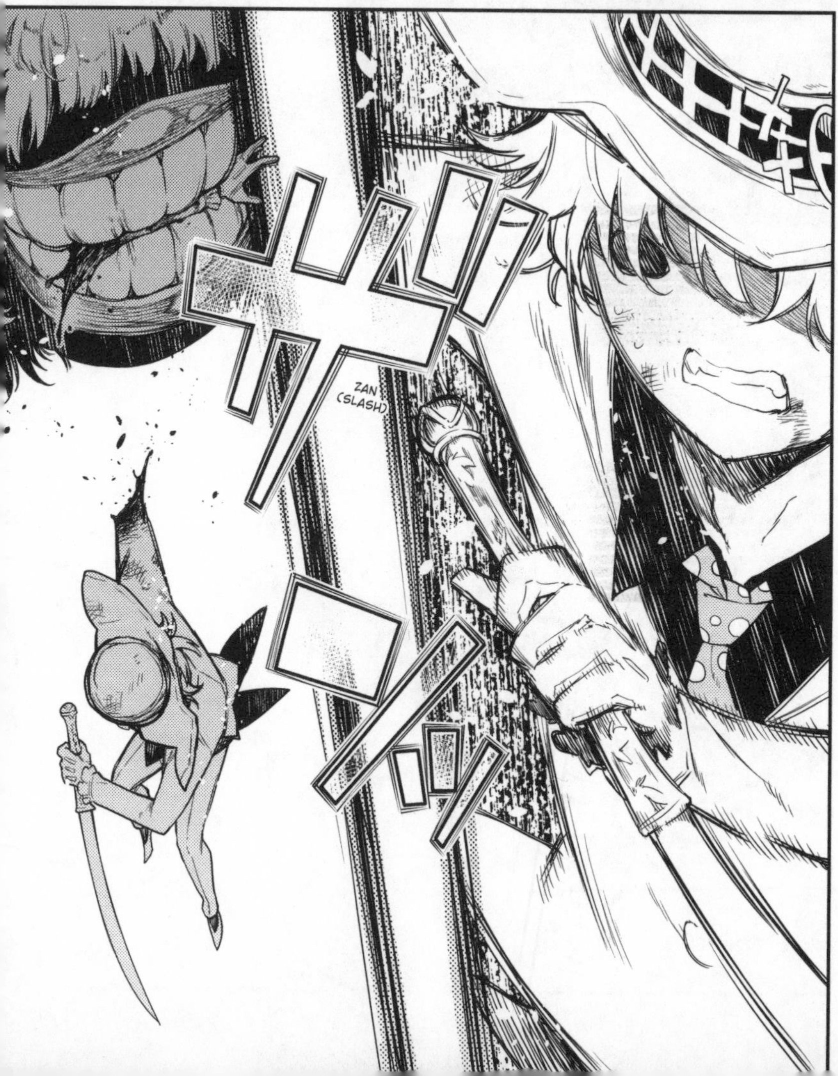
ZAN
(SLASH)

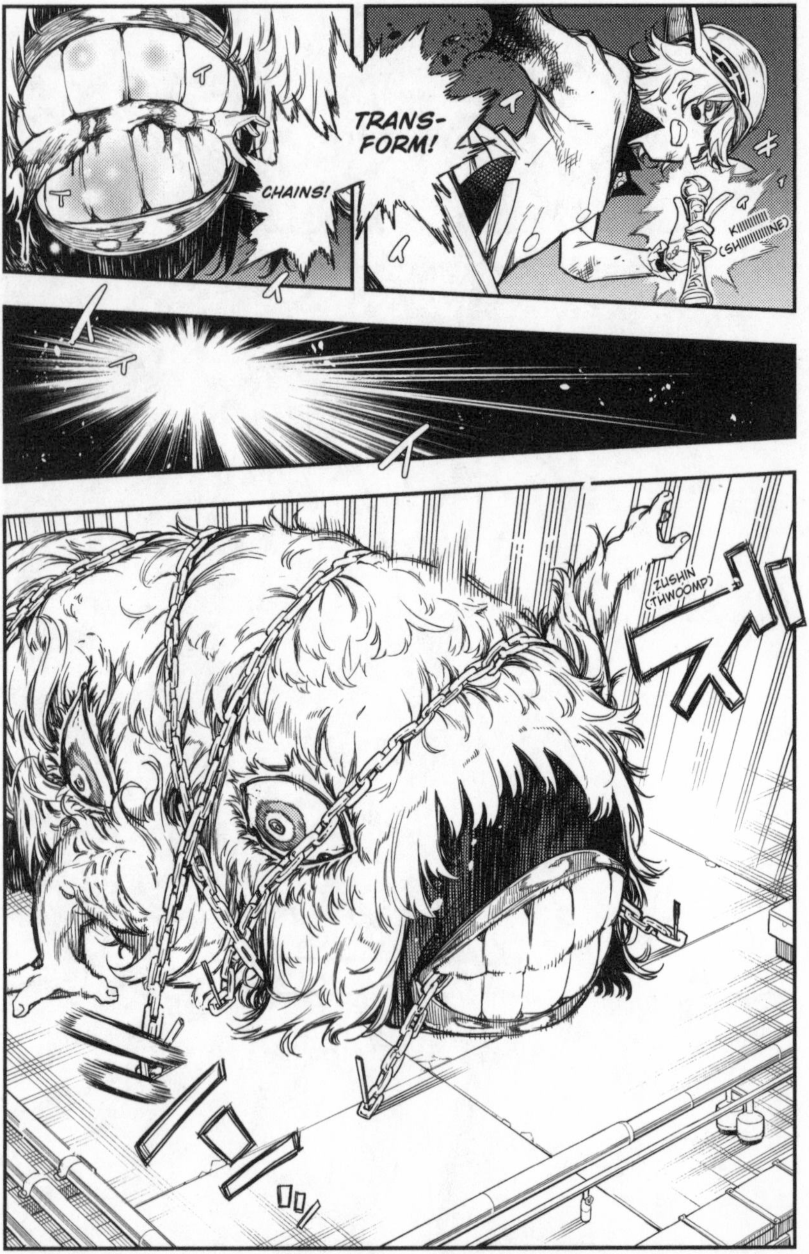

TRANS-FORM!
KIIIIIIIIIII (SHIIIIIIIIIIINE)
CHAINS!
ZUSHIN (THWOOMP)

GISHI (CREAK)
OH MY!
YOU'RE DEAD!

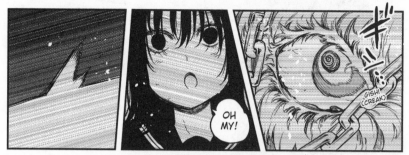

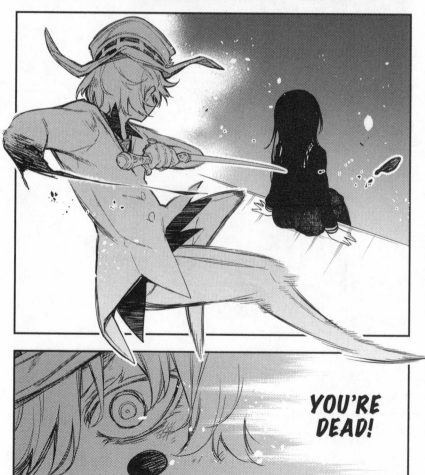

PITA
(HALT)

IT SEEMS YOU HAVE THE WRONG IMPRESSION.

HOW COULD I, JOR-CHAN'S MASTER, POSSIBLY BE WEAK?

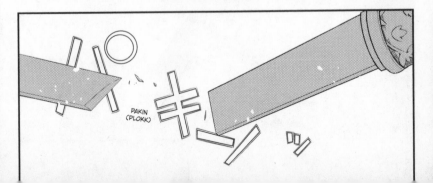

PAKIN
(PLOKK)

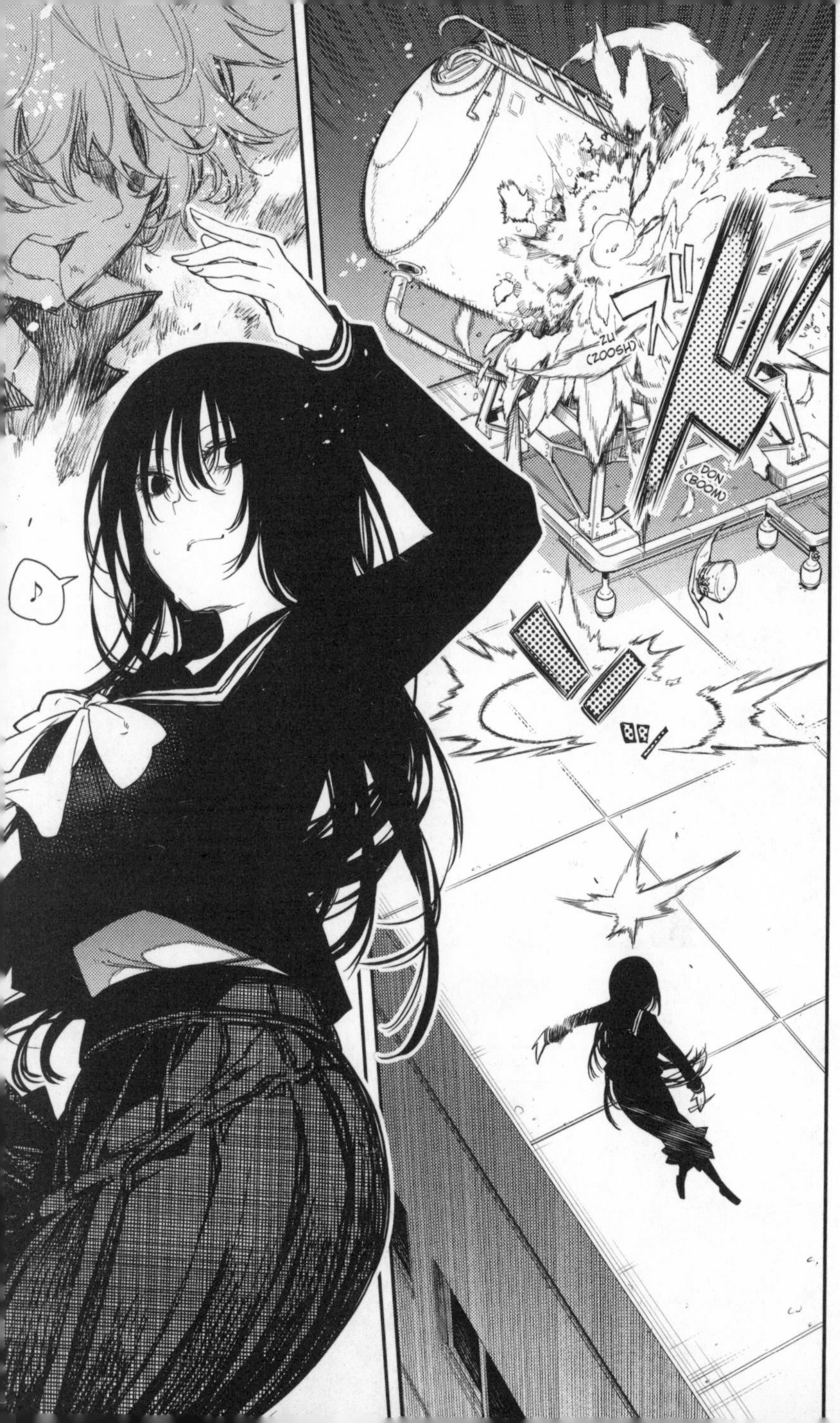
ZU
(ZOOSH)
DON
(BOOM)
♪

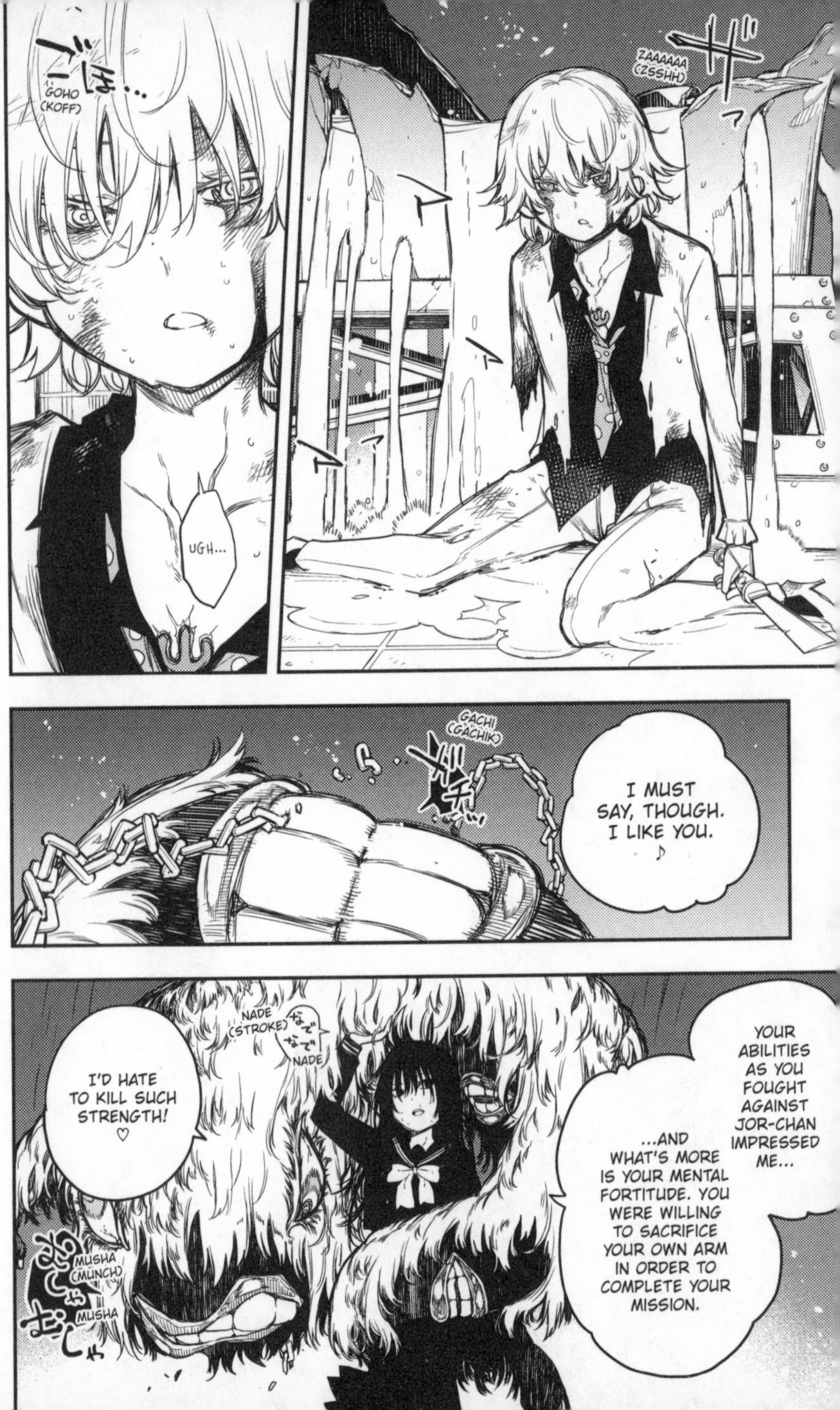
ZAAAAAA (ZSSHH)
GOHO (KOFF)
ごほ…
UGH...
GACHI (GACHIK)
I MUST SAY, THOUGH. I LIKE YOU. ♪
YOUR ABILITIES AS YOU FOUGHT AGAINST JOR-CHAN IMPRESSED ME...
...AND WHAT'S MORE IS YOUR MENTAL FORTITUDE. YOU WERE WILLING TO SACRIFICE YOUR OWN ARM IN ORDER TO COMPLETE YOUR MISSION.
NADE (STROKE) なで なで NADE
I'D HATE TO KILL SUCH STRENGTH! ♡
MUSHA (MUNCH) MUSHA

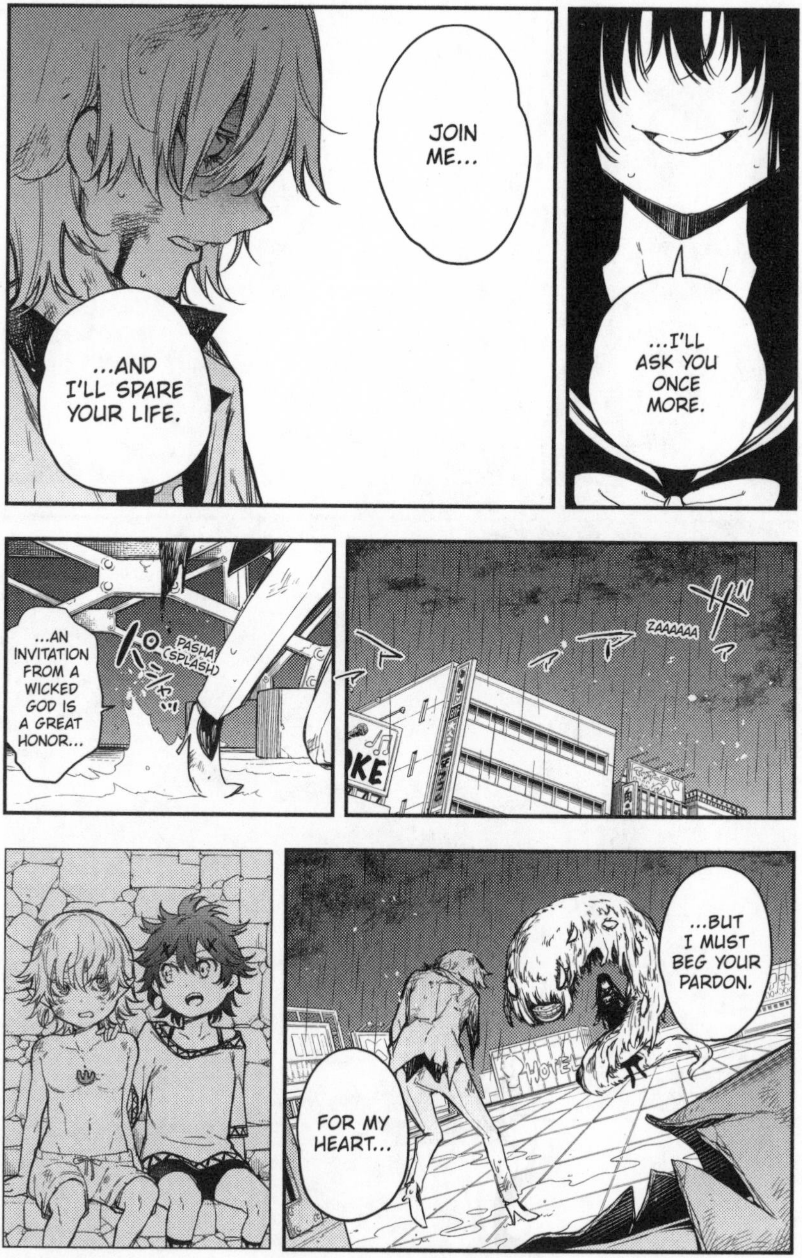
…I'LL ASK YOU ONCE MORE.
JOIN ME…
…AND I'LL SPARE YOUR LIFE.
ZAAAAAA
PASHA (SPLASH)
…AN INVITATION FROM A WICKED GOD IS A GREAT HONOR…
…BUT I MUST BEG YOUR PARDON.
FOR MY HEART…

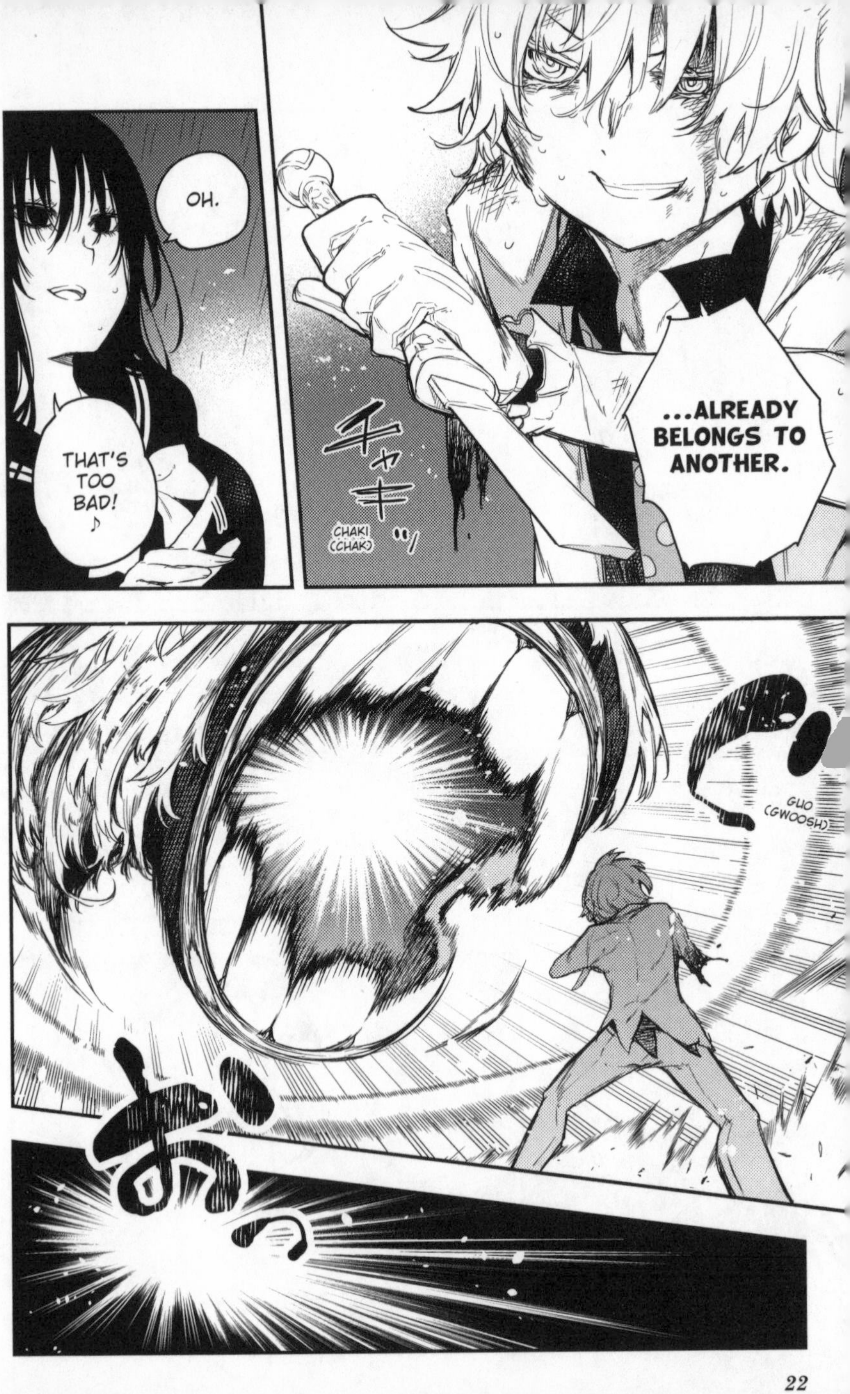
...ALREADY BELONGS TO ANOTHER.
CHAKI (CHAK)
OH.
THAT'S TOO BAD! ♪
GUO (GWOOSH)

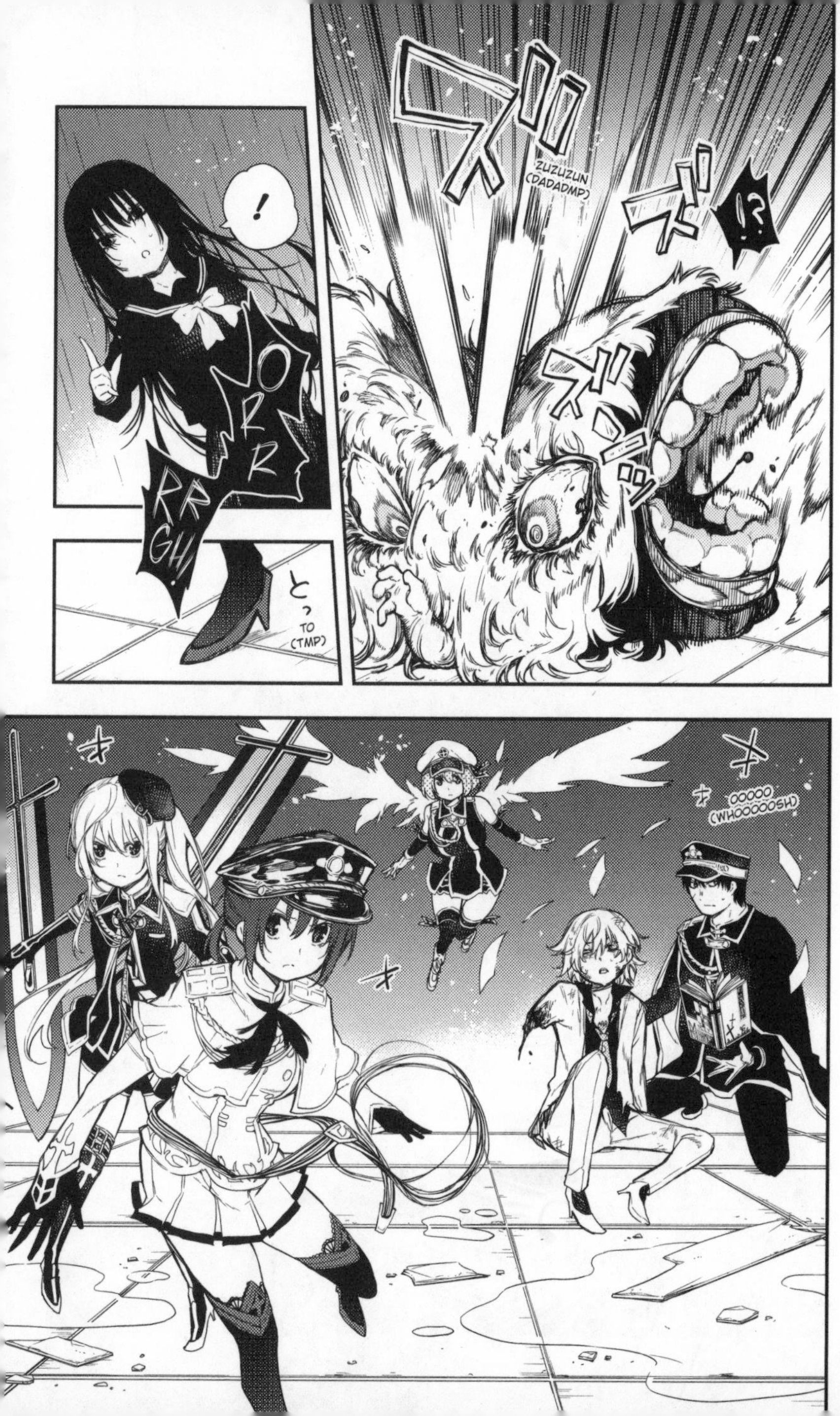
ZUZUZUN (DADADMP)
!?
!
NORRR
RRGH!
とっ
TO (TMP)
OOOOO (WHOOOOOSH)

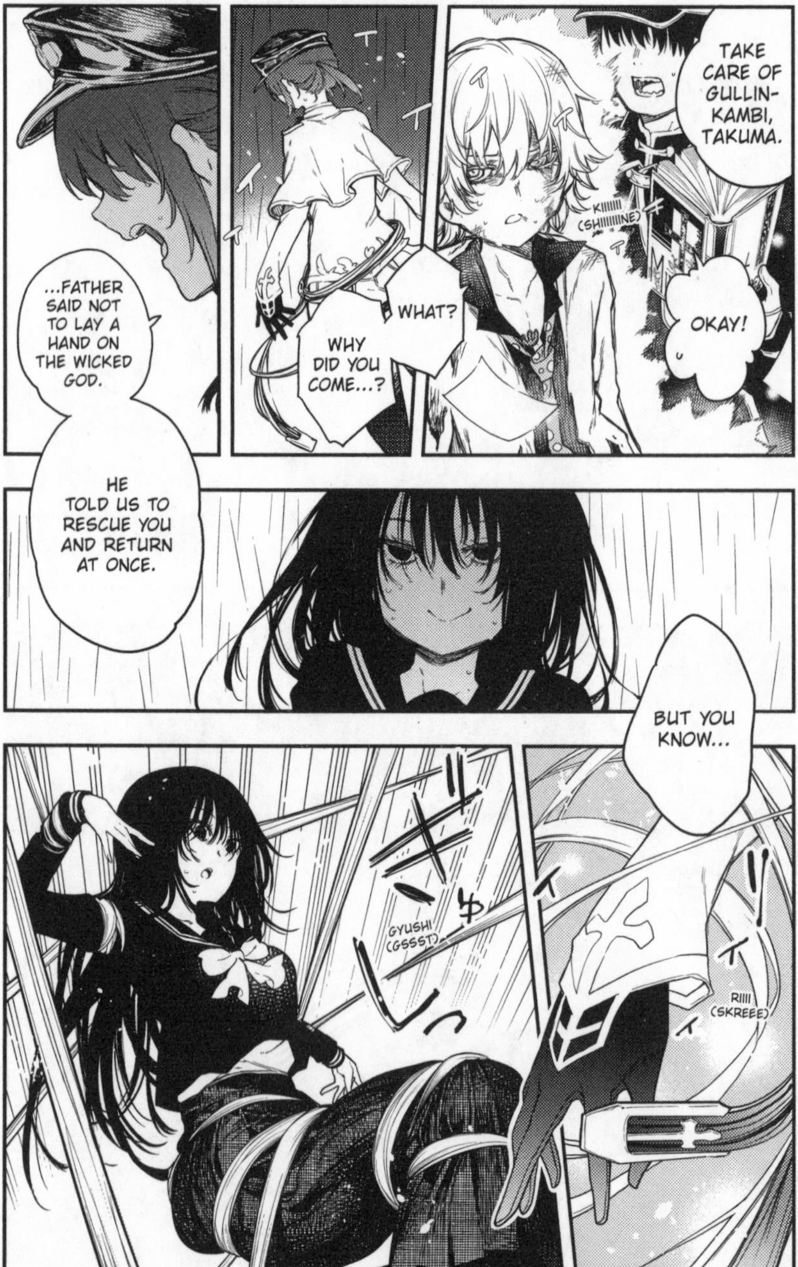
TAKE CARE OF GULLIN-KAMBI, TAKUMA.
KIIIIIII (SHIIIIIINE)
OKAY!
WHAT?
WHY DID YOU COME...?
...FATHER SAID NOT TO LAY A HAND ON THE WICKED GOD.
HE TOLD US TO RESCUE YOU AND RETURN AT ONCE.
BUT YOU KNOW...
RIIII (SKREEE)
GYUSHI (GSSST)

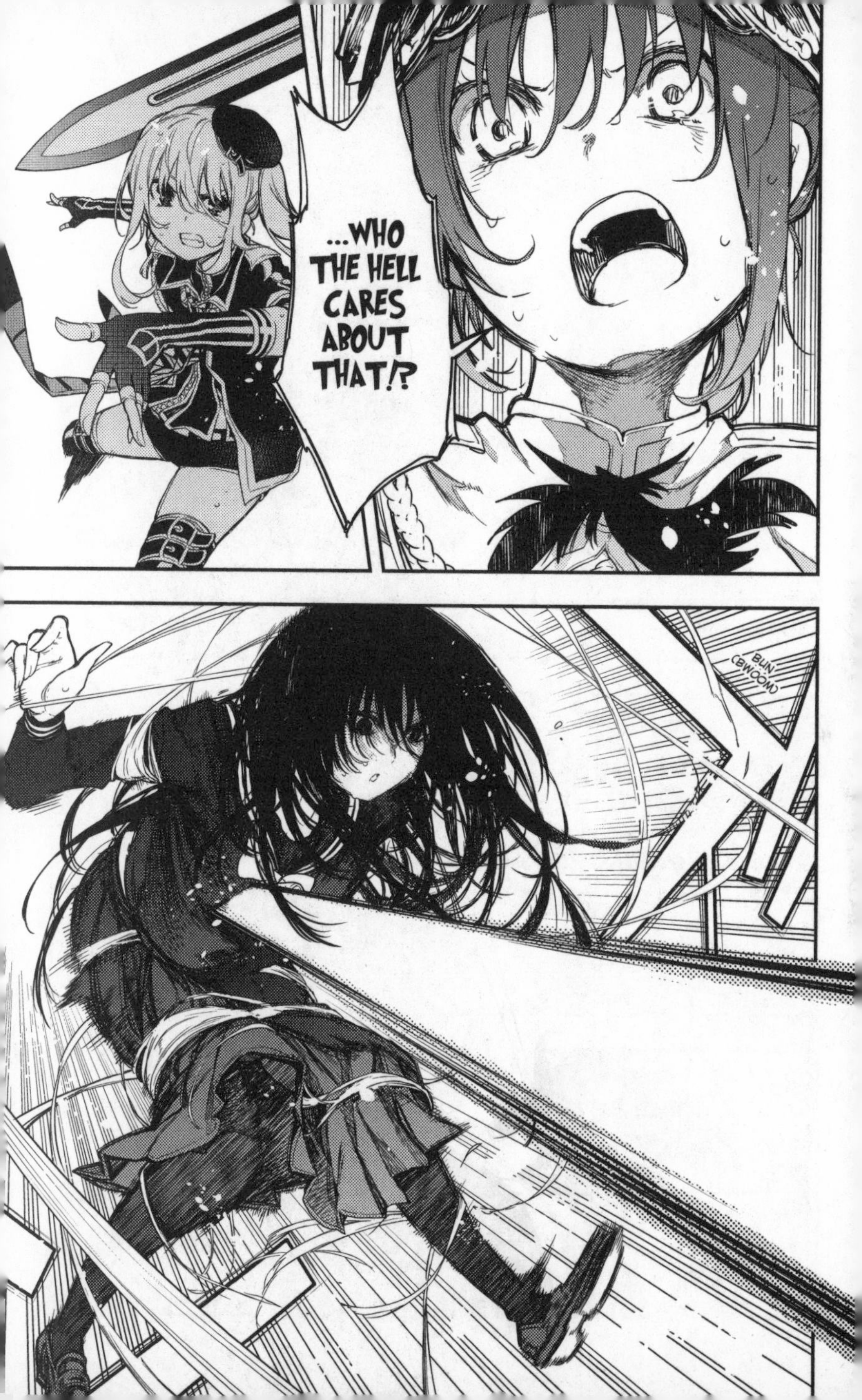
...WHO THE HELL CARES ABOUT THAT!?
BUN (BWOOM)

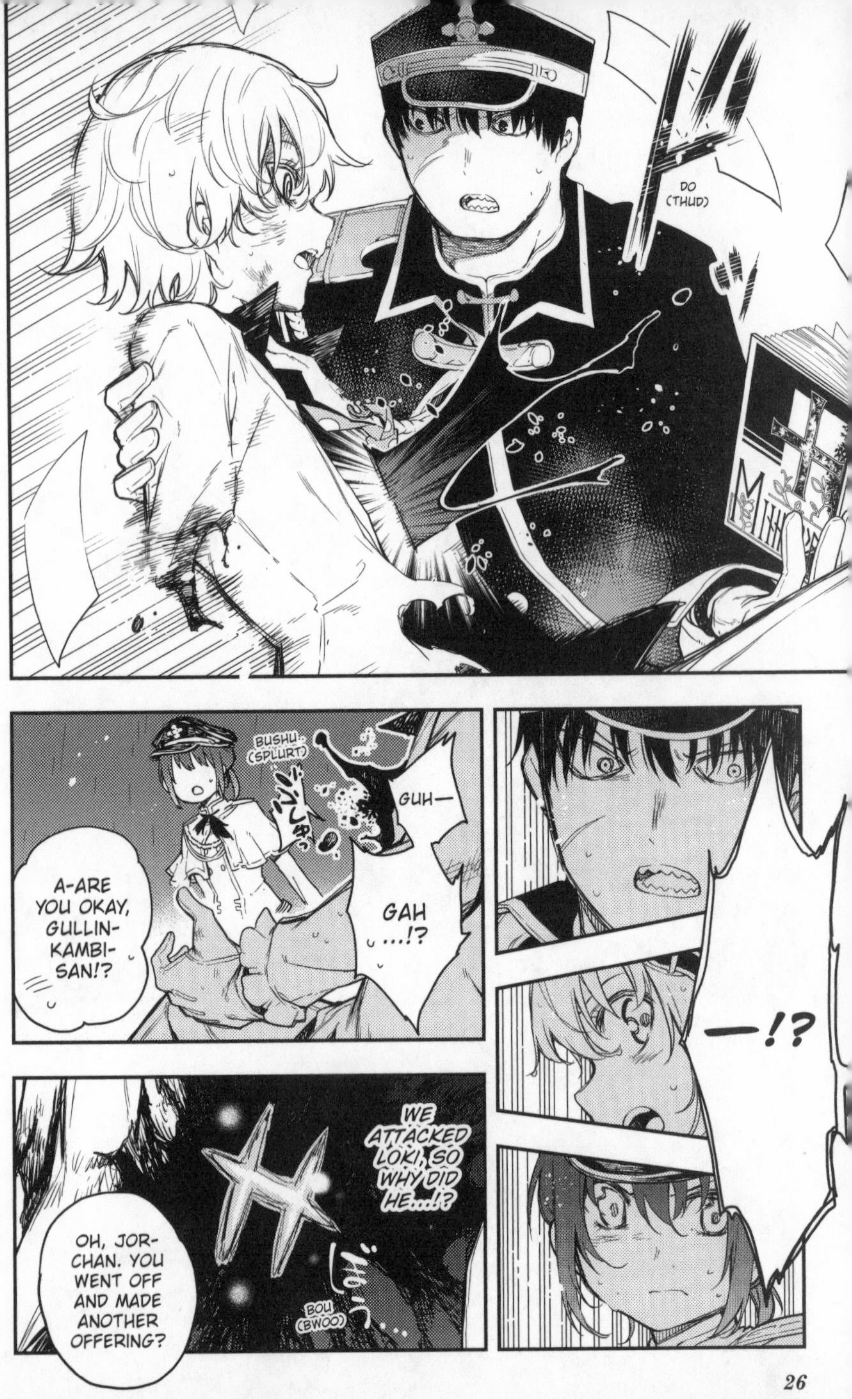
DO
(THUD)
—!?
GUH—
BUSHU
(SPLURT)
GAH
...!?
A-ARE
YOU OKAY,
GULLIN-
KAMBI-
SAN!?
WE
ATTACKED
LOKI, SO
WHY DID
HE...!?
BOU
(BWOO)
OH, JOR-
CHAN. YOU
WENT OFF
AND MADE
ANOTHER
OFFERING?

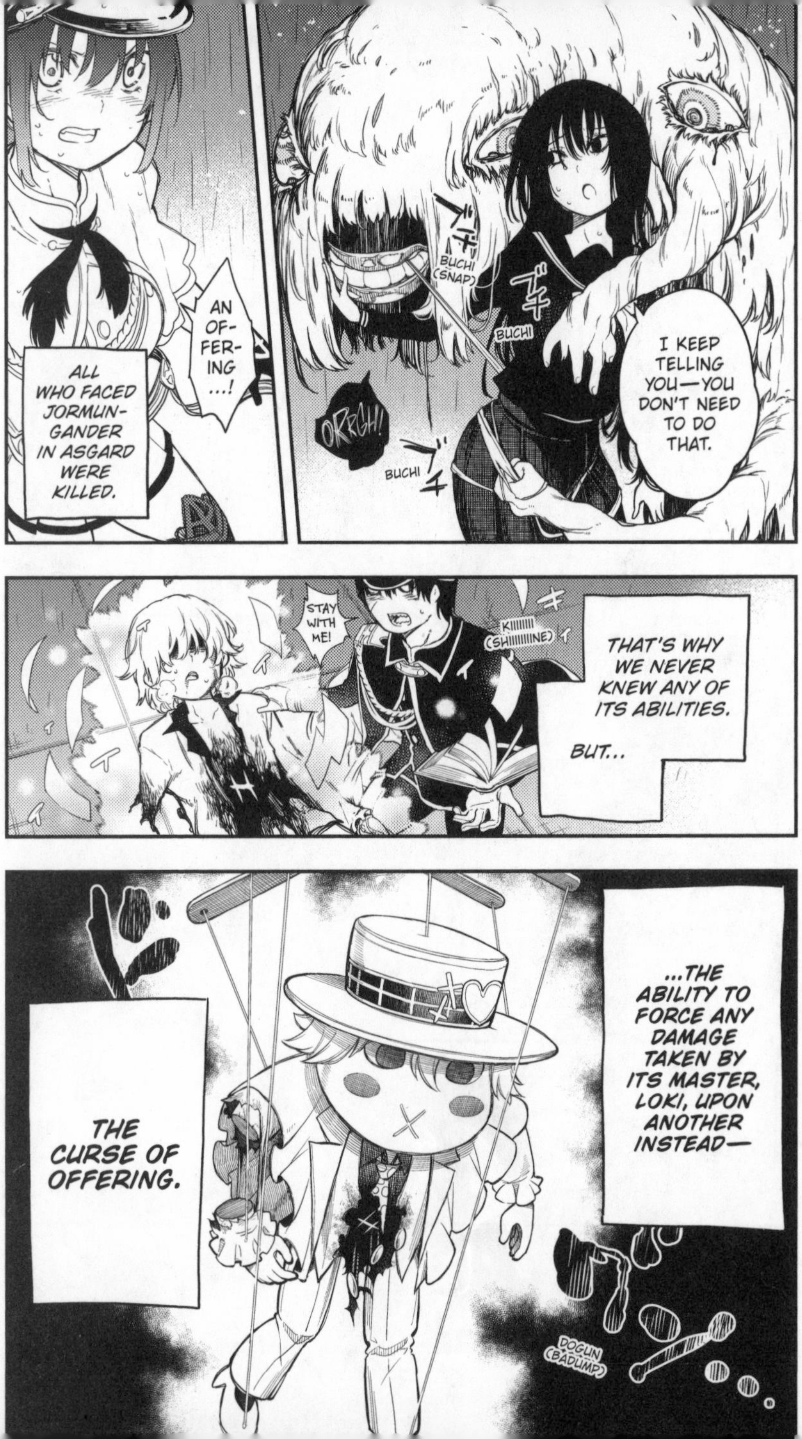
BUCHI (SNAP)
BUCHI
I KEEP TELLING YOU—YOU DON'T NEED TO DO THAT.
ORRGH!
BUCHI
AN OFF-ERING...!
ALL WHO FACED JORMUNGANDER IN ASGARD WERE KILLED.
THAT'S WHY WE NEVER KNEW ANY OF ITS ABILITIES.
BUT...
KIIIIII (SHIIIIIIINE)
STAY WITH ME!
...THE ABILITY TO FORCE ANY DAMAGE TAKEN BY ITS MASTER, LOKI, UPON ANOTHER INSTEAD—
THE CURSE OF OFFERING.
DOGUN (BADUMP)

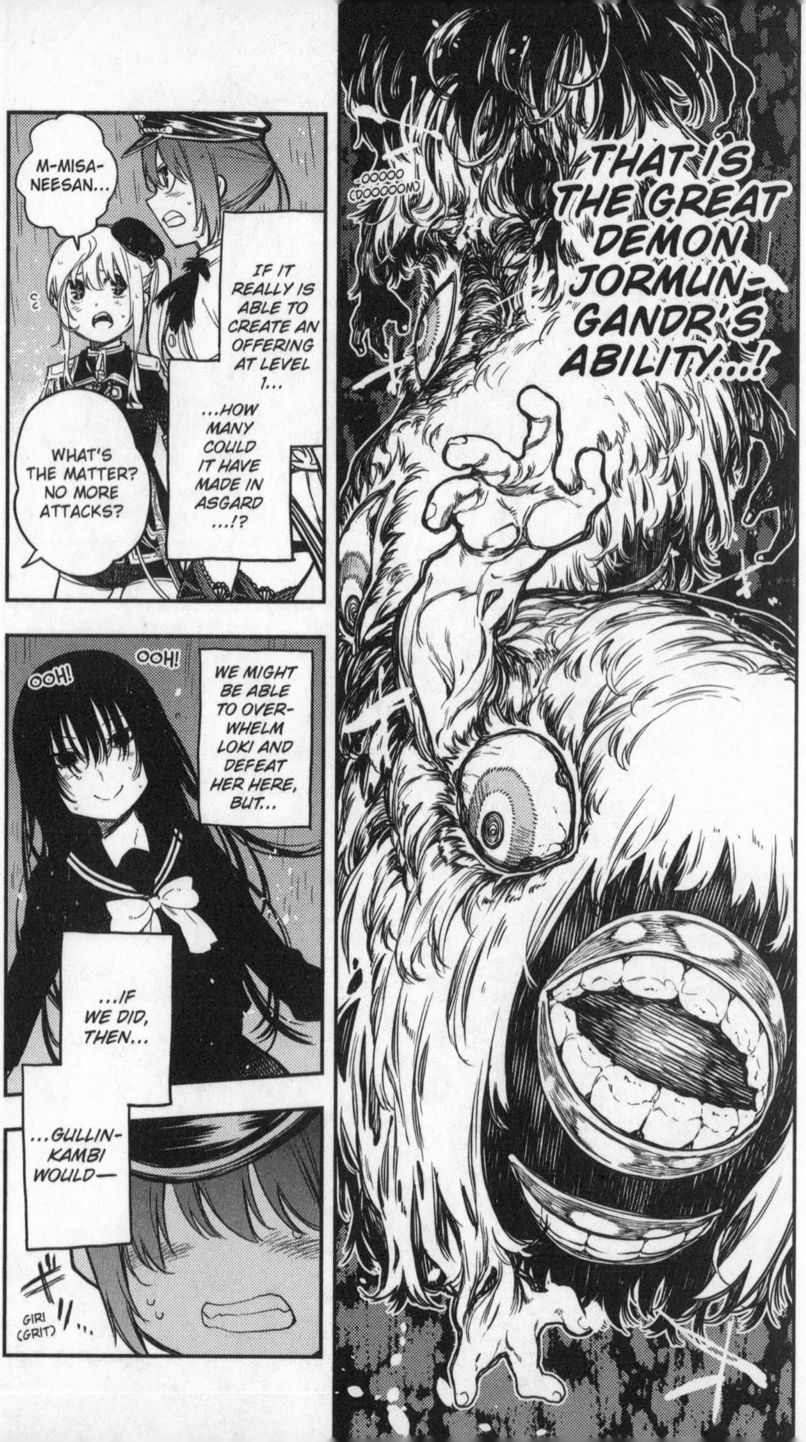
...OOOOO (DOOOOOM)
THAT IS THE GREAT DEMON JORMUN-GANDR'S ABILITY...!
IF IT REALLY IS ABLE TO CREATE AN OFFERING AT LEVEL 1...
M-MISA-NEESAN...
...HOW MANY COULD IT HAVE MADE IN ASGARD ...!?
WHAT'S THE MATTER? NO MORE ATTACKS?
OOH!
OOH!
WE MIGHT BE ABLE TO OVER-WHELM LOKI AND DEFEAT HER HERE, BUT...
...IF WE DID, THEN...
...GULLIN-KAMBI WOULD—
GIRI (GRIT)

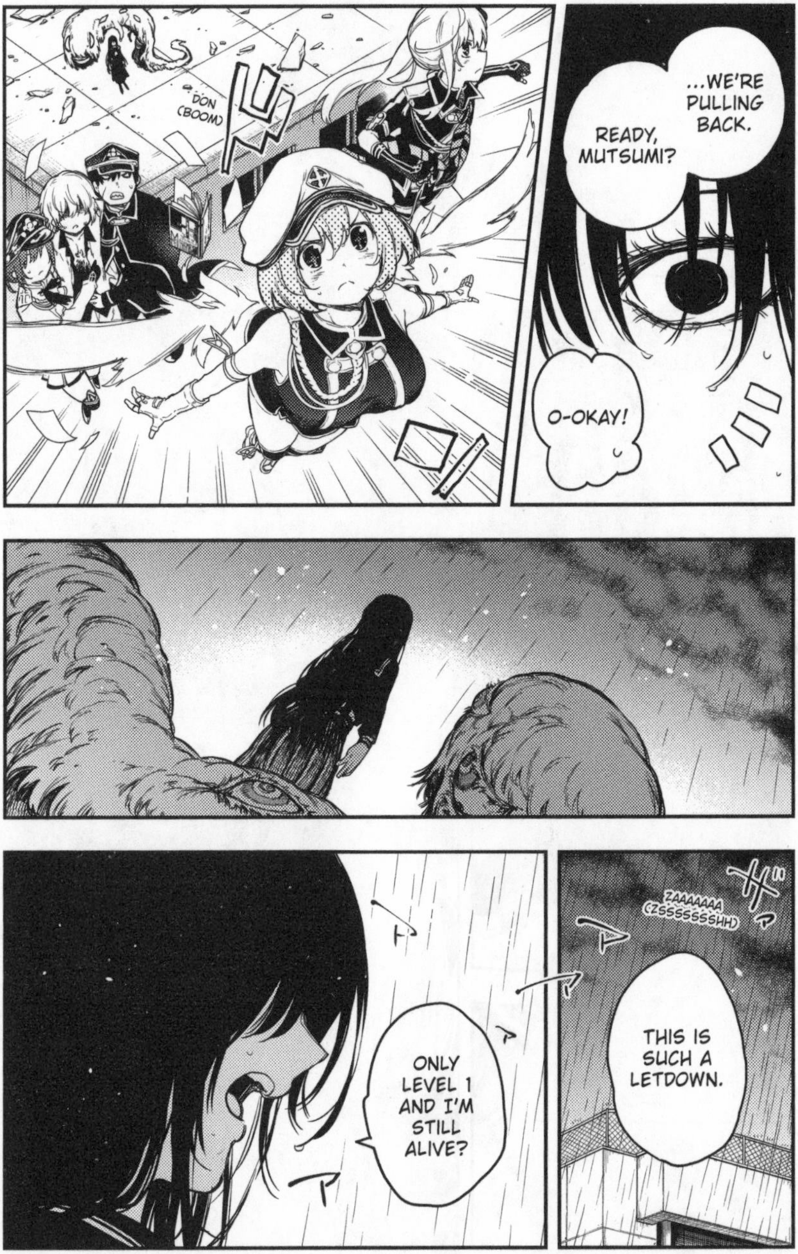
...WE'RE PULLING BACK.
READY, MUTSUMI?
O-OKAY!
DON (BOOM)
ZAAAAAAA (ZSSSSSSSHH)
THIS IS SUCH A LETDOWN.
ONLY LEVEL 1 AND I'M STILL ALIVE?

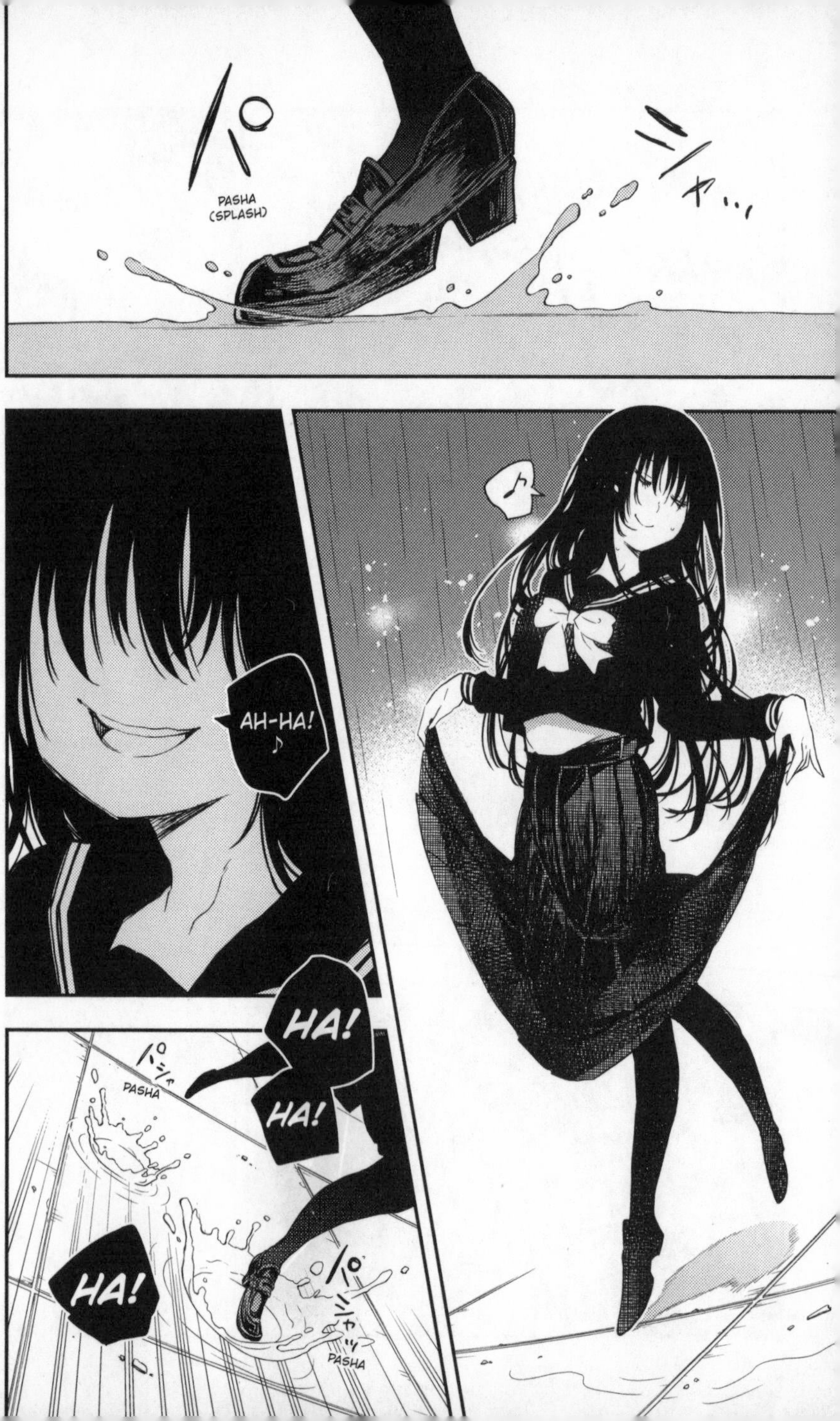
パ
PASHA (SPLASH)
シャ…
♪
AH-HA! ♪
HA!
HA!
パシャ
PASHA
HA!
パシャッ
PASHA

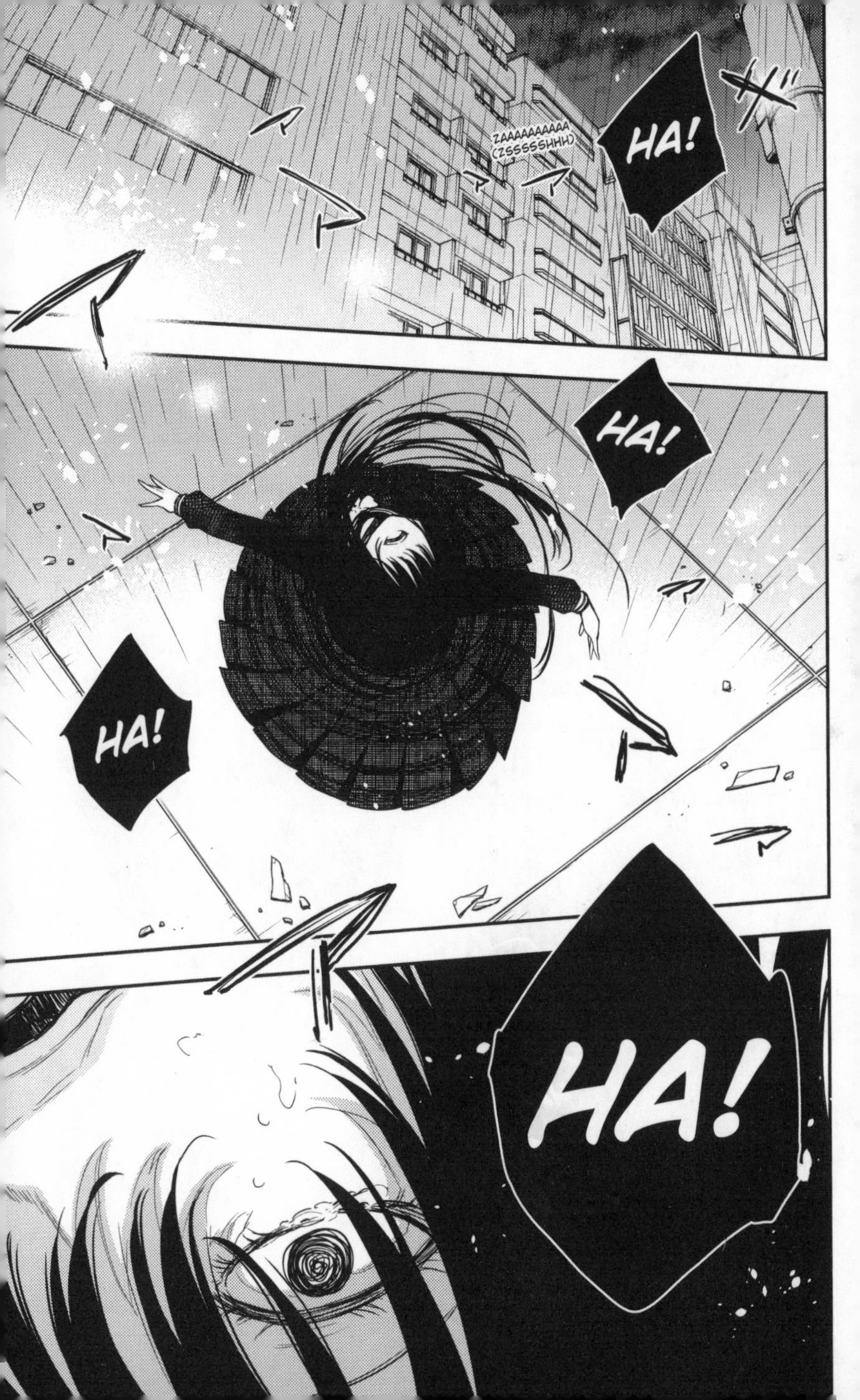
HA!
ZAAAAAAAAAA
(ZSSSSSHHH)
HA!
HA!
HA!

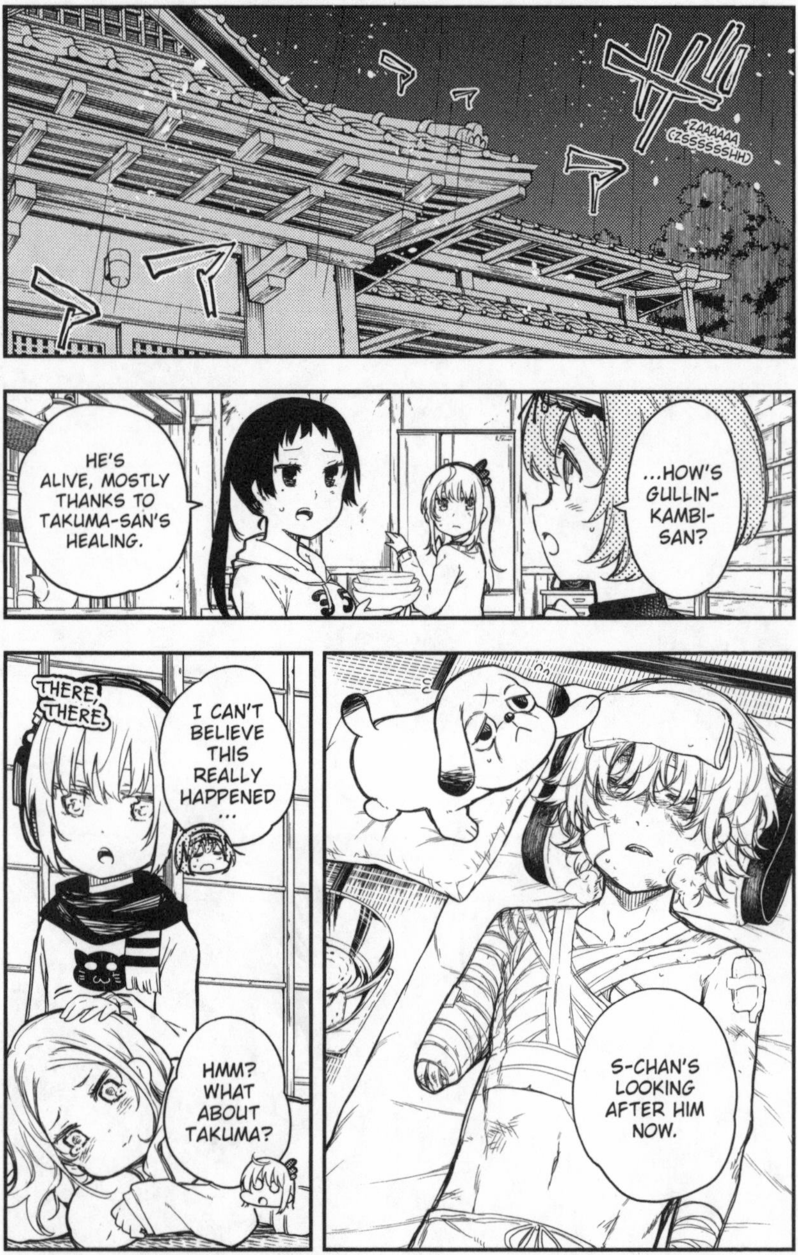
ZAAAAAA (ZSSSSSSHH)
...HOW'S GULLIN-KAMBI-SAN?
HE'S ALIVE, MOSTLY THANKS TO TAKUMA-SAN'S HEALING.
S-CHAN'S LOOKING AFTER HIM NOW.
I CAN'T BELIEVE THIS REALLY HAPPENED...
THERE, THERE.
HMM? WHAT ABOUT TAKUMA?

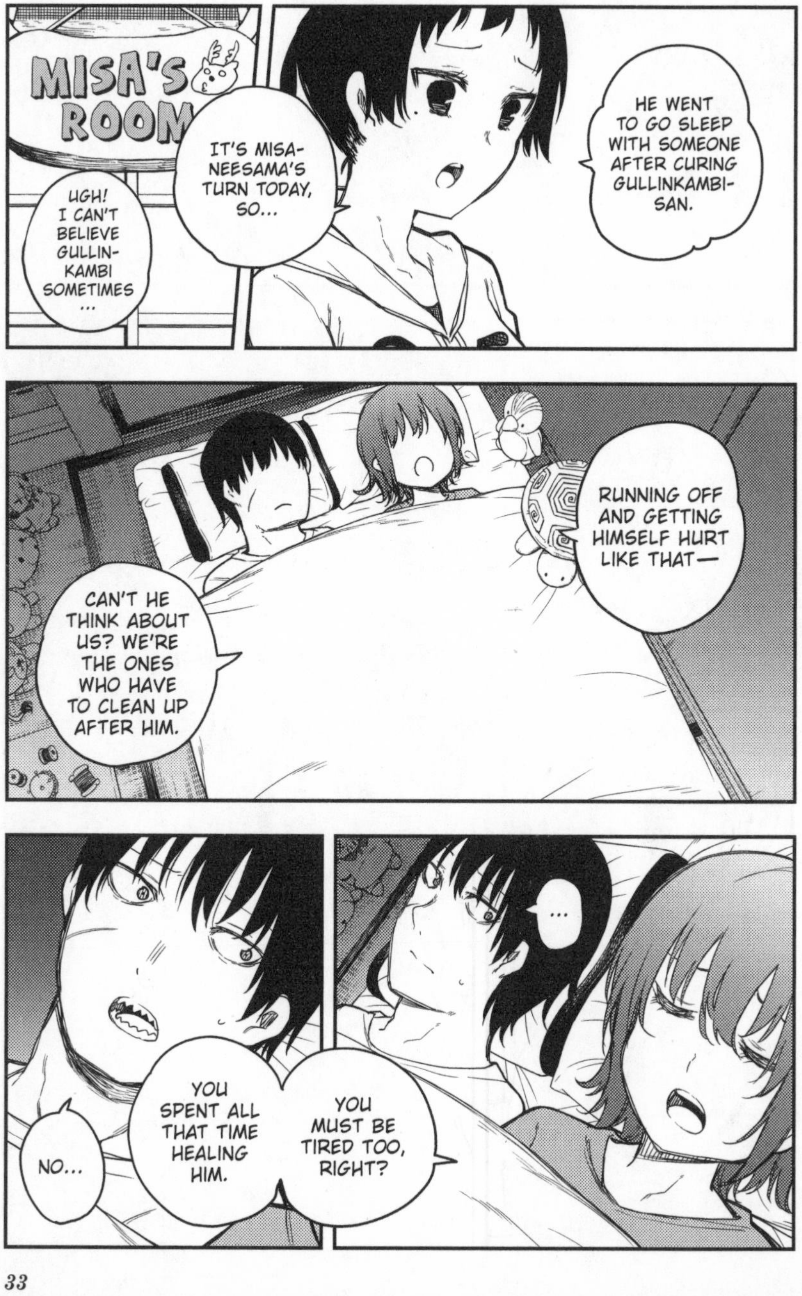
HE WENT TO GO SLEEP WITH SOMEONE AFTER CURING GULLINKAMBI-SAN.
IT'S MISA-NEESAMA'S TURN TODAY, SO...
MISA'S ROOM
UGH! I CAN'T BELIEVE GULLIN-KAMBI SOMETIMES ...
RUNNING OFF AND GETTING HIMSELF HURT LIKE THAT—
CAN'T HE THINK ABOUT US? WE'RE THE ONES WHO HAVE TO CLEAN UP AFTER HIM.
...
YOU MUST BE TIRED TOO, RIGHT?
YOU SPENT ALL THAT TIME HEALING HIM.
NO...

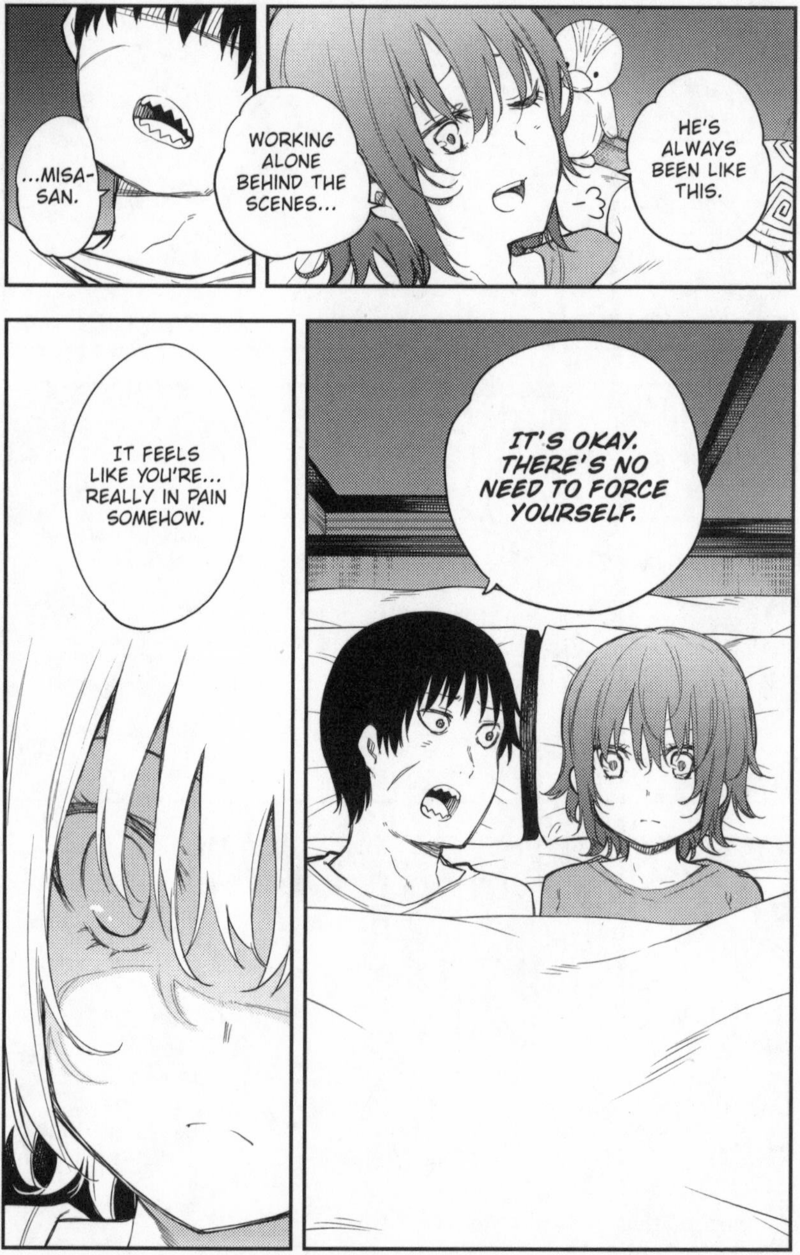
HE'S ALWAYS BEEN LIKE THIS.
WORKING ALONE BEHIND THE SCENES...
...MISA-SAN.
IT'S OKAY. THERE'S NO NEED TO FORCE YOURSELF.
IT FEELS LIKE YOU'RE... REALLY IN PAIN SOMEHOW.

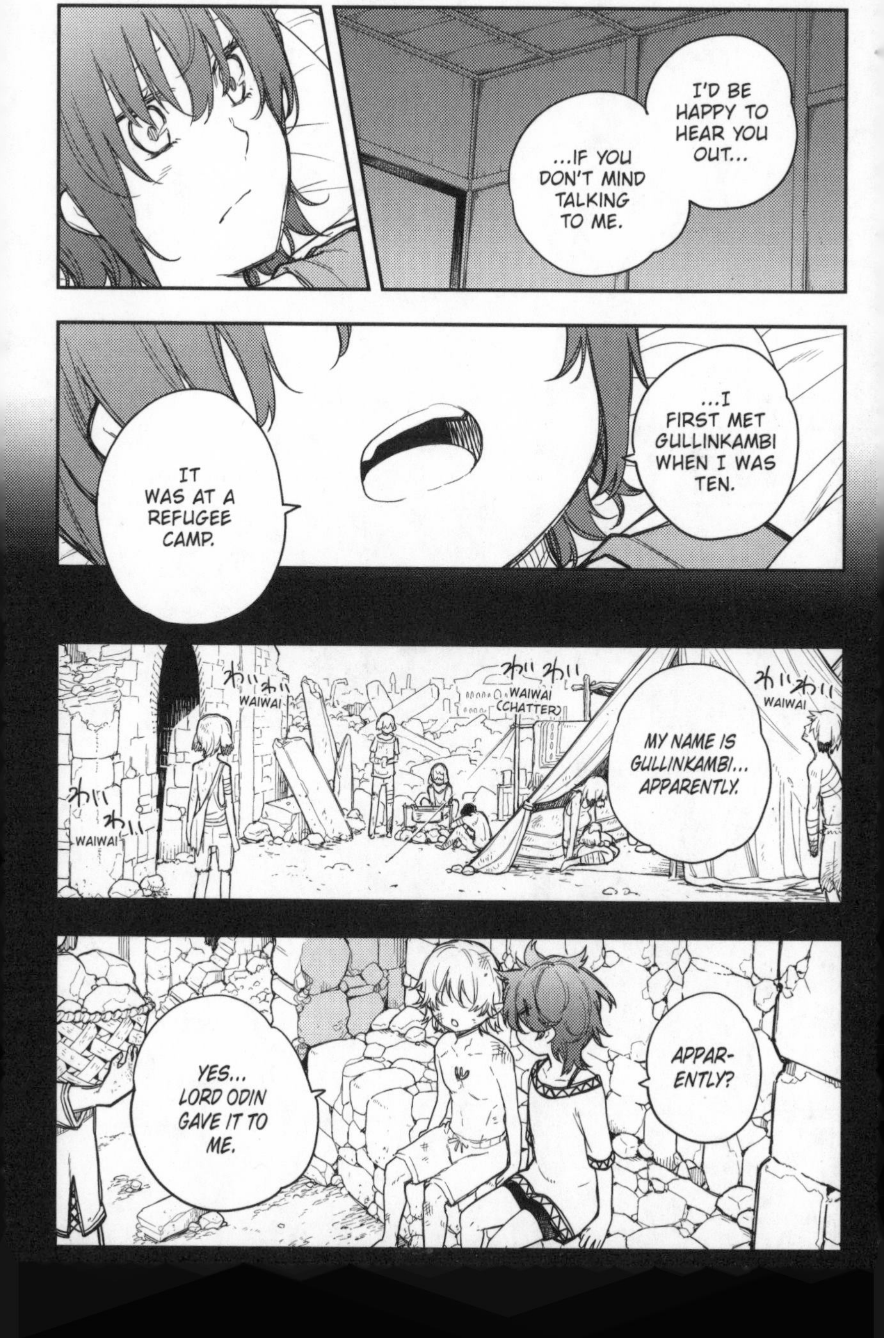

I'D BE HAPPY TO HEAR YOU OUT...
...IF YOU DON'T MIND TALKING TO ME.
...I FIRST MET GULLINKAMBI WHEN I WAS TEN.
IT WAS AT A REFUGEE CAMP.
わいわい WAIWAI
MY NAME IS GULLINKAMBI... APPARENTLY.
わいわい WAIWAI (CHATTER)
わいわい WAIWAI
わいわい WAIWAI
APPAR-ENTLY?
YES... LORD ODIN GAVE IT TO ME.

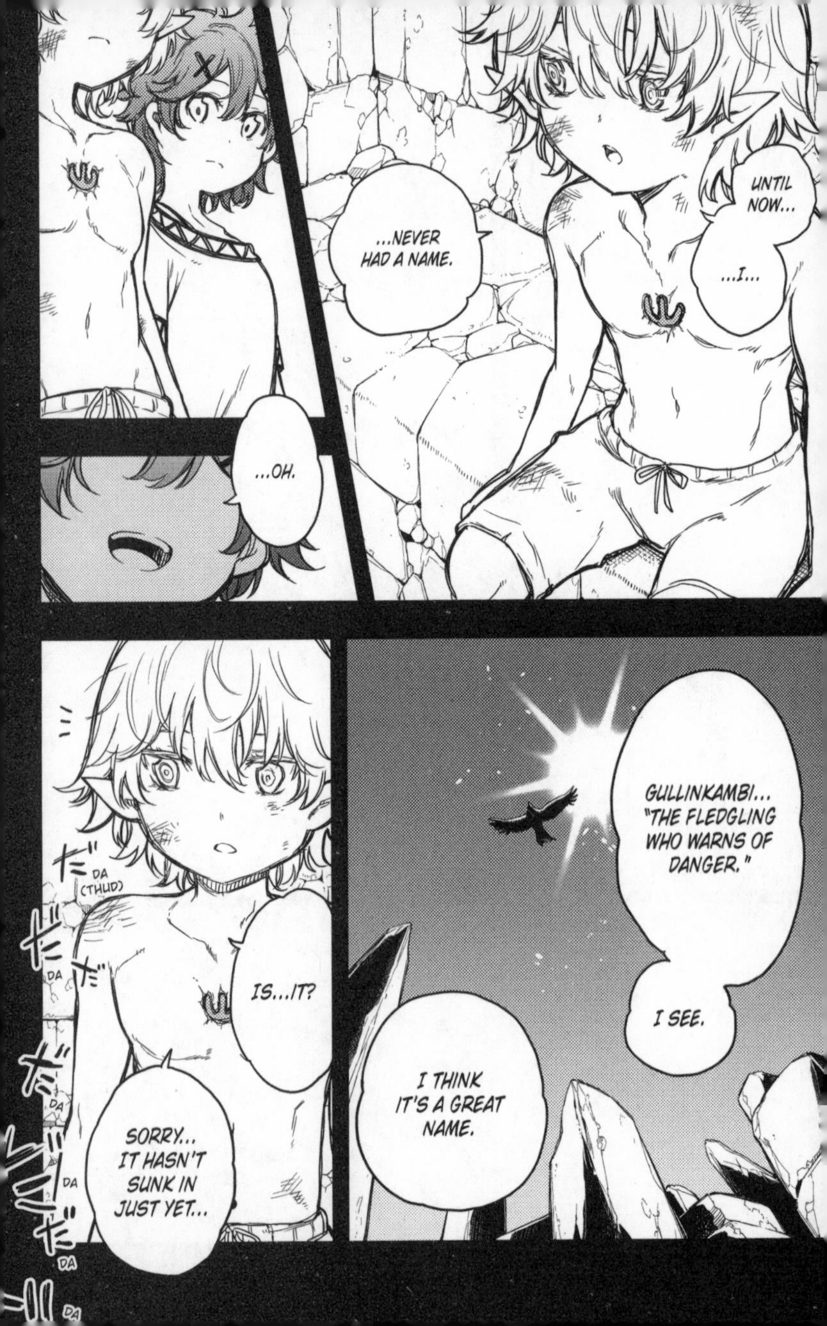
UNTIL NOW...
...I...
...NEVER HAD A NAME.
...OH.
GULLINKAMBI... "THE FLEDGLING WHO WARNS OF DANGER."
I SEE.
I THINK IT'S A GREAT NAME.
IS...IT?
DA (THUD)
DA
DA
DA
DA
DA
SORRY... IT HASN'T SUNK IN JUST YET...

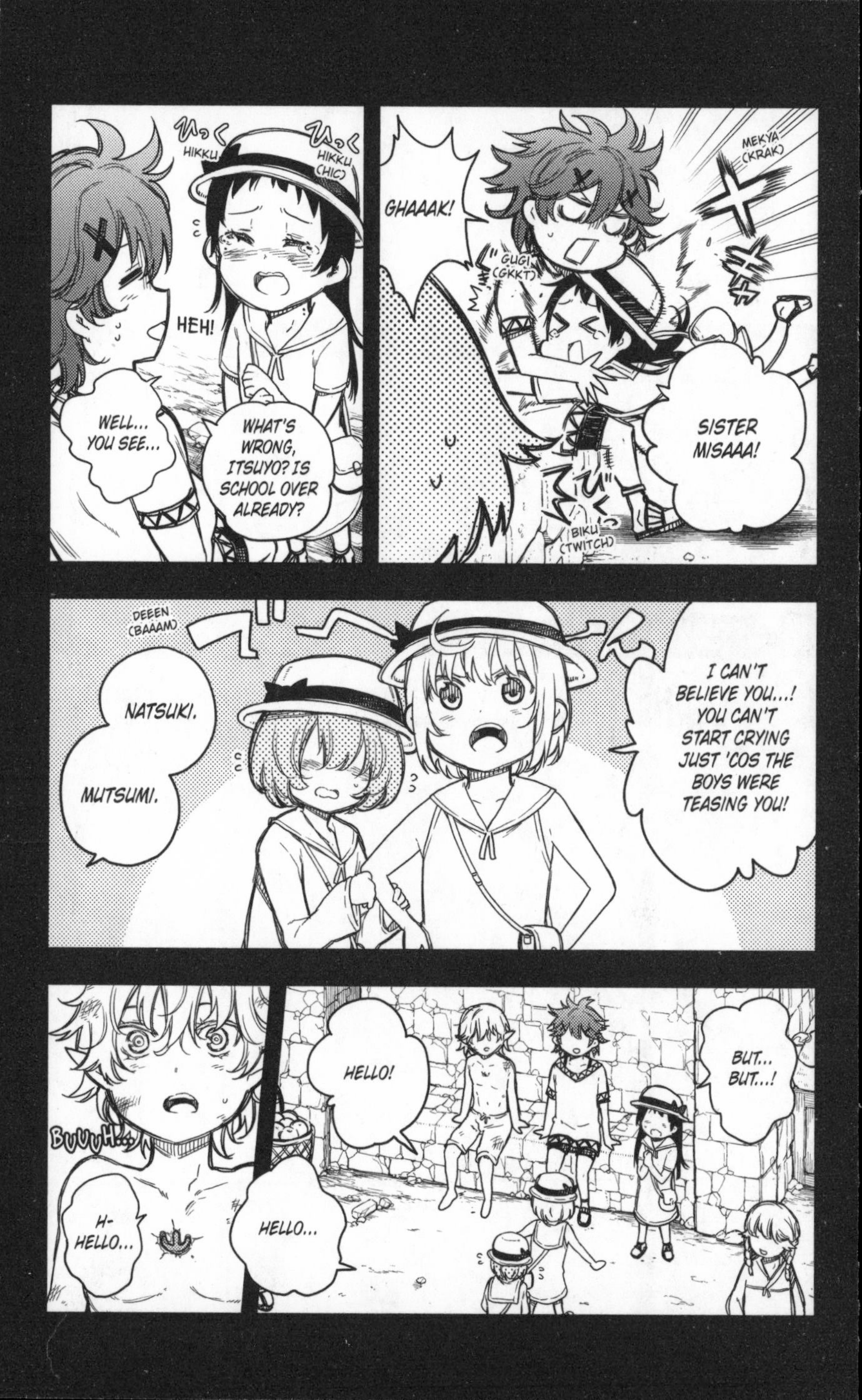

MEKYA (KRAK)
GHAAAK!
GUGI (GKKT)
SISTER MISAAA!
BIKU (TWITCH)
ひっく
HIKKU (HIC)
ひっく
HIKKU
HEH!
WHAT'S WRONG, ITSUYO? IS SCHOOL OVER ALREADY?
WELL... YOU SEE...
DEEEN (BAAAM)
I CAN'T BELIEVE YOU...! YOU CAN'T START CRYING JUST 'COS THE BOYS WERE TEASING YOU!
NATSUKI.
MUTSUMI.
BUT... BUT...!
HELLO!
BUUUH...
HELLO...
H-HELLO...

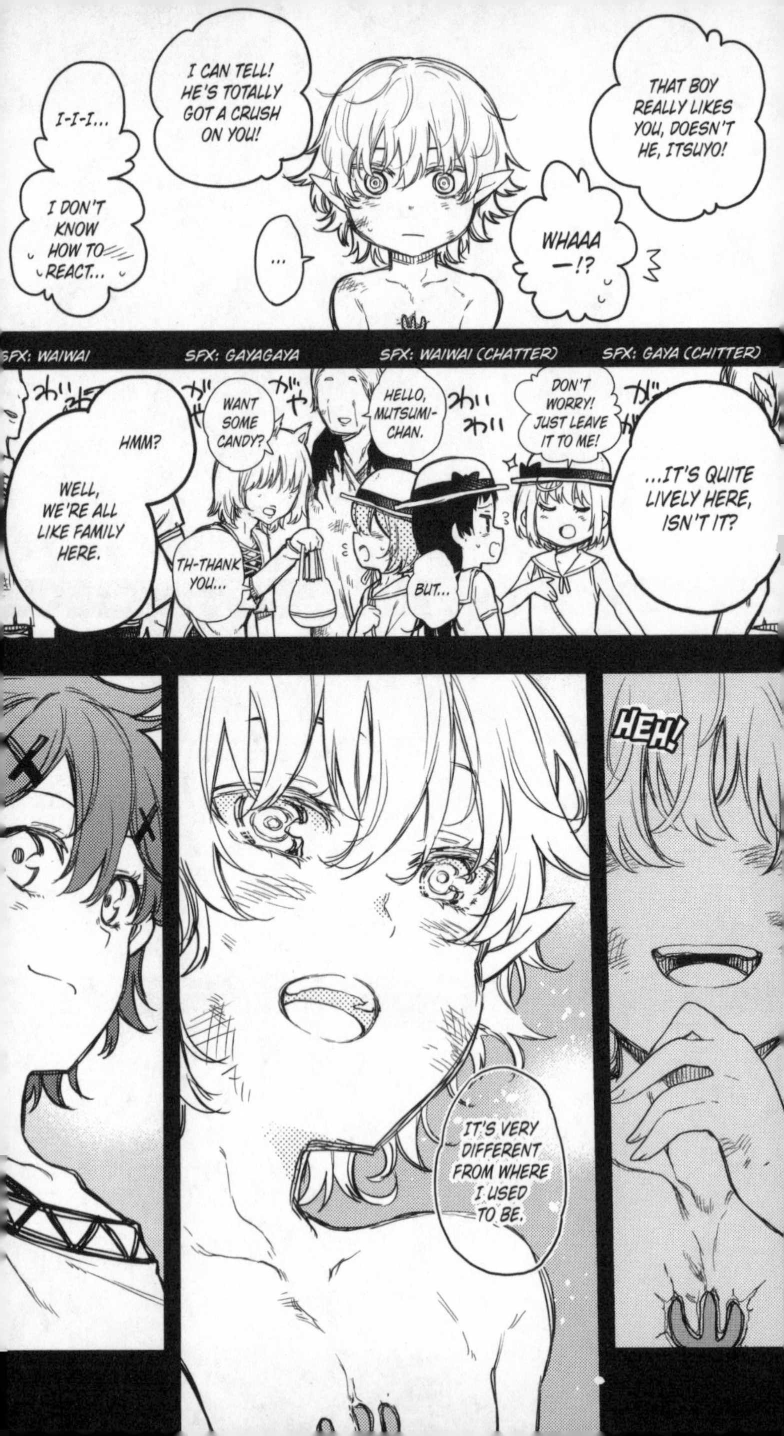
THAT BOY REALLY LIKES YOU, DOESN'T HE, ITSUYO!
WHAAA—!?
I CAN TELL! HE'S TOTALLY GOT A CRUSH ON YOU!
...
I-I-I...
I DON'T KNOW HOW TO REACT...
SFX: GAYA (CHITTER)
SFX: WAIWAI (CHATTER)
SFX: GAYAGAYA
SFX: WAIWAI
...IT'S QUITE LIVELY HERE, ISN'T IT?
DON'T WORRY! JUST LEAVE IT TO ME!
BUT...
HELLO, MUTSUMI-CHAN.
WANT SOME CANDY?
TH-THANK YOU...
HMM?
WELL, WE'RE ALL LIKE FAMILY HERE.
HEH!
IT'S VERY DIFFERENT FROM WHERE I USED TO BE.

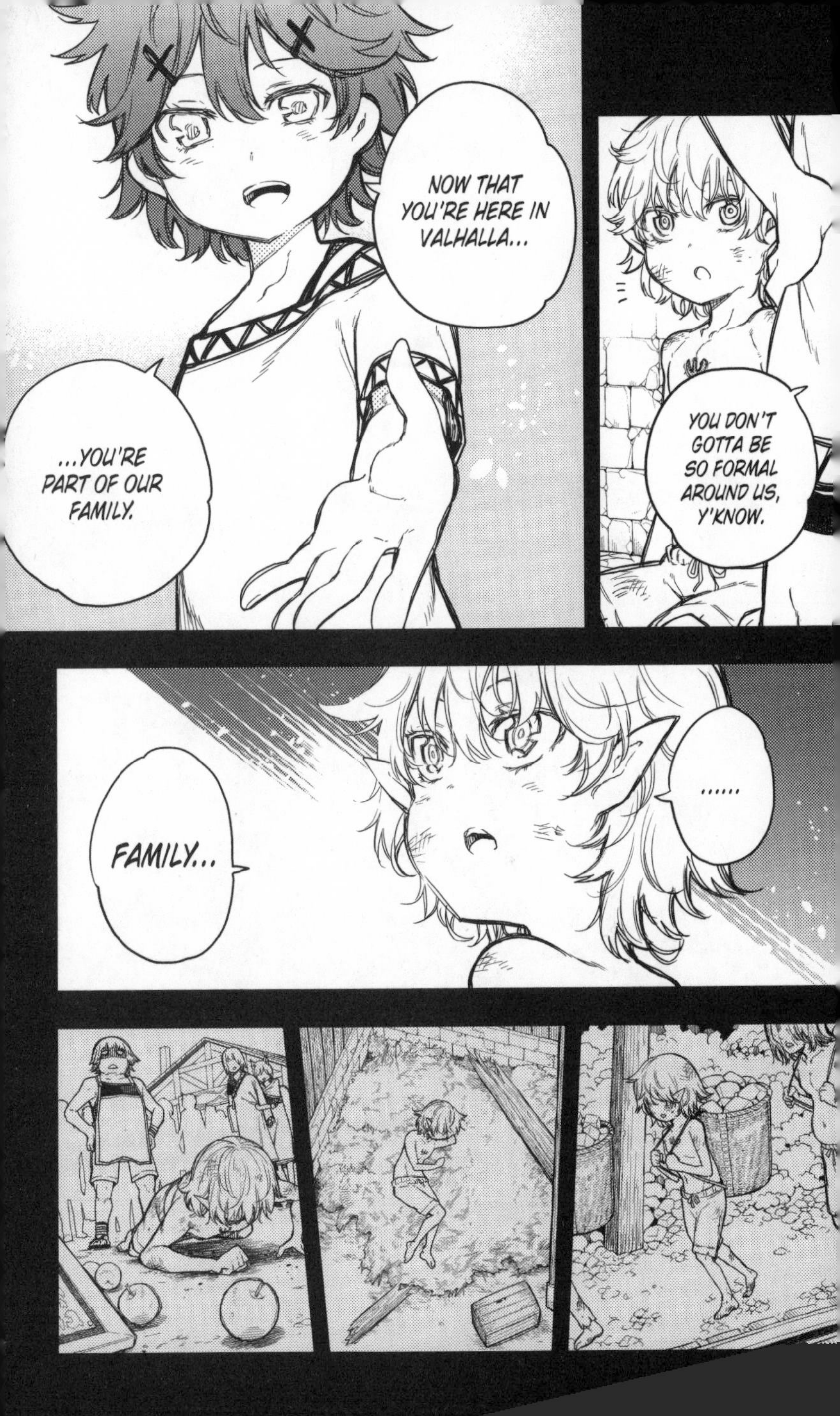
YOU DON'T GOTTA BE SO FORMAL AROUND US, Y'KNOW.
NOW THAT YOU'RE HERE IN VALHALLA...
...YOU'RE PART OF OUR FAMILY.
......
FAMILY...

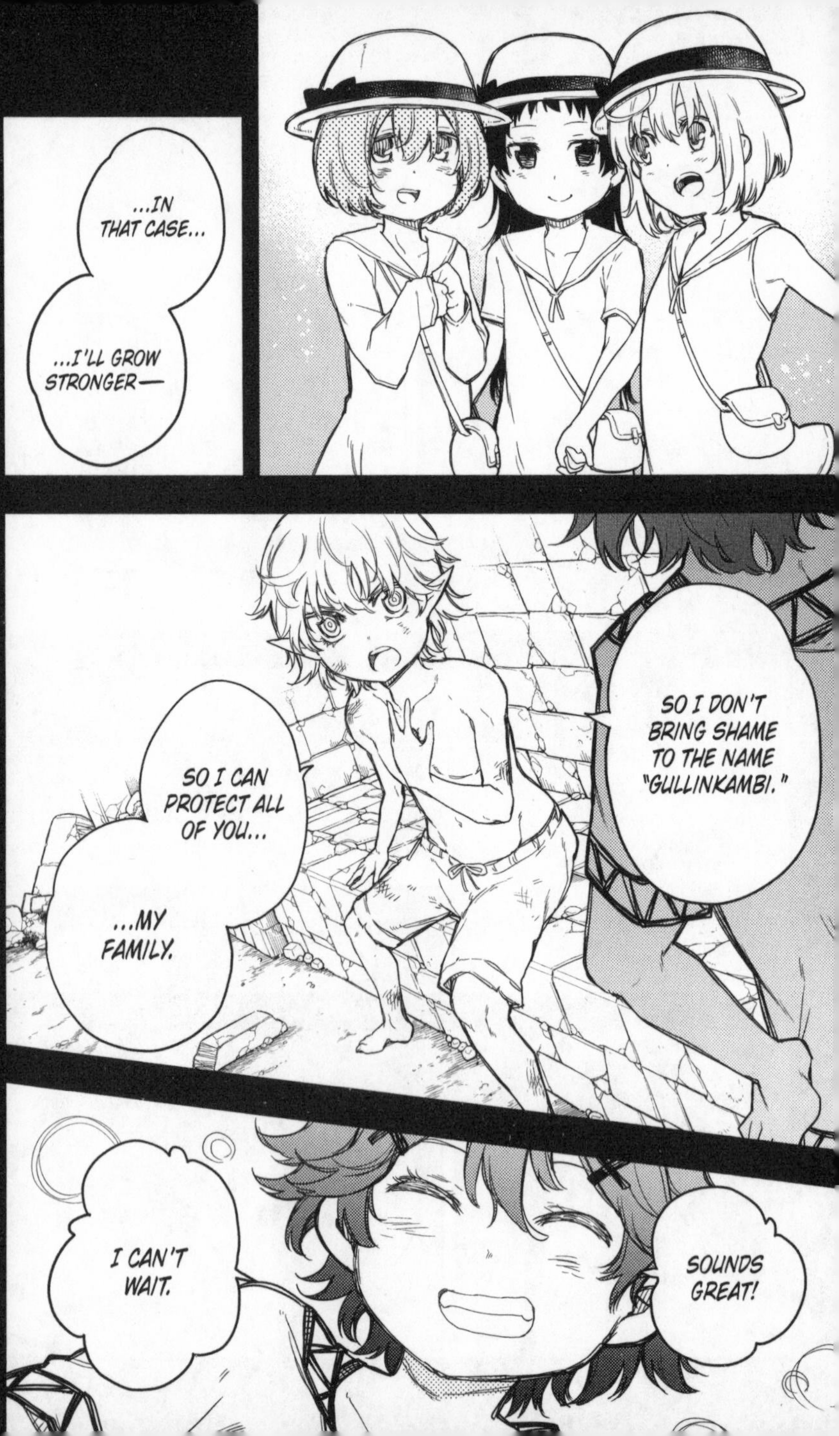
...IN THAT CASE...
...I'LL GROW STRONGER—
SO I DON'T BRING SHAME TO THE NAME "GULLINKAMBI."
SO I CAN PROTECT ALL OF YOU...
...MY FAMILY.
SOUNDS GREAT!
I CAN'T WAIT.

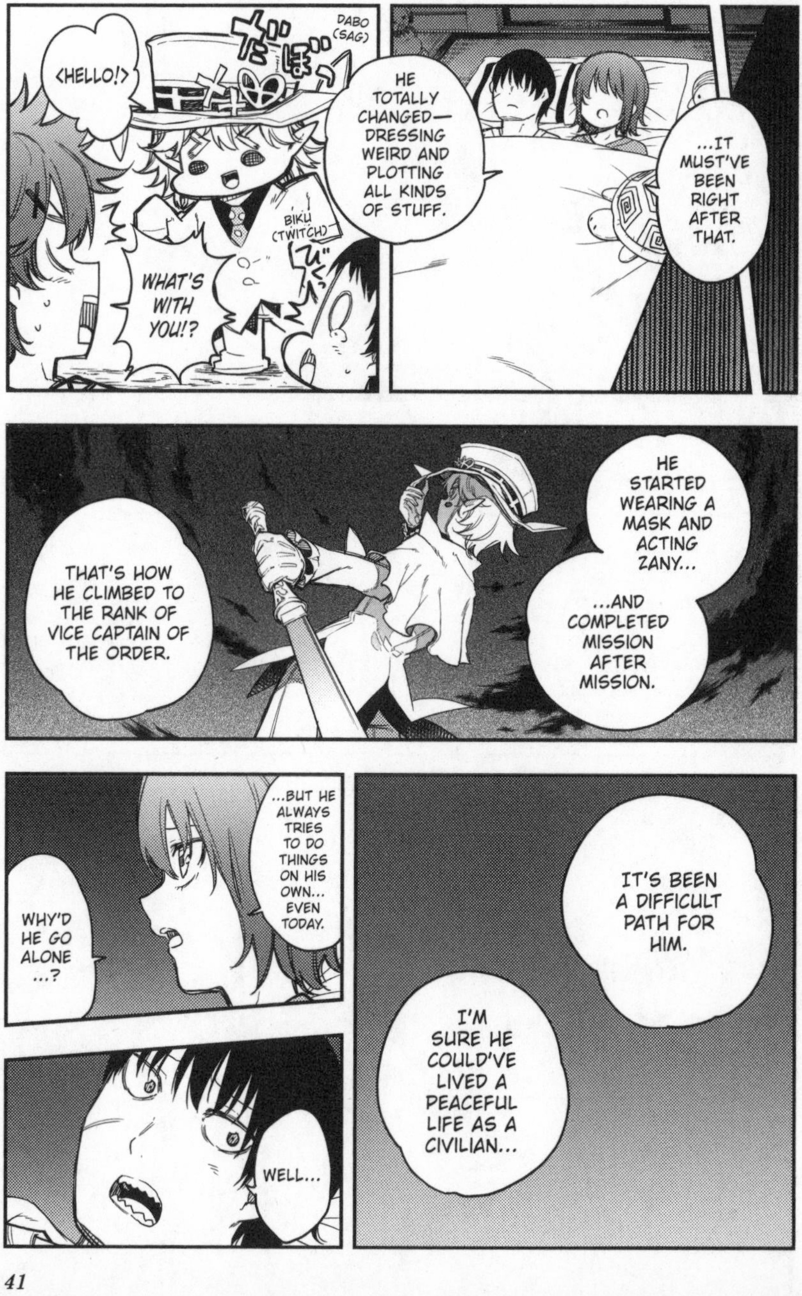
...IT MUST'VE BEEN RIGHT AFTER THAT.
HE TOTALLY CHANGED— DRESSING WEIRD AND PLOTTING ALL KINDS OF STUFF.
DABO (SAG)
<HELLO!>
BIKU (TWITCH)
WHAT'S WITH YOU!?
HE STARTED WEARING A MASK AND ACTING ZANY...
...AND COMPLETED MISSION AFTER MISSION.
THAT'S HOW HE CLIMBED TO THE RANK OF VICE CAPTAIN OF THE ORDER.
IT'S BEEN A DIFFICULT PATH FOR HIM.
I'M SURE HE COULD'VE LIVED A PEACEFUL LIFE AS A CIVILIAN...
...BUT HE ALWAYS TRIES TO DO THINGS ON HIS OWN... EVEN TODAY.
WHY'D HE GO ALONE ...?
WELL...

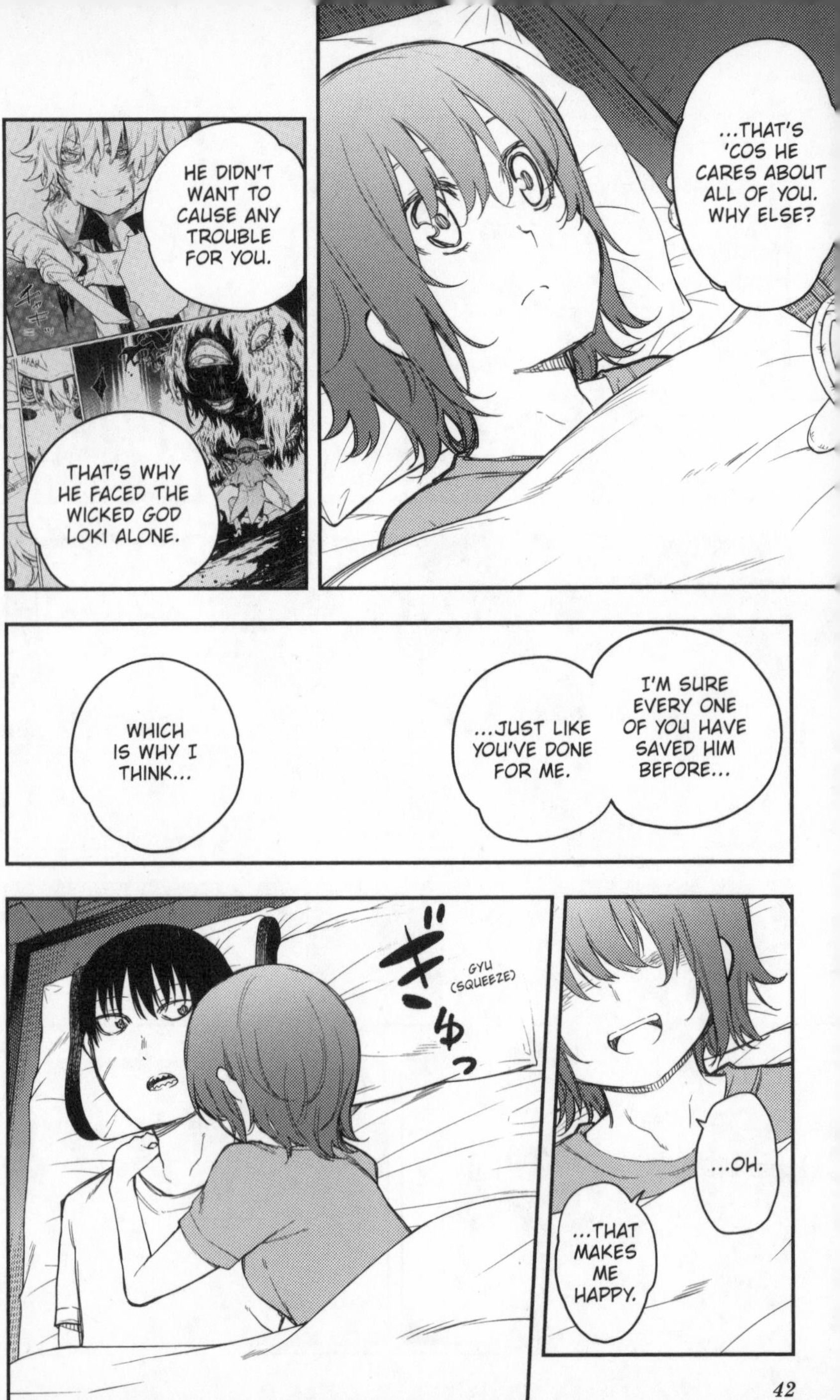
...THAT'S 'COS HE CARES ABOUT ALL OF YOU. WHY ELSE?
HE DIDN'T WANT TO CAUSE ANY TROUBLE FOR YOU.
THAT'S WHY HE FACED THE WICKED GOD LOKI ALONE.
I'M SURE EVERY ONE OF YOU HAVE SAVED HIM BEFORE...
...JUST LIKE YOU'VE DONE FOR ME.
WHICH IS WHY I THINK...
...OH.
...THAT MAKES ME HAPPY.
ぎゅっ
GYU (SQUEEZE)

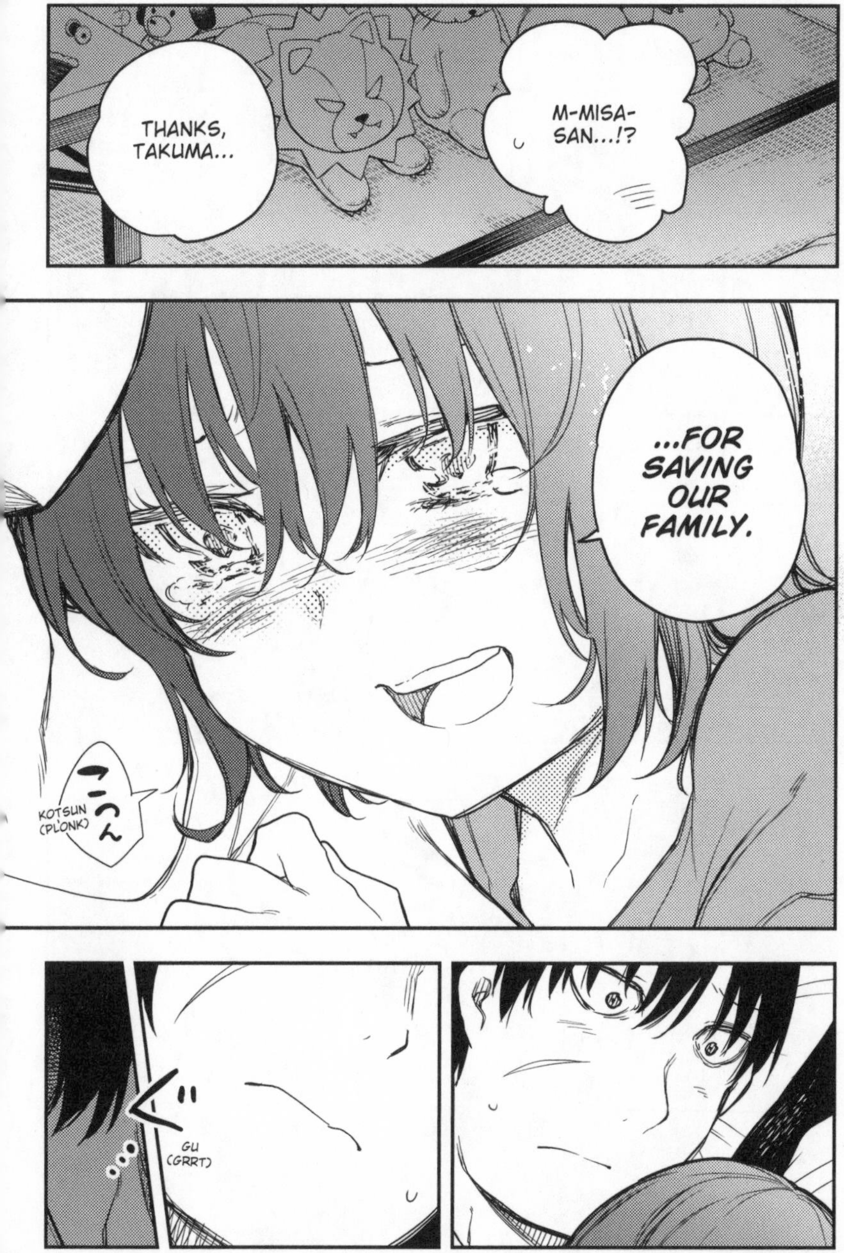
M-MISA-SAN...!?
THANKS, TAKUMA...
...FOR SAVING OUR FAMILY.
こつん
KOTSUN (PLONK)
ぐっ
GU (GRRT)
...

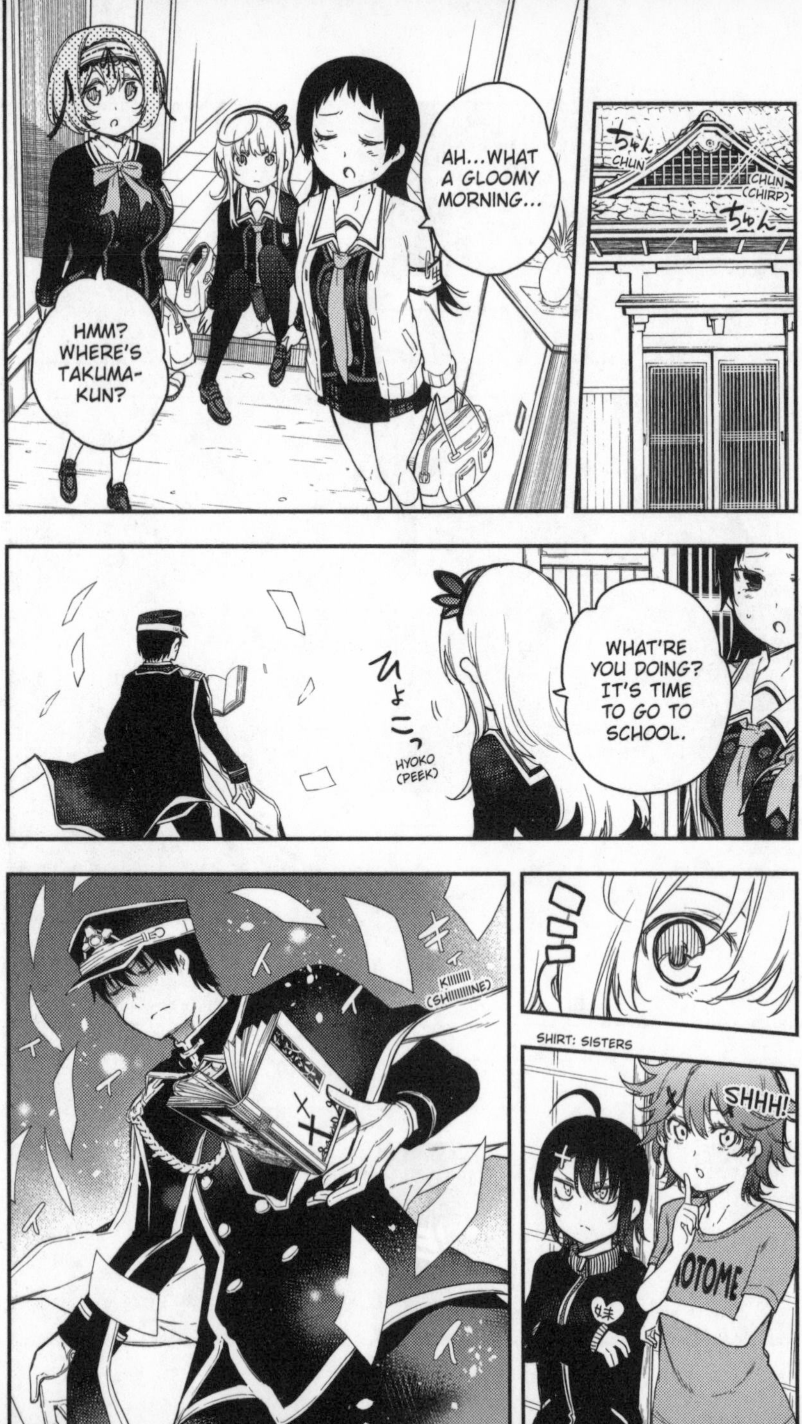
ちゅん
CHUN
CHUN (CHIRP)
ちゅん
AH...WHAT A GLOOMY MORNING...
HMM? WHERE'S TAKUMA-KUN?
WHAT'RE YOU DOING? IT'S TIME TO GO TO SCHOOL.
ひょこっ
HYOKO (PEEK)
SHIRT: SISTERS
SHHH!
キィィィィィ
KIIIIIIII (SHIIIIIIIINE)

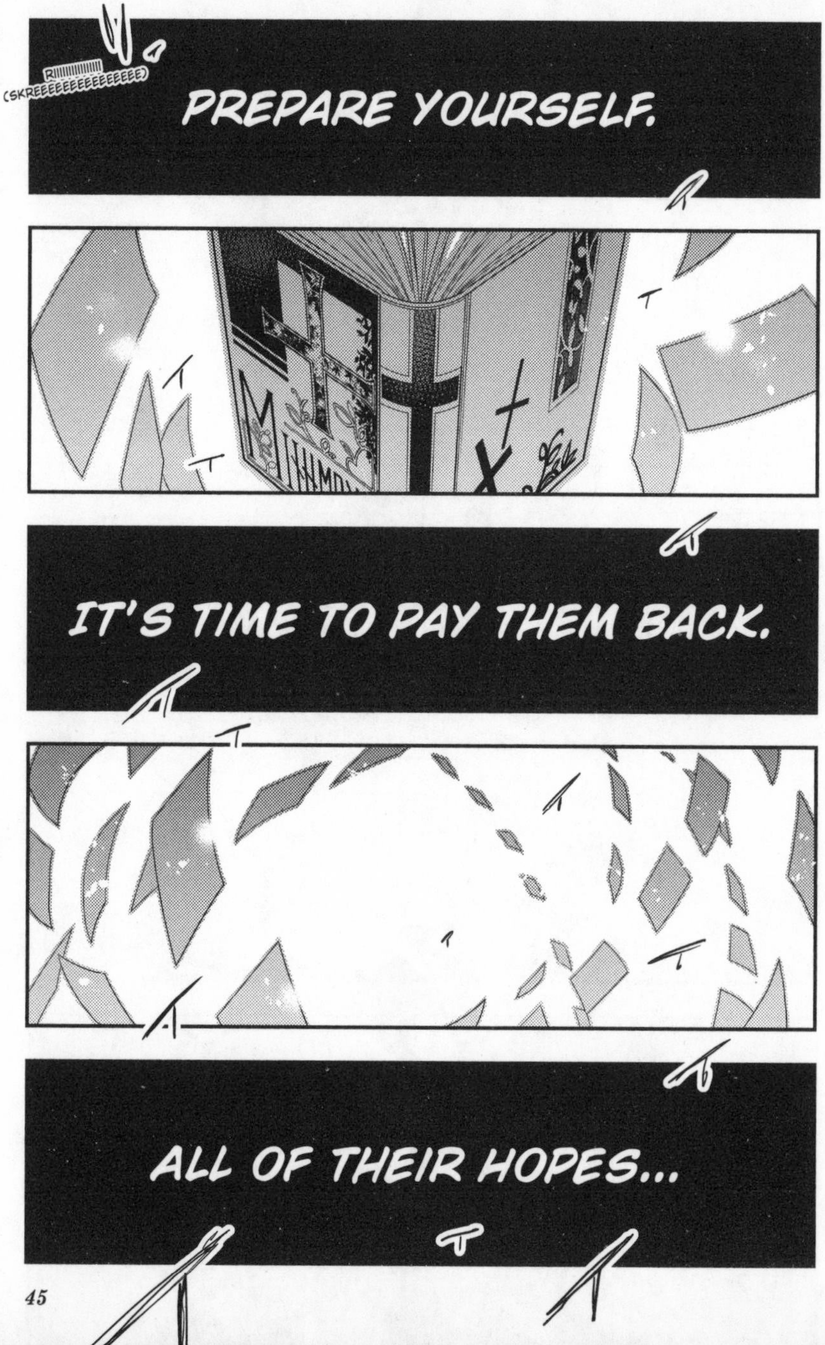
RIIIIIIIIIIIIIIIII
(SKREEEEEEEEEEEEEEEEE)
PREPARE YOURSELF.
IT'S TIME TO PAY THEM BACK.
ALL OF THEIR HOPES...

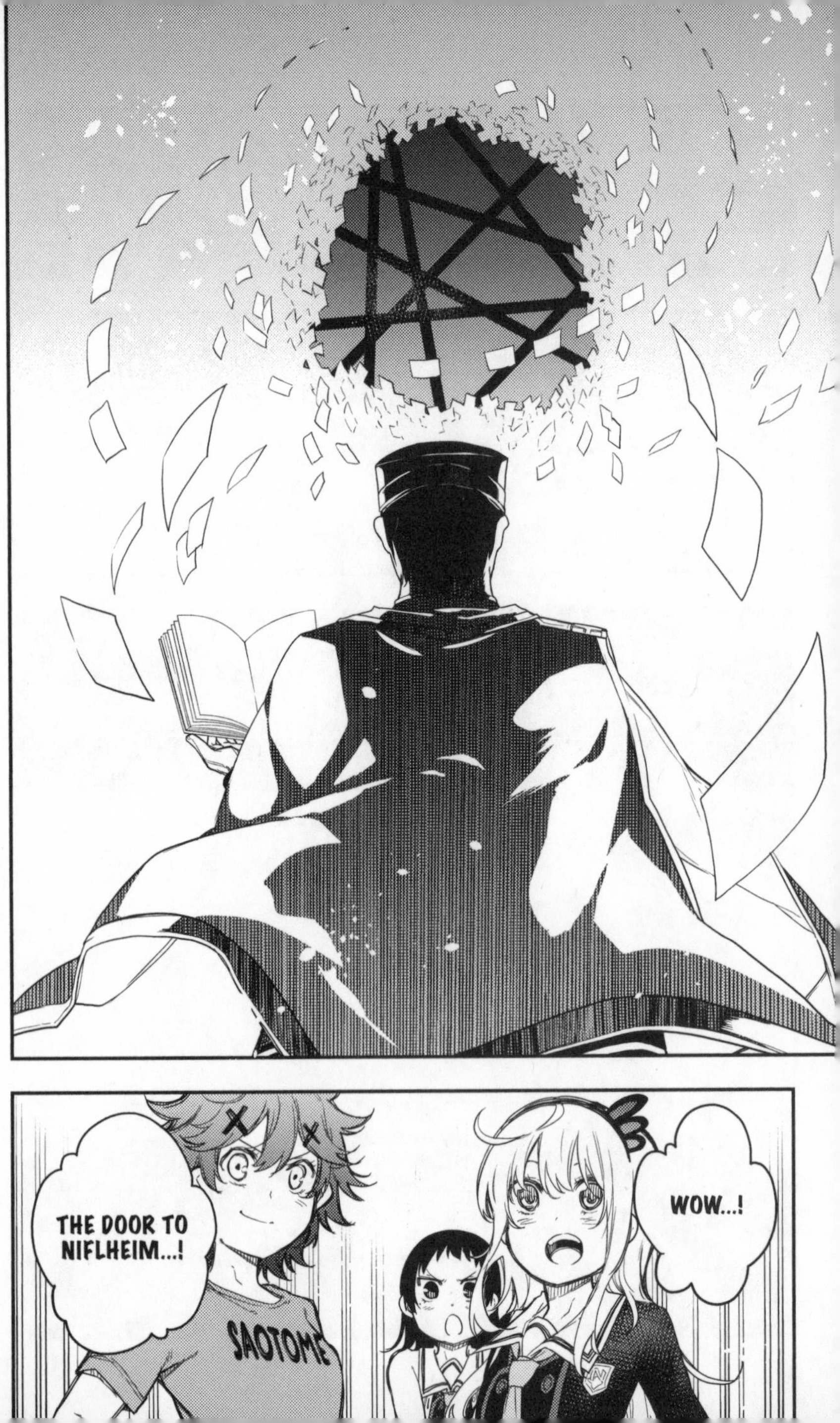
WOW...!
THE DOOR TO NIFLHEIM...!
SAOTOME

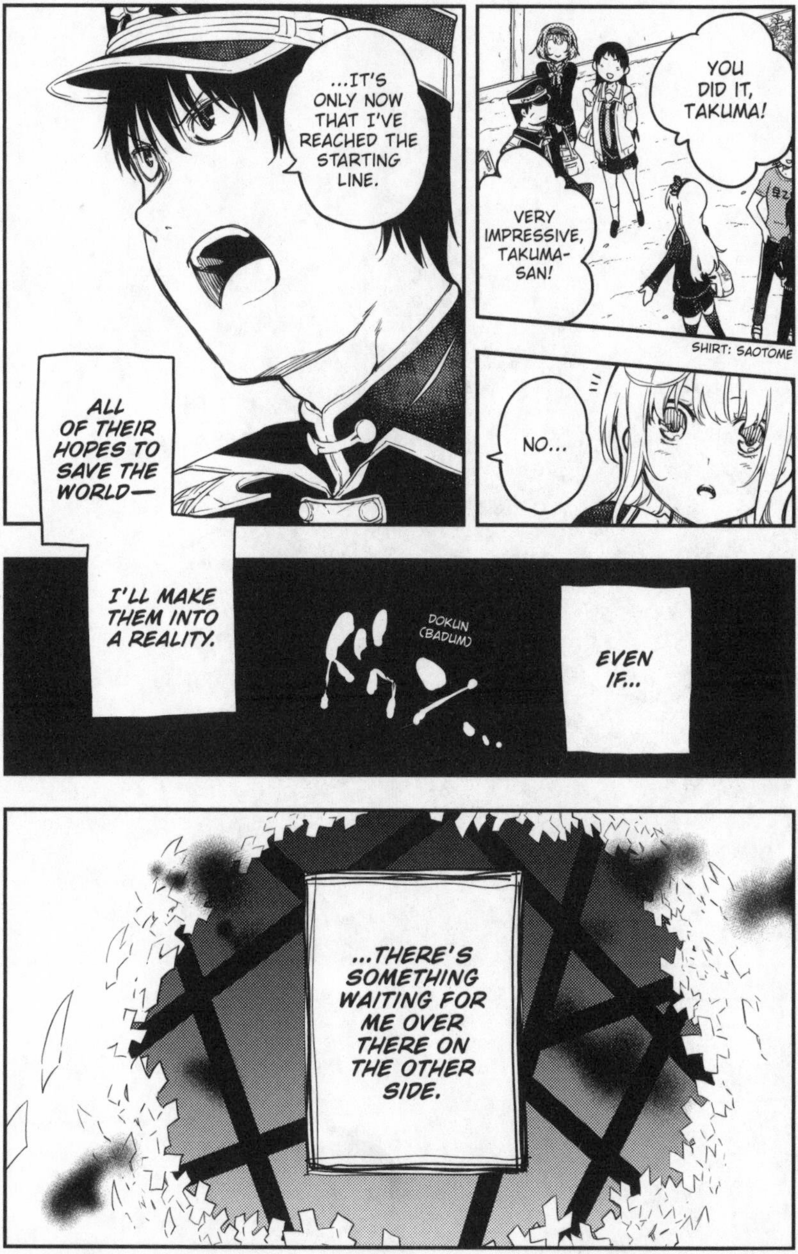
YOU DID IT, TAKUMA!
VERY IMPRESSIVE, TAKUMA-SAN!
SHIRT: SAOTOME
NO...
...IT'S ONLY NOW THAT I'VE REACHED THE STARTING LINE.
ALL OF THEIR HOPES TO SAVE THE WORLD—
I'LL MAKE THEM INTO A REALITY.
EVEN IF...
DOKUN (BADUM)
...THERE'S SOMETHING WAITING FOR ME OVER THERE ON THE OTHER SIDE.

Val × Love

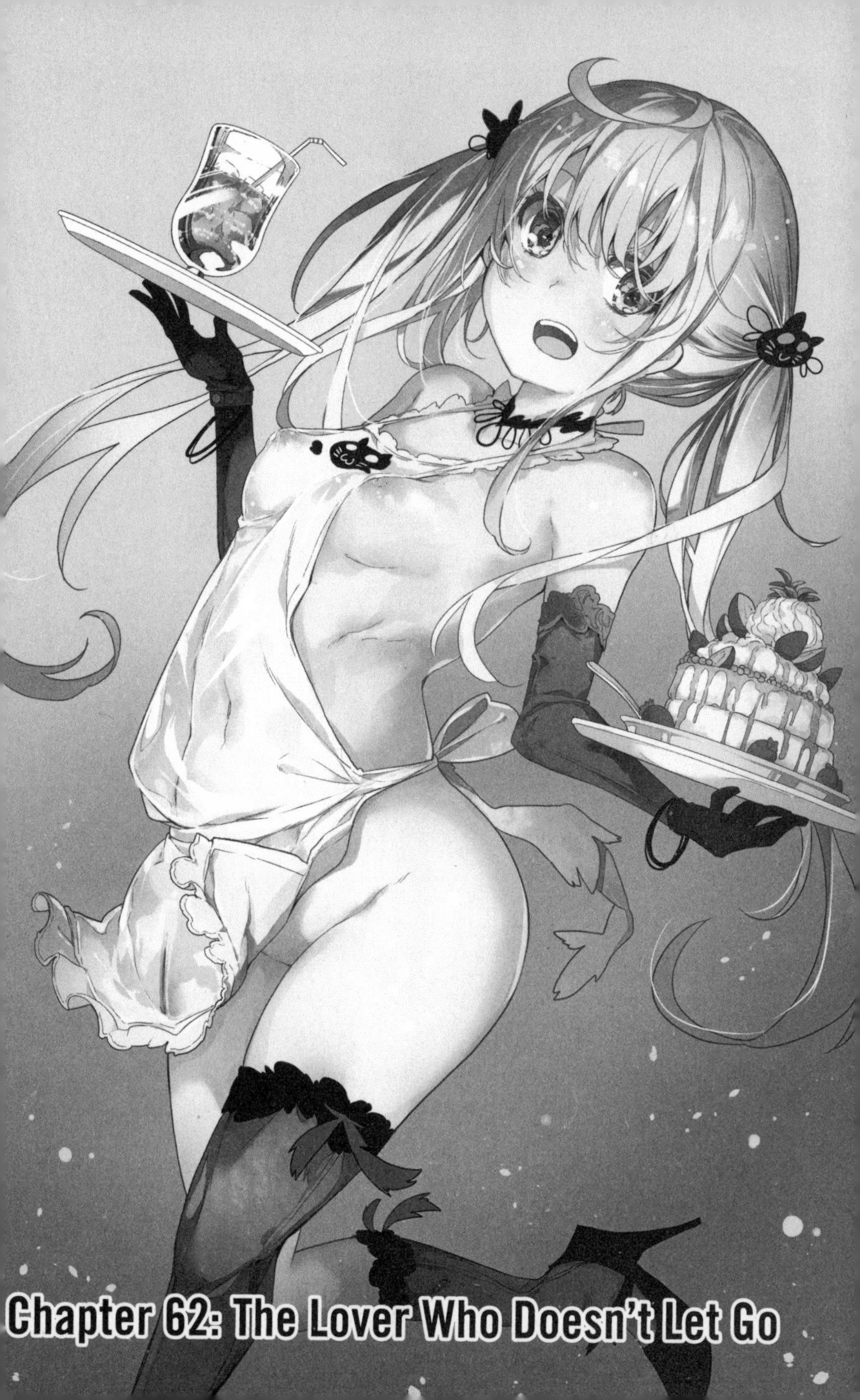

Chapter 62: The Lover Who Doesn't Let Go

Val X Love

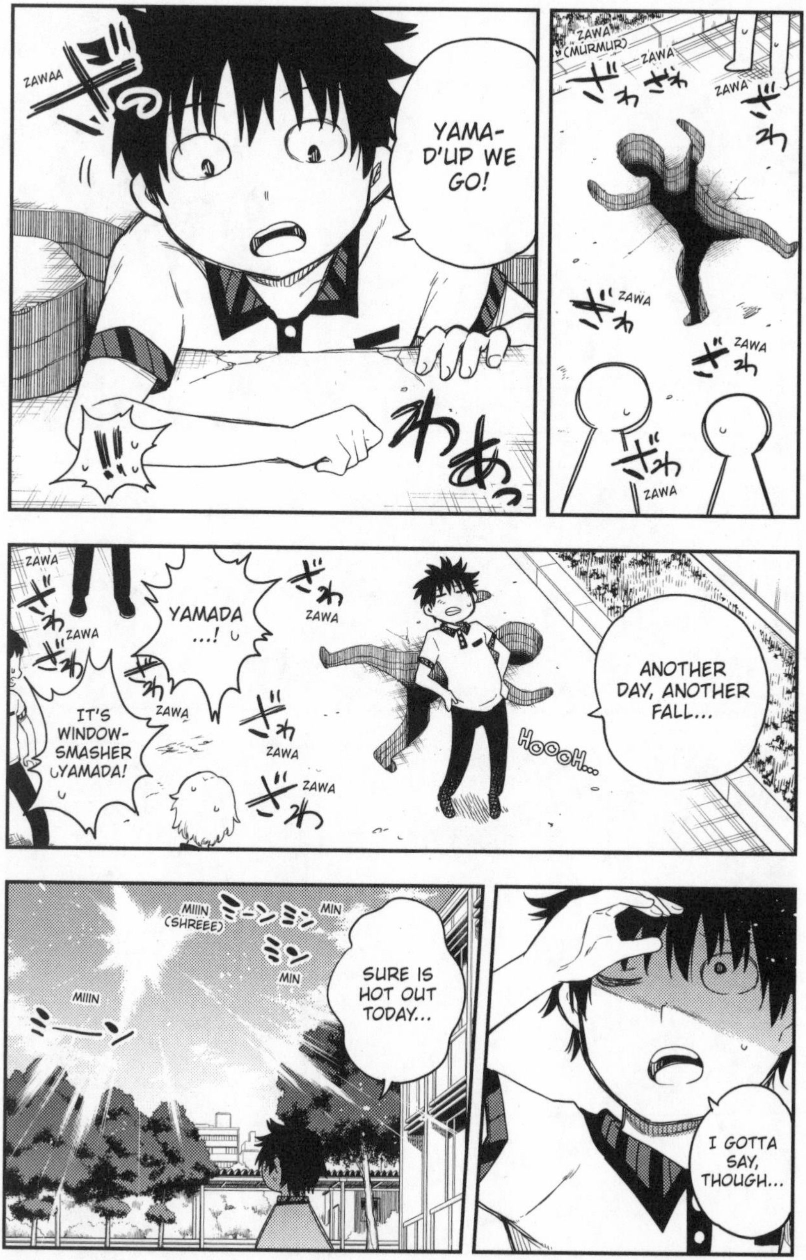
ZAWA (MURMUR)
ZAWA
ZAWA
ZAWA
ZAWA
ZAWA
YAMA-D'UP WE GO!
ZAWAA
!!
ANOTHER DAY, ANOTHER FALL...
HOOOH...
ZAWA
ZAWA
ZAWA
YAMADA...!
ZAWA
ZAWA
ZAWA
IT'S WINDOW-SMASHER YAMADA!
I GOTTA SAY, THOUGH...
SURE IS HOT OUT TODAY...
MIN
MIIN (SHREEE)
MIN
MIIN

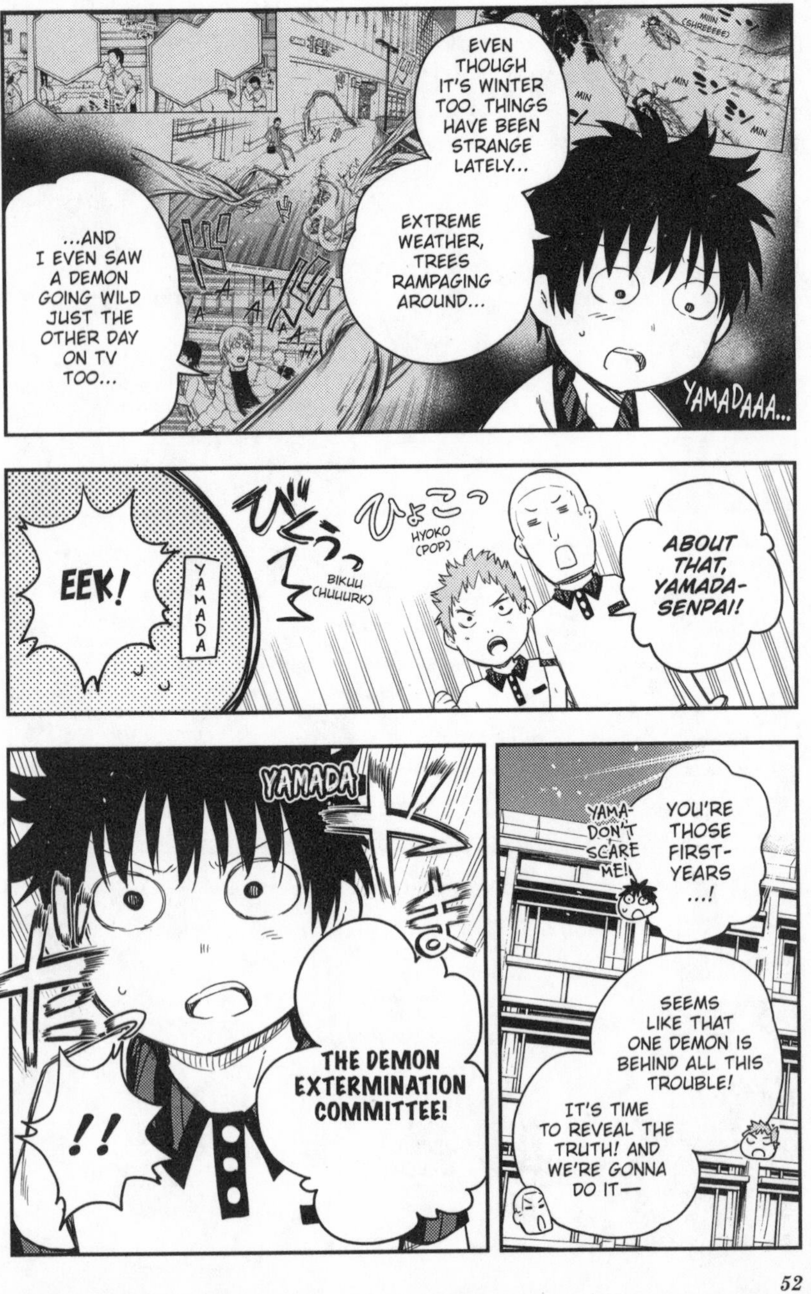
MIIN (SHREEEEE)
MIN
MIN
MIN
EVEN THOUGH IT'S WINTER TOO. THINGS HAVE BEEN STRANGE LATELY...
EXTREME WEATHER, TREES RAMPAGING AROUND...
...AND I EVEN SAW A DEMON GOING WILD JUST THE OTHER DAY ON TV TOO...
YAMADAAA...
ABOUT THAT, YAMADA-SENPAI!
HYOKO (POP)
BIKUU (HUUURK)
EEK!
YAMADA
YOU'RE THOSE FIRST-YEARS ...!
YAMA- DON'T SCARE ME!
SEEMS LIKE THAT ONE DEMON IS BEHIND ALL THIS TROUBLE!
IT'S TIME TO REVEAL THE TRUTH! AND WE'RE GONNA DO IT—
YAMADA
THE DEMON EXTERMINATION COMMITTEE!
!!

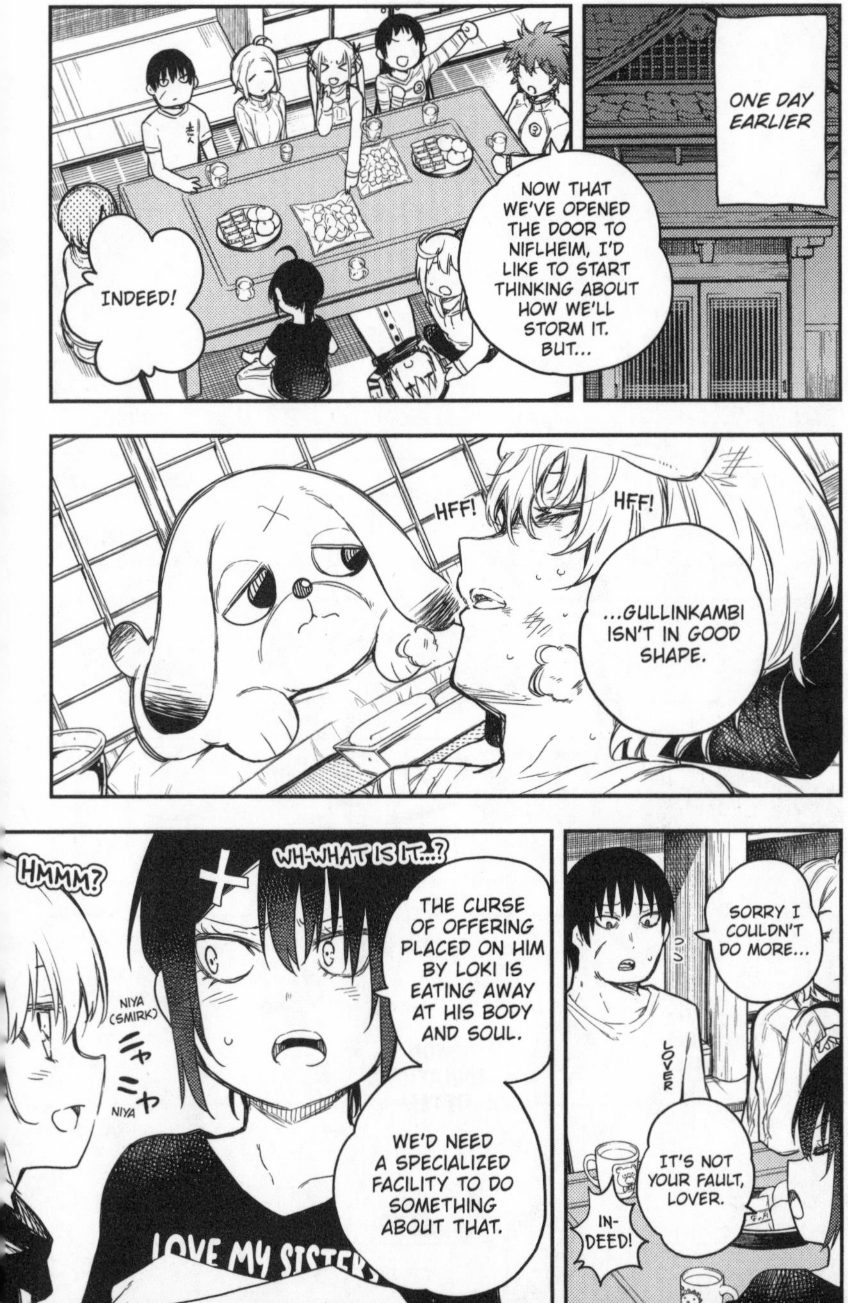
ONE DAY EARLIER
NOW THAT WE'VE OPENED THE DOOR TO NIFLHEIM, I'D LIKE TO START THINKING ABOUT HOW WE'LL STORM IT. BUT...
INDEED!
HFF!
HFF!
...GULLINKAMBI ISN'T IN GOOD SHAPE.
SORRY I COULDN'T DO MORE...
LOVER
IT'S NOT YOUR FAULT, LOVER.
IN-DEED!
WH-WHAT IS IT...?
THE CURSE OF OFFERING PLACED ON HIM BY LOKI IS EATING AWAY AT HIS BODY AND SOUL.
HMMM?
NIYA (SMIRK)
ニヤニヤ
NIYA
WE'D NEED A SPECIALIZED FACILITY TO DO SOMETHING ABOUT THAT.
LOVE MY SISTER

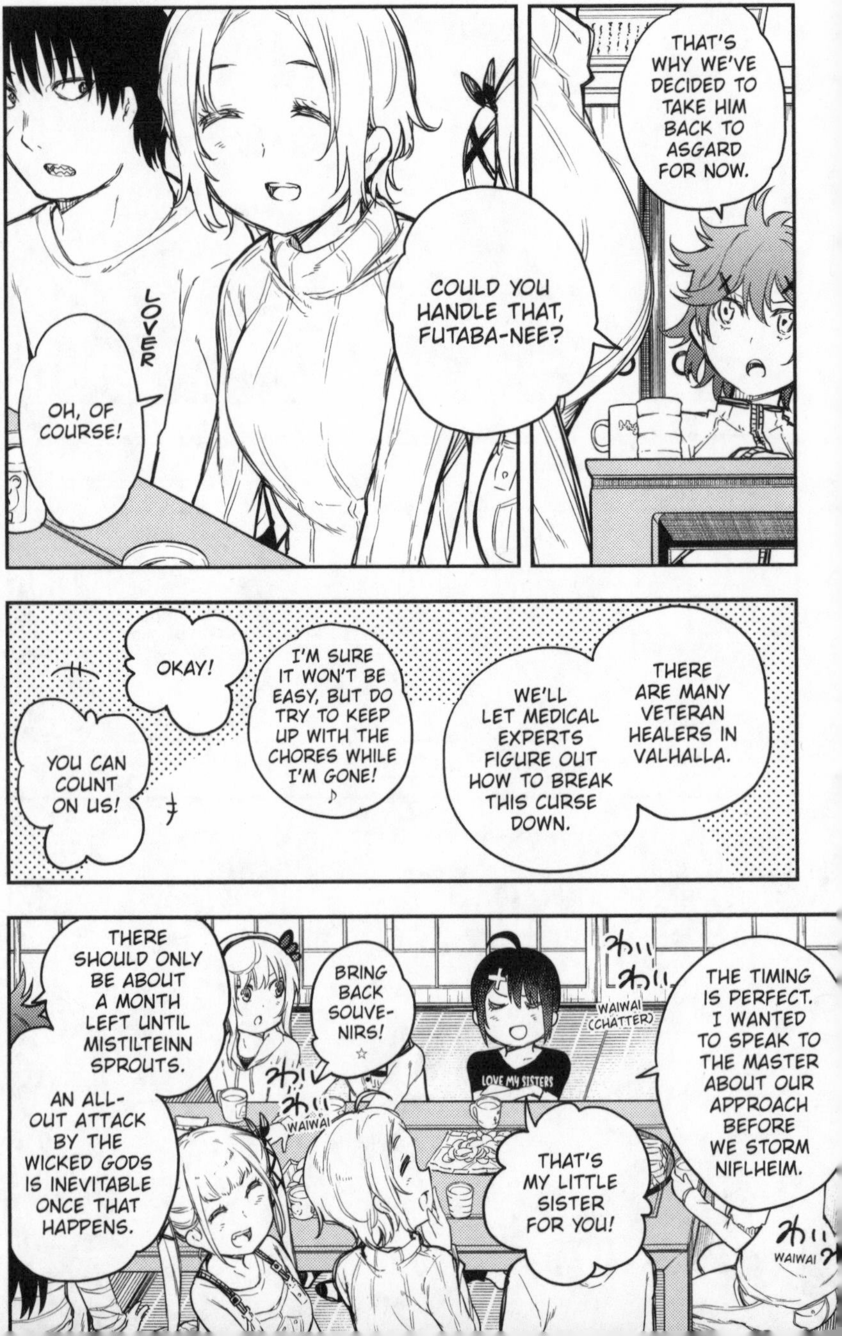
THAT'S WHY WE'VE DECIDED TO TAKE HIM BACK TO ASGARD FOR NOW.
COULD YOU HANDLE THAT, FUTABA-NEE?
LOVER
OH, OF COURSE!
THERE ARE MANY VETERAN HEALERS IN VALHALLA.
WE'LL LET MEDICAL EXPERTS FIGURE OUT HOW TO BREAK THIS CURSE DOWN.
I'M SURE IT WON'T BE EASY, BUT DO TRY TO KEEP UP WITH THE CHORES WHILE I'M GONE! ♪
OKAY!
YOU CAN COUNT ON US!
THE TIMING IS PERFECT. I WANTED TO SPEAK TO THE MASTER ABOUT OUR APPROACH BEFORE WE STORM NIFLHEIM.
WAIWAI
WAIWAI (CHATTER)
THAT'S MY LITTLE SISTER FOR YOU!
LOVE MY SISTERS
BRING BACK SOUVENIRS! ☆
WAIWAI
THERE SHOULD ONLY BE ABOUT A MONTH LEFT UNTIL MISTILTEINN SPROUTS.
AN ALL-OUT ATTACK BY THE WICKED GODS IS INEVITABLE ONCE THAT HAPPENS.

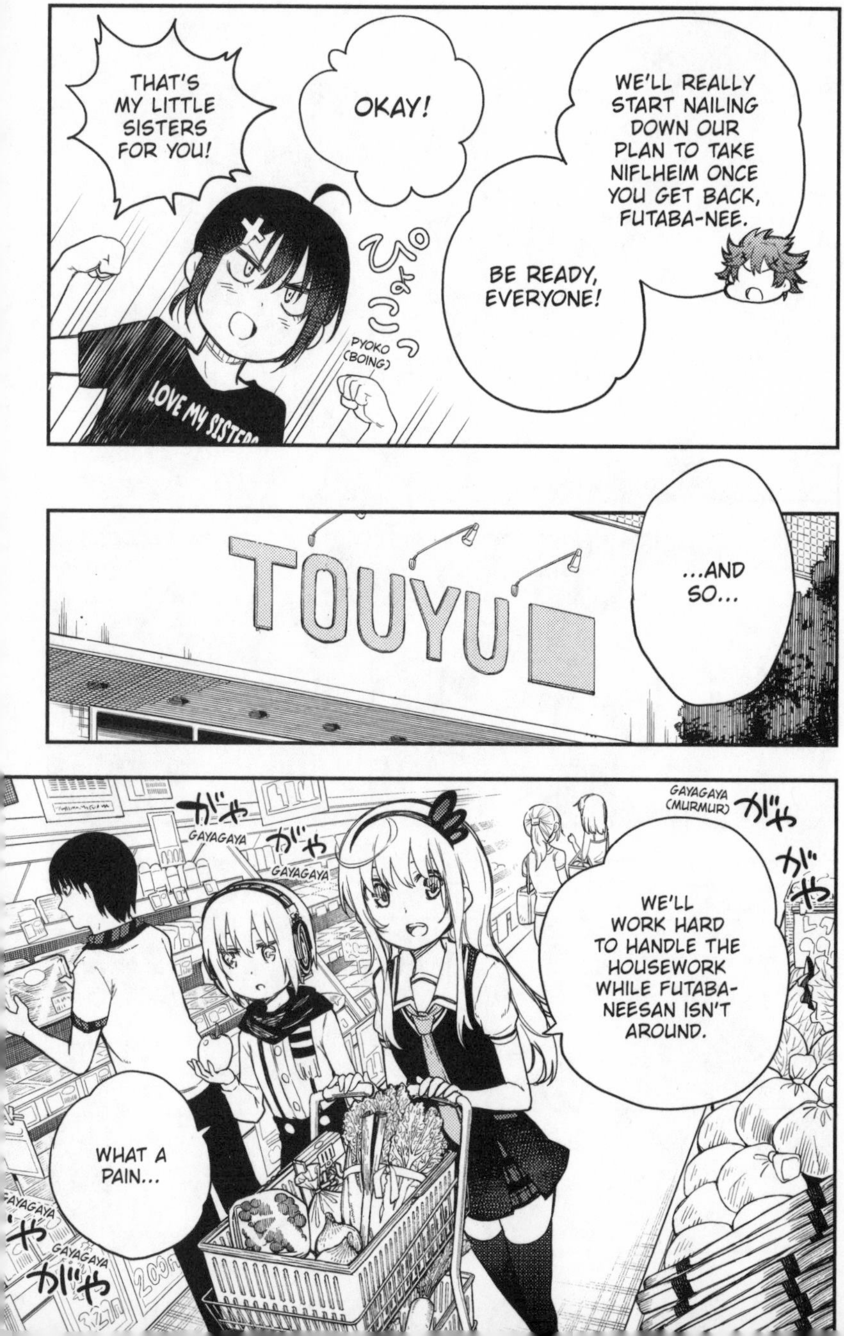
WE'LL REALLY START NAILING DOWN OUR PLAN TO TAKE NIFLHEIM ONCE YOU GET BACK, FUTABA-NEE.
BE READY, EVERYONE!
OKAY!
ぴょこっ
PYOKO (BOING)
THAT'S MY LITTLE SISTERS FOR YOU!
...AND SO...
TOUYU
GAYAGAYA (MURMUR) がや
がや
WE'LL WORK HARD TO HANDLE THE HOUSEWORK WHILE FUTABA-NEESAN ISN'T AROUND.
がや
GAYAGAYA
がや
GAYAGAYA
WHAT A PAIN...
GAYAGAYA
や
GAYAGAYA
がや

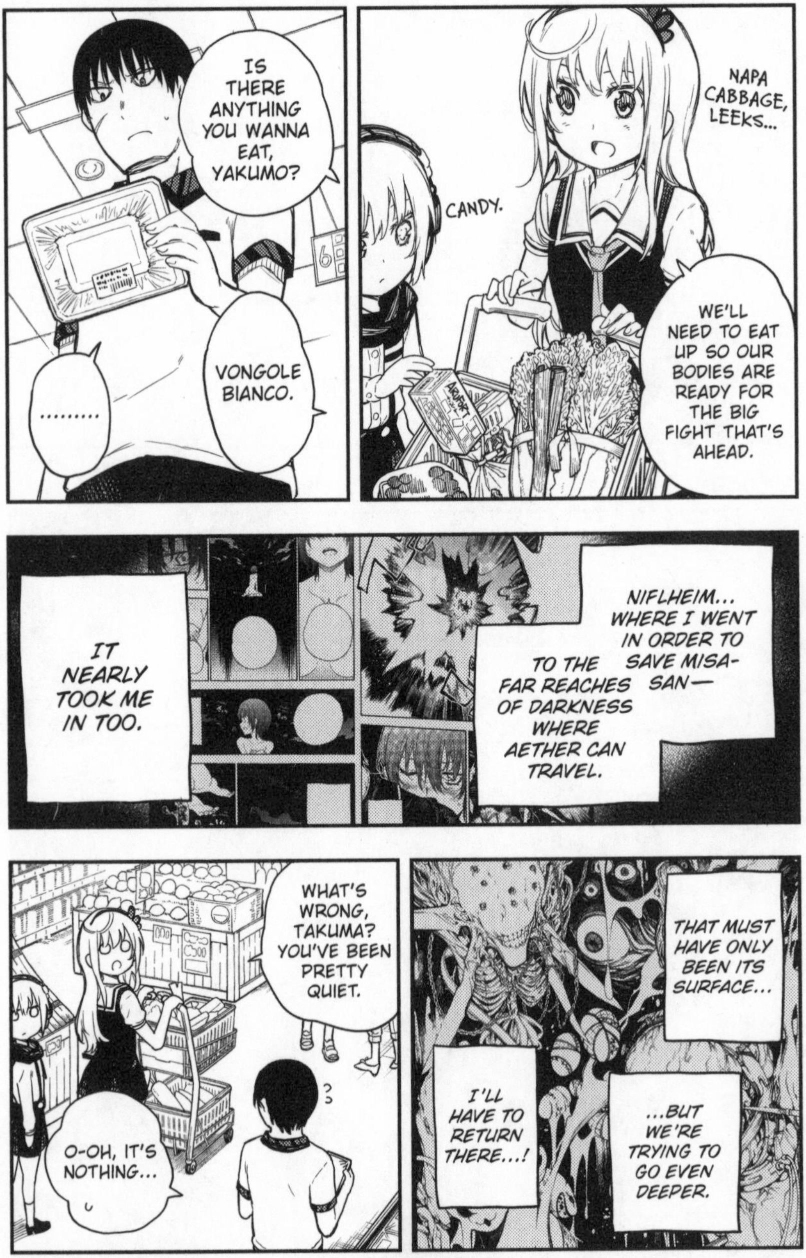
NAPA CABBAGE, LEEKS...
CANDY.
WE'LL NEED TO EAT UP SO OUR BODIES ARE READY FOR THE BIG FIGHT THAT'S AHEAD.
IS THERE ANYTHING YOU WANNA EAT, YAKUMO?
VONGOLE BIANCO.
....
NIFLHEIM... WHERE I WENT IN ORDER TO SAVE MISA-SAN—
TO THE FAR REACHES OF DARKNESS WHERE AETHER CAN TRAVEL.
IT NEARLY TOOK ME IN TOO.
THAT MUST HAVE ONLY BEEN ITS SURFACE...
...BUT WE'RE TRYING TO GO EVEN DEEPER.
I'LL HAVE TO RETURN THERE...!
WHAT'S WRONG, TAKUMA? YOU'VE BEEN PRETTY QUIET.
O-OH, IT'S NOTHING...

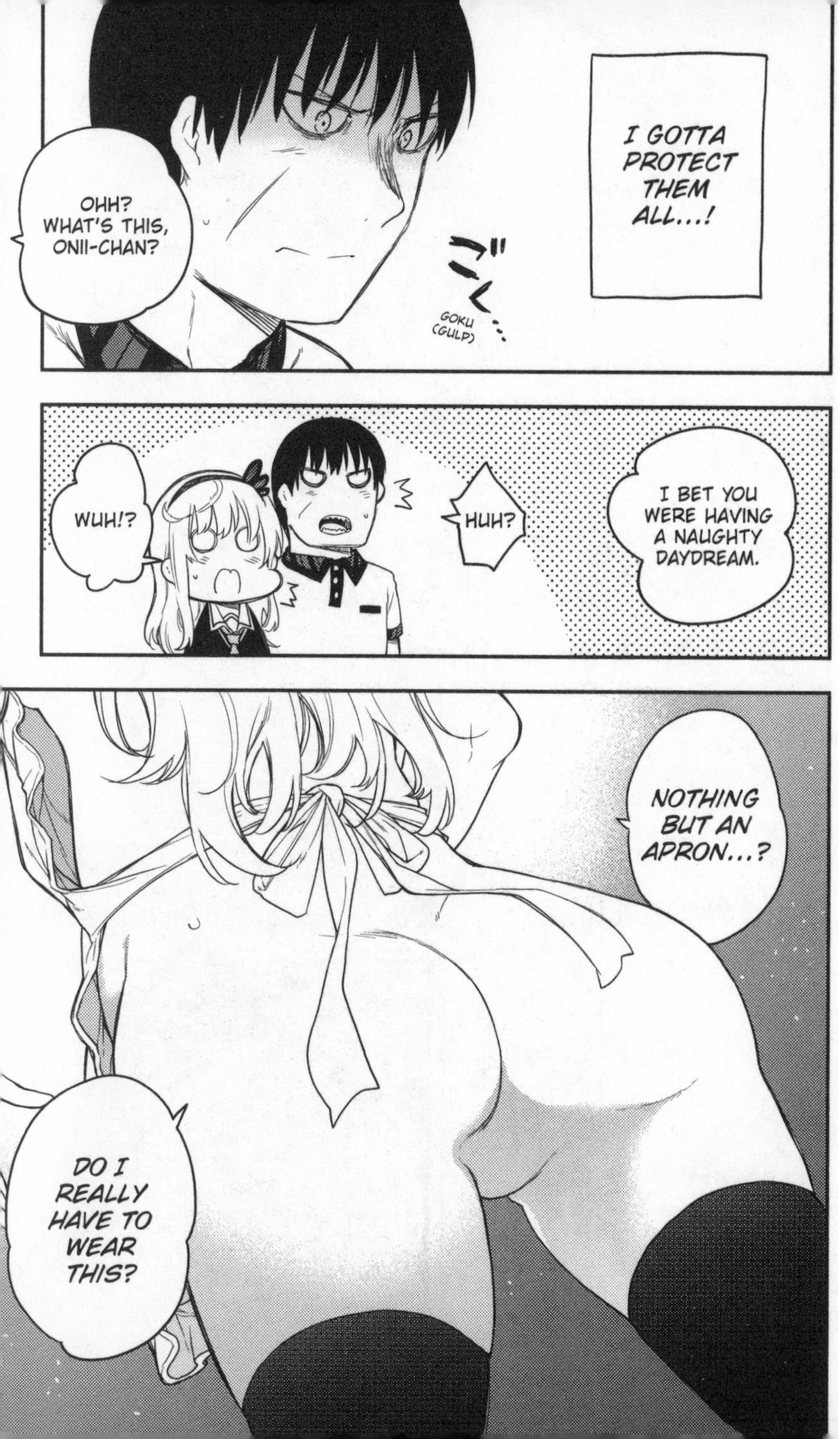
I GOTTA PROTECT THEM ALL...!
ごく
GOKU (GULP)
OHH? WHAT'S THIS, ONII-CHAN?
I BET YOU WERE HAVING A NAUGHTY DAYDREAM.
HUH?
WUH!?
NOTHING BUT AN APRON...?
DO I REALLY HAVE TO WEAR THIS?

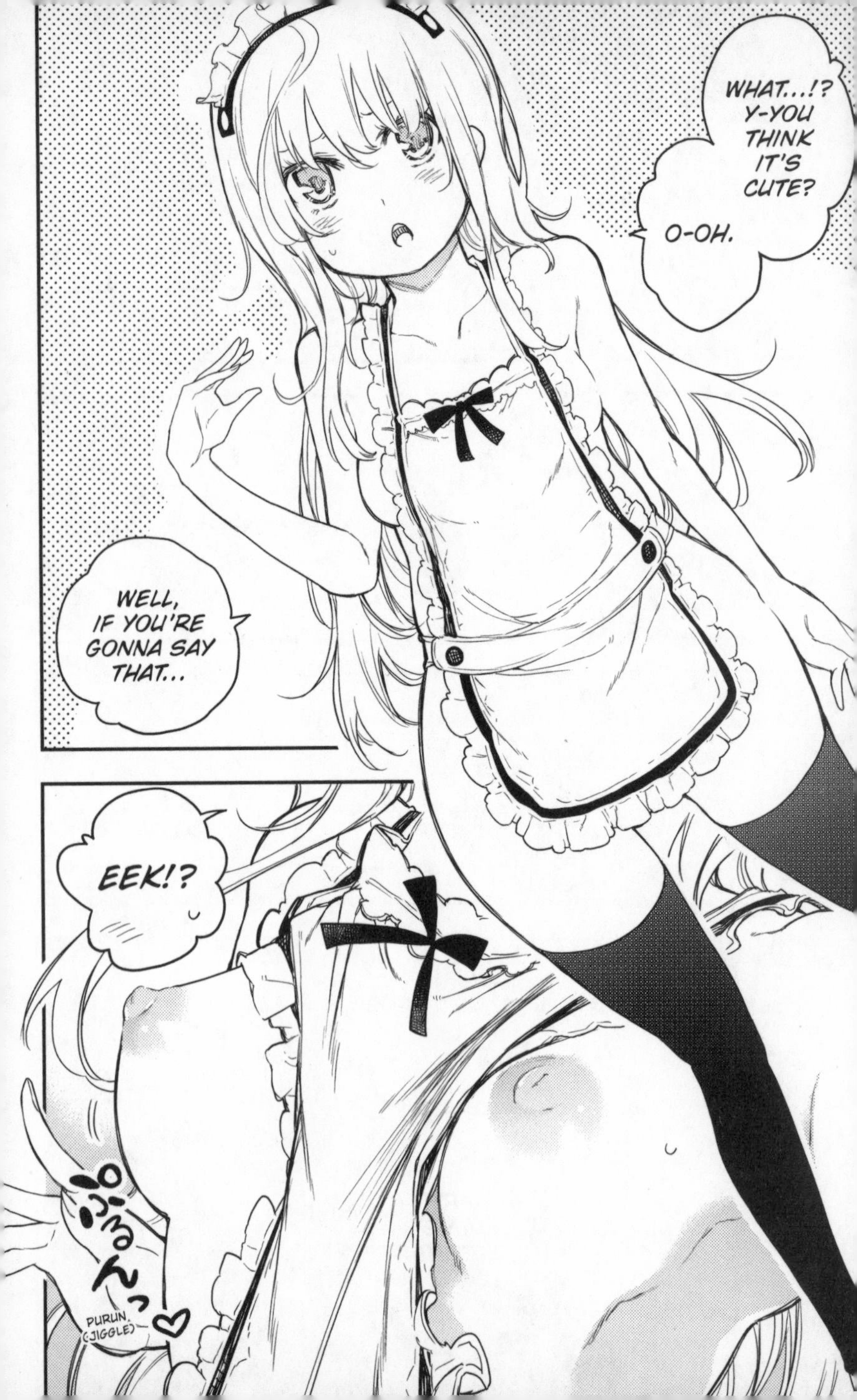
WHAT...!? Y-YOU THINK IT'S CUTE?
O-OH.
WELL, IF YOU'RE GONNA SAY THAT...
EEK!?
ぷるんっ♡
PURUN. (JIGGLE)

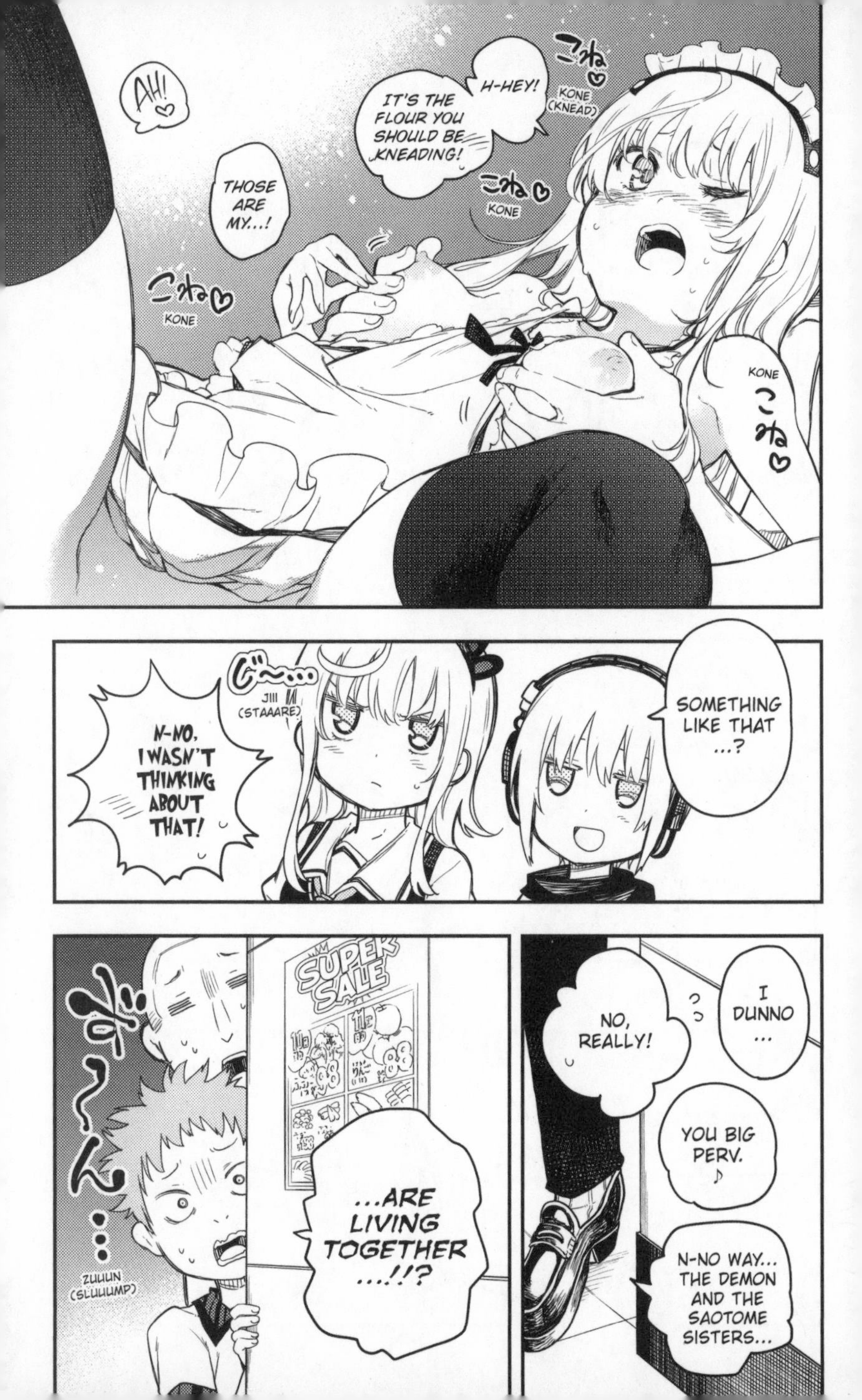
こね♡
KONE (KNEAD)
H-HEY!
IT'S THE FLOUR YOU SHOULD BE KNEADING!
AH!♡
こね♡
KONE
THOSE ARE MY...!
KONE
こね♡
こね♡
KONE
SOMETHING LIKE THAT ...?
じ〜...
JIII (STAAARE)
N-NO, I WASN'T THINKING ABOUT THAT!
I DUNNO ...
NO, REALLY!
YOU BIG PERV. ♪
N-NO WAY... THE DEMON AND THE SAOTOME SISTERS...
SUPER SALE
...ARE LIVING TOGETHER ....!!?
ZUUUN (SLUUUMP)

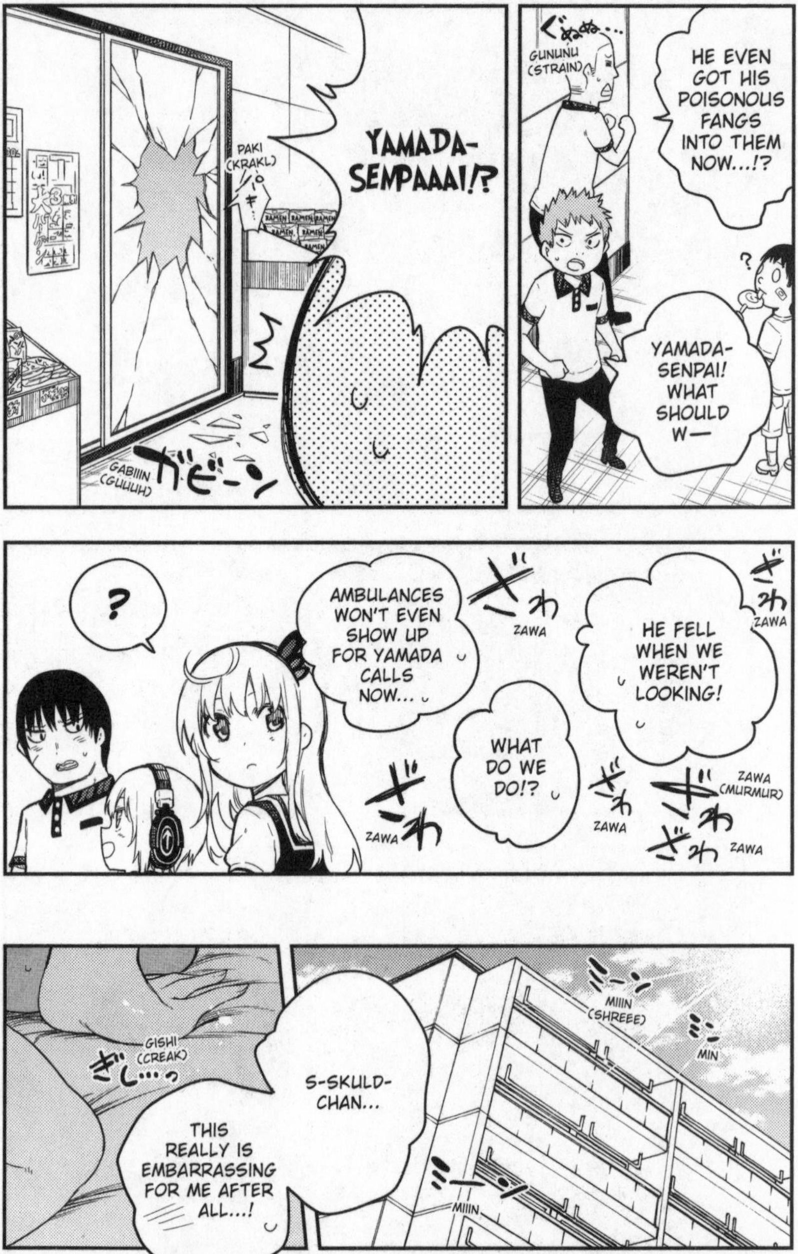
ぐぬぬ…
GUNUNU (STRAIN)
HE EVEN GOT HIS POISONOUS FANGS INTO THEM NOW...!?
?
YAMADA-SENPAI! WHAT SHOULD W—
YAMADA-SENPAAAI!?
PAKI (KRAKL)
RAMEN
ガビーン
GABIIIN (GUUUH)
ざわ
ZAWA
HE FELL WHEN WE WEREN'T LOOKING!
ざわ
ZAWA
AMBULANCES WON'T EVEN SHOW UP FOR YAMADA CALLS NOW...
WHAT DO WE DO!?
ZAWA (MURMUR)
ZAWA
ZAWA
ZAWA
?
MIIN (SHREEE)
MIN
MIIN
S-SKULD-CHAN...
THIS REALLY IS EMBARRASSING FOR ME AFTER ALL...!
GISHI (CREAK)

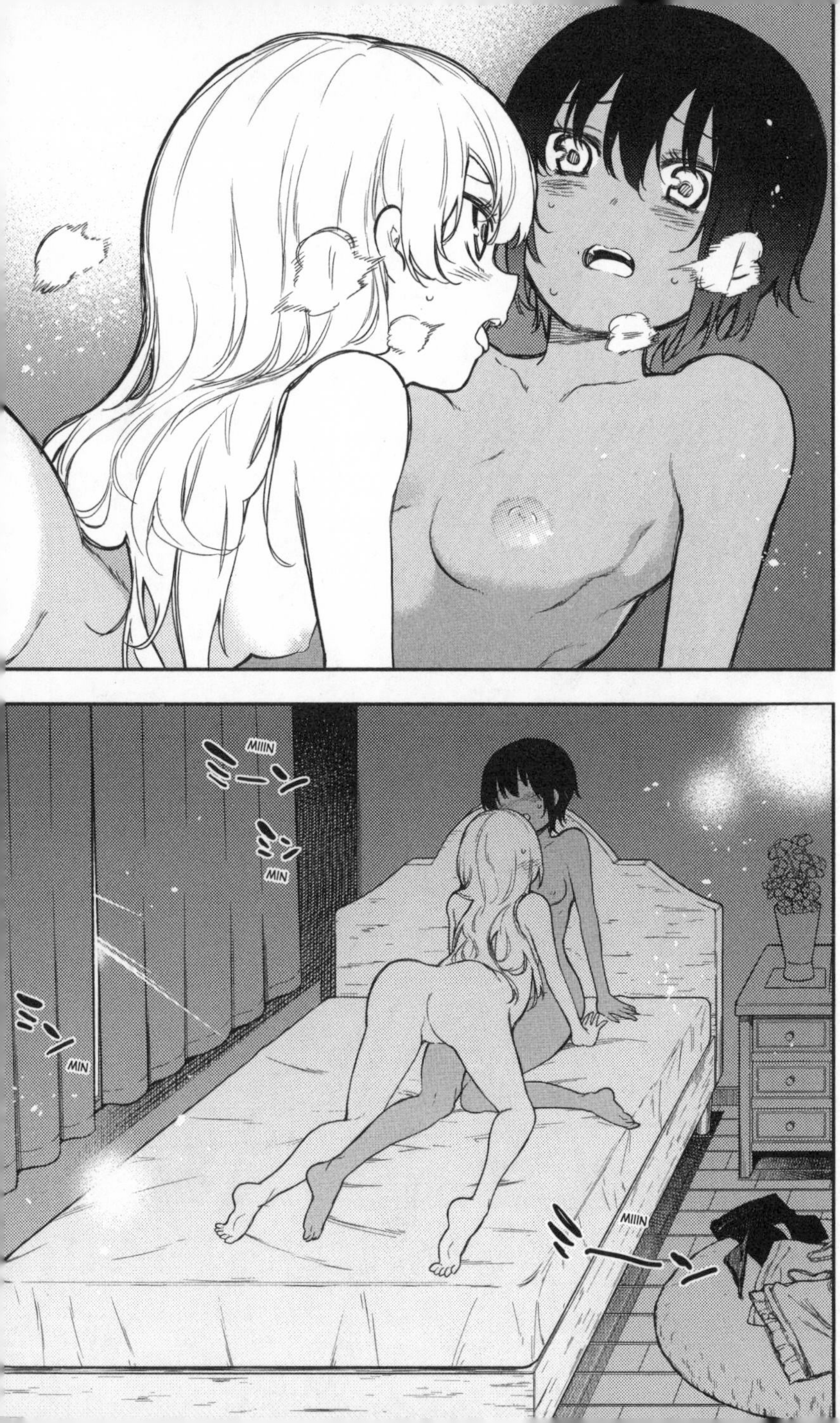

MIIN
MIN
MIN
MIIN

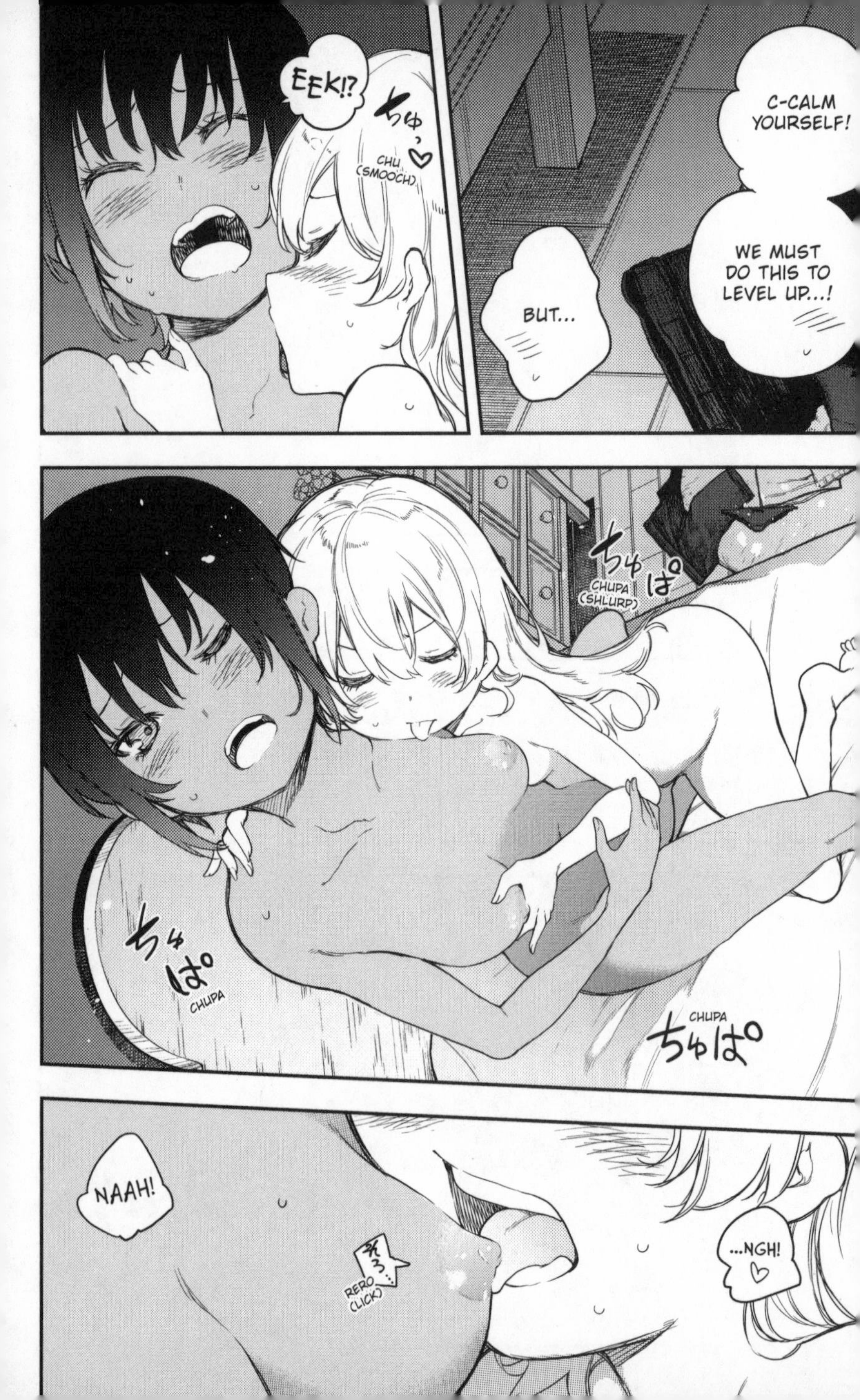
C-CALM YOURSELF!
WE MUST DO THIS TO LEVEL UP...!
BUT...
EEK!?
ちゅっ
CHU (SMOOCH)
ちゅぱ
CHUPA (SHLURP)
CHUPA
ちゅぱ
ちゅぱ
CHUPA
...NGH!
れろ…
RERO (LICK)
NAAH!

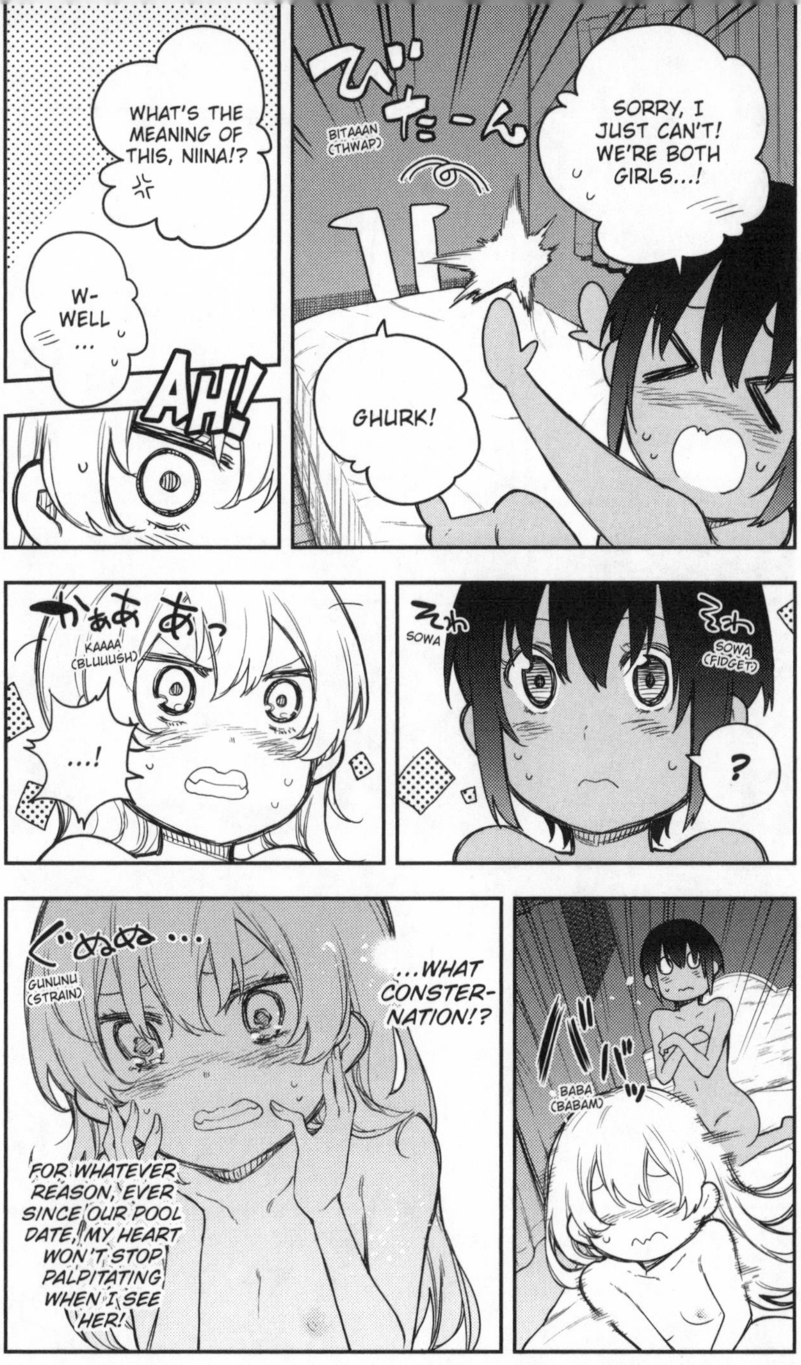
びたーん
BITAAAN (THWAP)
SORRY, I JUST CAN'T! WE'RE BOTH GIRLS...!
GHURK!
WHAT'S THE MEANING OF THIS, NIINA!?
W-WELL ...
AH!!
そわ
SOWA
そわ
SOWA (FIDGET)
?
かぁぁあっ
KAAAA (BLUUUSH)
...!
ババッ
BABA (BABAM)
ぐぬぬ…
GUNUNU (STRAIN)
...WHAT CONSTER-NATION!?
FOR WHATEVER REASON, EVER SINCE OUR POOL DATE, MY HEART WON'T STOP PALPITATING WHEN I SEE HER!

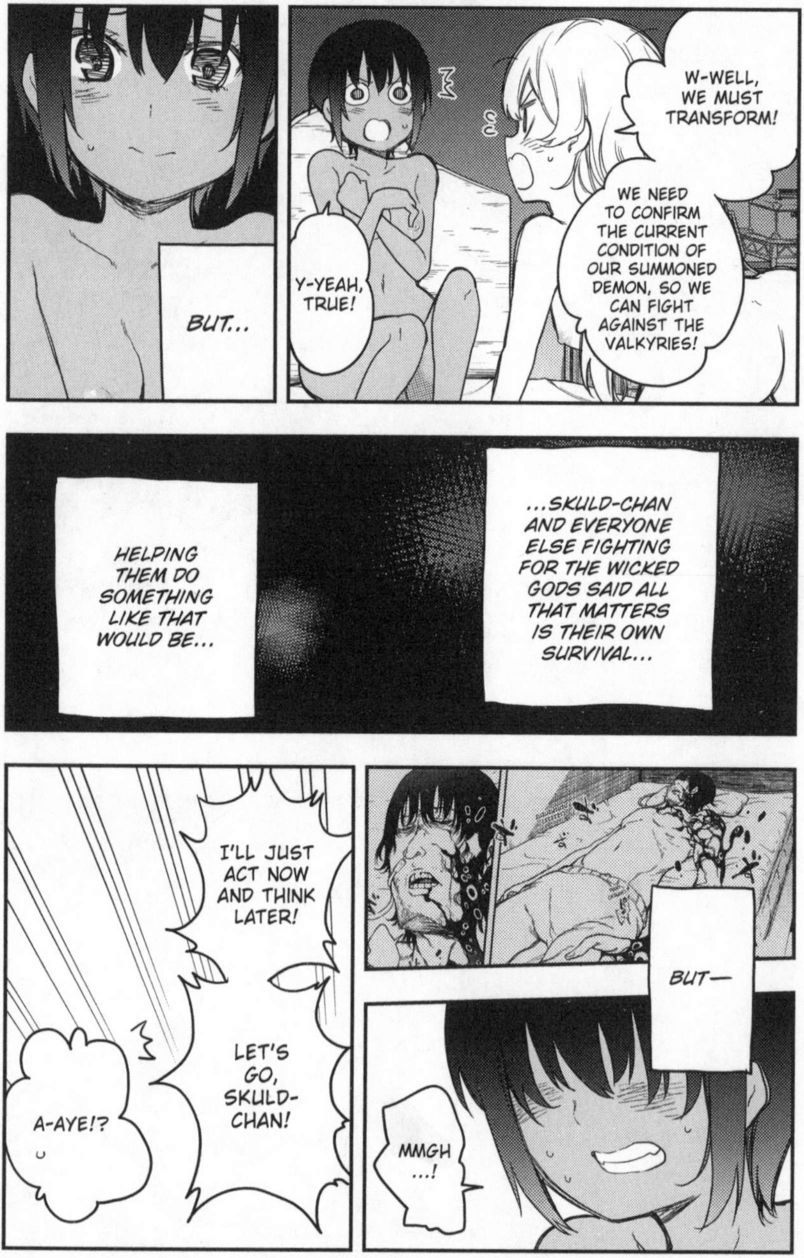
W-WELL, WE MUST TRANSFORM!
WE NEED TO CONFIRM THE CURRENT CONDITION OF OUR SUMMONED DEMON, SO WE CAN FIGHT AGAINST THE VALKYRIES!
Y-YEAH, TRUE!
BUT...
...SKULD-CHAN AND EVERYONE ELSE FIGHTING FOR THE WICKED GODS SAID ALL THAT MATTERS IS THEIR OWN SURVIVAL...
HELPING THEM DO SOMETHING LIKE THAT WOULD BE...
BUT—
MMGH ...!
I'LL JUST ACT NOW AND THINK LATER!
LET'S GO, SKULD-CHAN!
A-AYE!?

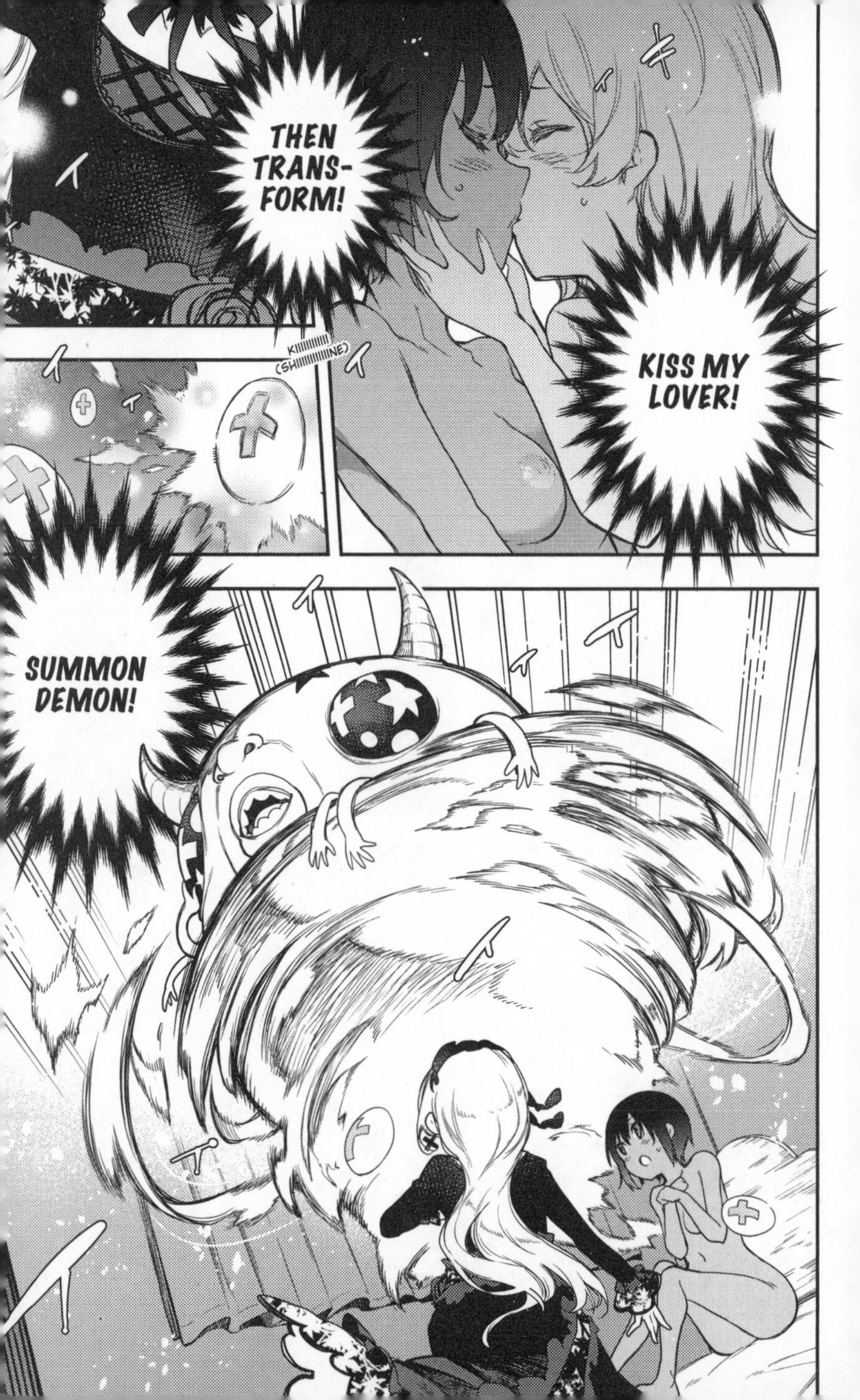
THEN TRANS-FORM!
KISS MY LOVER!
KIIIIIIIIIIIII (SHIIIIIIIIIIIIINE)
SUMMON DEMON!

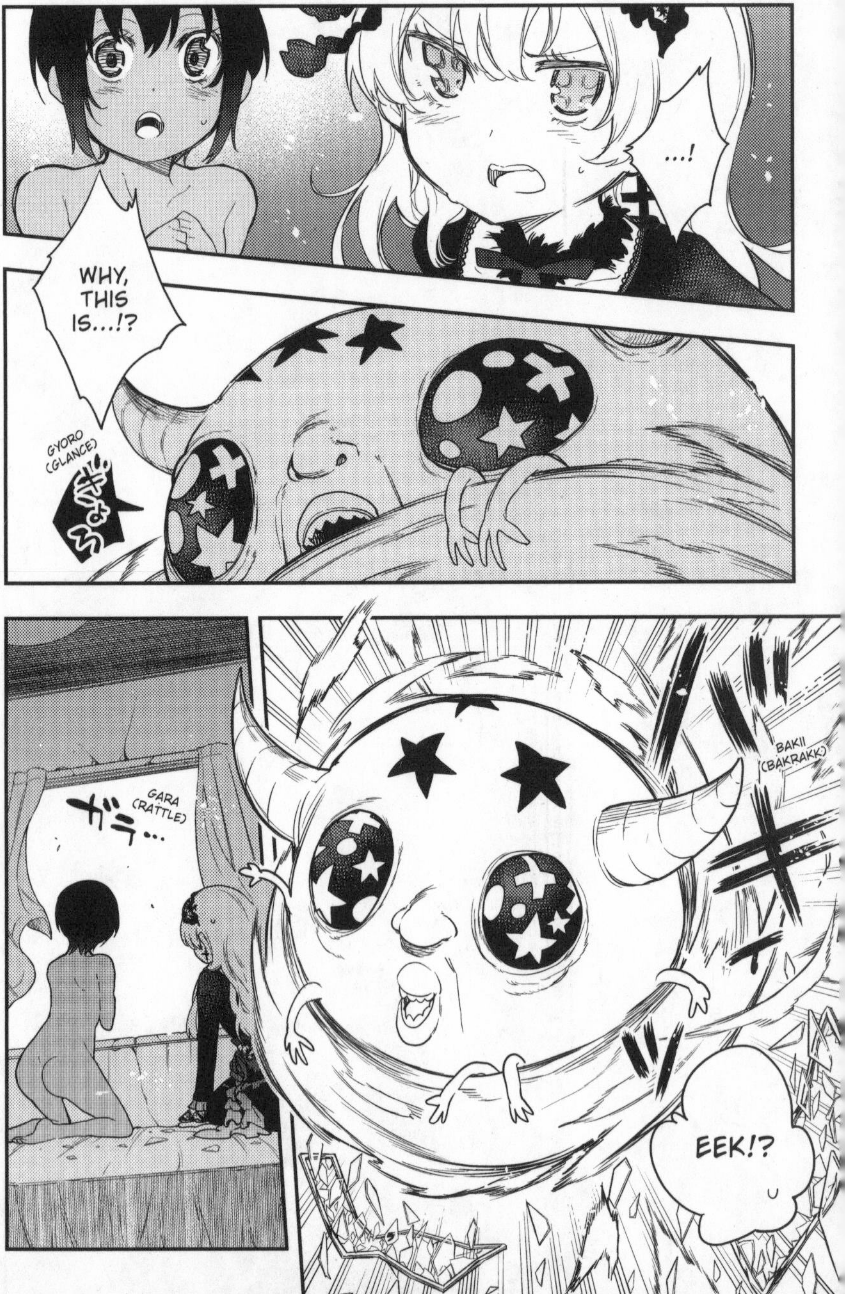
...!
WHY, THIS IS...!?
GYORO (GLANCE)
ぎょろ
BAKII (BAKRAKK)
EEK!?
GARA (RATTLE)
ガラ…

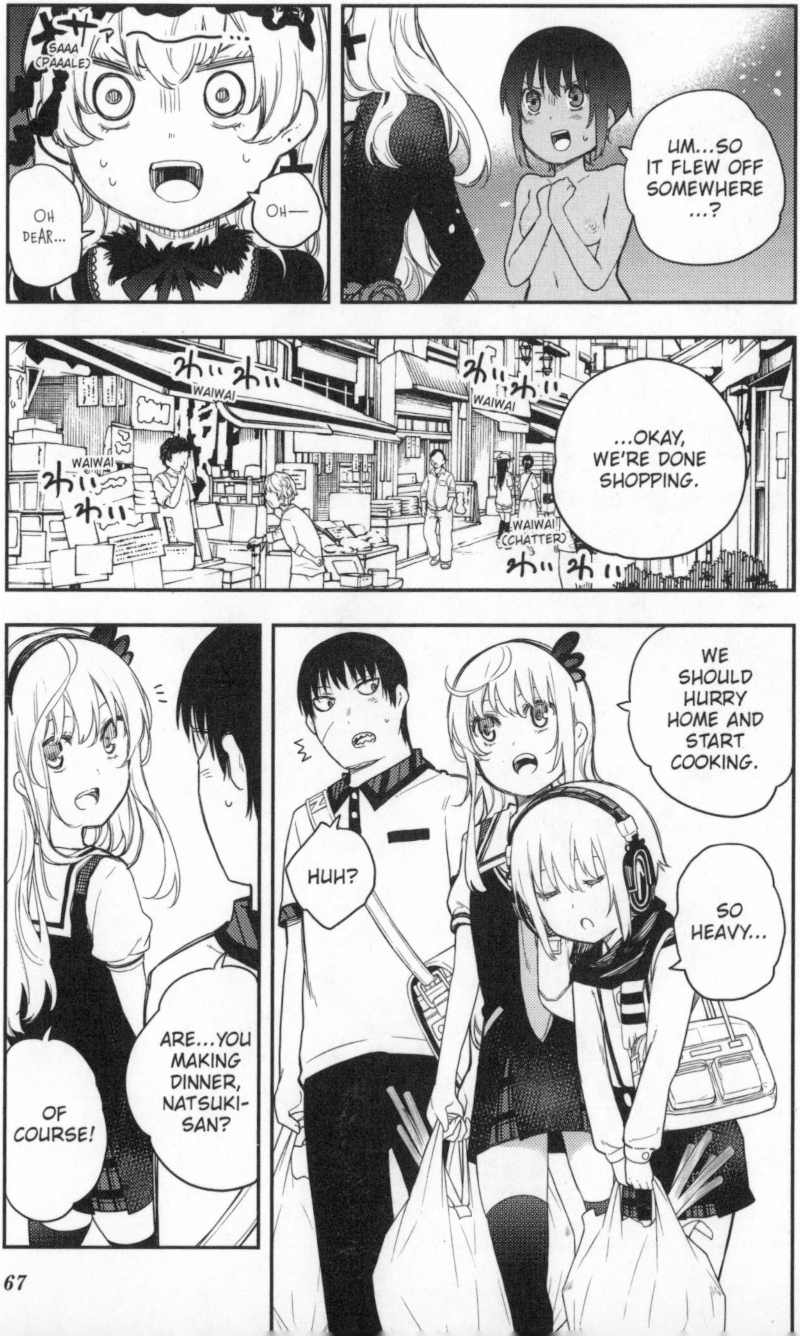
UM...SO IT FLEW OFF SOMEWHERE ...?
SAAA (PAAALE)
OH—
OH DEAR...
WAIWAI
WAIWAI
...OKAY, WE'RE DONE SHOPPING.
WAIWAI (CHATTER)
WAIWAI
WE SHOULD HURRY HOME AND START COOKING.
SO HEAVY...
HUH?
ARE...YOU MAKING DINNER, NATSUKI-SAN?
OF COURSE!

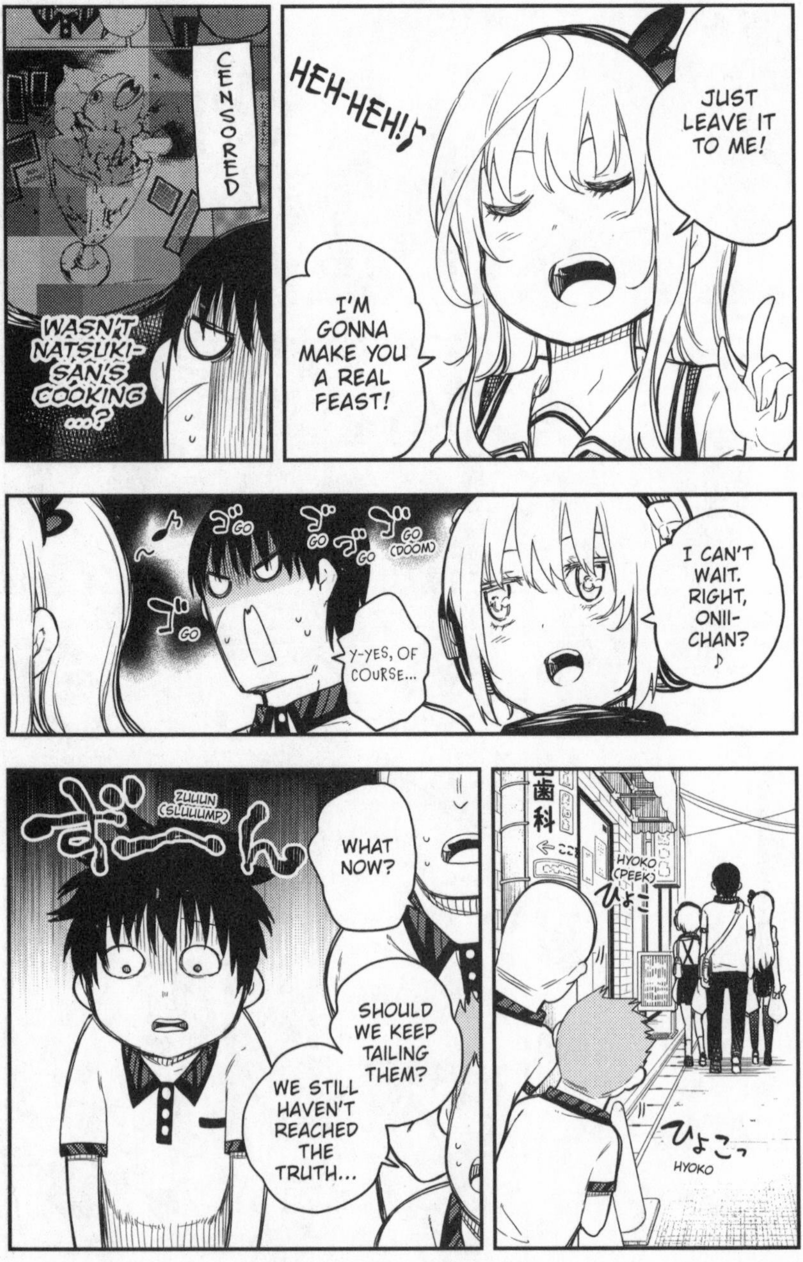
JUST LEAVE IT TO ME!
HEH-HEH!♪
I'M GONNA MAKE YOU A REAL FEAST!
CENSORED
WASN'T NATSUKI-SAN'S COOKING ...?
I CAN'T WAIT. RIGHT, ONII-CHAN? ♪
ゴ GO ゴ GO ゴ GO ゴ GO (DOOM)
ゴ GO
Y-YES, OF COURSE...
歯科
HYOKO (PEEK)
ひょこ
ひょこっ
HYOKO
WHAT NOW?
ずーん
ZUUUN (SLUUUMP)
SHOULD WE KEEP TAILING THEM?
WE STILL HAVEN'T REACHED THE TRUTH...

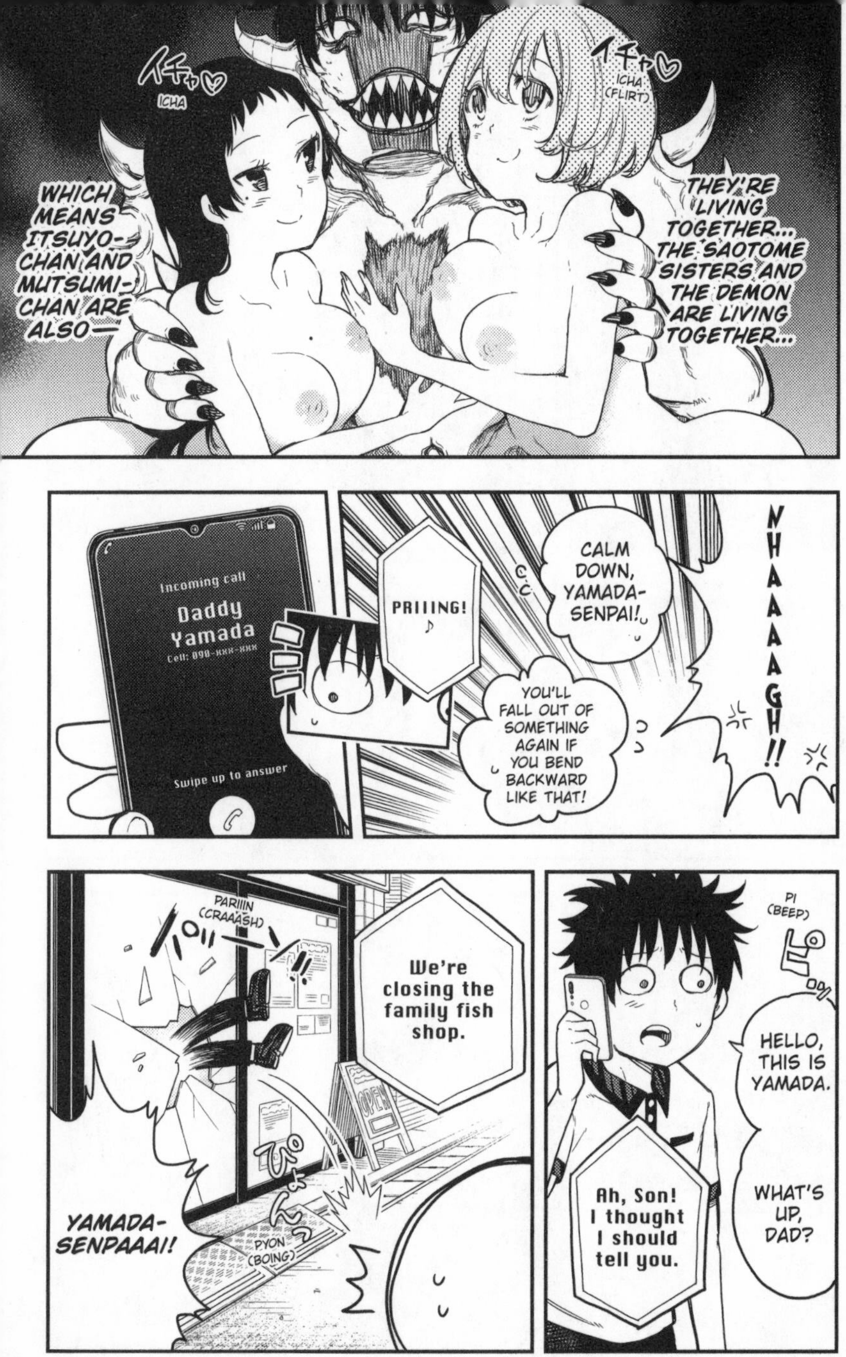
イチャ♡
ICHA (FLIRT)
THEY'RE LIVING TOGETHER... THE SAOTOME SISTERS AND THE DEMON ARE LIVING TOGETHER...
イチャ♡
ICHA
WHICH MEANS ITSUYO-CHAN AND MUTSUMI-CHAN ARE ALSO—
NHAAAAAGH!!
CALM DOWN, YAMADA-SENPAI!
YOU'LL FALL OUT OF SOMETHING AGAIN IF YOU BEND BACKWARD LIKE THAT!
PRIIING! ♪
Incoming call
Daddy Yamada
Cell: 090-XXX-XXX
Swipe up to answer
PI (BEEP)
HELLO, THIS IS YAMADA.
WHAT'S UP, DAD?
Ah, Son! I thought I should tell you.
PARIIIN (CRAAASH)
We're closing the family fish shop.
OPEN
YAMADA-SENPAAAI!
ぴょんっ
PYON (BOING)

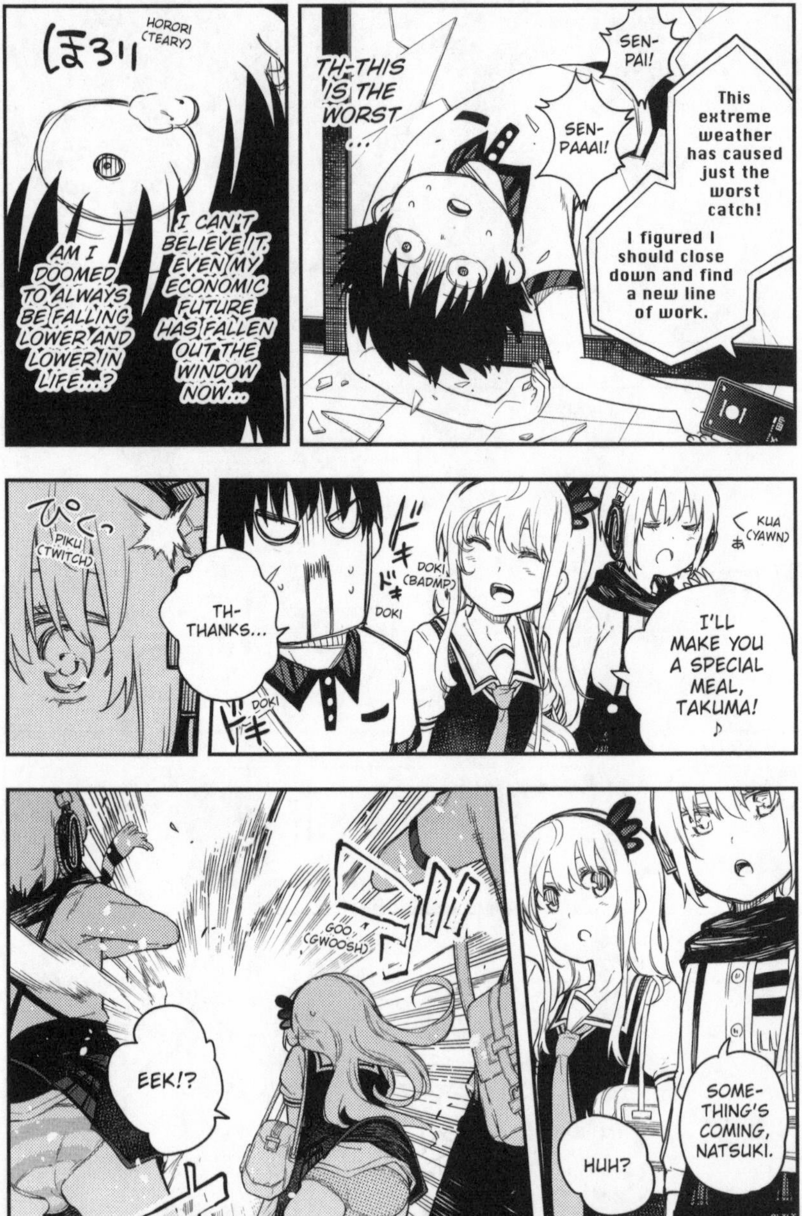
SEN-PAI!
This extreme weather has caused just the worst catch!
I figured I should close down and find a new line of work.
SEN-PAAAI!
TH-THIS IS THE WORST...
ほろり
HORORI (TEARY)
I CAN'T BELIEVE IT. EVEN MY ECONOMIC FUTURE HAS FALLEN OUT THE WINDOW NOW...
AM I DOOMED TO ALWAYS BE FALLING LOWER AND LOWER IN LIFE...?
KUA (YAWN)
I'LL MAKE YOU A SPECIAL MEAL, TAKUMA! ♪
DOKI (BADMP)
DOKI
TH-THANKS...
DOKI
PIKU (TWITCH)
SOME-THING'S COMING, NATSUKI.
HUH?
GOO (GWOOSH)
EEK!?

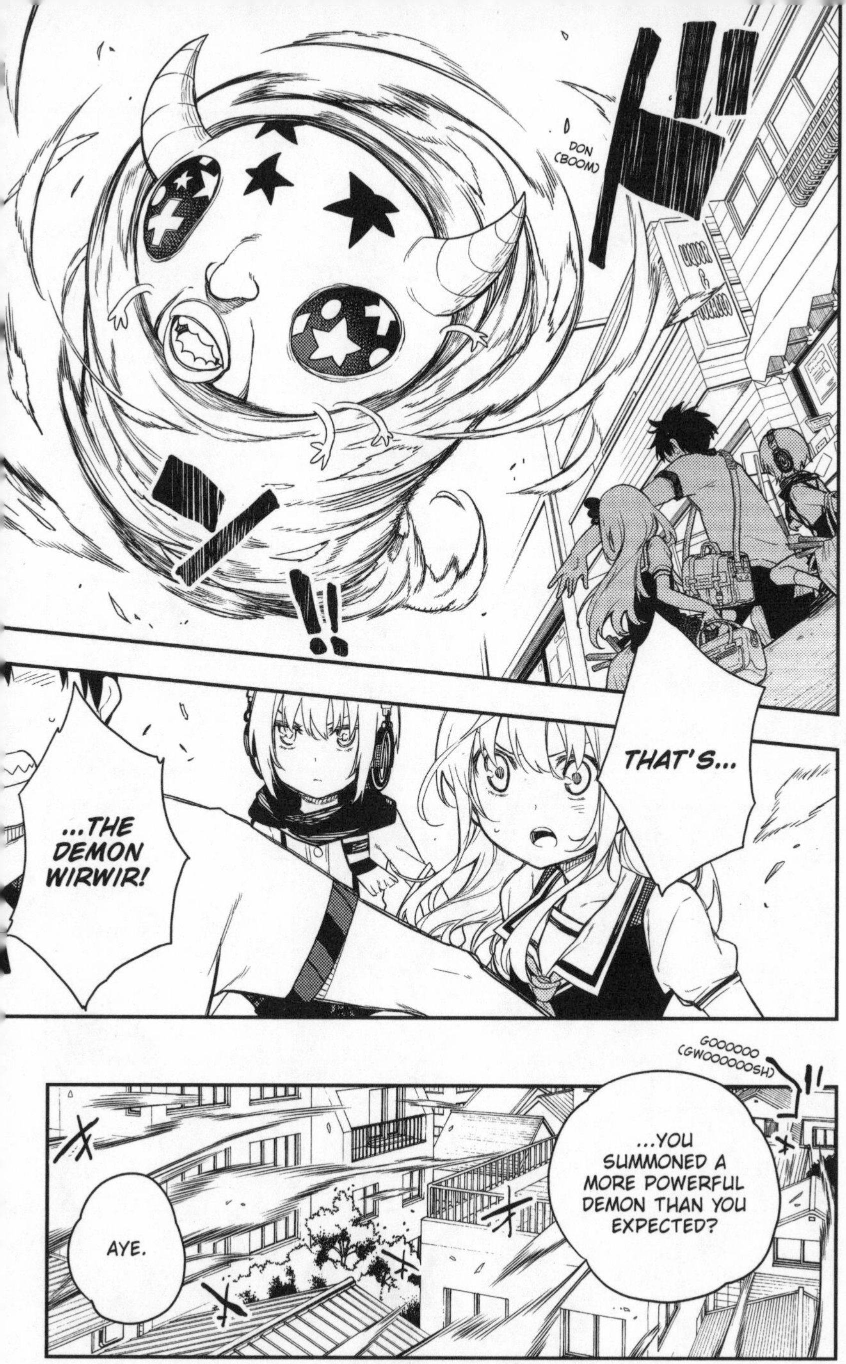
DON (BOOM)
THAT'S...
...THE DEMON WIRWIR!
GOOOOOO (GWOOOOOOSH)
...YOU SUMMONED A MORE POWERFUL DEMON THAN YOU EXPECTED?
AYE.

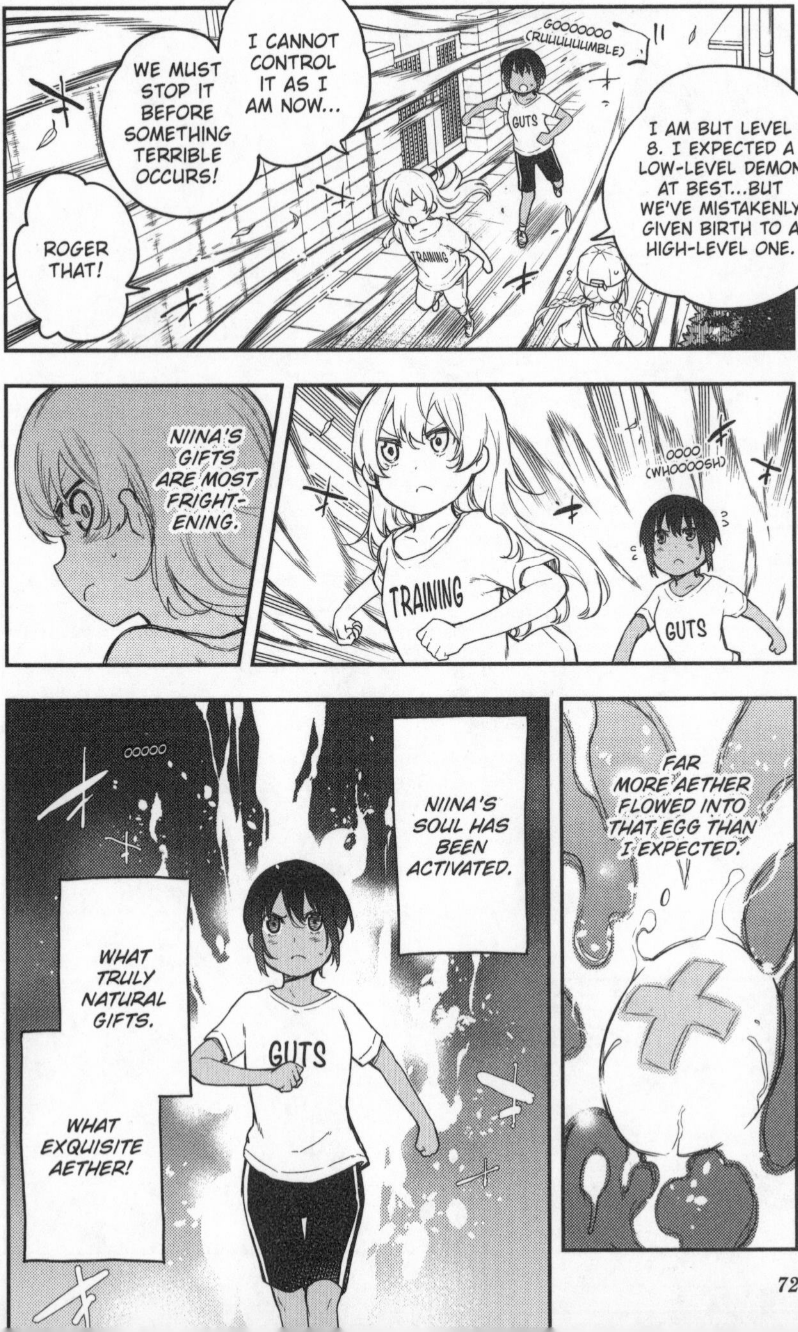
I AM BUT LEVEL 8. I EXPECTED A LOW-LEVEL DEMON AT BEST...BUT WE'VE MISTAKENLY GIVEN BIRTH TO A HIGH-LEVEL ONE.
GOOOOOOO (RUUUUUUMBLE)
I CANNOT CONTROL IT AS I AM NOW...
WE MUST STOP IT BEFORE SOMETHING TERRIBLE OCCURS!
ROGER THAT!
GUTS
TRAINING
OOOO (WHOOOOSH)
TRAINING
GUTS
NIINA'S GIFTS ARE MOST FRIGHT-ENING.
FAR MORE AETHER FLOWED INTO THAT EGG THAN I EXPECTED.
NIINA'S SOUL HAS BEEN ACTIVATED.
OOOOO
WHAT TRULY NATURAL GIFTS.
WHAT EXQUISITE AETHER!
GUTS

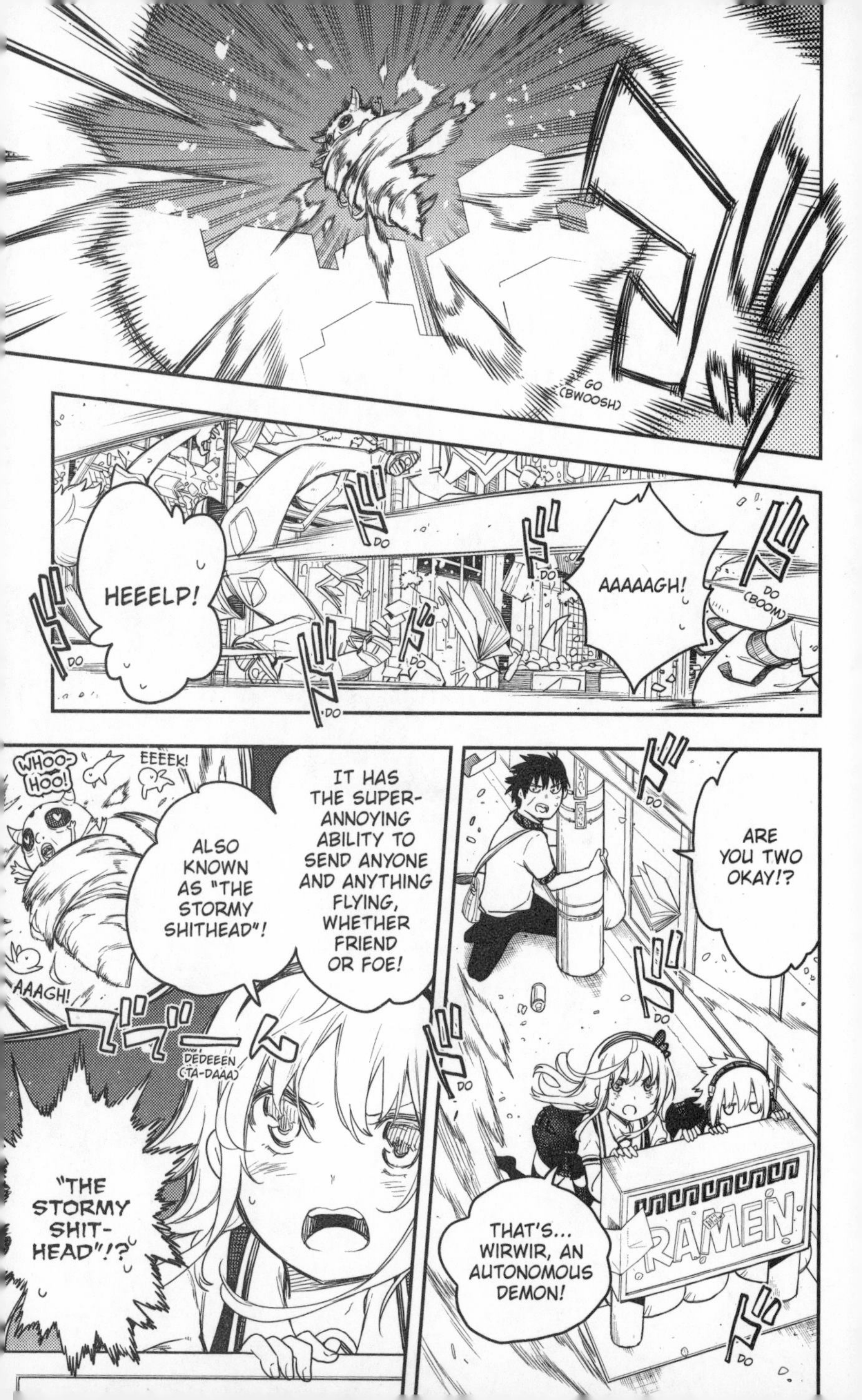

GO (BWOOSH)
DO (BOOM)
AAAAAGH!
DO
DO
DO
HEEELP!
DO
DO
DO
ARE YOU TWO OKAY!?
DO
DO
THAT'S... WIRWIR, AN AUTONOMOUS DEMON!
RAMEN
DO
IT HAS THE SUPER-ANNOYING ABILITY TO SEND ANYONE AND ANYTHING FLYING, WHETHER FRIEND OR FOE!
ALSO KNOWN AS "THE STORMY SHITHEAD"!
EEEEK!
WHOO-HOO!
AAAGH!
DEDEEEN (TA-DAAA)
"THE STORMY SHIT-HEAD"!?

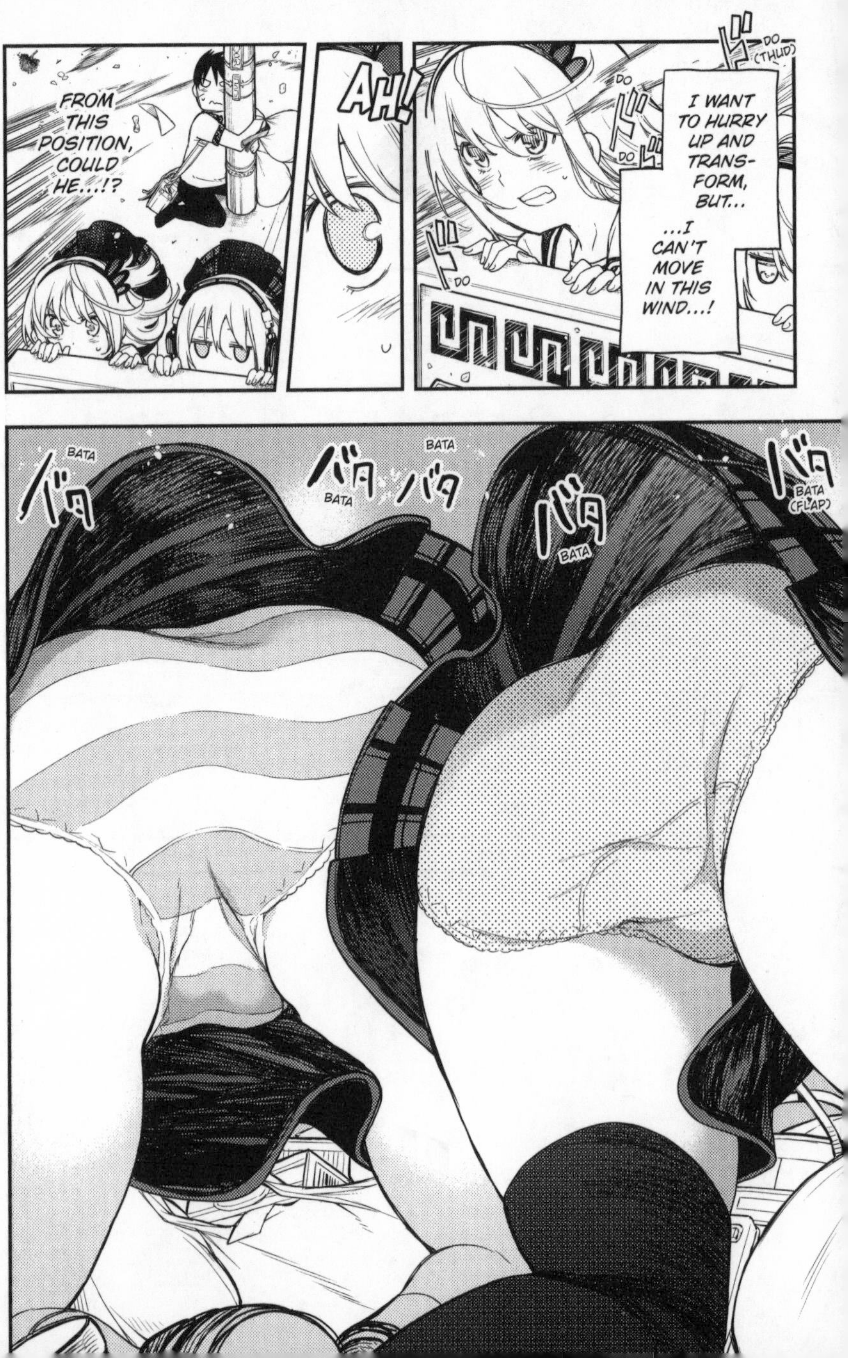

ド
DO (THUD)
ド
DO
ド
DO
I WANT TO HURRY UP AND TRANS-FORM, BUT...
...I CAN'T MOVE IN THIS WIND...!
ド
DO
AH!
FROM THIS POSITION, COULD HE...!?
バタ
BATA (FLAP)
バタ
BATA
バタ
BATA
バタ
BATA
バタ
BATA

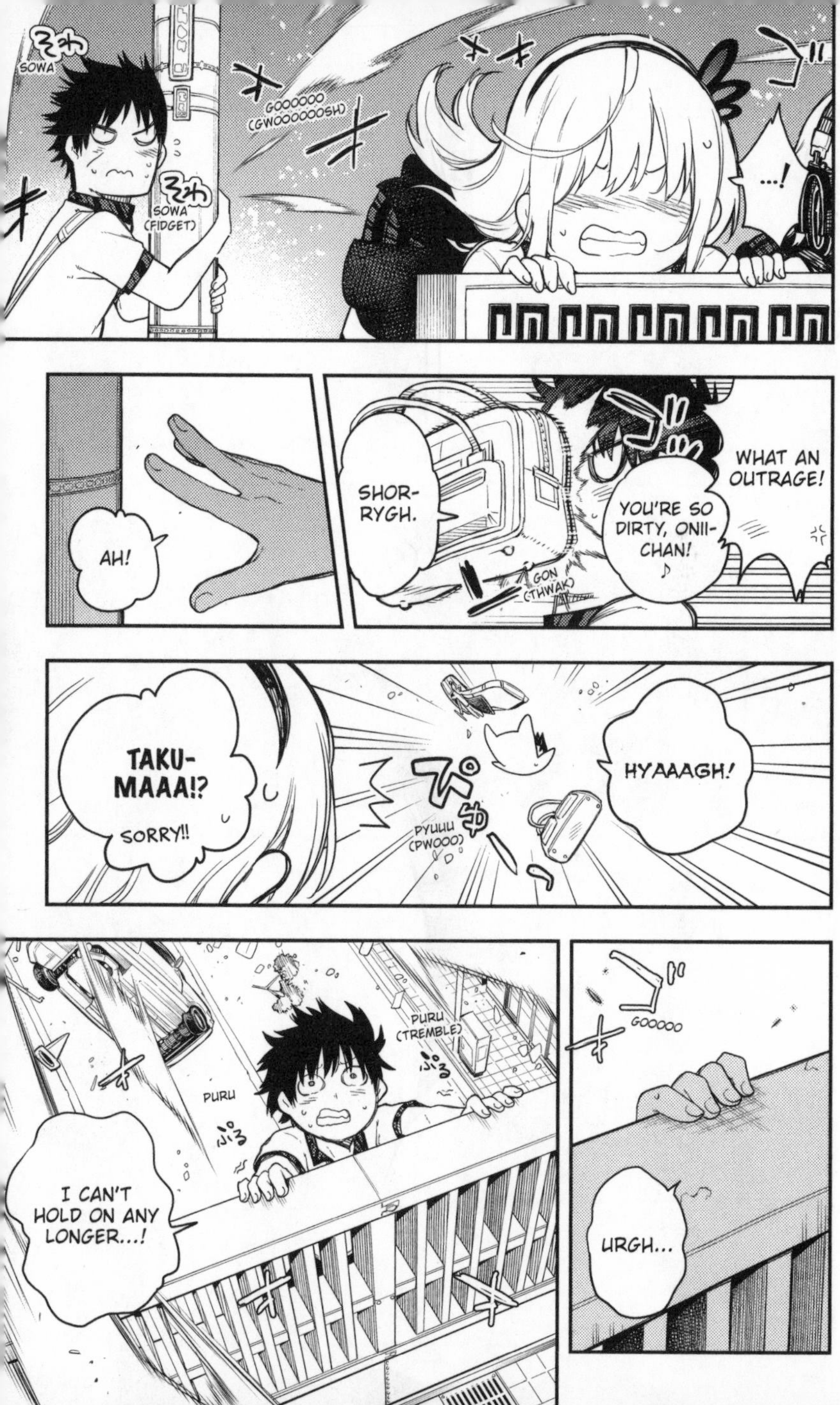
...!
GOOOOOO (GWOOOOOOSH)
SOWA (FIDGET)
SOWA
WHAT AN OUTRAGE!
YOU'RE SO DIRTY, ONII-CHAN! ♪
SHOR-RYGH.
GON (THWAK)
AH!
HYAAAGH!
PYUUU (PWOOO)
TAKU-MAAA!? SORRY!!
GOOOOO
URGH...
PURU (TREMBLE)
PURU
I CAN'T HOLD ON ANY LONGER...!

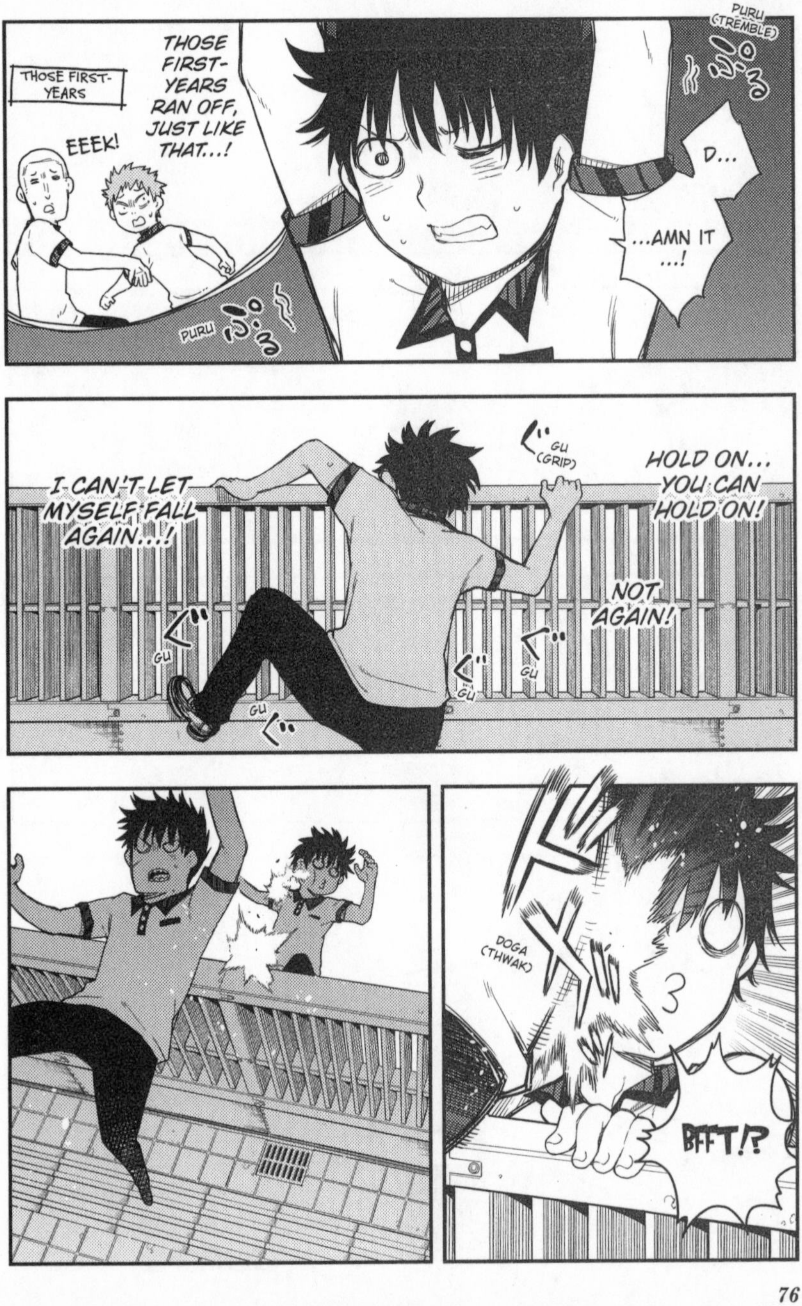
PURU (TREMBLE)
ぷる
D...
...AMN IT ...!
THOSE FIRST-YEARS RAN OFF, JUST LIKE THAT...!
THOSE FIRST-YEARS
EEEK!
PURU
ぷる
HOLD ON... YOU CAN HOLD ON!
ぐ
GU (GRIP)
NOT AGAIN!
ぐ
GU
ぐ
GU
ぐ
GU
ぐ
GU
I-CAN'T-LET MYSELF FALL AGAIN...!
DOGA (THWAK)
BFFT!?

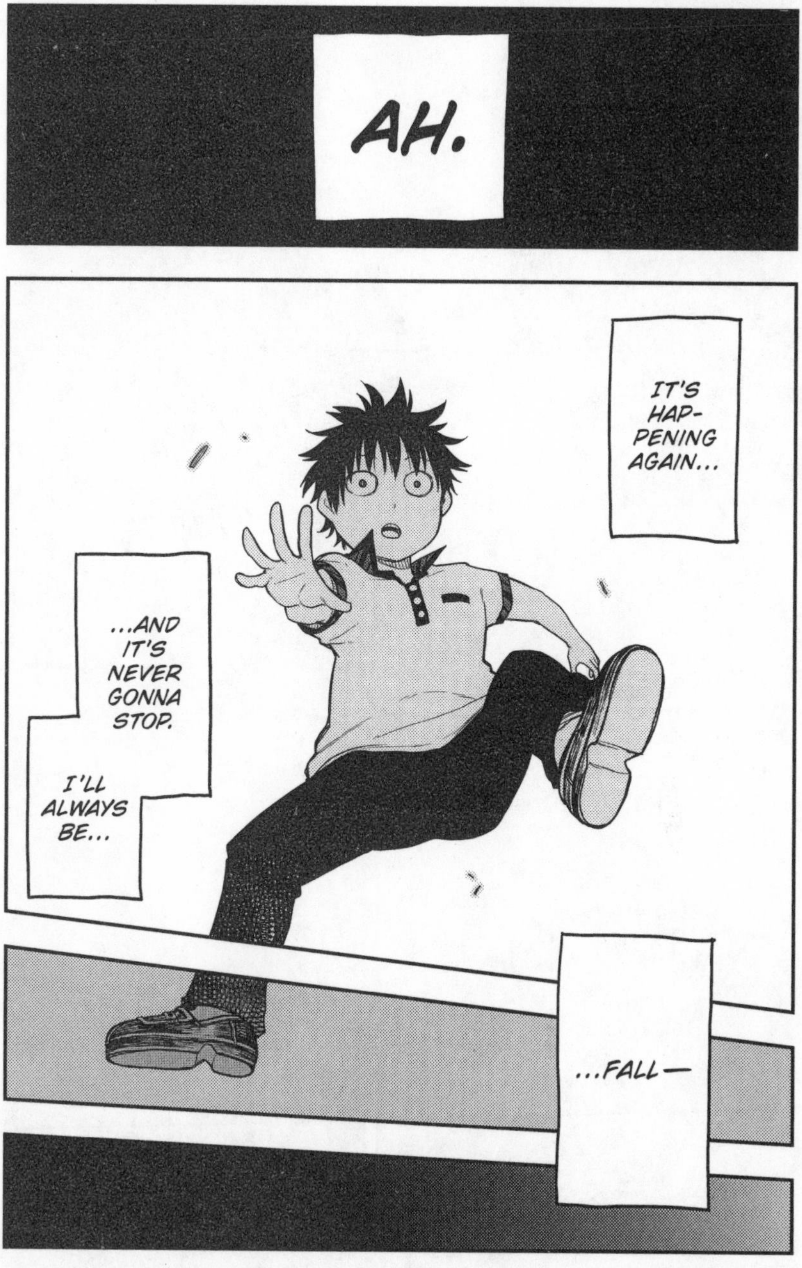
AH.
IT'S HAP-PENING AGAIN...
...AND IT'S NEVER GONNA STOP.
I'LL ALWAYS BE...
...FALL—

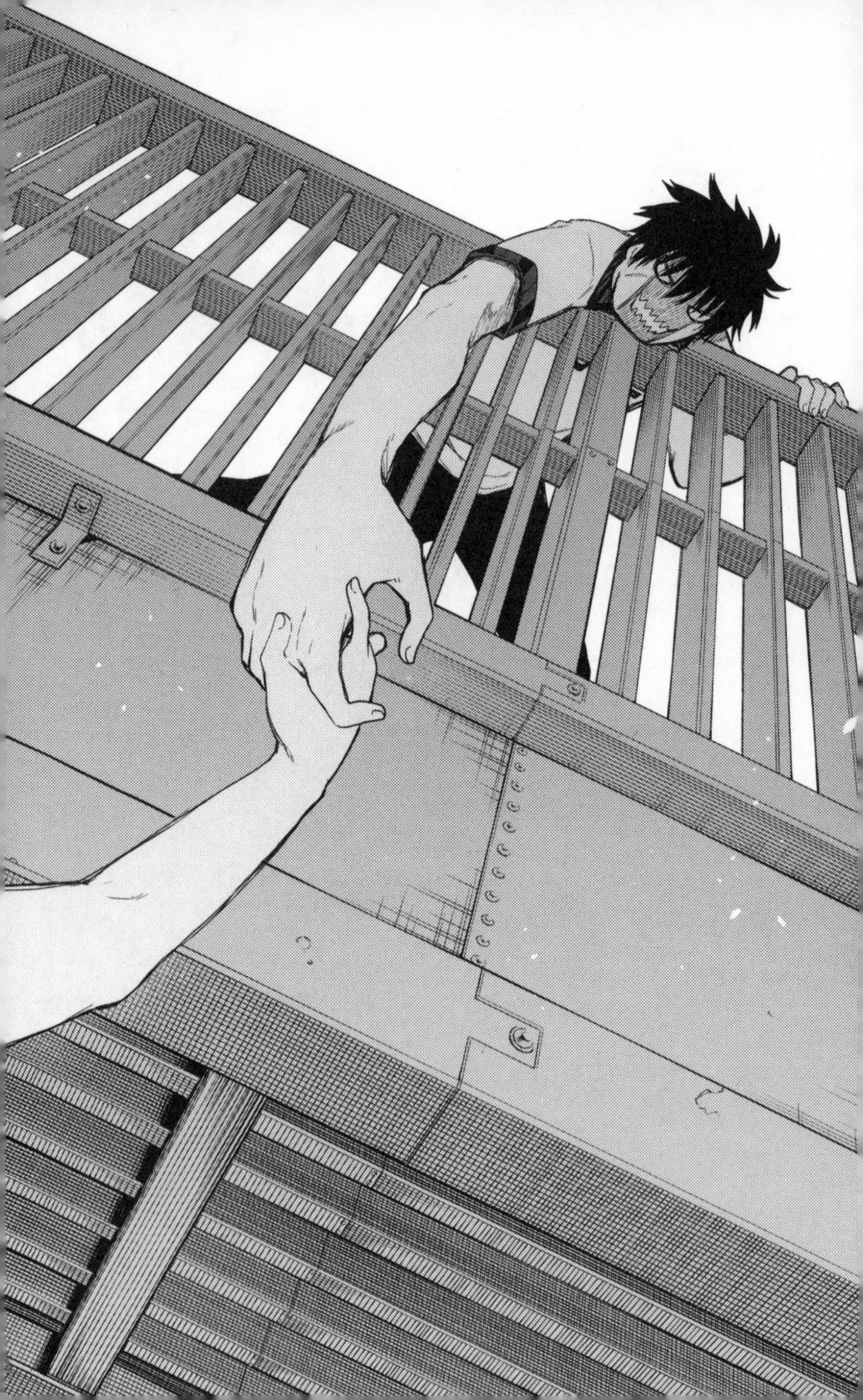

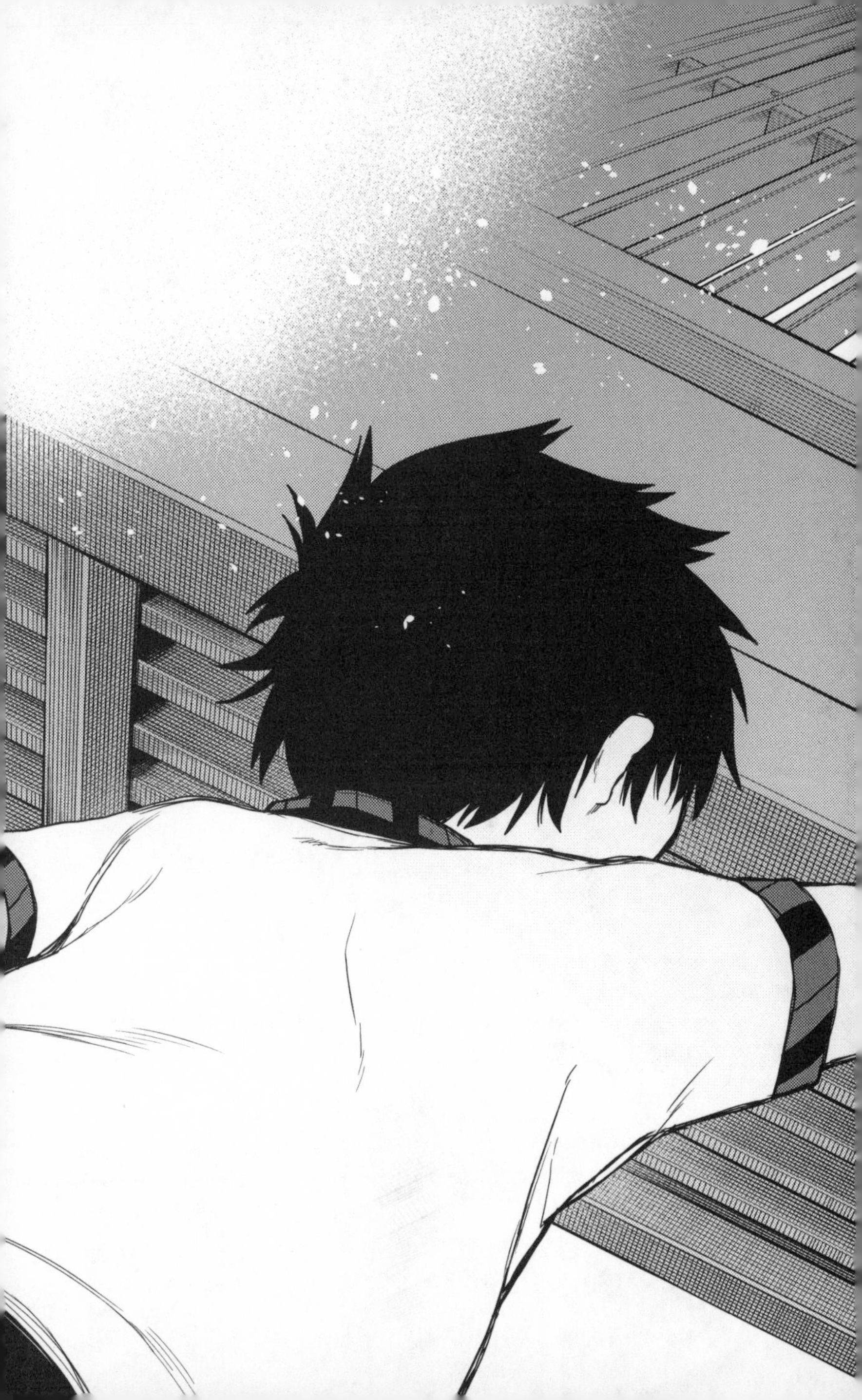

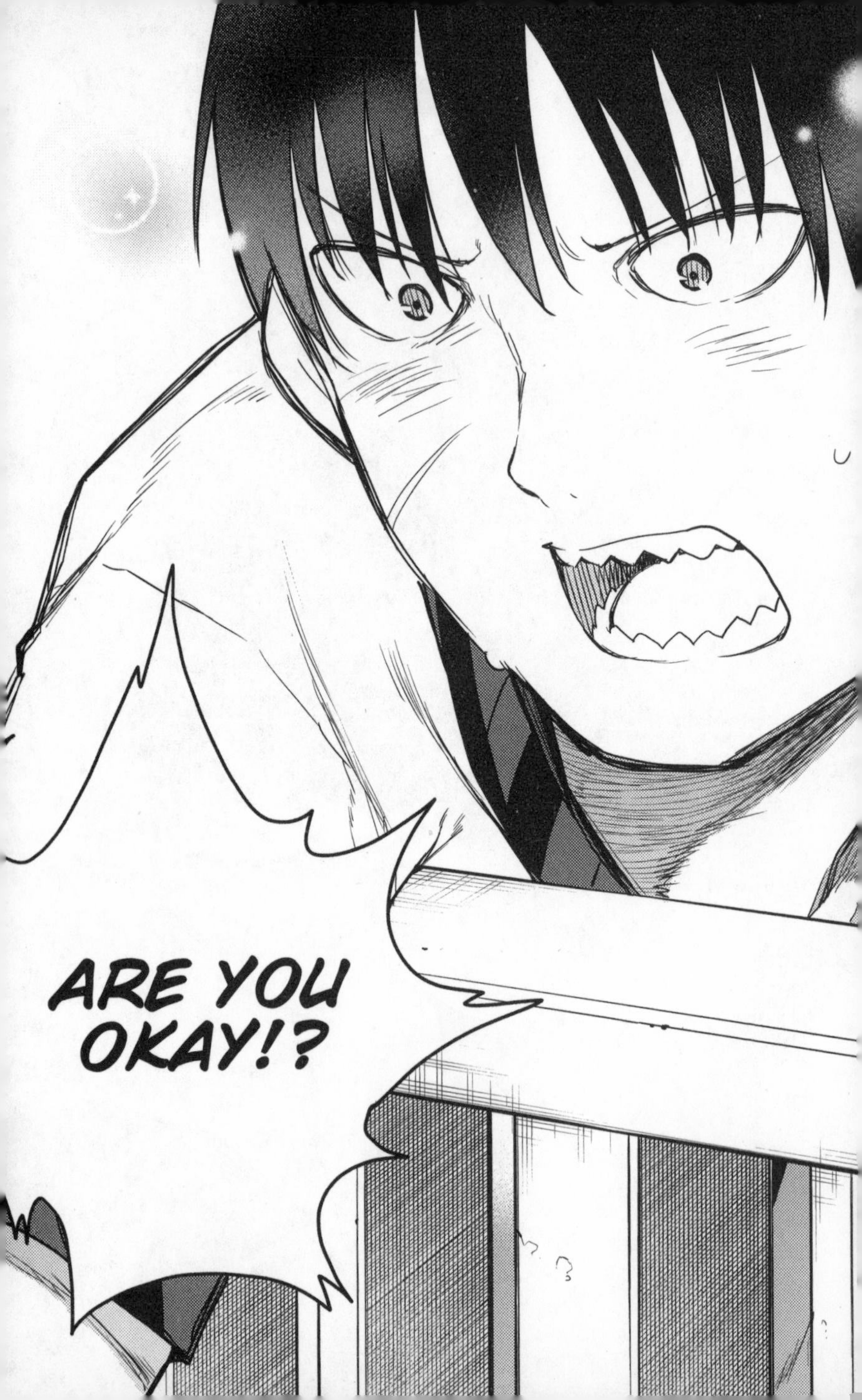
ARE YOU OKAY!?

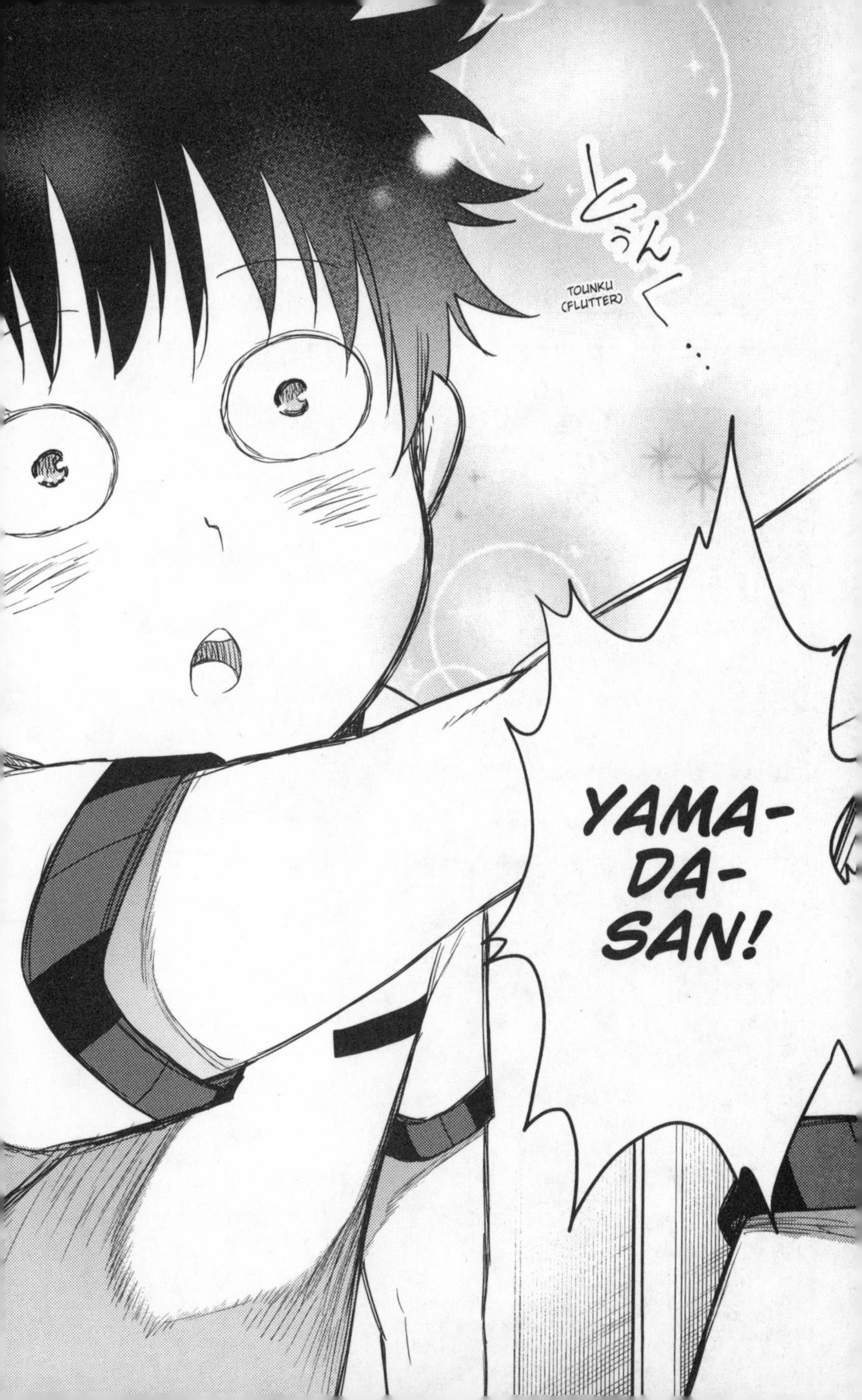
とぅんく
TOUNKU (FLUTTER)
...
YAMA-DA-SAN!

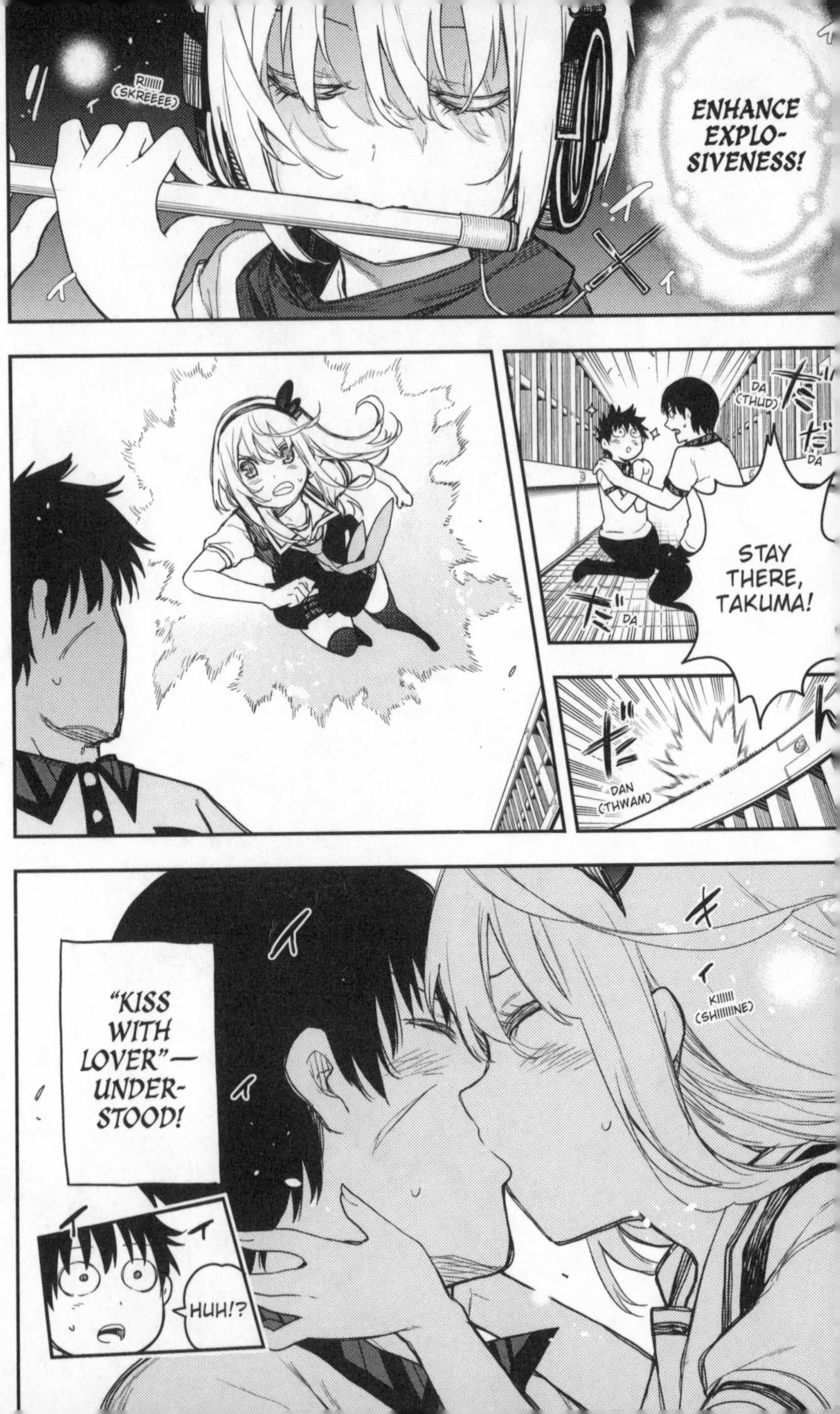
ENHANCE EXPLO-SIVENESS!
RIIIII (SKREEEE)
DA (THUD)
DA
STAY THERE, TAKUMA!
DA
DAN (THWAM)
KIIIII (SHIIIIINE)
"KISS WITH LOVER"—UNDER-STOOD!
HUH!?

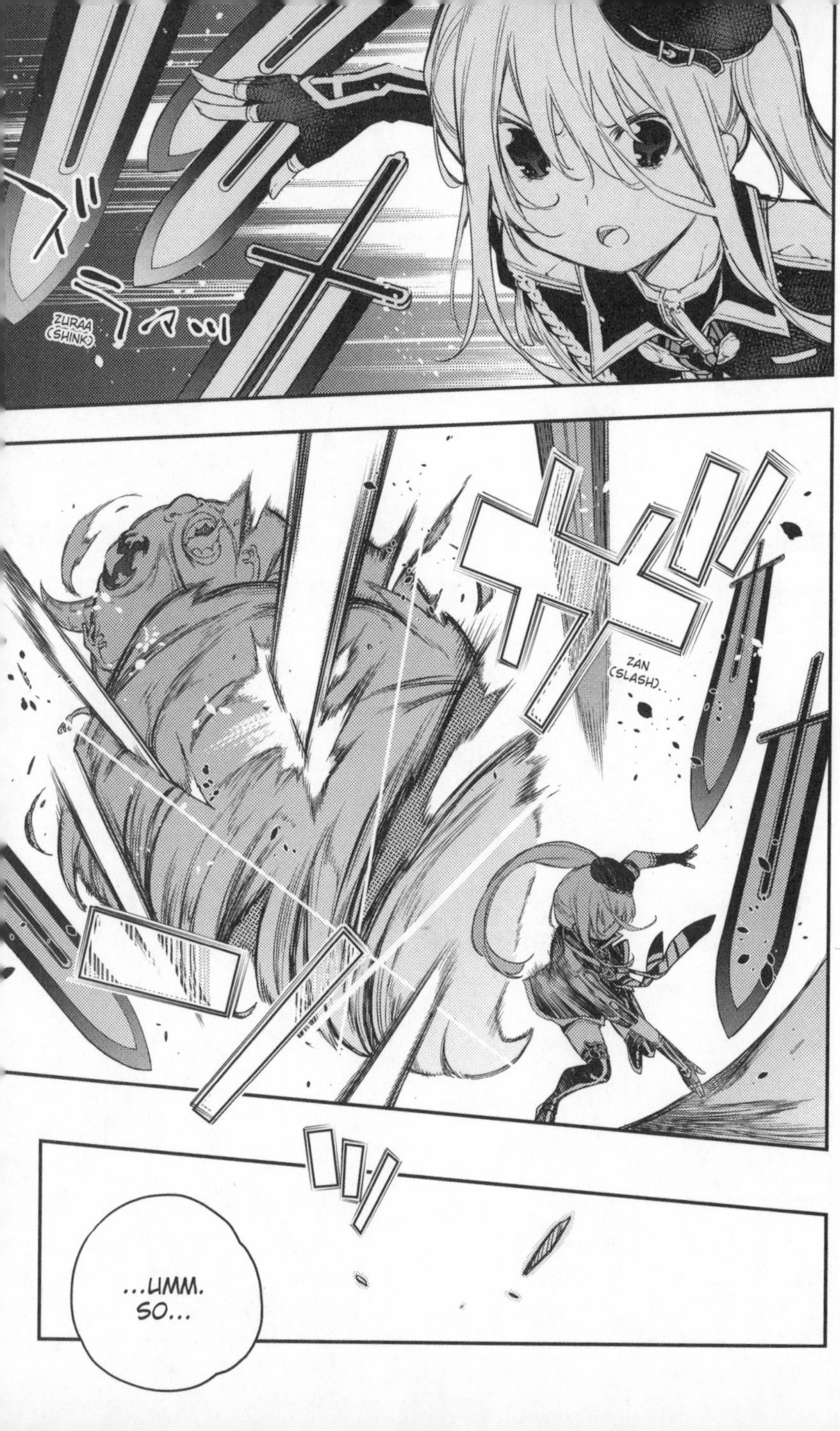
ZURAA (SHINK)
ZAN (SLASH)...
...UMM. SO...

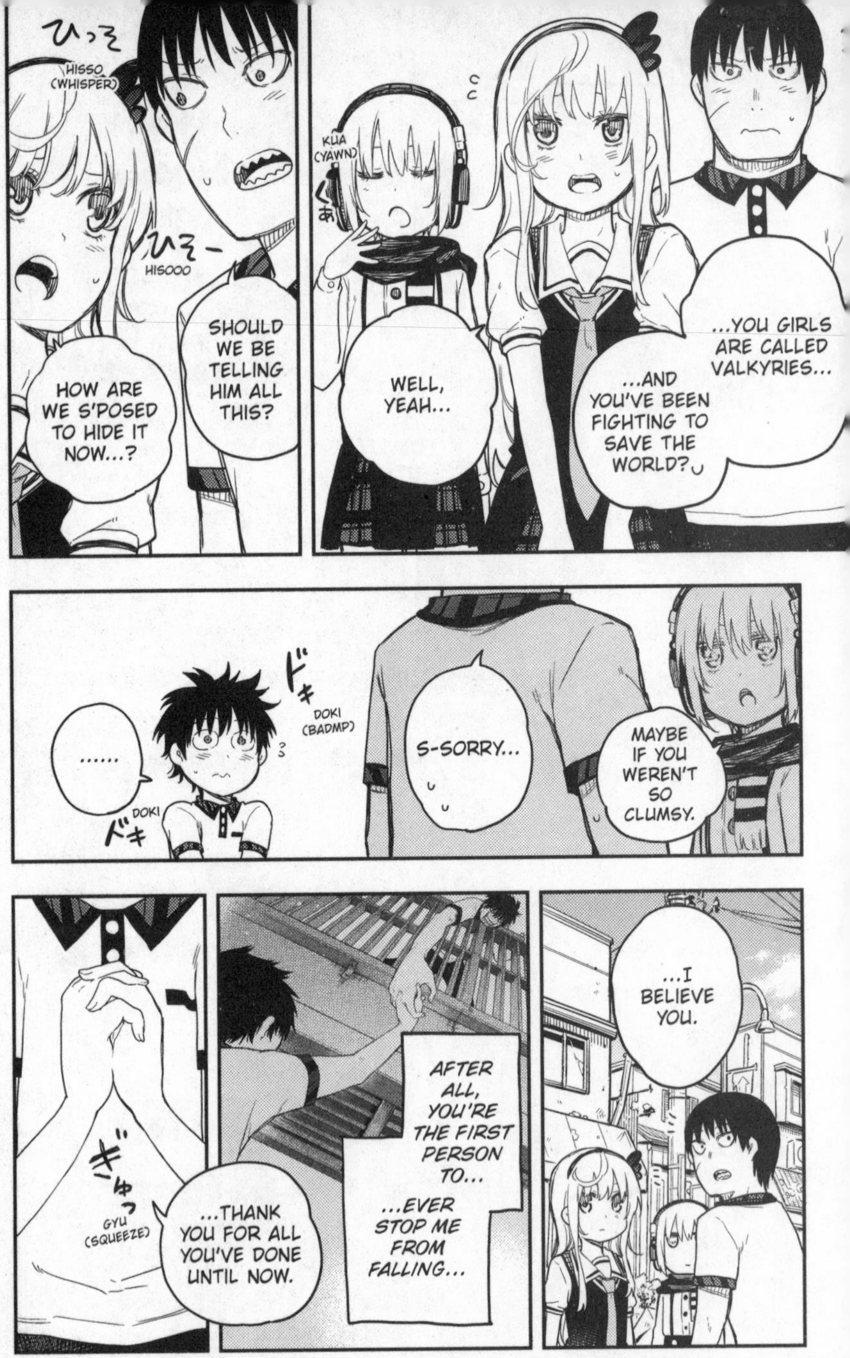
...YOU GIRLS ARE CALLED VALKYRIES...
...AND YOU'VE BEEN FIGHTING TO SAVE THE WORLD?
くぁ
KUA (YAWN)
WELL, YEAH...
ひっそ
HISSO (WHISPER)
SHOULD WE BE TELLING HIM ALL THIS?
ひそー
HISOOO
HOW ARE WE S'POSED TO HIDE IT NOW...?
MAYBE IF YOU WEREN'T SO CLUMSY.
S-SORRY...
ドキ
DOKI (BADMP)
......
ドキ
DOKI
...I BELIEVE YOU.
AFTER ALL, YOU'RE THE FIRST PERSON TO...
...EVER STOP ME FROM FALLING...
ぎゅっ
GYU (SQUEEZE)
...THANK YOU FOR ALL YOU'VE DONE UNTIL NOW.

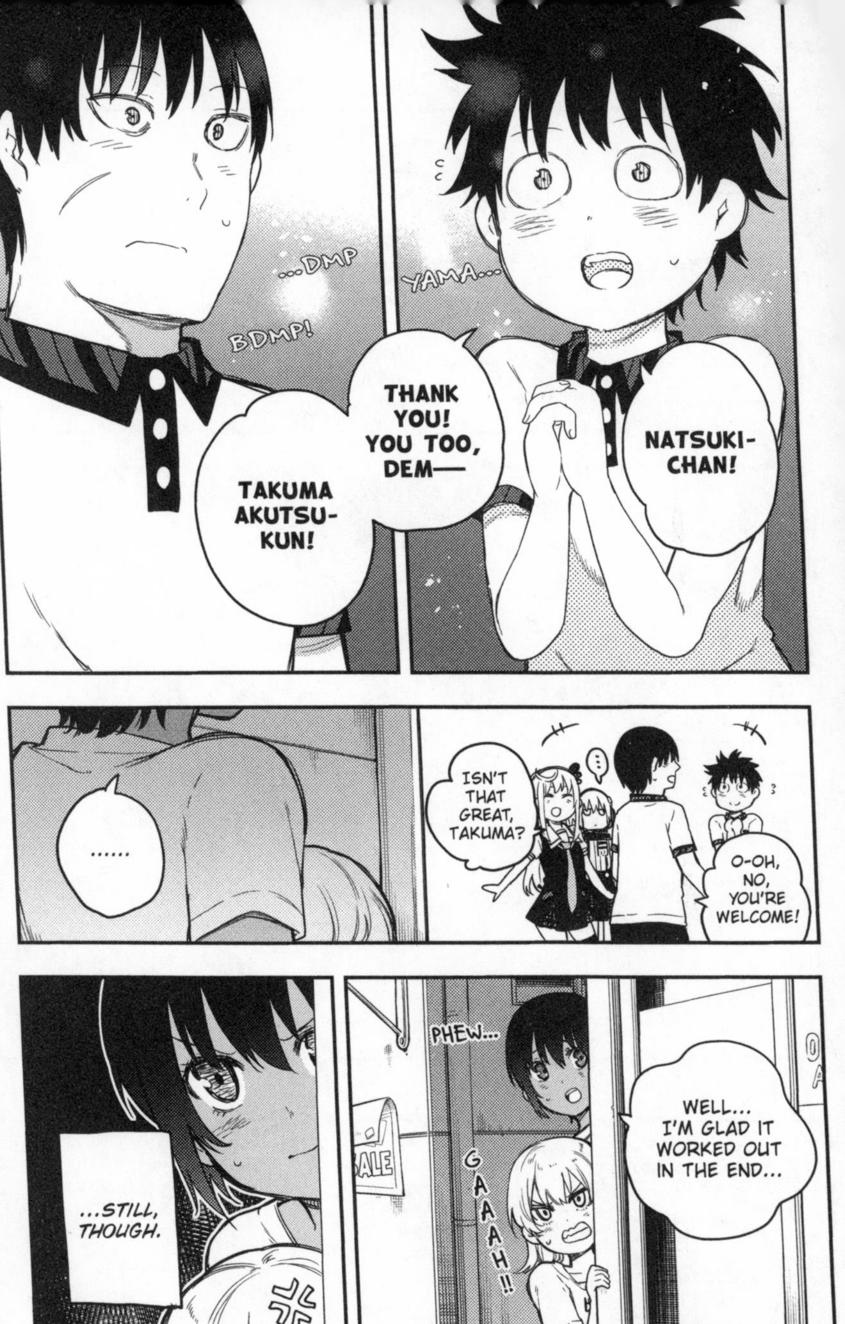
YAMA...
NATSUKI-CHAN!
THANK YOU! YOU TOO, DEM—
...DMP
BDMP!
TAKUMA AKUTSU-KUN!
ISN'T THAT GREAT, TAKUMA?
O-OH, NO, YOU'RE WELCOME!
......
PHEW...
WELL... I'M GLAD IT WORKED OUT IN THE END...
GAAAAH!!
...STILL, THOUGH.

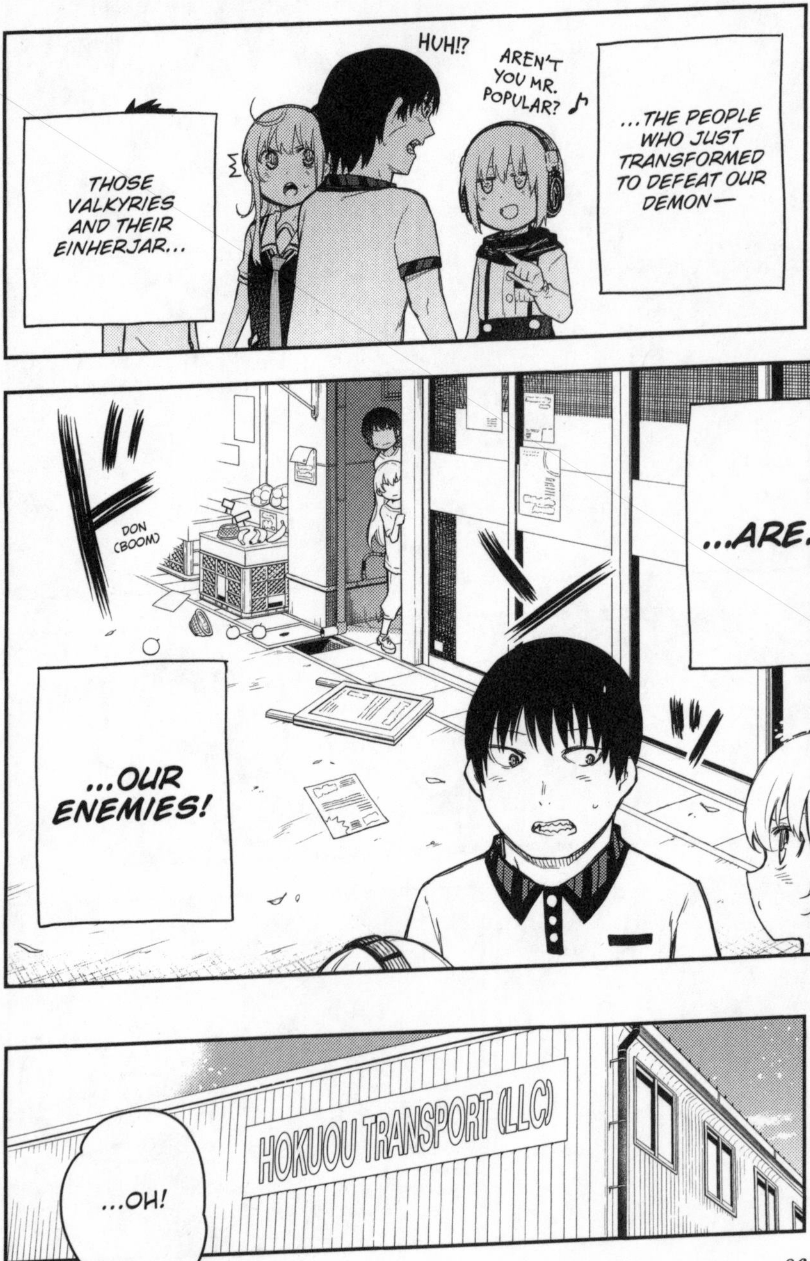
...THE PEOPLE WHO JUST TRANSFORMED TO DEFEAT OUR DEMON—
AREN'T YOU MR. POPULAR? ♪
HUH!?
THOSE VALKYRIES AND THEIR EINHERJAR...
...ARE...
DON (BOOM)
...OUR ENEMIES!
HOKUOU TRANSPORT (LLC)
...OH!

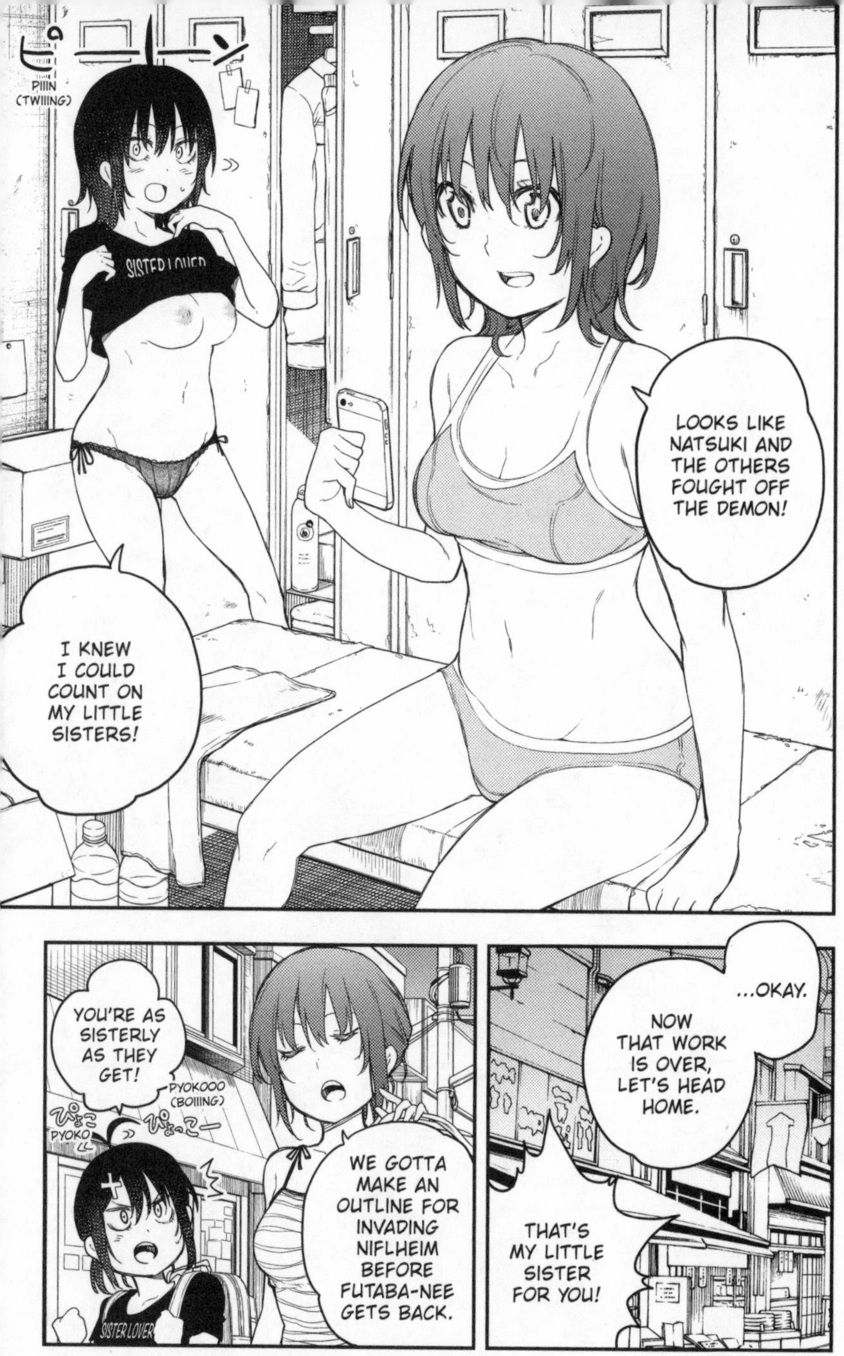
LOOKS LIKE NATSUKI AND THE OTHERS FOUGHT OFF THE DEMON!
ぴーーン
PIIIN (TWIIING)
SISTER LOVER
I KNEW I COULD COUNT ON MY LITTLE SISTERS!
...OKAY.
NOW THAT WORK IS OVER, LET'S HEAD HOME.
THAT'S MY LITTLE SISTER FOR YOU!
WE GOTTA MAKE AN OUTLINE FOR INVADING NIFLHEIM BEFORE FUTABA-NEE GETS BACK.
YOU'RE AS SISTERLY AS THEY GET!
ぴょっこー
PYOKOOO (BOIIING)
ぴょこ
PYOKO
SISTER LOVER

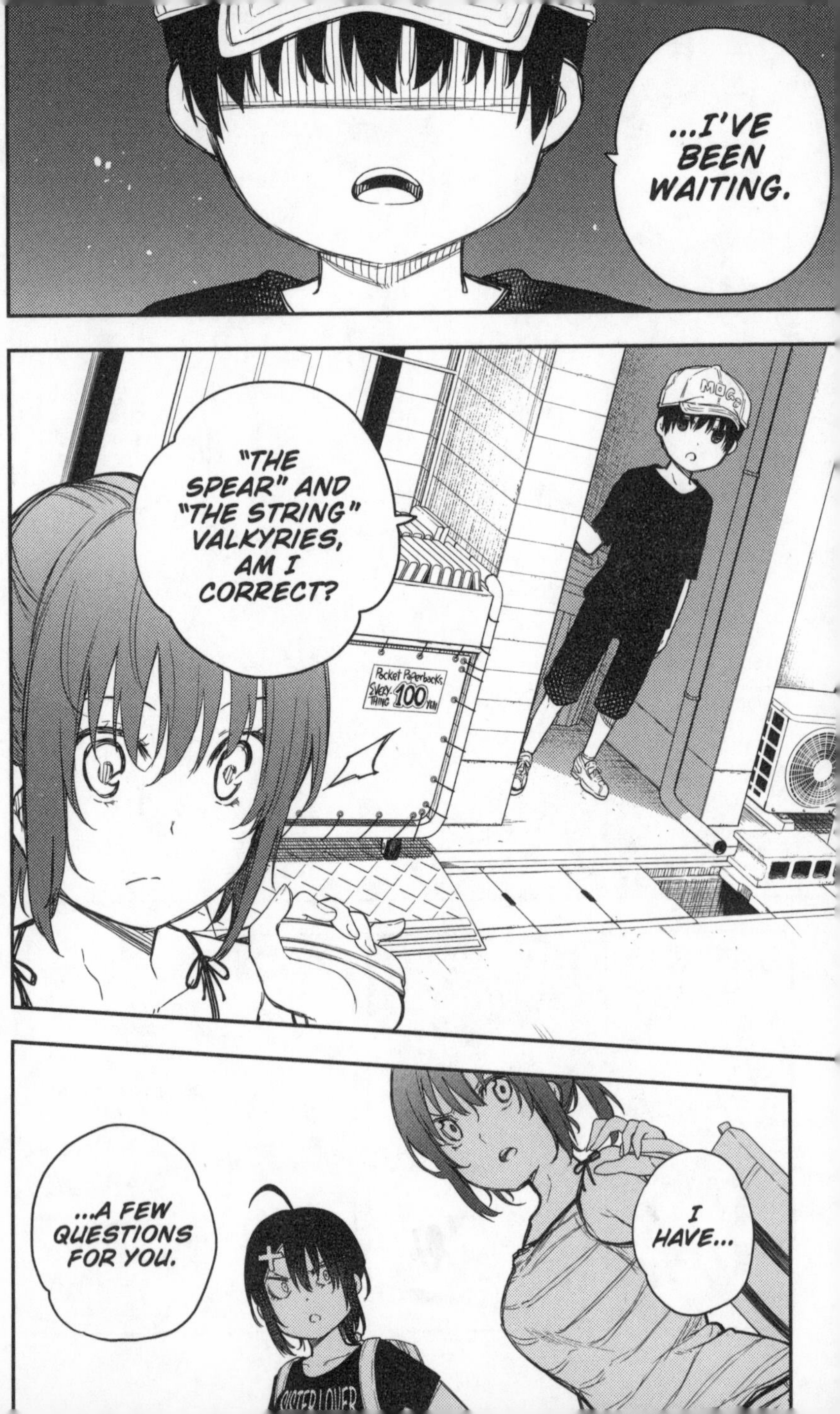
...I'VE BEEN WAITING.
"THE SPEAR" AND "THE STRING" VALKYRIES, AM I CORRECT?
Pocket Paperbacks EVERY-THING 100 YEN
I HAVE...
...A FEW QUESTIONS FOR YOU.

Val × Löve

THE BIGGEST PUSHOVER IN THE WHOLE SERIES

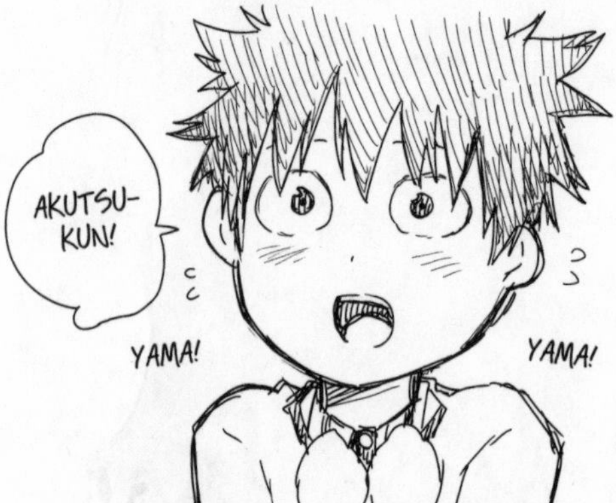
AKUTSU-KUN!
YAMA!
YAMA!

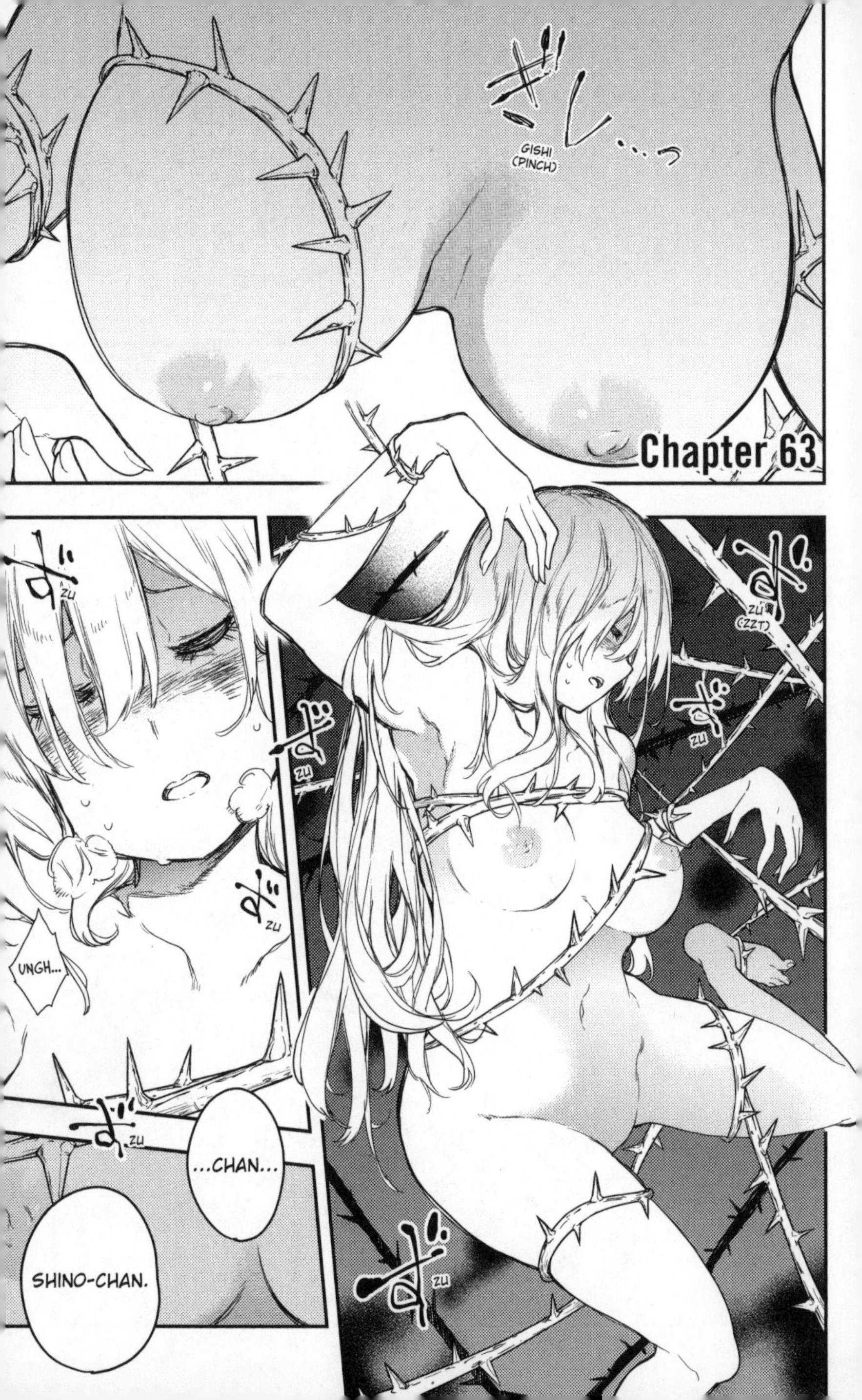
GISHI
(PINCH)
Chapter 63
ZU
(ZZT)
ZU
ZU
ZU
ZU
ZU
UNGH...
ZU
...CHAN...
SHINO-CHAN.

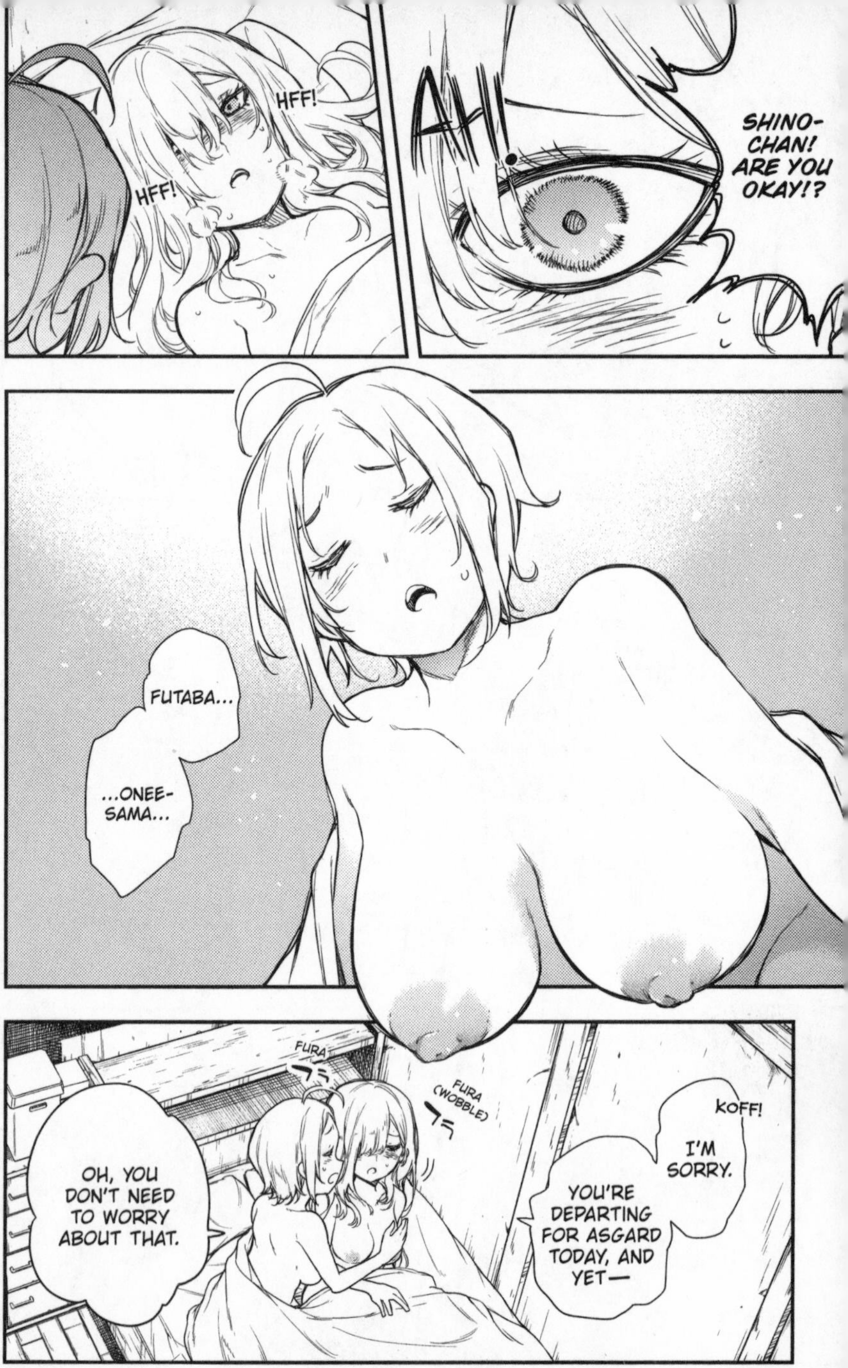
AH!
SHINO-CHAN! ARE YOU OKAY!?
HFF!
HFF!
FUTABA...
...ONEE-SAMA...
KOFF!
I'M SORRY.
YOU'RE DEPARTING FOR ASGARD TODAY, AND YET—
FURA (WOBBLE)
FURA
OH, YOU DON'T NEED TO WORRY ABOUT THAT.

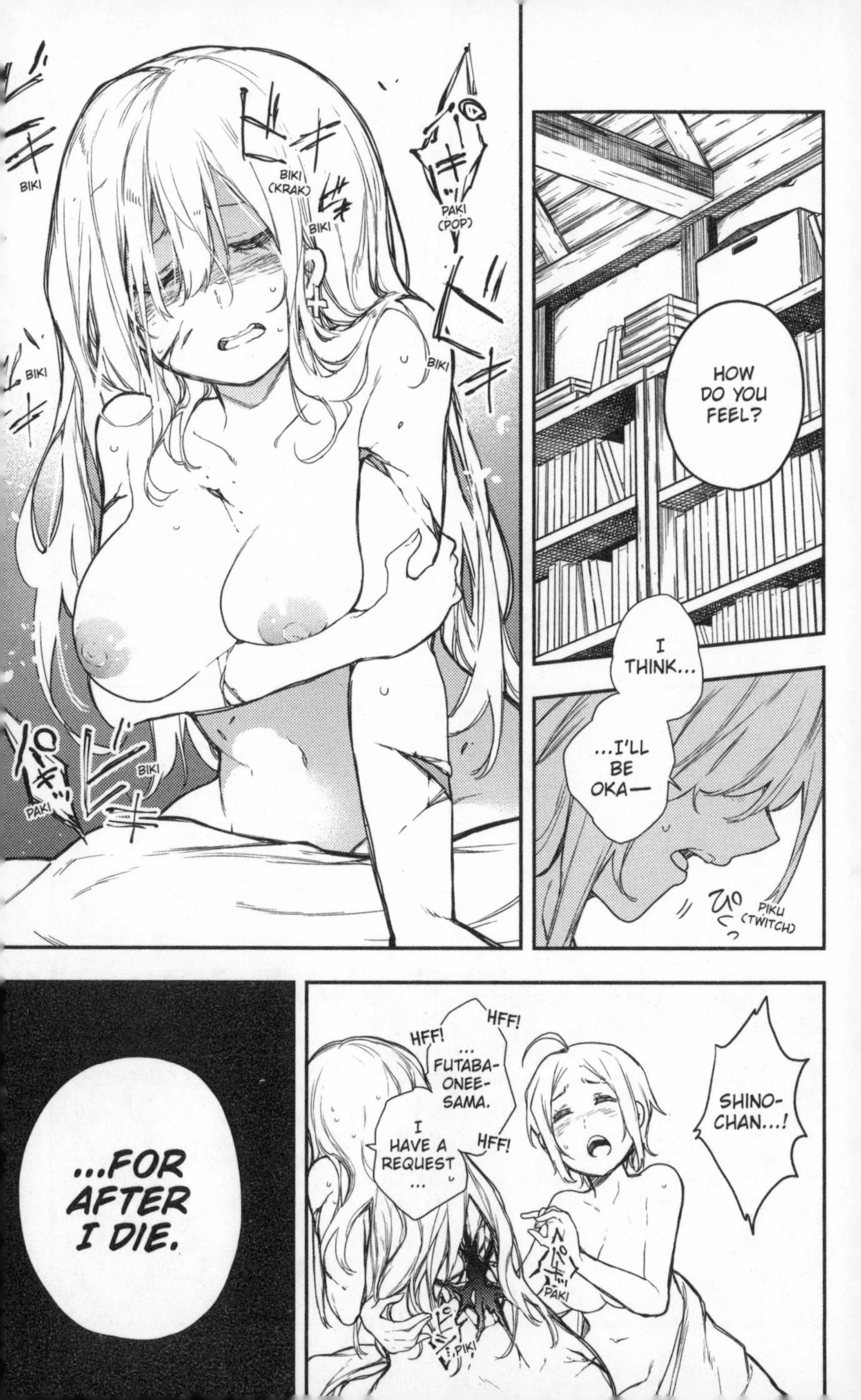
HOW DO YOU FEEL?
I THINK...
...I'LL BE OKA—
PIKU (TWITCH)
PAKI (POP)
BIKI (KRAK)
BIKI
BIKI
BIKI
BIKI
BIKI
BIKI
PAKI
SHINO-CHAN...!
HFF!
HFF!
...FUTABA-ONEE-SAMA.
HFF!
I HAVE A REQUEST...
PAKI
PIKI
...FOR AFTER I DIE.

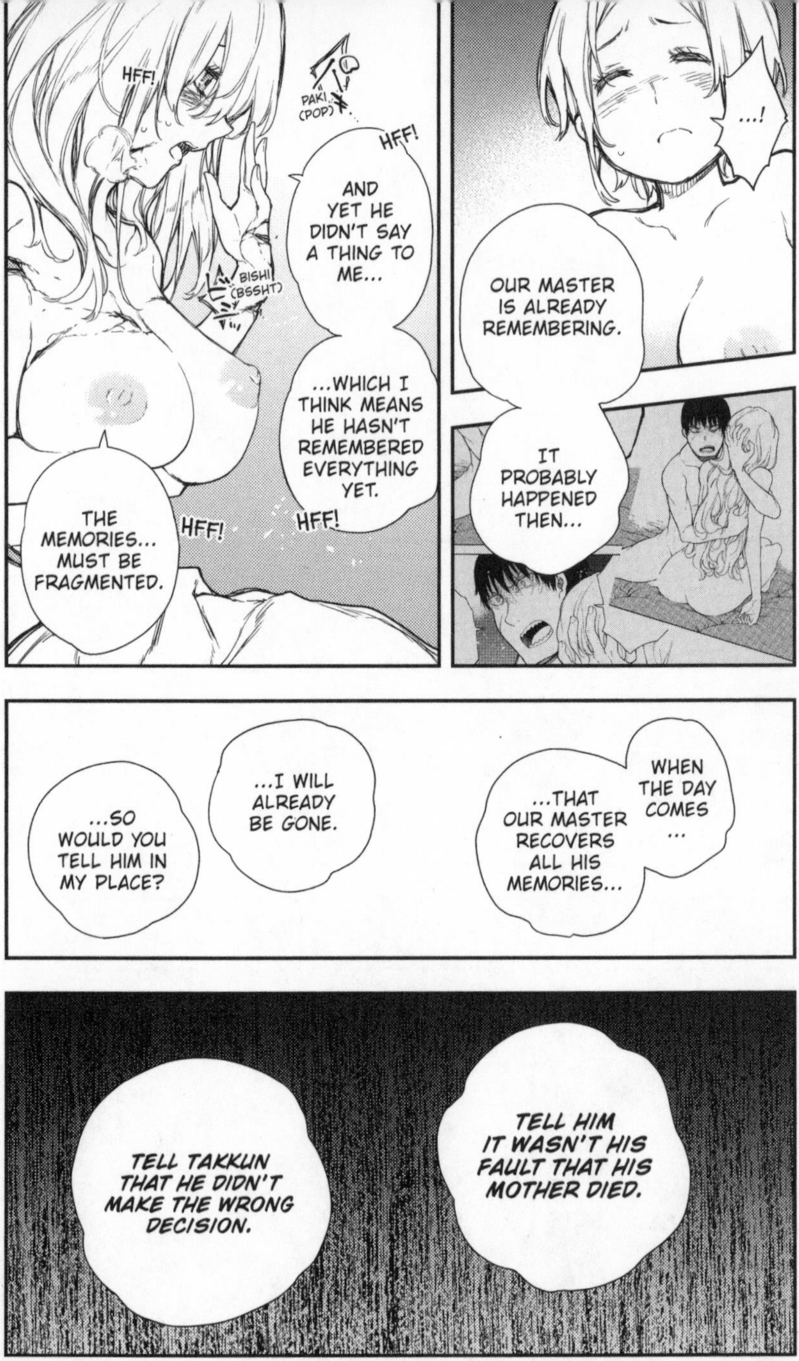
...!
OUR MASTER IS ALREADY REMEMBERING.
IT PROBABLY HAPPENED THEN...
PAKI (POP)
HFF!
AND YET HE DIDN'T SAY A THING TO ME...
...WHICH I THINK MEANS HE HASN'T REMEMBERED EVERYTHING YET.
HFF!
BISHI (BSSHT)
HFF!
THE MEMORIES... MUST BE FRAGMENTED.
HFF!
WHEN THE DAY COMES...
...THAT OUR MASTER RECOVERS ALL HIS MEMORIES...
...I WILL ALREADY BE GONE.
...SO WOULD YOU TELL HIM IN MY PLACE?
TELL HIM IT WASN'T HIS FAULT THAT HIS MOTHER DIED.
TELL TAKKUN THAT HE DIDN'T MAKE THE WRONG DECISION.

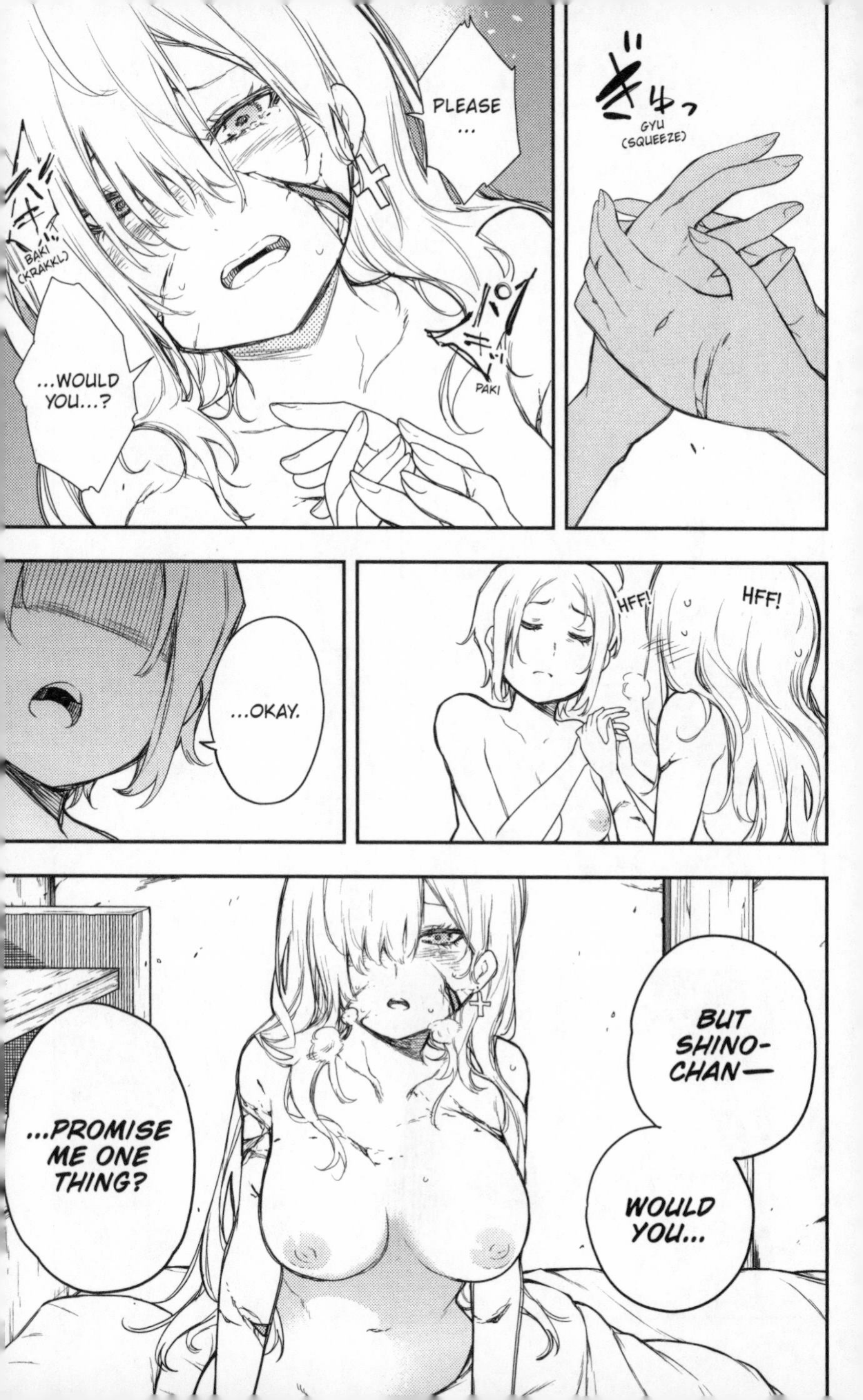
ぎゅっ
GYU (SQUEEZE)
PLEASE ...
PAKI
BAKI (KRAKKL)
...WOULD YOU...?
HFF!
HFF!
...OKAY.
BUT SHINO-CHAN—
WOULD YOU...
...PROMISE ME ONE THING?

Chapter 63: The Returning Maiden

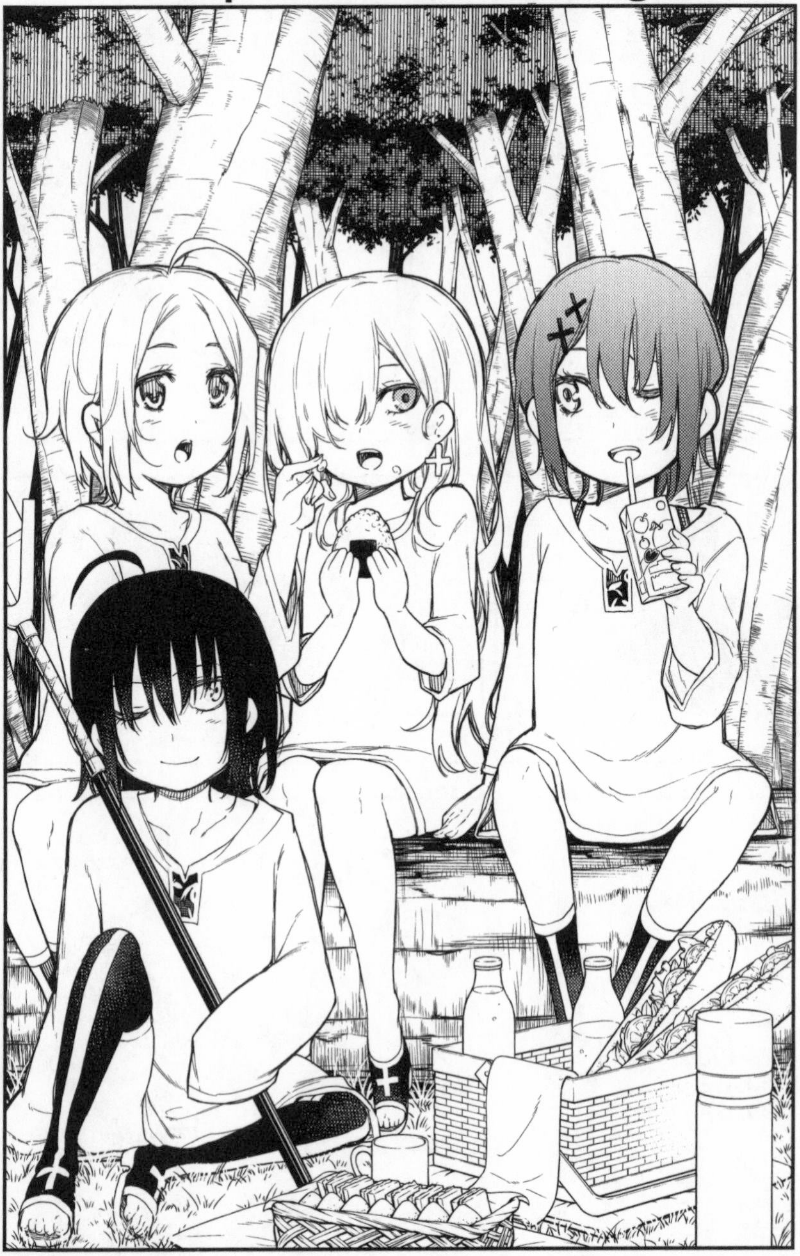

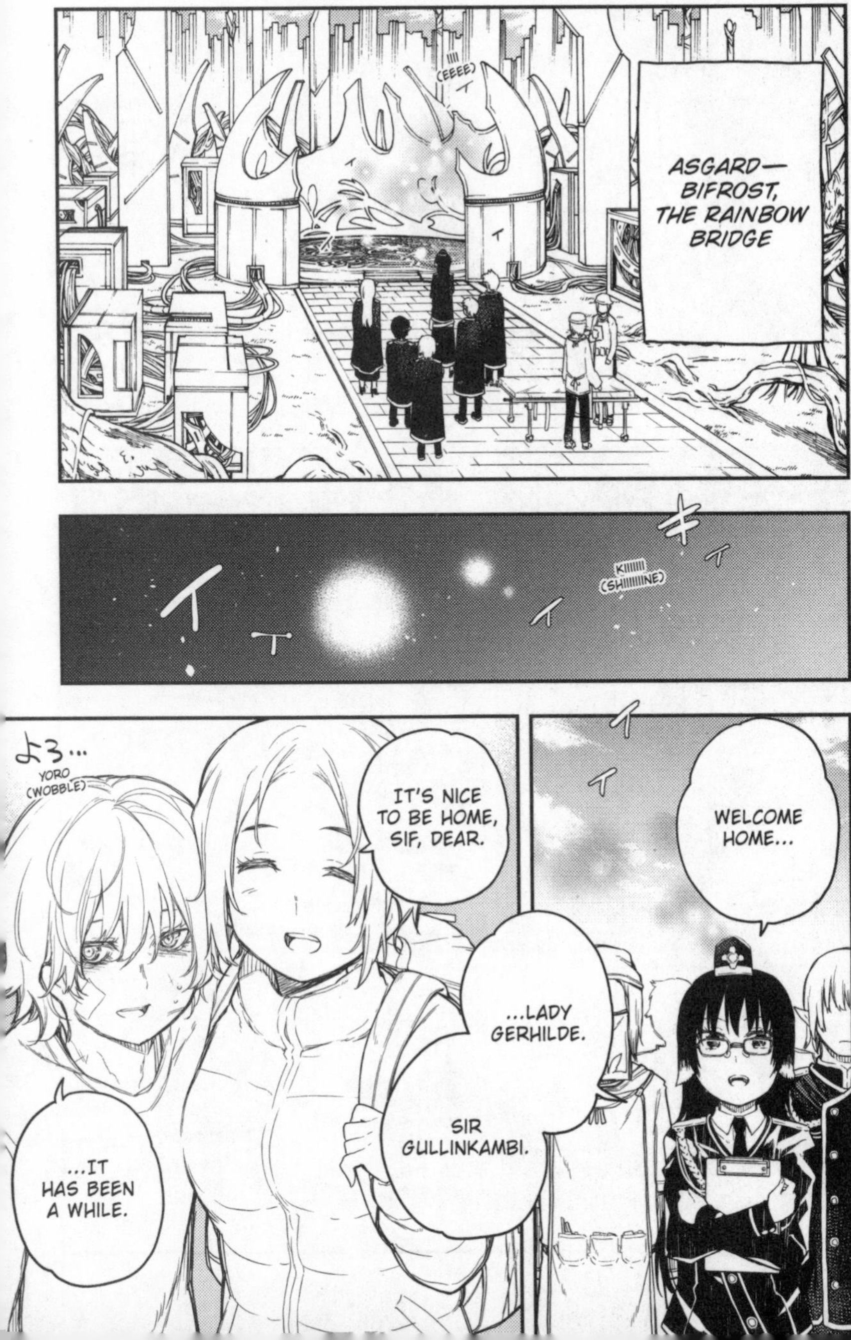

ASGARD—BIFROST, THE RAINBOW BRIDGE
IIII (EEEE)
KIIIIII (SHIIIIIINE)
WELCOME HOME...
...LADY GERHILDE.
SIR GULLINKAMBI.
IT'S NICE TO BE HOME, SIF, DEAR.
よろ…
YORO (WOBBLE)
...IT HAS BEEN A WHILE.

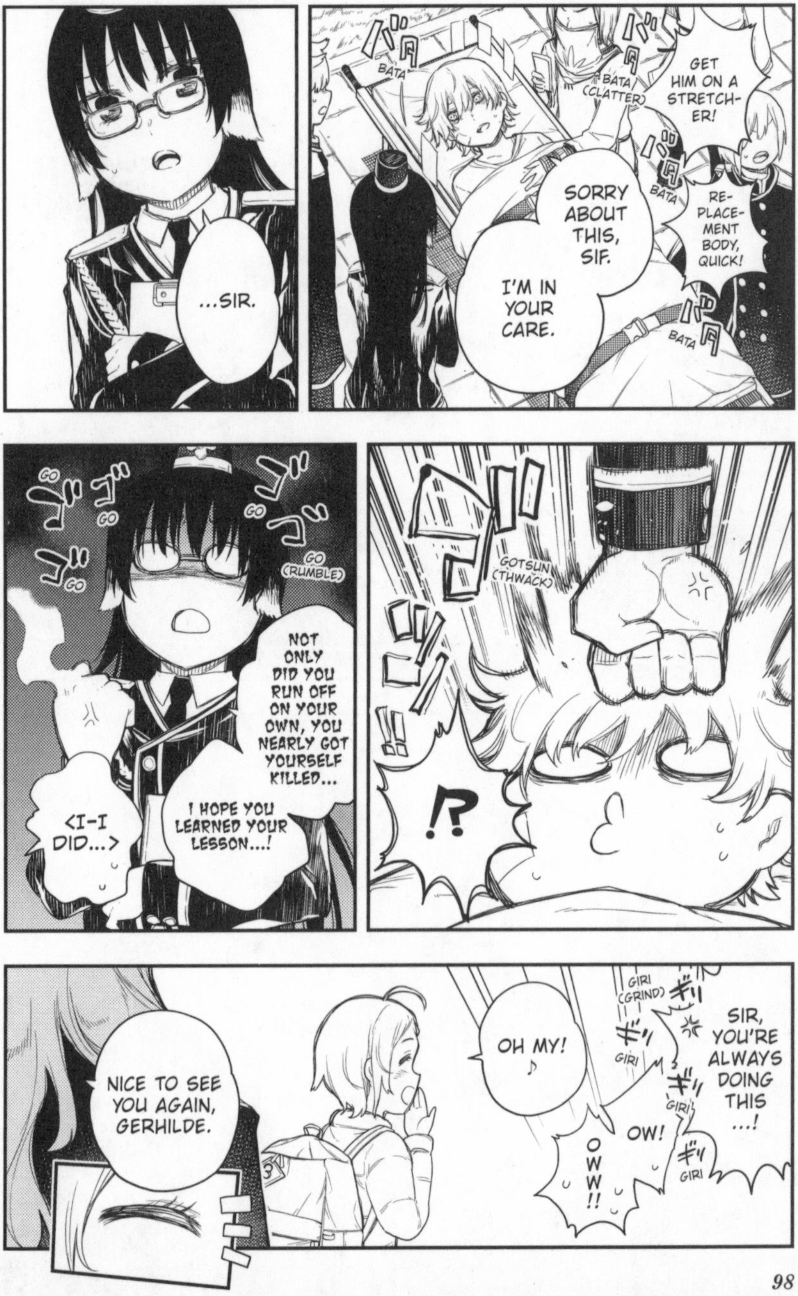
GET HIM ON A STRETCHER!
BATA (CLATTER)
BATA
BATA
REPLACEMENT BODY, QUICK!
SORRY ABOUT THIS, SIF.
I'M IN YOUR CARE.
BATA
...SIR.
GOTSUN (THWACK)
!?
GO (RUMBLE)
GO
GO
GO
NOT ONLY DID YOU RUN OFF ON YOUR OWN, YOU NEARLY GOT YOURSELF KILLED...
I HOPE YOU LEARNED YOUR LESSON...!
<I-I DID...>
SIR, YOU'RE ALWAYS DOING THIS ...!
GIRI (GRIND)
GIRI
GIRI
GIRI
OW!
OWW!!
OH MY! ♪
NICE TO SEE YOU AGAIN, GERHILDE.

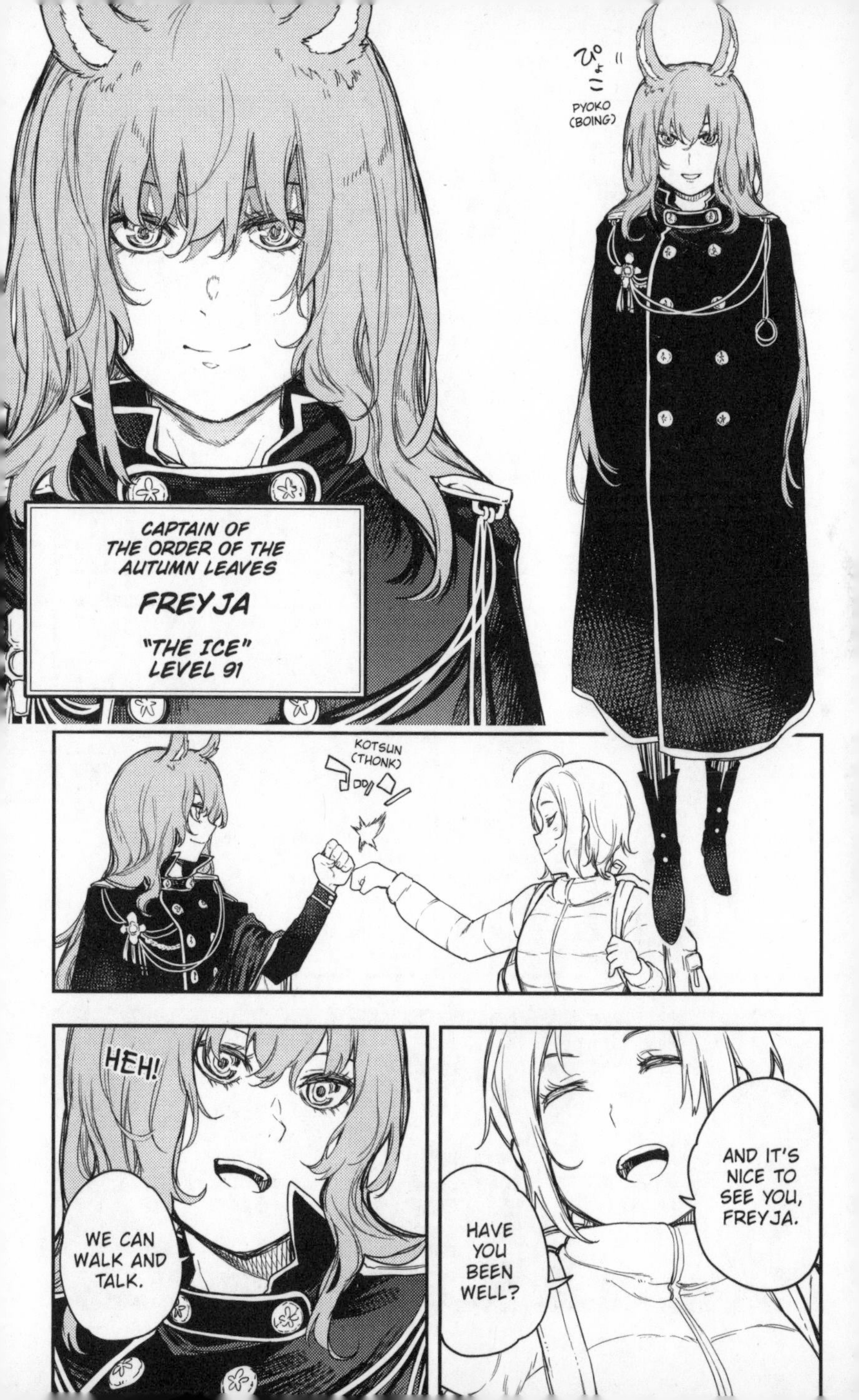
ぴょこ
PYOKO (BOING)
CAPTAIN OF THE ORDER OF THE AUTUMN LEAVES
FREYJA
"THE ICE"
LEVEL 91
KOTSUN (THONK)
AND IT'S NICE TO SEE YOU, FREYJA.
HAVE YOU BEEN WELL?
HEH!
WE CAN WALK AND TALK.

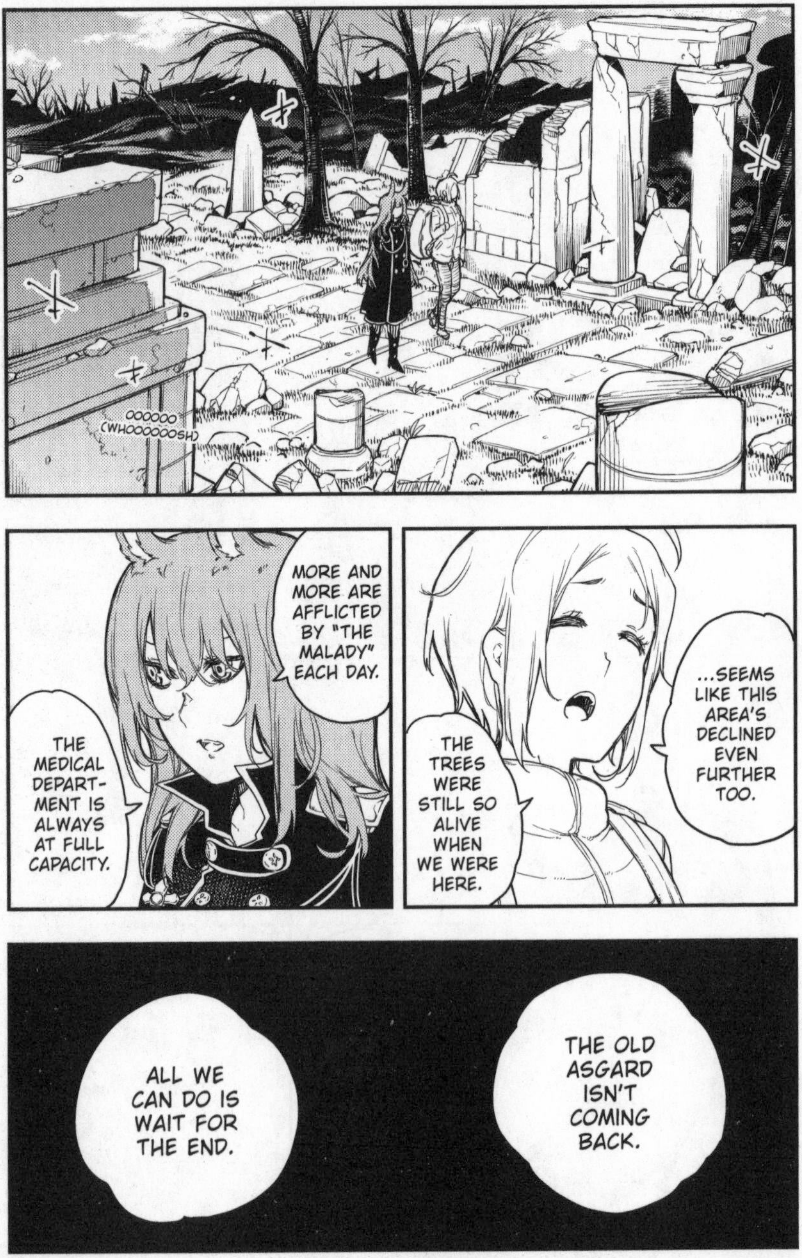
OOOOOO (WHOOOOOOSH)
...SEEMS LIKE THIS AREA'S DECLINED EVEN FURTHER TOO.
THE TREES WERE STILL SO ALIVE WHEN WE WERE HERE.
MORE AND MORE ARE AFFLICTED BY "THE MALADY" EACH DAY.
THE MEDICAL DEPARTMENT IS ALWAYS AT FULL CAPACITY.
THE OLD ASGARD ISN'T COMING BACK.
ALL WE CAN DO IS WAIT FOR THE END.

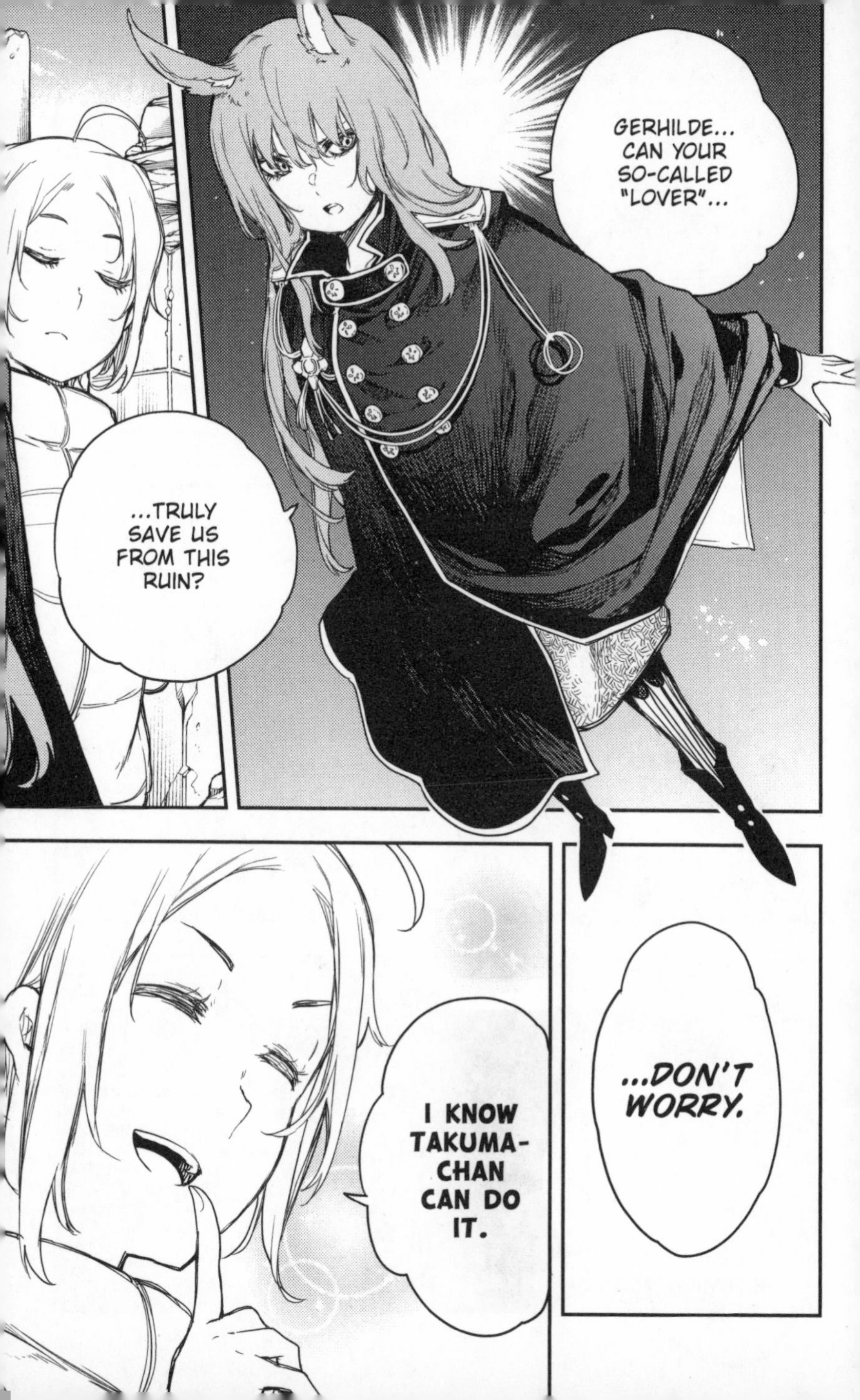
GERHILDE... CAN YOUR SO-CALLED "LOVER"...
...TRULY SAVE US FROM THIS RUIN?
...DON'T WORRY.
I KNOW TAKUMA-CHAN CAN DO IT.

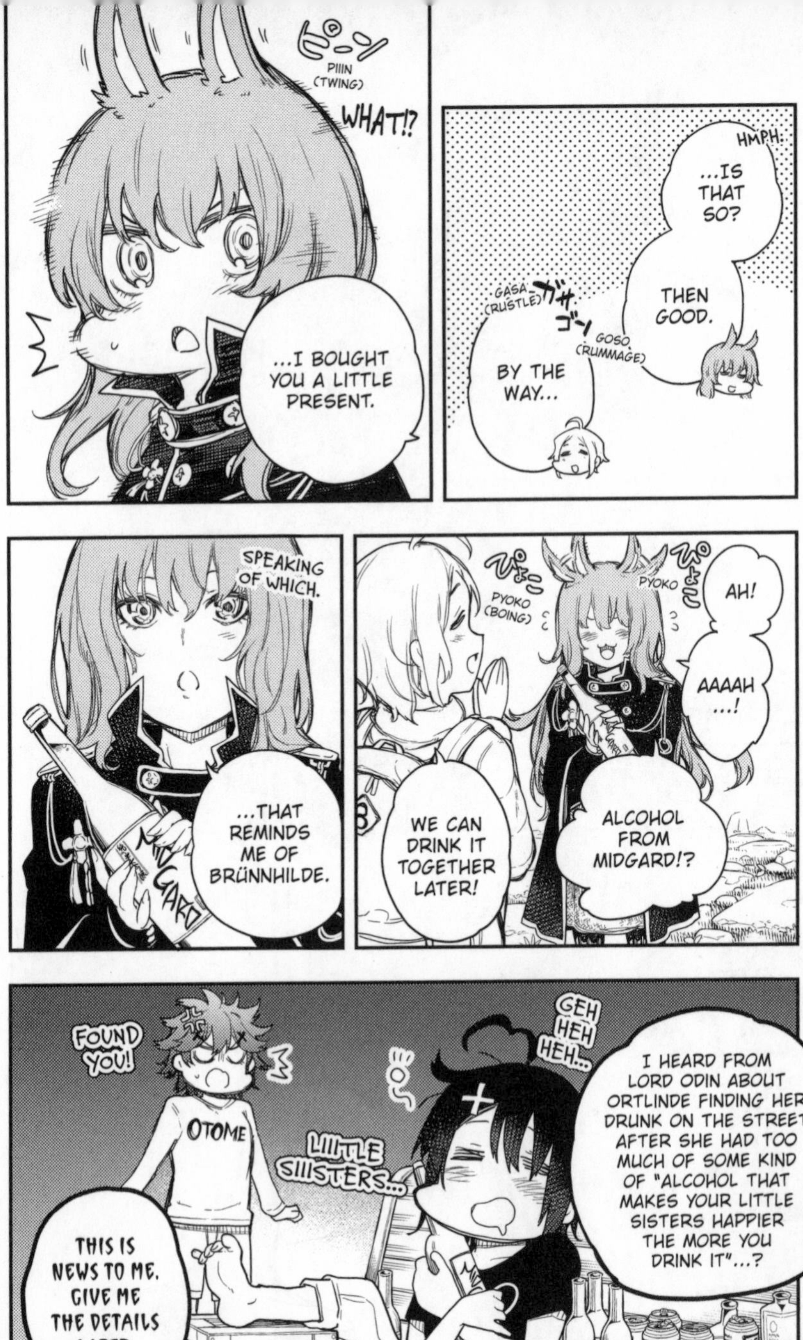
HMPH.
...IS THAT SO?
THEN GOOD.
GASA (RUSTLE)
GOSO (RUMMAGE)
BY THE WAY...
PIIIN (TWING)
WHAT!?
...I BOUGHT YOU A LITTLE PRESENT.
PYOKO
AH!
AAAAH...!
PYOKO (BOING)
ALCOHOL FROM MIDGARD!?
WE CAN DRINK IT TOGETHER LATER!
SPEAKING OF WHICH.
...THAT REMINDS ME OF BRÜNNHILDE.
MIDGARD
I HEARD FROM LORD ODIN ABOUT ORTLINDE FINDING HER DRUNK ON THE STREET AFTER SHE HAD TOO MUCH OF SOME KIND OF "ALCOHOL THAT MAKES YOUR LITTLE SISTERS HAPPIER THE MORE YOU DRINK IT"...?
GEH HEH HEH...
LIIITLE SIIISTERS...
FOUND YOU!
OTOME
THIS IS NEWS TO ME. GIVE ME THE DETAILS LATER.

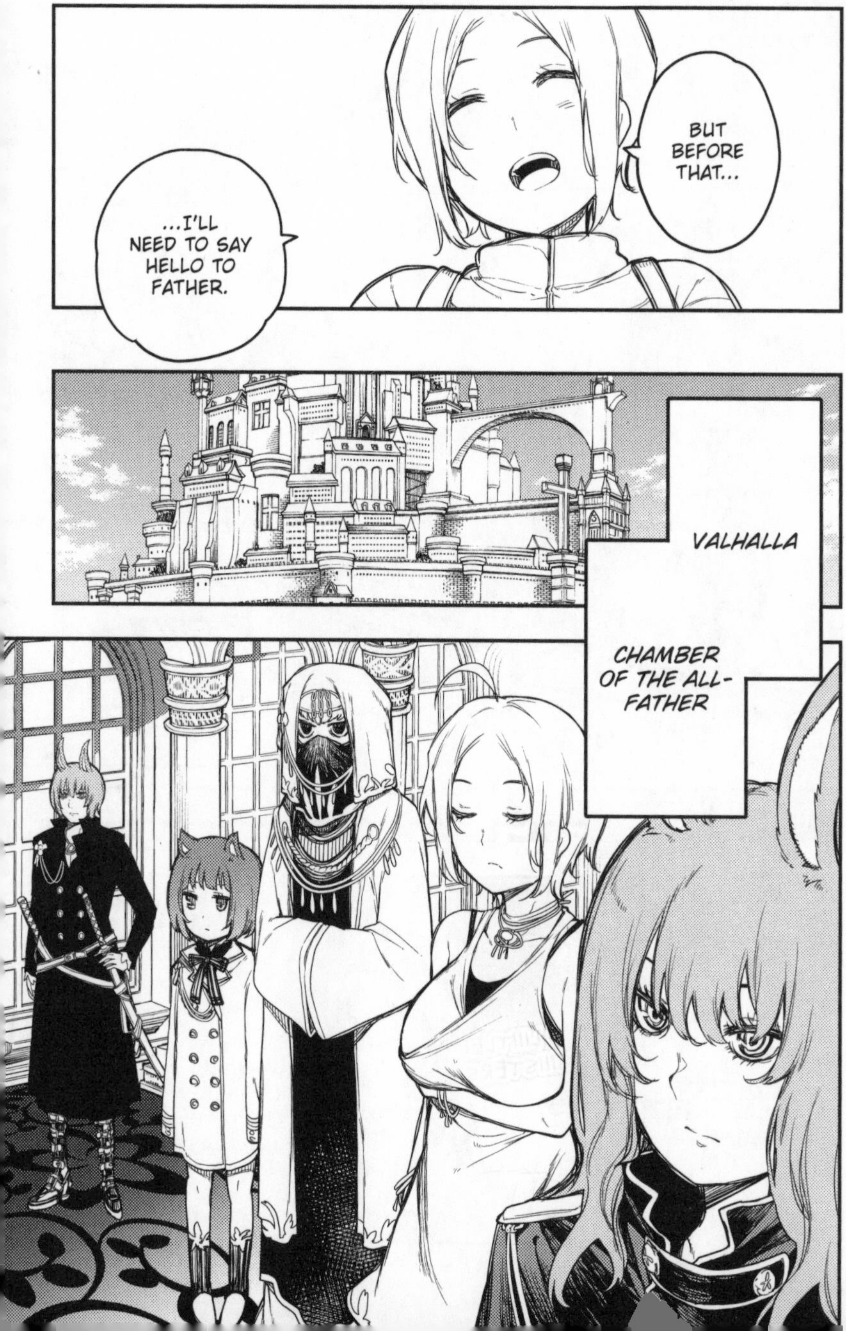
BUT BEFORE THAT...
...I'LL NEED TO SAY HELLO TO FATHER.
VALHALLA
CHAMBER OF THE ALL-FATHER

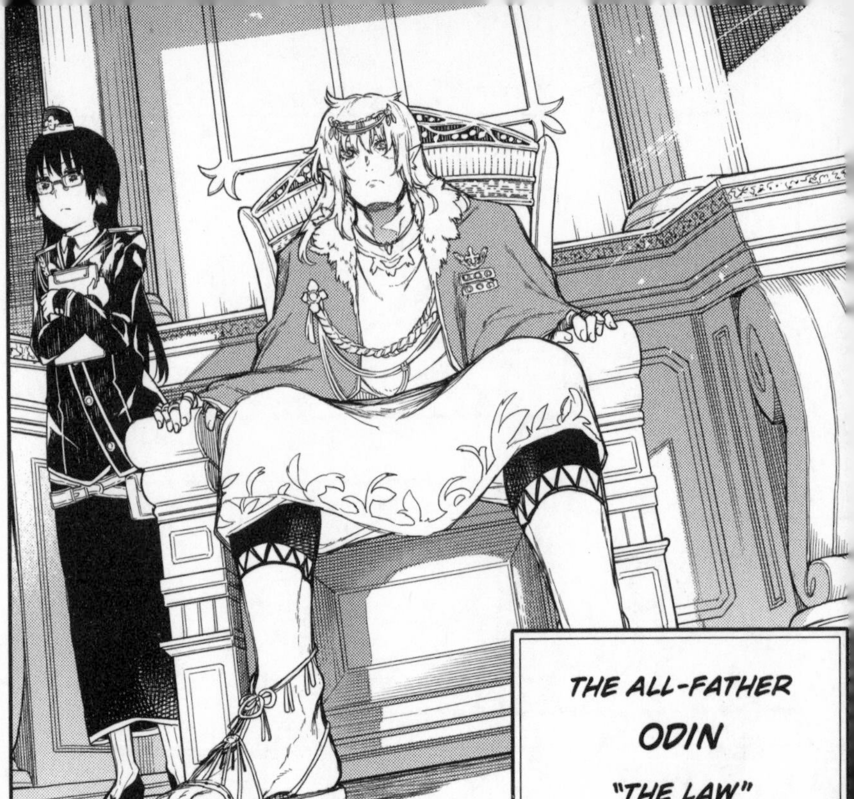
THE ALL-FATHER
ODIN
"THE LAW"
LEVEL 100
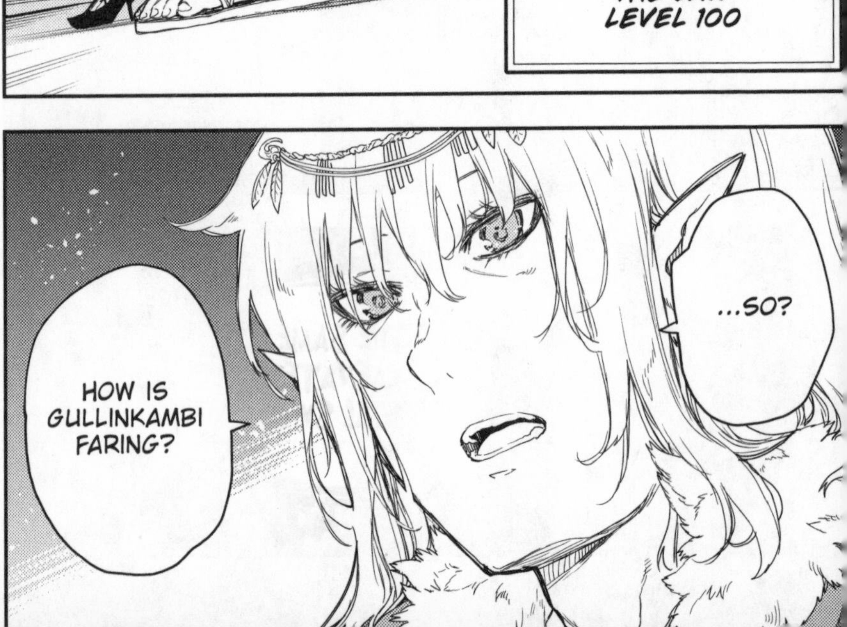
...SO?
HOW IS GULLINKAMBI FARING?

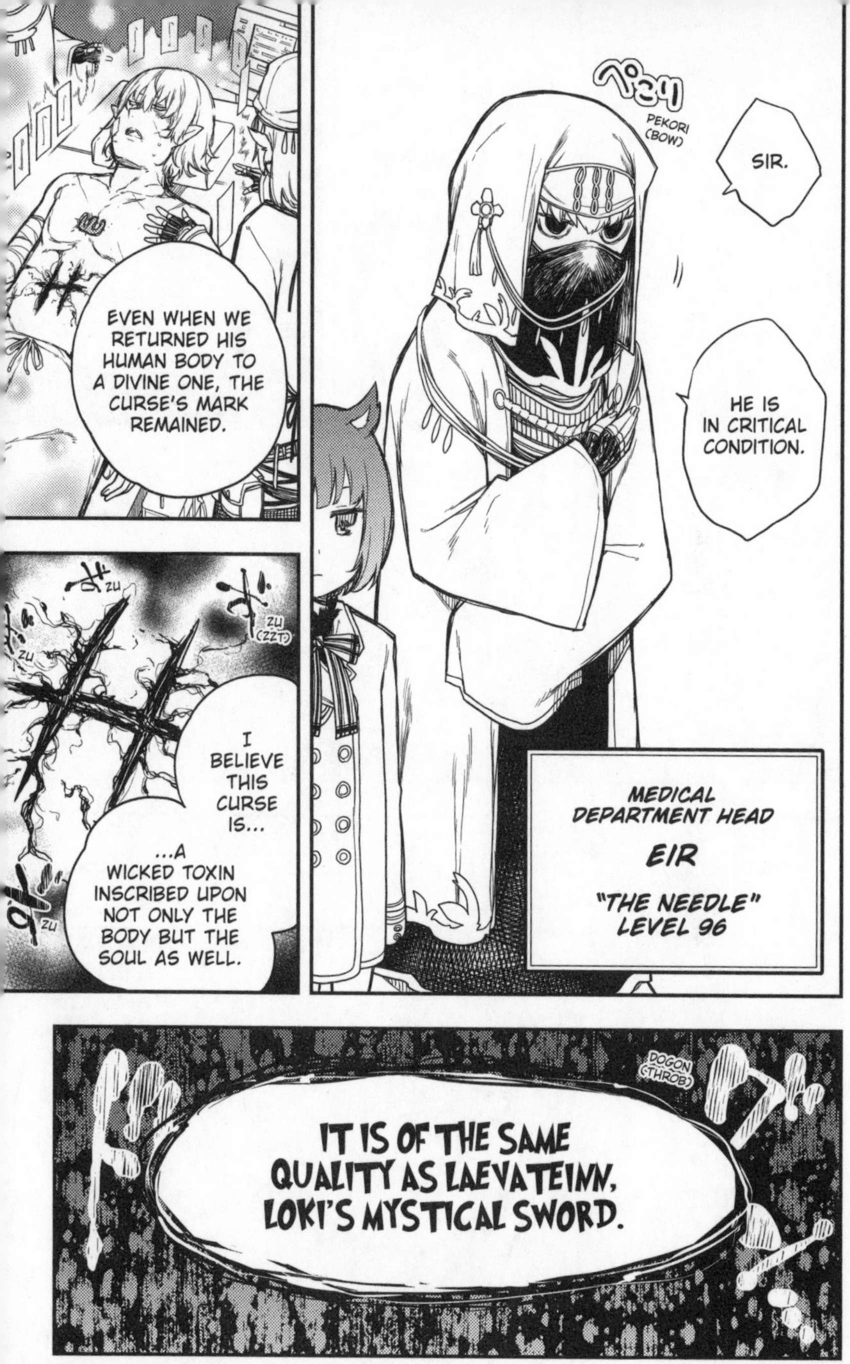
PEKORI (BOW)
SIR.
HE IS IN CRITICAL CONDITION.
MEDICAL DEPARTMENT HEAD
EIR
"THE NEEDLE" LEVEL 96
EVEN WHEN WE RETURNED HIS HUMAN BODY TO A DIVINE ONE, THE CURSE'S MARK REMAINED.
ZU
ZU (ZZT)
ZU
I BELIEVE THIS CURSE IS...
...A WICKED TOXIN INSCRIBED UPON NOT ONLY THE BODY BUT THE SOUL AS WELL.
ZU
DOGON (THROB)
IT IS OF THE SAME QUALITY AS LAEVATEINN, LOKI'S MYSTICAL SWORD.

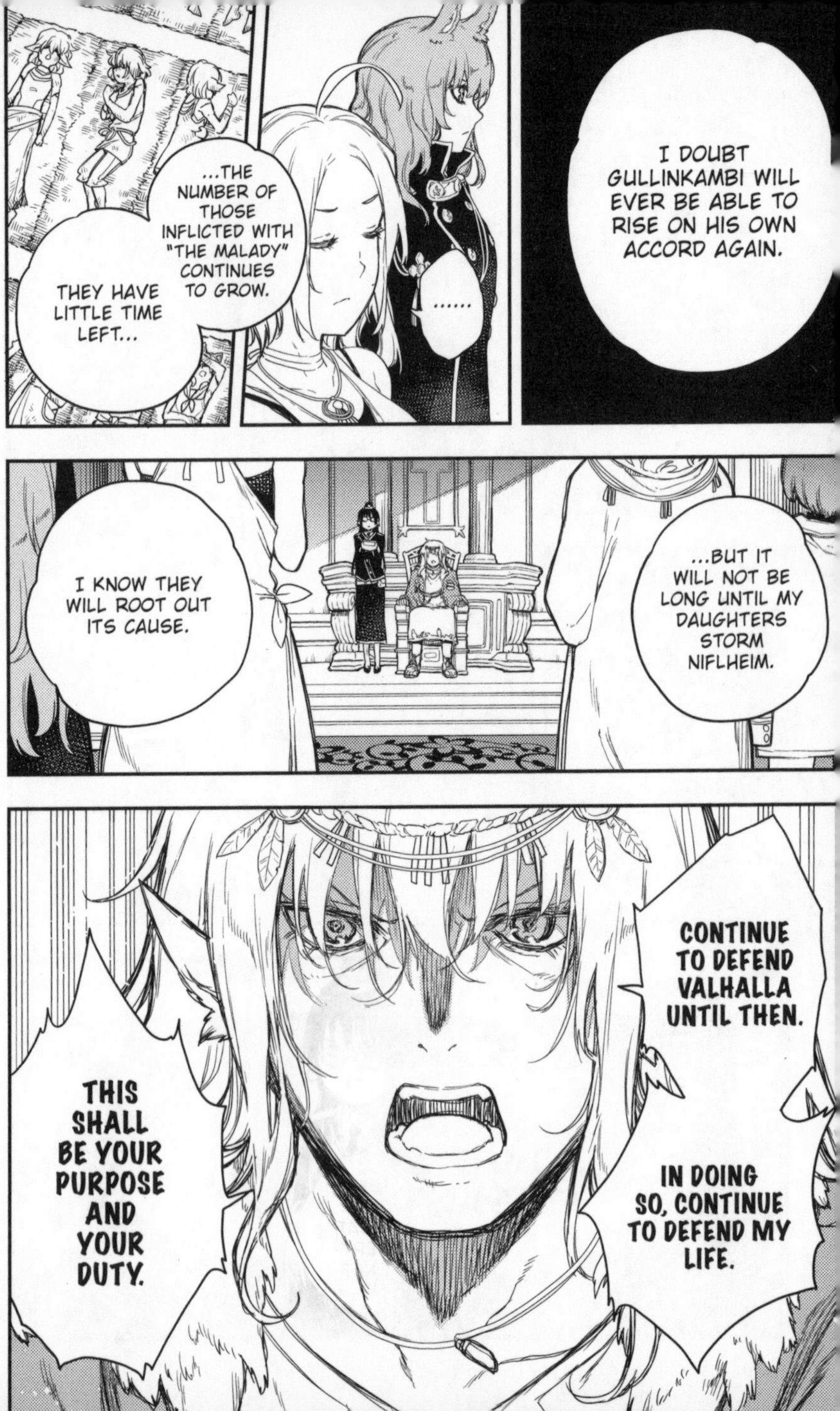
I DOUBT GULLINKAMBI WILL EVER BE ABLE TO RISE ON HIS OWN ACCORD AGAIN.
......
...THE NUMBER OF THOSE INFLICTED WITH "THE MALADY" CONTINUES TO GROW.
THEY HAVE LITTLE TIME LEFT...
...BUT IT WILL NOT BE LONG UNTIL MY DAUGHTERS STORM NIFLHEIM.
I KNOW THEY WILL ROOT OUT ITS CAUSE.
CONTINUE TO DEFEND VALHALLA UNTIL THEN.
IN DOING SO, CONTINUE TO DEFEND MY LIFE.
THIS SHALL BE YOUR PURPOSE AND YOUR DUTY.

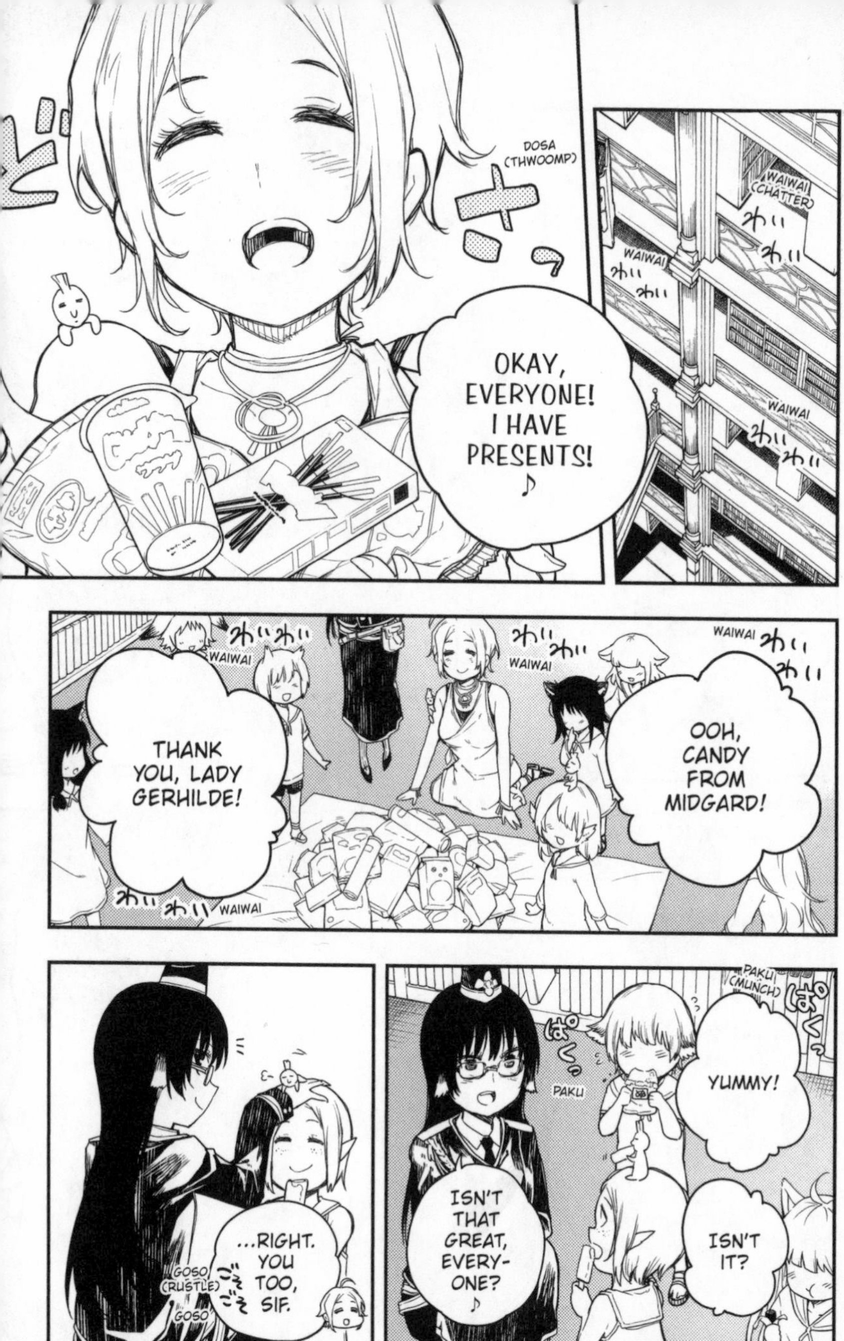
WAIWAI (CHATTER)
WAIWAI
WAIWAI
DOSA (THWOOMP)
OKAY, EVERYONE! I HAVE PRESENTS! ♪
WAIWAI
OOH, CANDY FROM MIDGARD!
WAIWAI
WAIWAI
THANK YOU, LADY GERHILDE!
WAIWAI
PAKU (MUNCH)
YUMMY!
PAKU
ISN'T IT?
ISN'T THAT GREAT, EVERYONE? ♪
...RIGHT. YOU TOO, SIF.
GOSO (RUSTLE)
GOSO

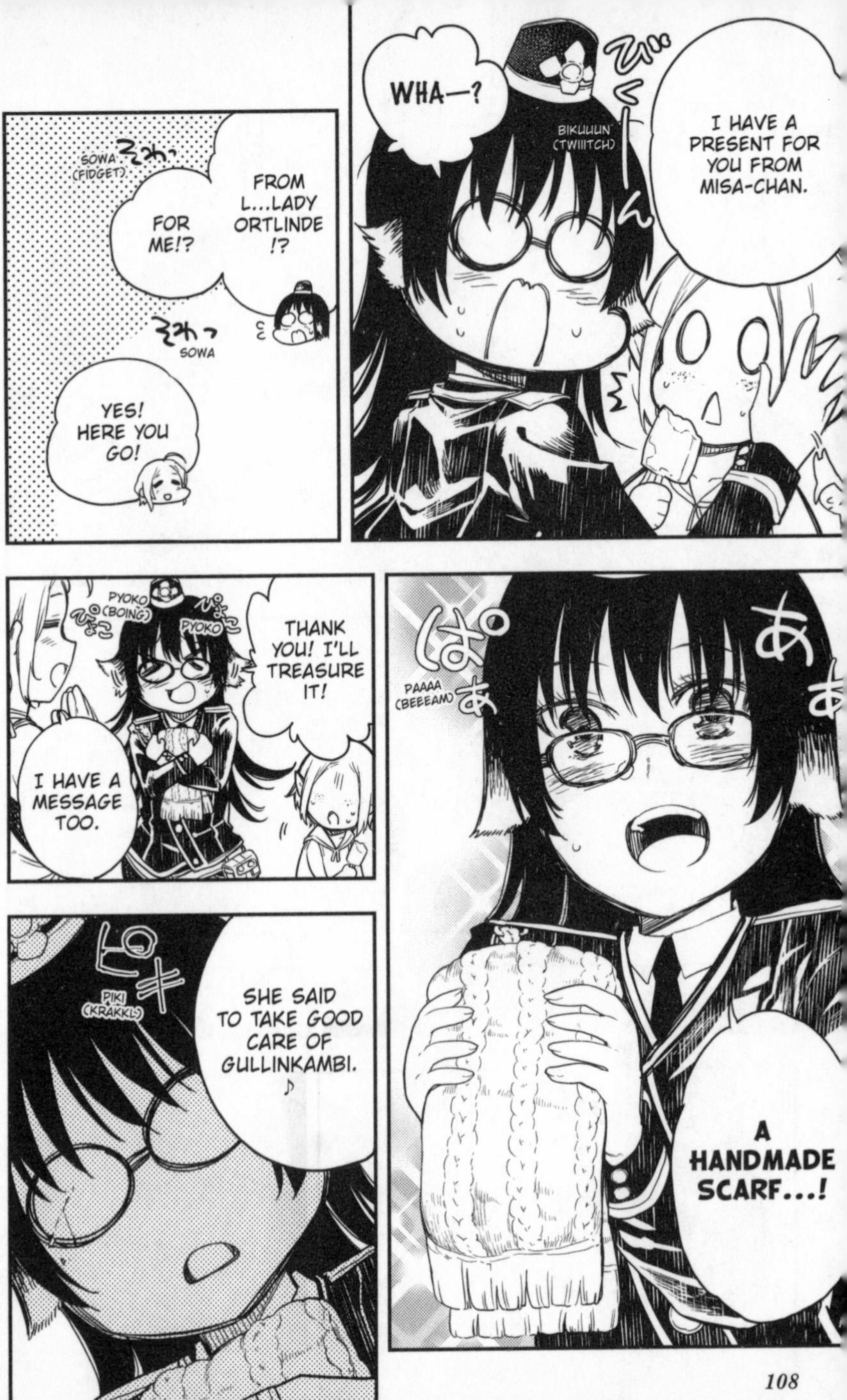
I HAVE A PRESENT FOR YOU FROM MISA-CHAN.
BIKUUUN (TWIIITCH)
WHA—?
SOWA (FIDGET)
FROM L...LADY ORTLINDE!?
FOR ME!?
SOWA
YES! HERE YOU GO!
PAAAA (BEEEAM)
A HANDMADE SCARF...!
THANK YOU! I'LL TREASURE IT!
PYOKO (BOING)
PYOKO
I HAVE A MESSAGE TOO.
PIKI (KRAKKL)
SHE SAID TO TAKE GOOD CARE OF GULLINKAMBI. ♪

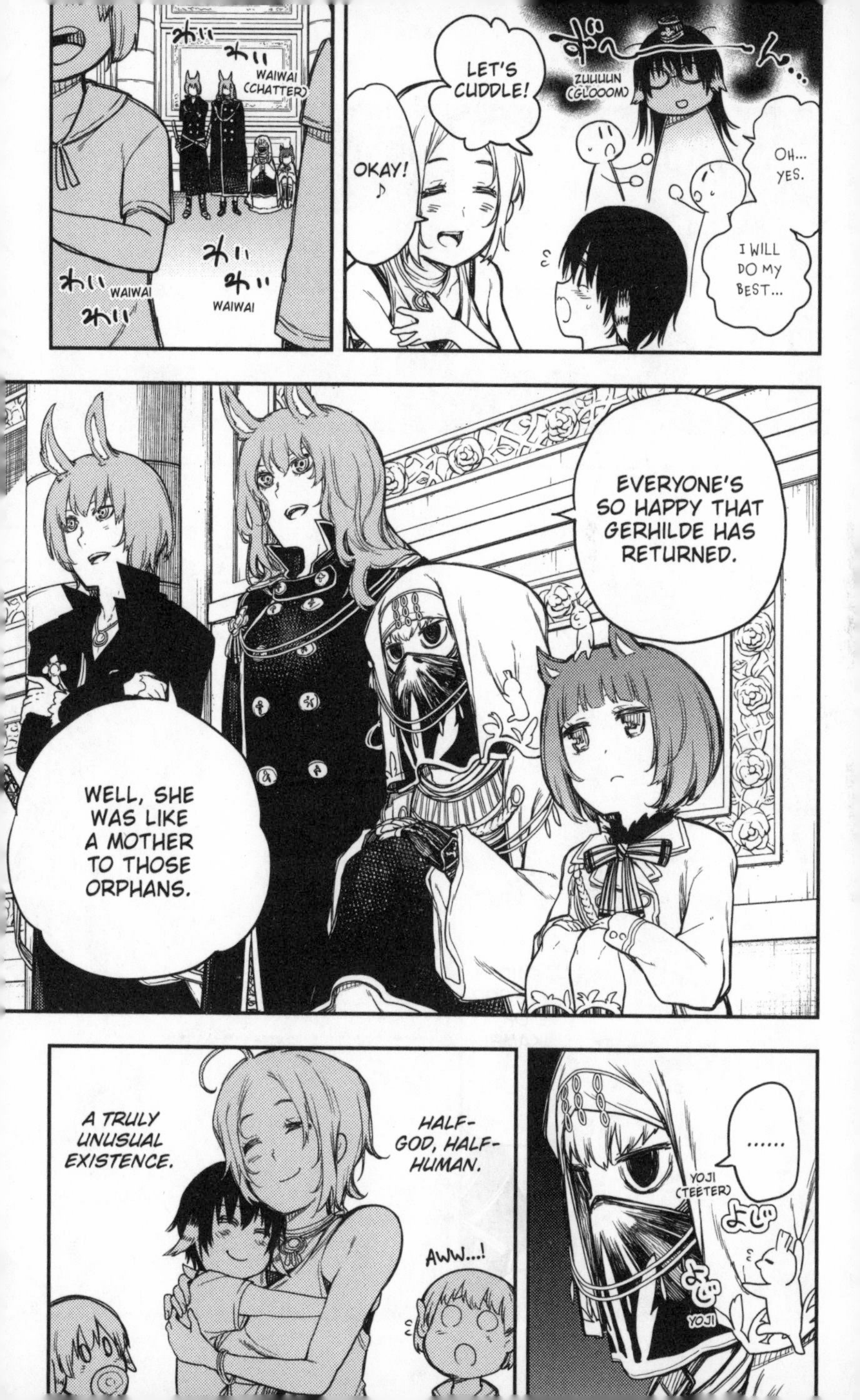
LET'S CUDDLE!
OKAY! ♪
ずへーーーん…
ZUUUUN (GLOOOM)
OH... YES.
I WILL DO MY BEST...
わい わい
WAIWAI (CHATTER)
わい わい
WAIWAI
わい わい
WAIWAI
EVERYONE'S SO HAPPY THAT GERHILDE HAS RETURNED.
WELL, SHE WAS LIKE A MOTHER TO THOSE ORPHANS.
......
よじ
YOJI (TEETER)
よじ
YOJI
HALF-GOD, HALF-HUMAN.
A TRULY UNUSUAL EXISTENCE.
AWW...!

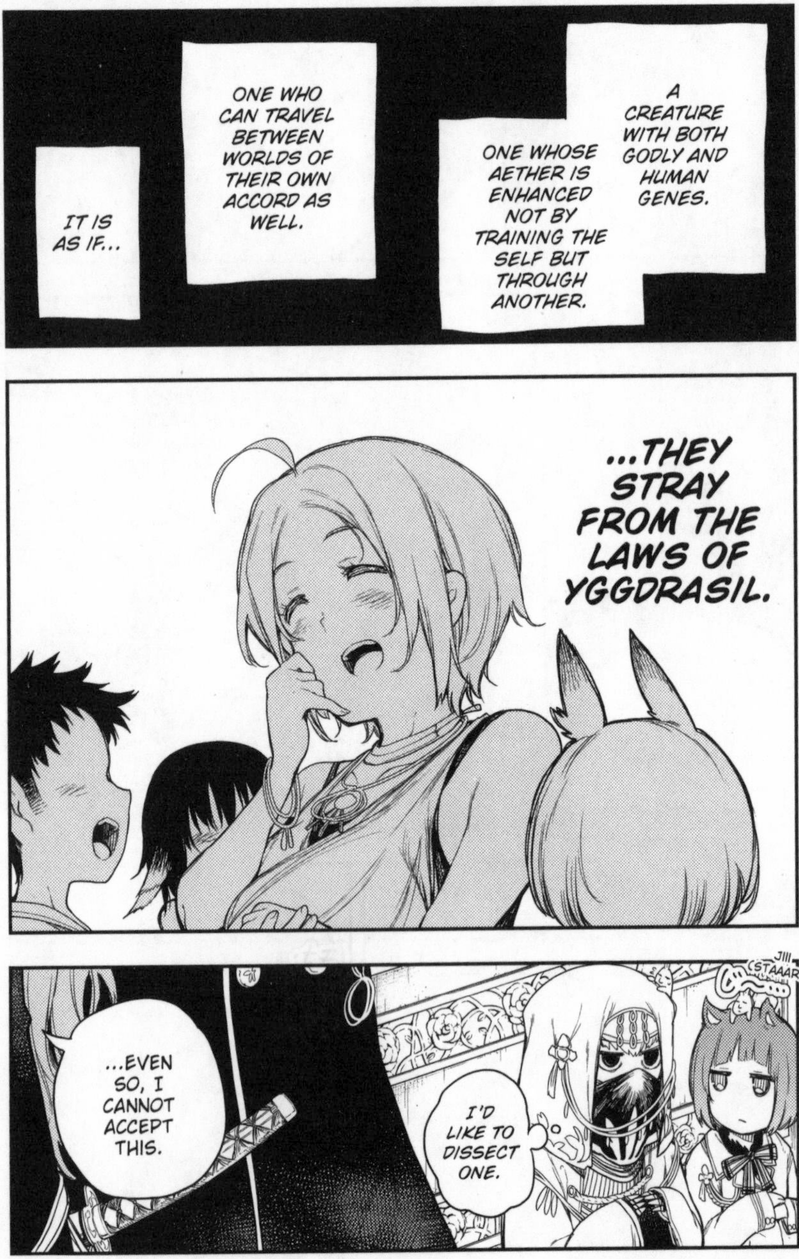
A CREATURE WITH BOTH GODLY AND HUMAN GENES.
ONE WHOSE AETHER IS ENHANCED NOT BY TRAINING THE SELF BUT THROUGH ANOTHER.
ONE WHO CAN TRAVEL BETWEEN WORLDS OF THEIR OWN ACCORD AS WELL.
IT IS AS IF...
...THEY STRAY FROM THE LAWS OF YGGDRASIL.
JIII (STAAARE)
I'D LIKE TO DISSECT ONE.
...EVEN SO, I CANNOT ACCEPT THIS.

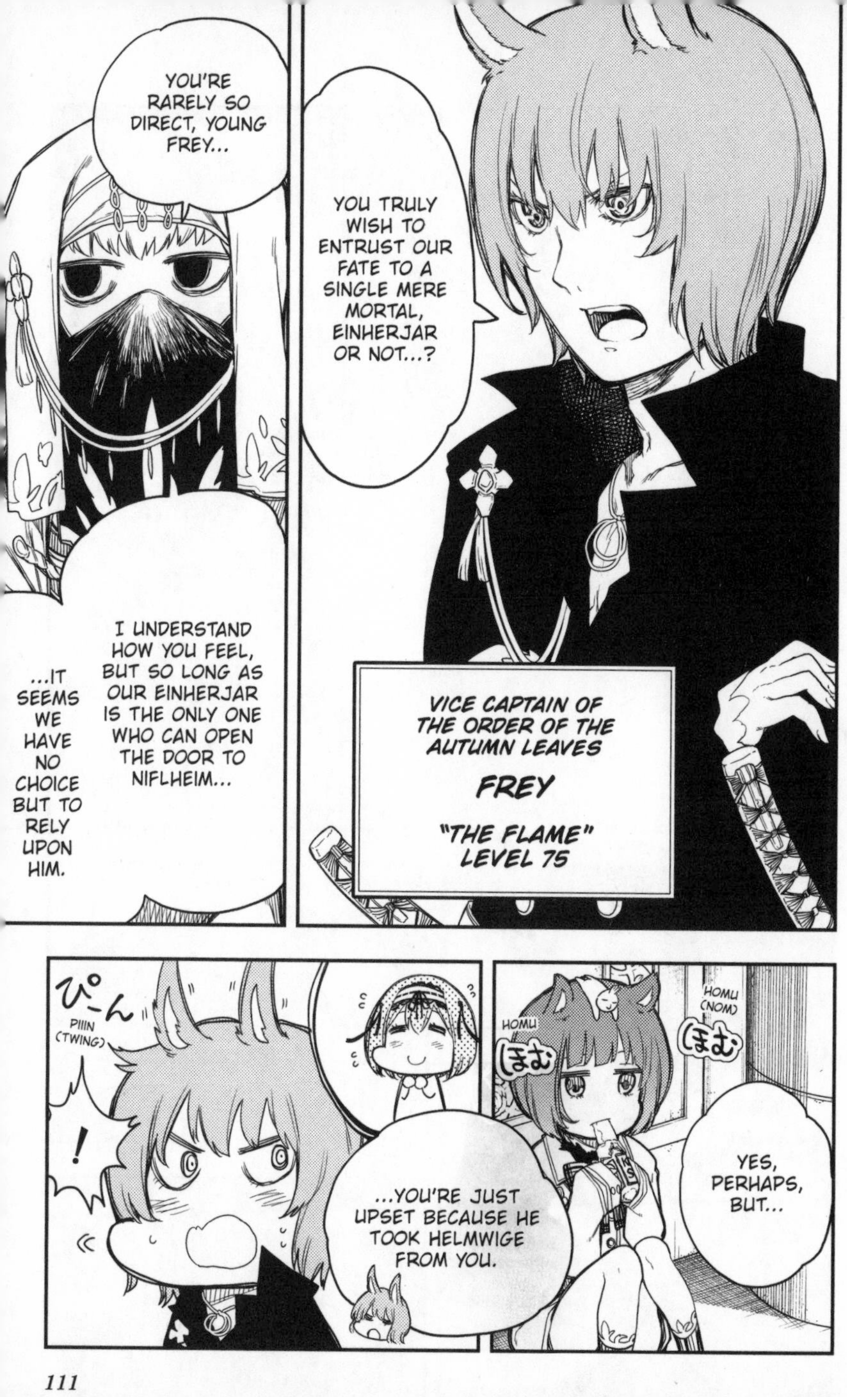
YOU TRULY WISH TO ENTRUST OUR FATE TO A SINGLE MERE MORTAL, EINHERJAR OR NOT...?
VICE CAPTAIN OF THE ORDER OF THE AUTUMN LEAVES
FREY
"THE FLAME"
LEVEL 75
YOU'RE RARELY SO DIRECT, YOUNG FREY...
I UNDERSTAND HOW YOU FEEL, BUT SO LONG AS OUR EINHERJAR IS THE ONLY ONE WHO CAN OPEN THE DOOR TO NIFLHEIM...
...IT SEEMS WE HAVE NO CHOICE BUT TO RELY UPON HIM.
ほむ
HOMU (NOM)
ほむ
HOMU
YES, PERHAPS, BUT...
...YOU'RE JUST UPSET BECAUSE HE TOOK HELMWIGE FROM YOU.
ぴーん
PIIIN (TWING)
!

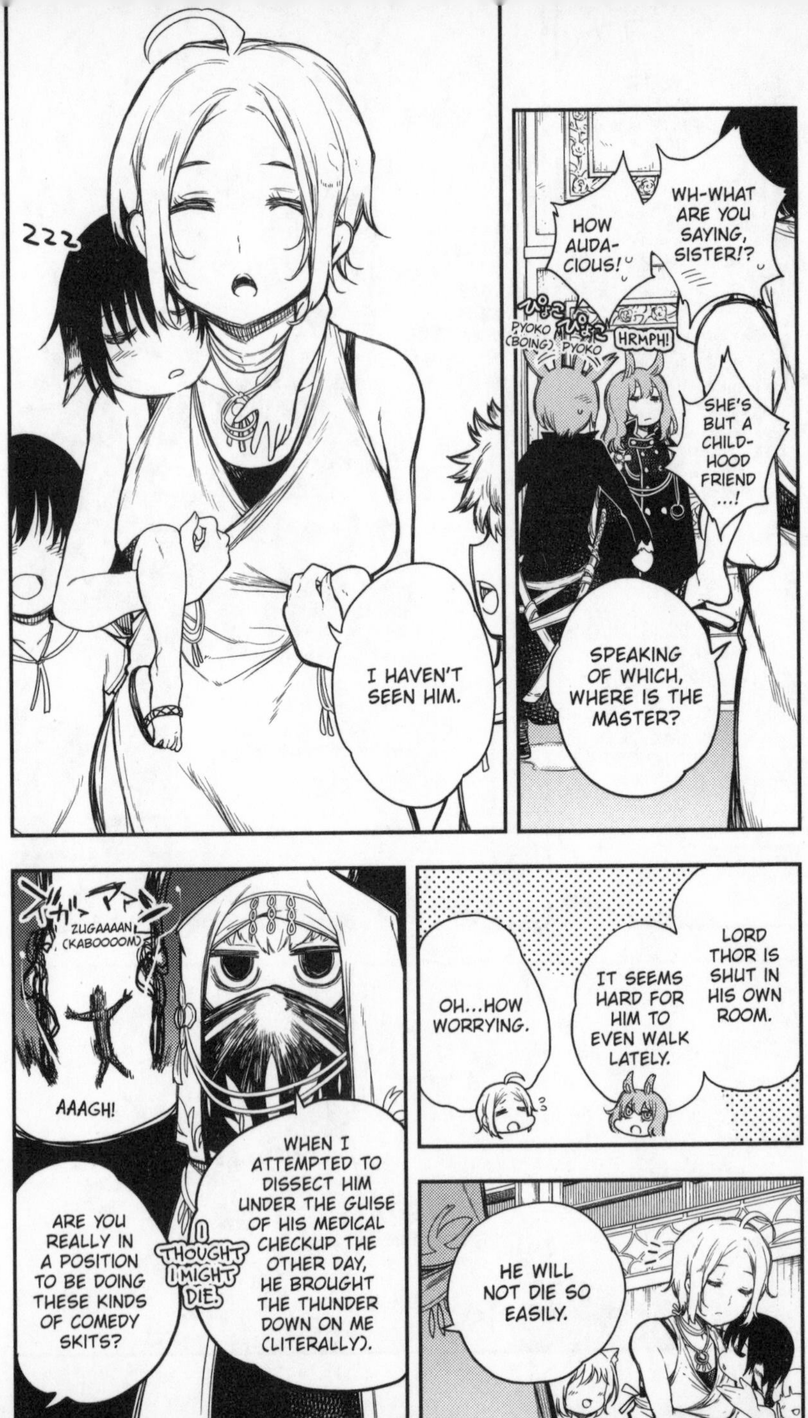
WH-WHAT ARE YOU SAYING, SISTER!?
HOW AUDA-CIOUS!
PYOKO (BOING) PYOKO
HRMPH!
SHE'S BUT A CHILD-HOOD FRIEND...!
SPEAKING OF WHICH, WHERE IS THE MASTER?
ZZZ
I HAVEN'T SEEN HIM.
LORD THOR IS SHUT IN HIS OWN ROOM.
IT SEEMS HARD FOR HIM TO EVEN WALK LATELY.
OH...HOW WORRYING.
HE WILL NOT DIE SO EASILY.
ZUGAAAAN (KABOOOOM)
AAAGH!
WHEN I ATTEMPTED TO DISSECT HIM UNDER THE GUISE OF HIS MEDICAL CHECKUP THE OTHER DAY, HE BROUGHT THE THUNDER DOWN ON ME (LITERALLY).
I THOUGHT I MIGHT DIE.
ARE YOU REALLY IN A POSITION TO BE DOING THESE KINDS OF COMEDY SKITS?

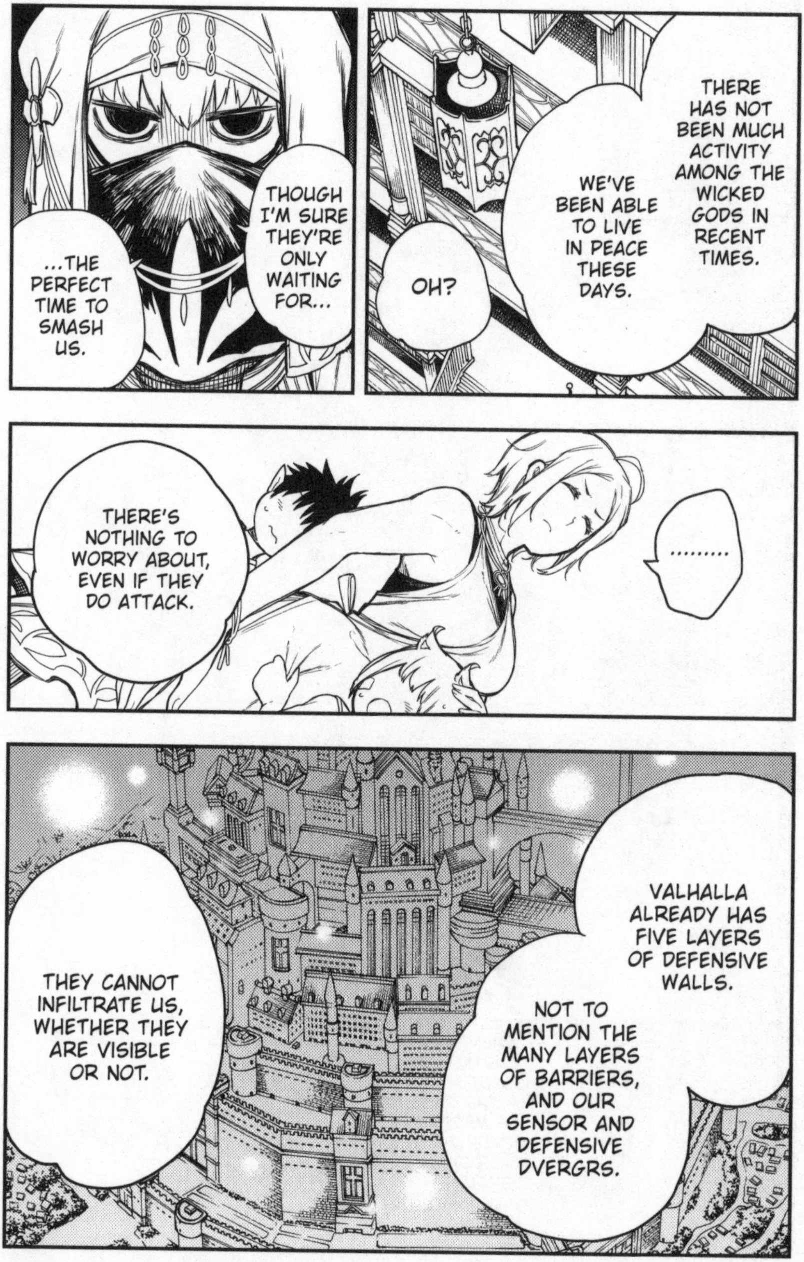
THERE HAS NOT BEEN MUCH ACTIVITY AMONG THE WICKED GODS IN RECENT TIMES.
WE'VE BEEN ABLE TO LIVE IN PEACE THESE DAYS.
OH?
THOUGH I'M SURE THEY'RE ONLY WAITING FOR...
...THE PERFECT TIME TO SMASH US.
....
THERE'S NOTHING TO WORRY ABOUT, EVEN IF THEY DO ATTACK.
VALHALLA ALREADY HAS FIVE LAYERS OF DEFENSIVE WALLS.
NOT TO MENTION THE MANY LAYERS OF BARRIERS, AND OUR SENSOR AND DEFENSIVE DVERGRS.
THEY CANNOT INFILTRATE US, WHETHER THEY ARE VISIBLE OR NOT.

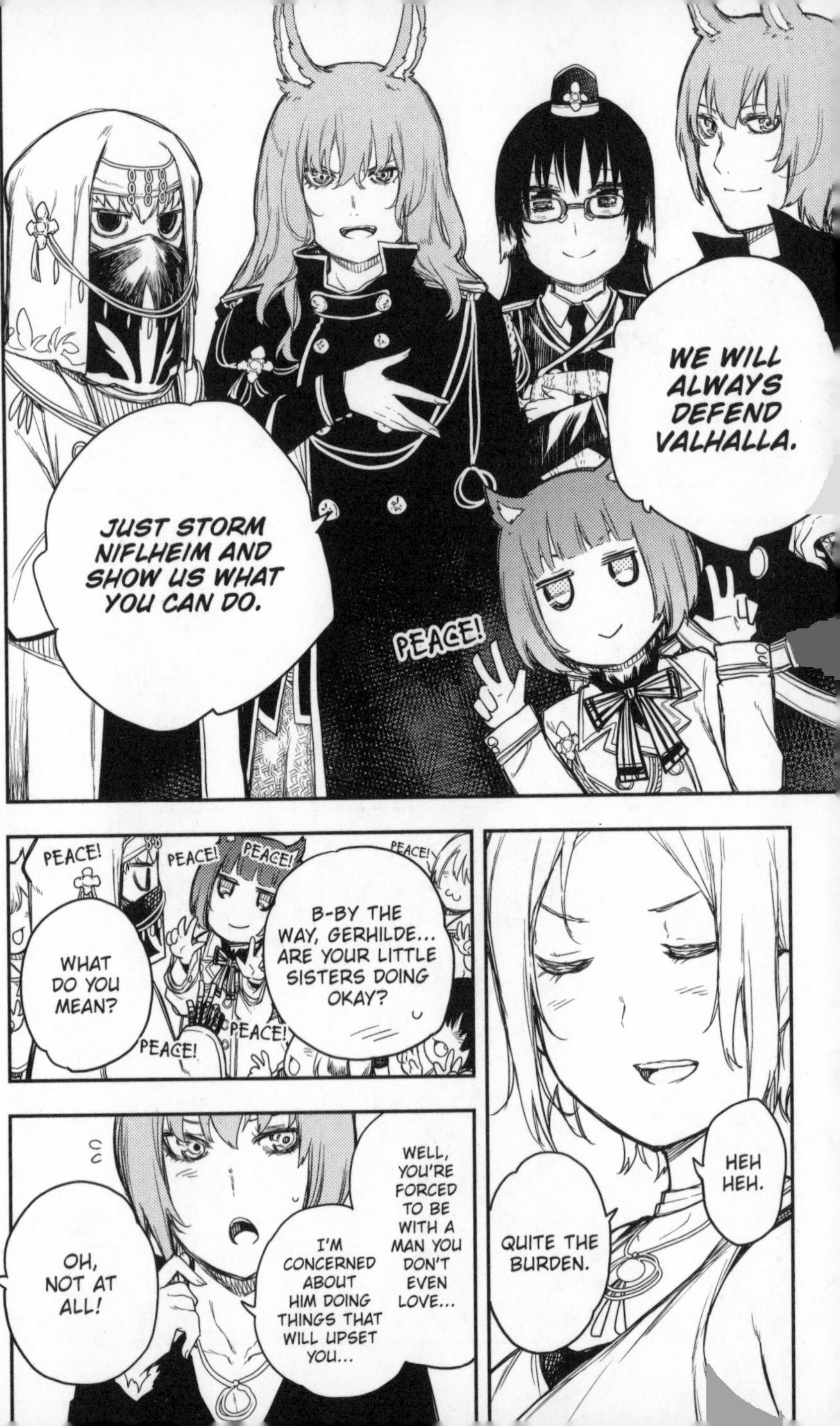
WE WILL ALWAYS DEFEND VALHALLA.
JUST STORM NIFLHEIM AND SHOW US WHAT YOU CAN DO.
PEACE!
HEH HEH.
QUITE THE BURDEN.
PEACE!
PEACE!
PEACE!
PEACE!
B-BY THE WAY, GERHILDE... ARE YOUR LITTLE SISTERS DOING OKAY?
WHAT DO YOU MEAN?
PEACE!
PEACE!
WELL, YOU'RE FORCED TO BE WITH A MAN YOU DON'T EVEN LOVE...
I'M CONCERNED ABOUT HIM DOING THINGS THAT WILL UPSET YOU...
OH, NOT AT ALL!

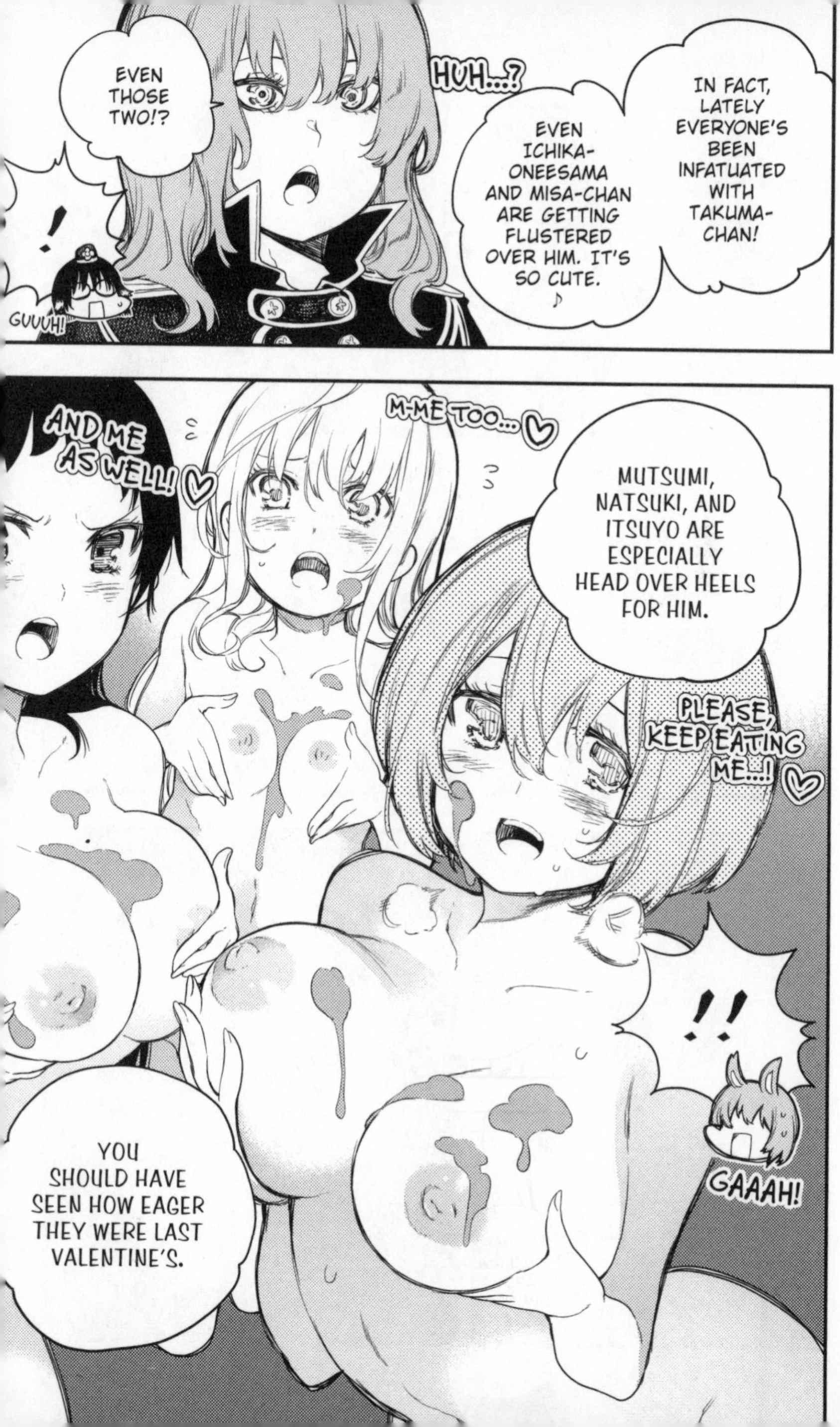
IN FACT, LATELY EVERYONE'S BEEN INFATUATED WITH TAKUMA-CHAN!
EVEN ICHIKA-ONEESAMA AND MISA-CHAN ARE GETTING FLUSTERED OVER HIM. IT'S SO CUTE. ♪
HUH...?
EVEN THOSE TWO!?
!
GUUUH!
MUTSUMI, NATSUKI, AND ITSUYO ARE ESPECIALLY HEAD OVER HEELS FOR HIM.
M-ME TOO... ♡
AND ME AS WELL! ♡
PLEASE, KEEP EATING ME...! ♡
!!
GAAAH!
YOU SHOULD HAVE SEEN HOW EAGER THEY WERE LAST VALENTINE'S.

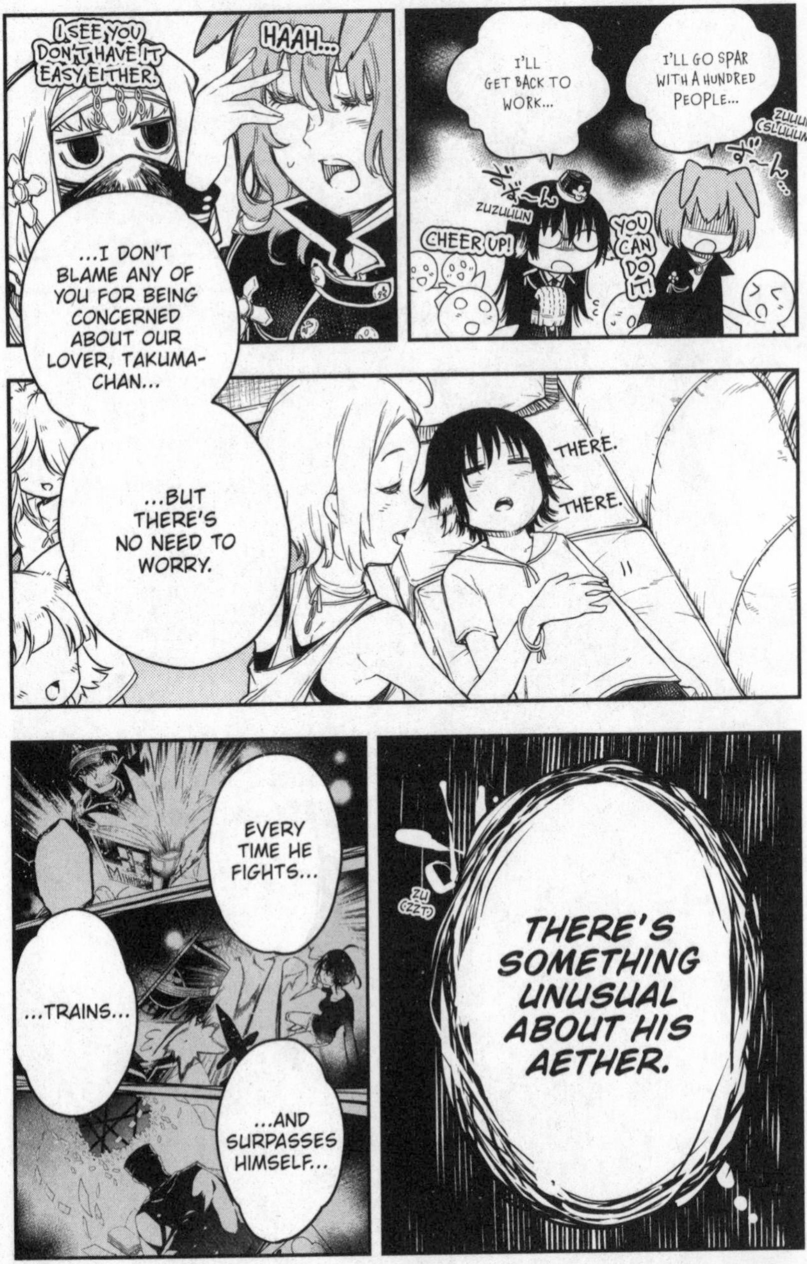
I'LL GO SPAR WITH A HUNDRED PEOPLE...
I'LL GET BACK TO WORK...
ZUUUN (SLUUUMP)
ず～ん…
ずず～ん
ZUZUUUN
YOU CAN DO IT!
CHEER UP!
HAAH...
I SEE YOU DON'T HAVE IT EASY EITHER.
...I DON'T BLAME ANY OF YOU FOR BEING CONCERNED ABOUT OUR LOVER, TAKUMA-CHAN...
THERE.
THERE.
...BUT THERE'S NO NEED TO WORRY.
ZU (ZZZT)
THERE'S SOMETHING UNUSUAL ABOUT HIS AETHER.
EVERY TIME HE FIGHTS...
...TRAINS...
...AND SURPASSES HIMSELF...

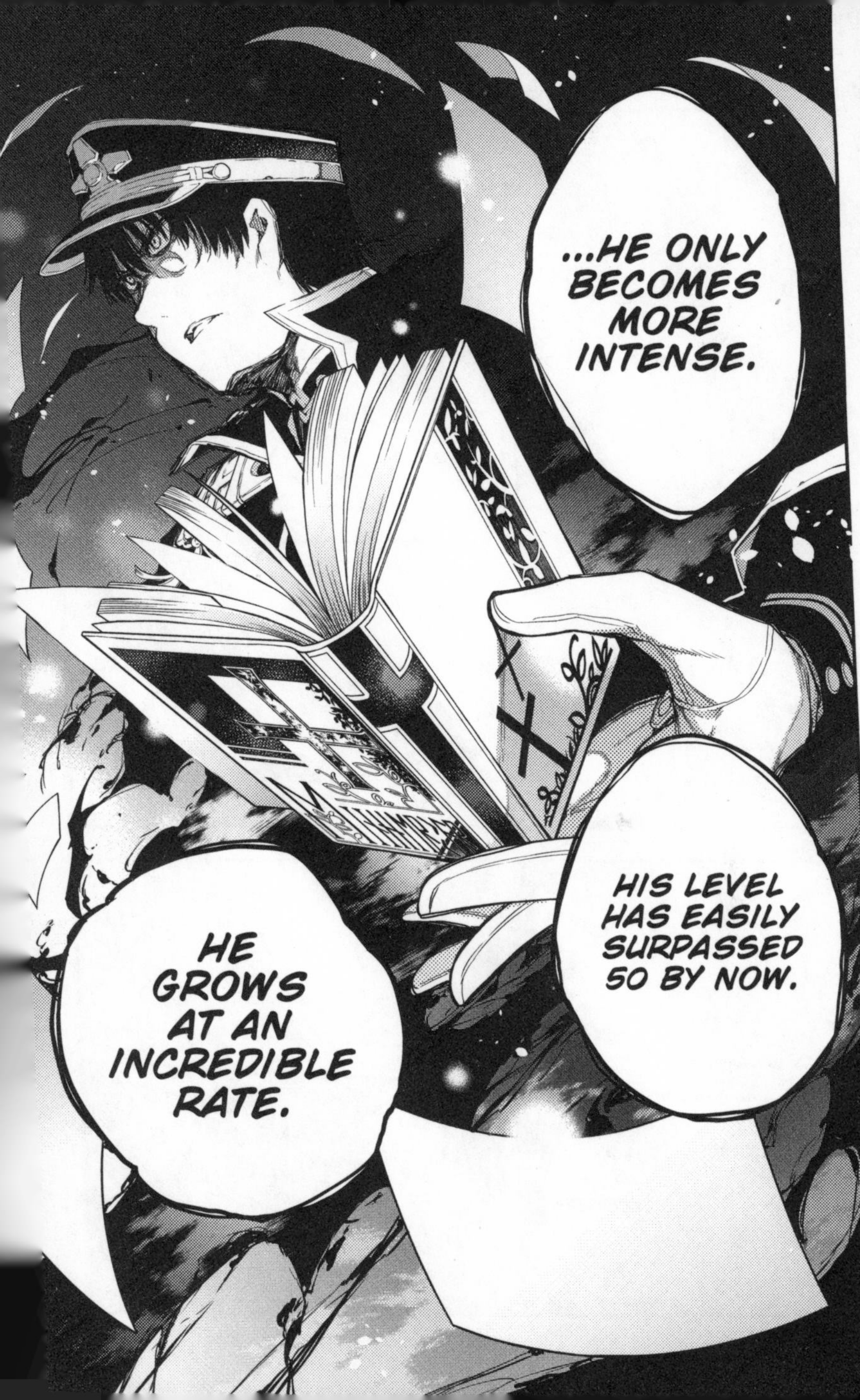
...HE ONLY BECOMES MORE INTENSE.
HIS LEVEL HAS EASILY SURPASSED 50 BY NOW.
HE GROWS AT AN INCREDIBLE RATE.

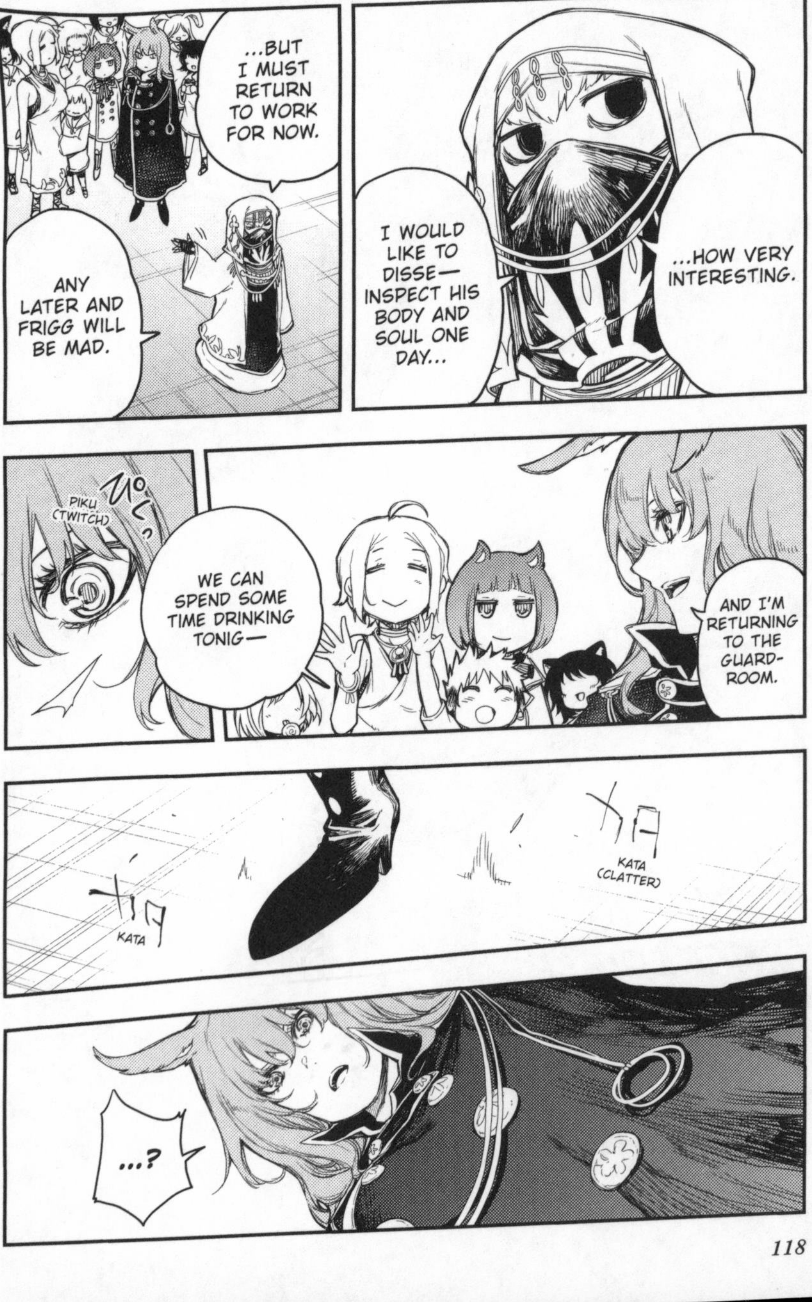
...HOW VERY INTERESTING.
I WOULD LIKE TO DISSE— INSPECT HIS BODY AND SOUL ONE DAY...
...BUT I MUST RETURN TO WORK FOR NOW.
ANY LATER AND FRIGG WILL BE MAD.
AND I'M RETURNING TO THE GUARD-ROOM.
WE CAN SPEND SOME TIME DRINKING TONIG—
PIKU (TWITCH)
KATA (CLATTER)
KATA
...?

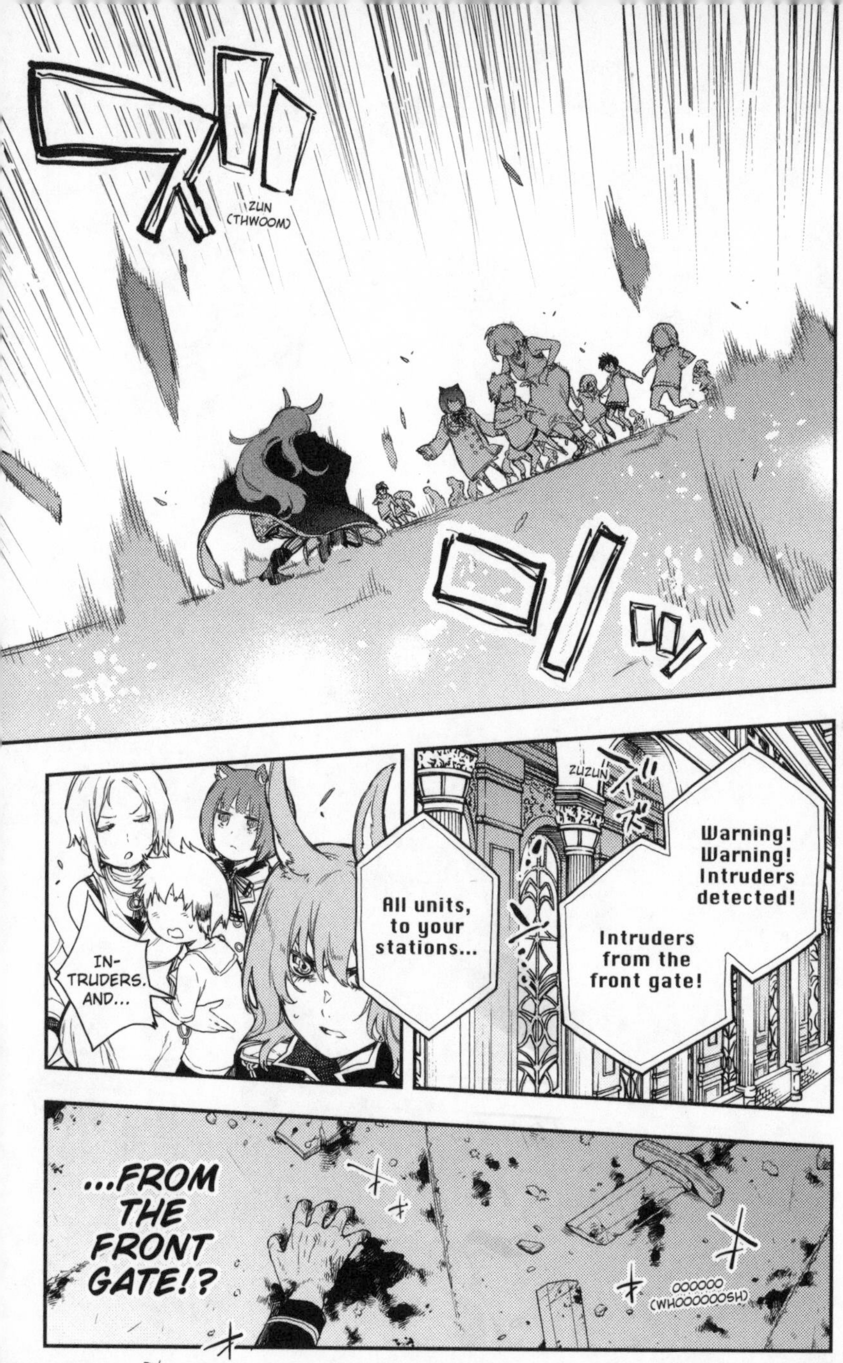
ZUN (THWOOM)
ZUZUN
Warning! Warning! Intruders detected!
Intruders from the front gate!
All units, to your stations...
IN-TRUDERS. AND...
...FROM THE FRONT GATE!?
OOOOOO (WHOOOOOOSH)

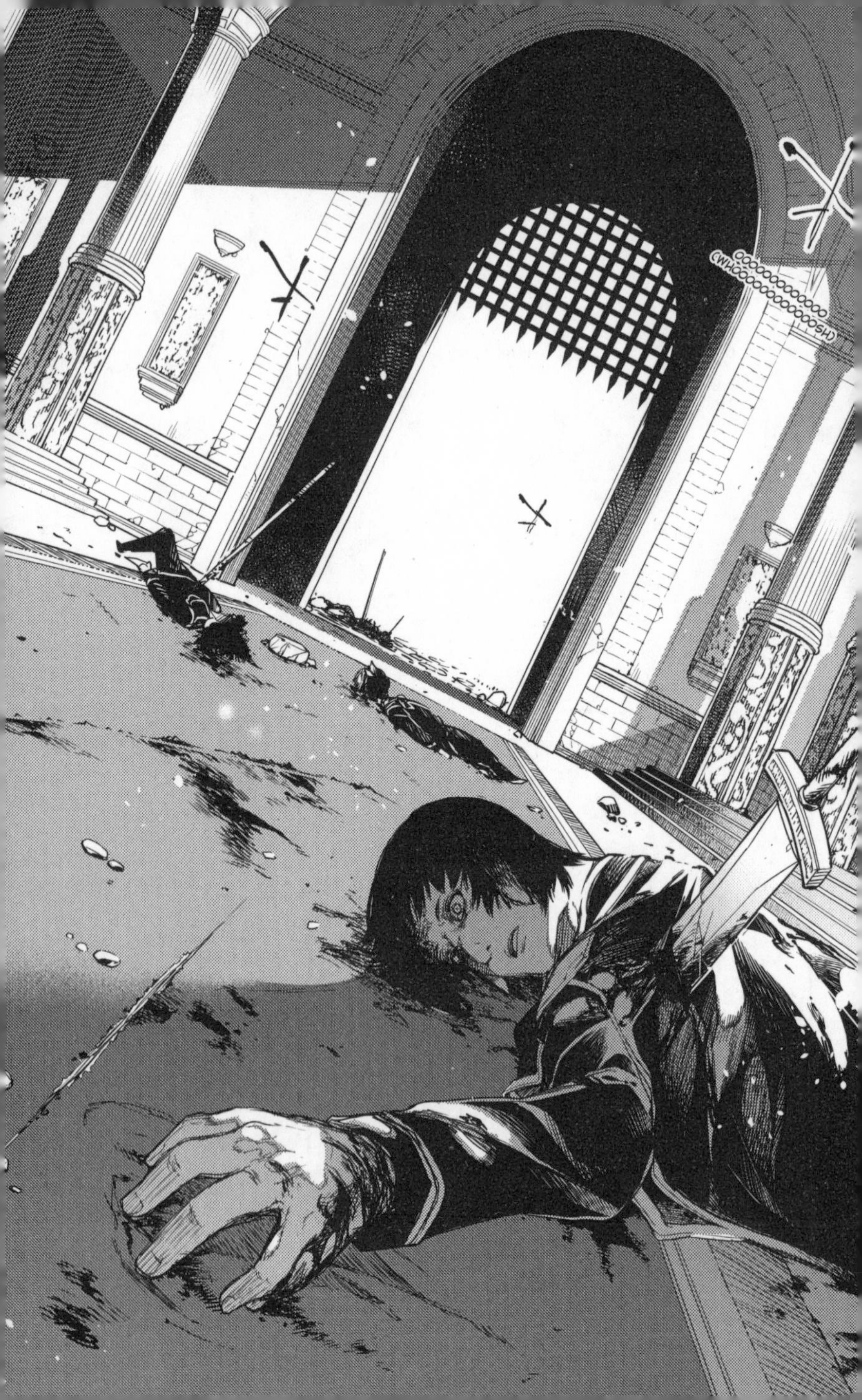
(WHOOOOOOOOOOOOOOOOOOOOOOOOSH)

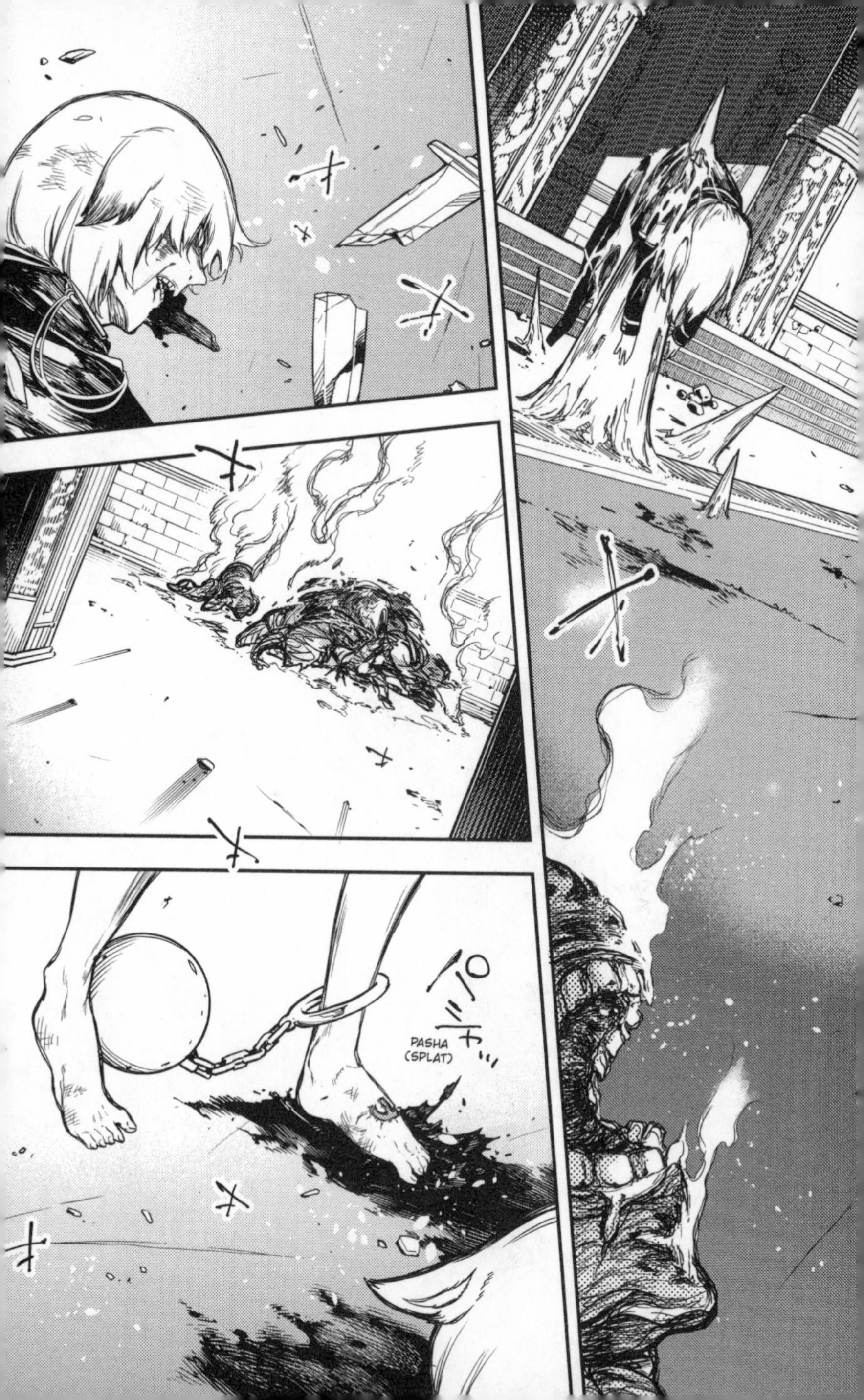
PASHA
(SPLAT)

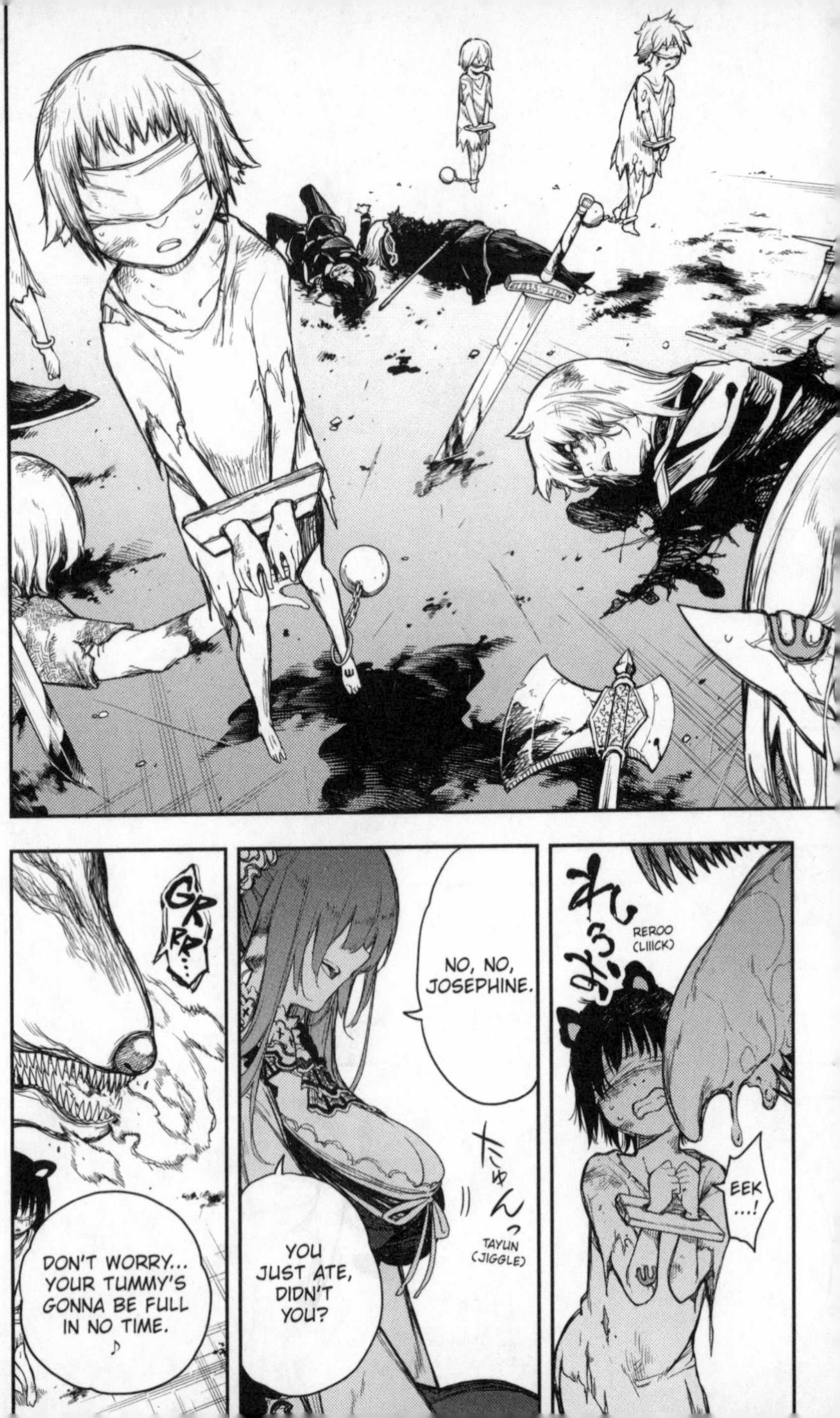

REROO (LIIICK)
EEK ...!
NO, NO, JOSEPHINE.
たゆんっ
TAYUN (JIGGLE)
YOU JUST ATE, DIDN'T YOU?
GRRR...
DON'T WORRY... YOUR TUMMY'S GONNA BE FULL IN NO TIME. ♪

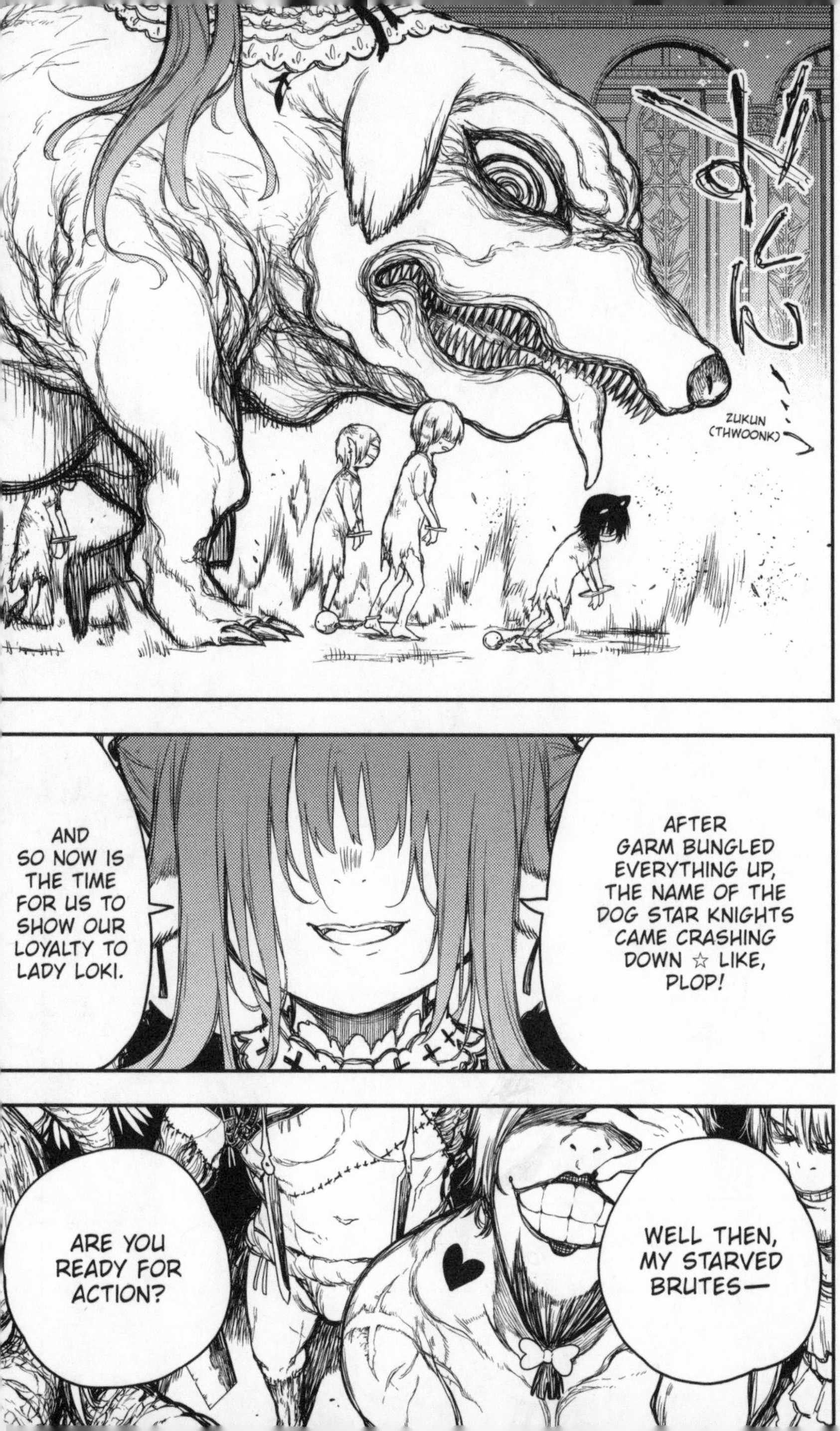
ずくん
ZUKUN (THWOONK)
AFTER GARM BUNGLED EVERYTHING UP, THE NAME OF THE DOG STAR KNIGHTS CAME CRASHING DOWN ☆ LIKE, PLOP!
AND SO NOW IS THE TIME FOR US TO SHOW OUR LOYALTY TO LADY LOKI.
WELL THEN, MY STARVED BRUTES—
ARE YOU READY FOR ACTION?

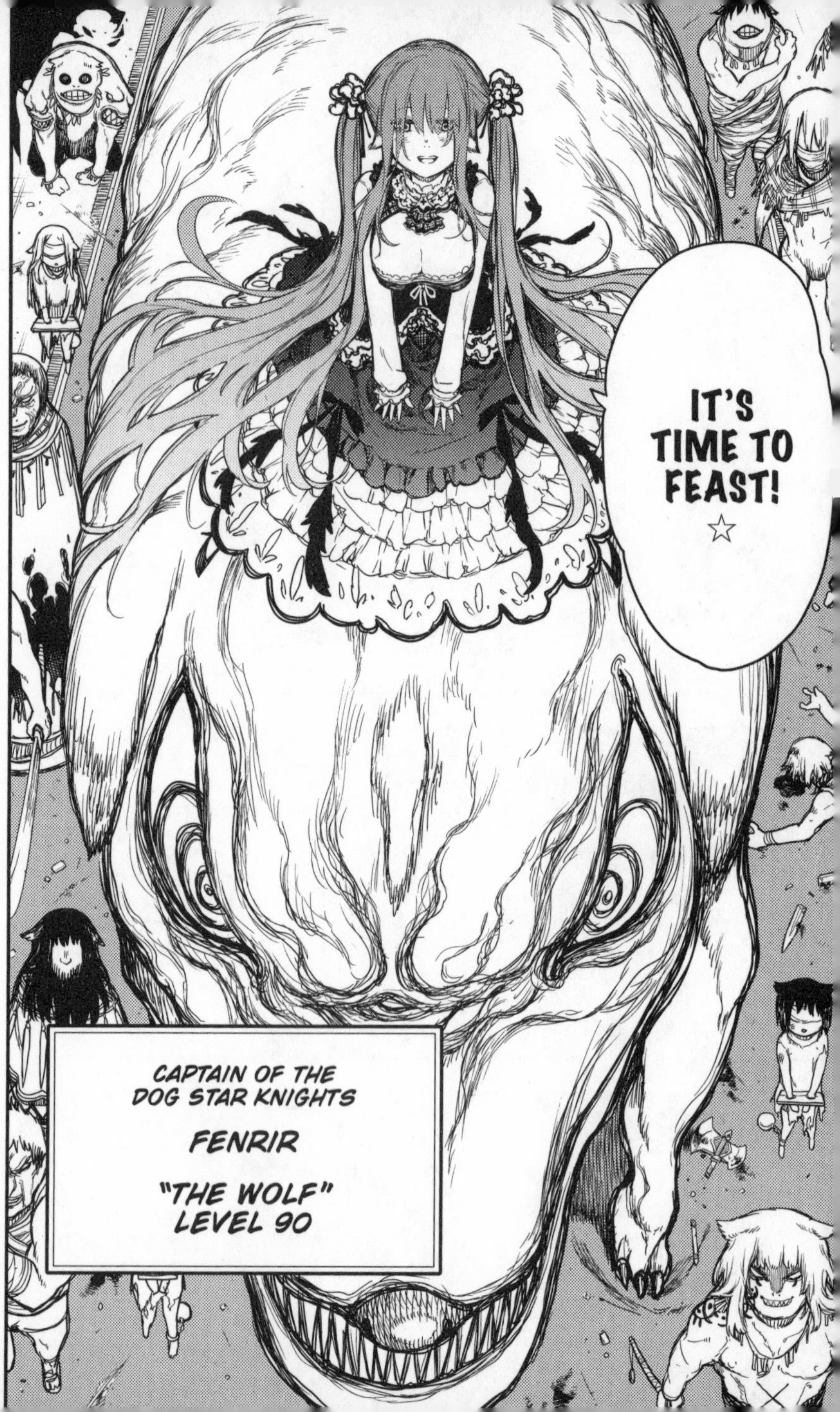
IT'S TIME TO FEAST! ☆
CAPTAIN OF THE DOG STAR KNIGHTS
FENRIR
"THE WOLF"
LEVEL 90

Val X Löve

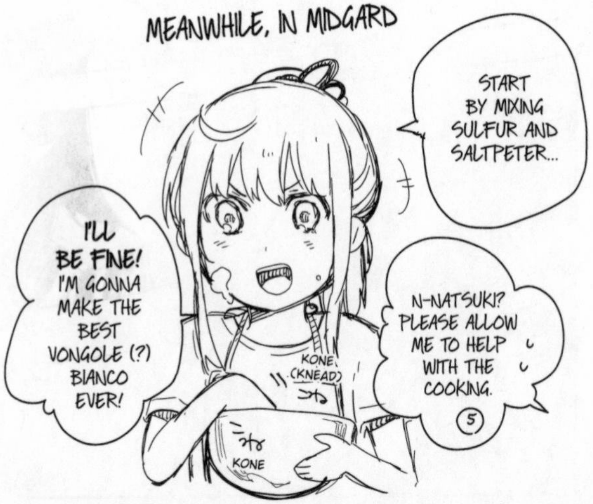
MEANWHILE, IN MIDGARD
START BY MIXING SULFUR AND SALTPETER...
N-NATSUKI? PLEASE ALLOW ME TO HELP WITH THE COOKING.
I'LL BE FINE! I'M GONNA MAKE THE BEST VONGOLE (?) BIANCO EVER!
KONE (KNEAD)
KONE

Chapter 64: The Impeding Maiden

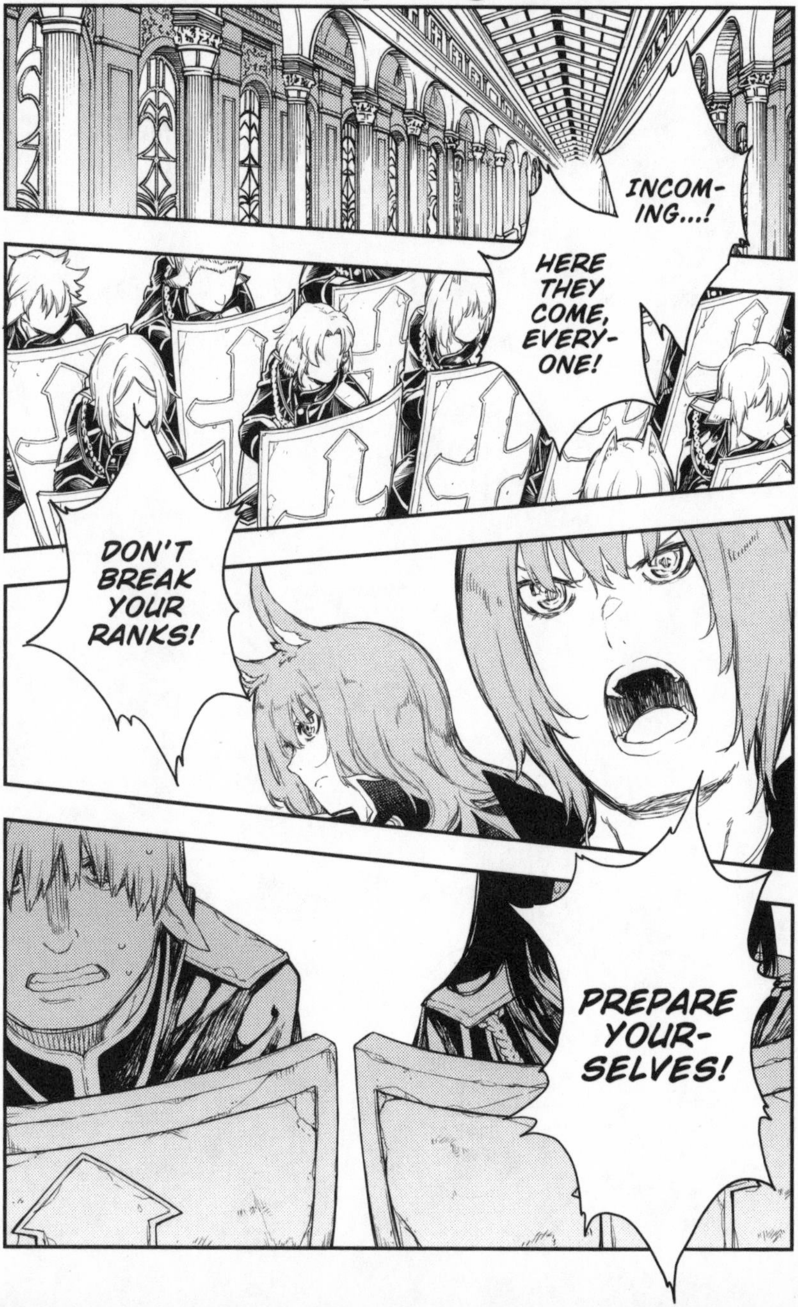
INCOMING...!
HERE THEY COME, EVERYONE!
DON'T BREAK YOUR RANKS!
PREPARE YOURSELVES!

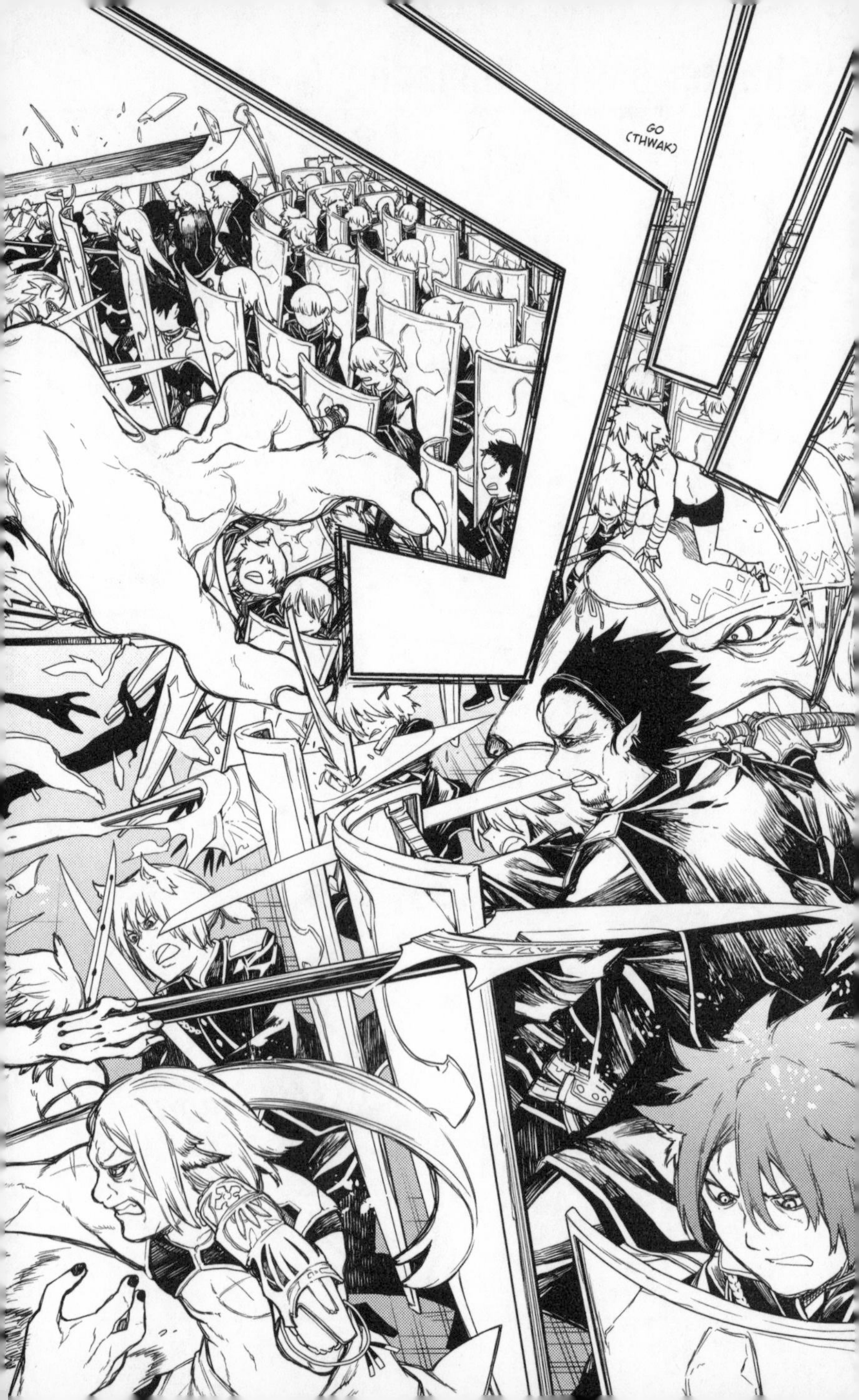
GO
(THWAK)

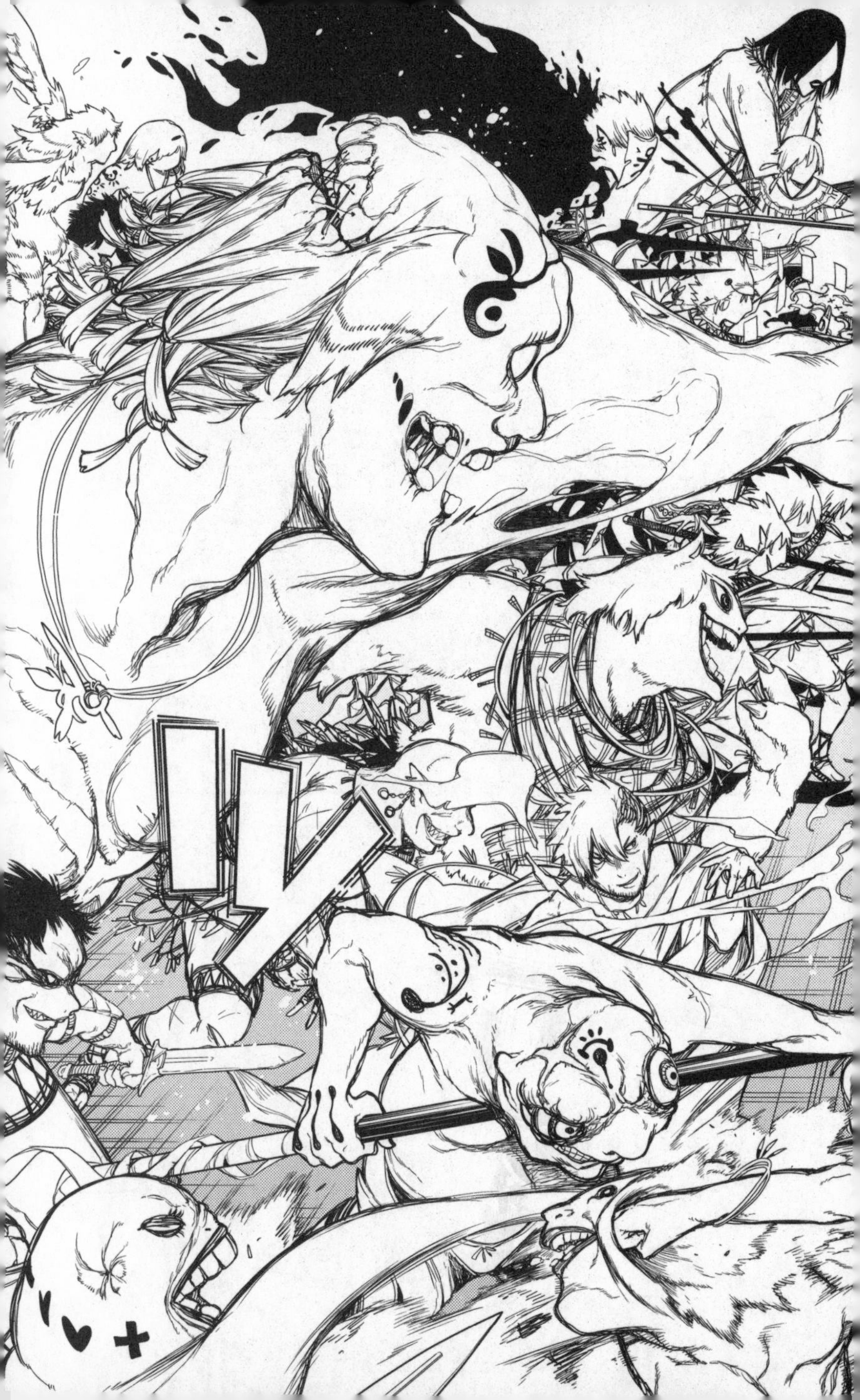

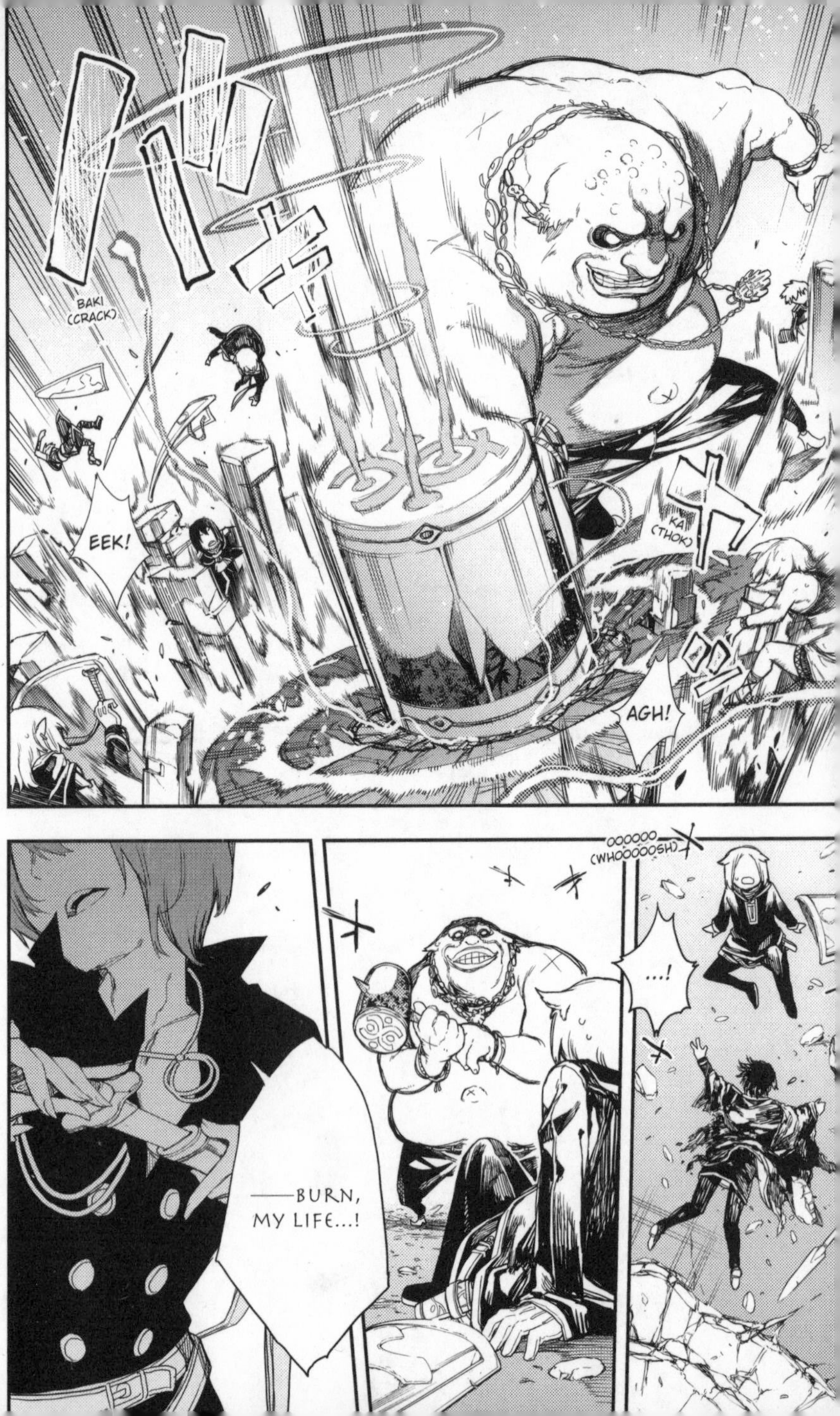
BAKI (CRACK)
KA (THOK)
EEK!
AGH!
OOOOOO (WHOOOOOSH)
...!
——BURN, MY LIFE...!

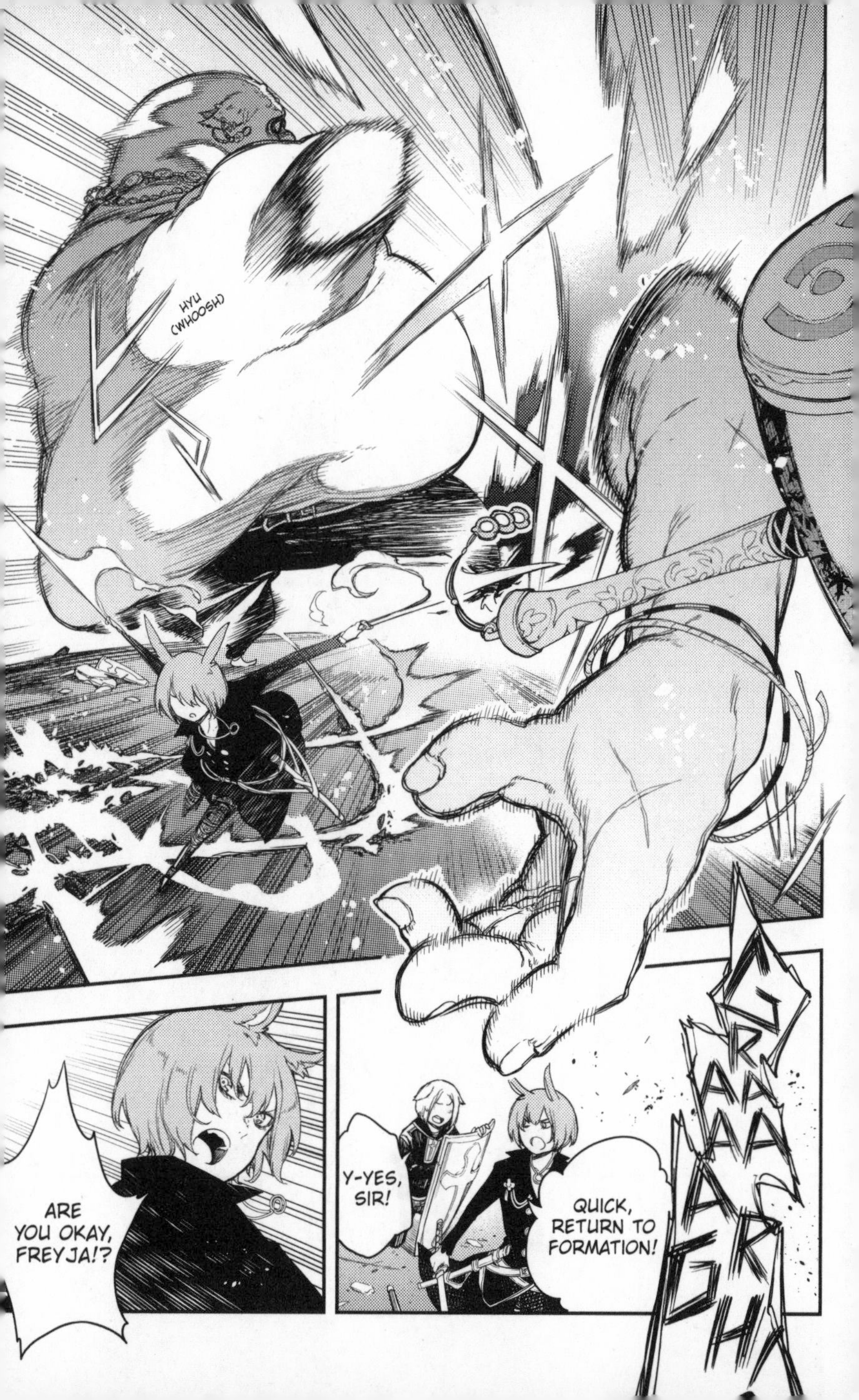
HYU (WHOOSH)
QUICK, RETURN TO FORMATION!
Y-YES, SIR!
ARE YOU OKAY, FREYJA!?

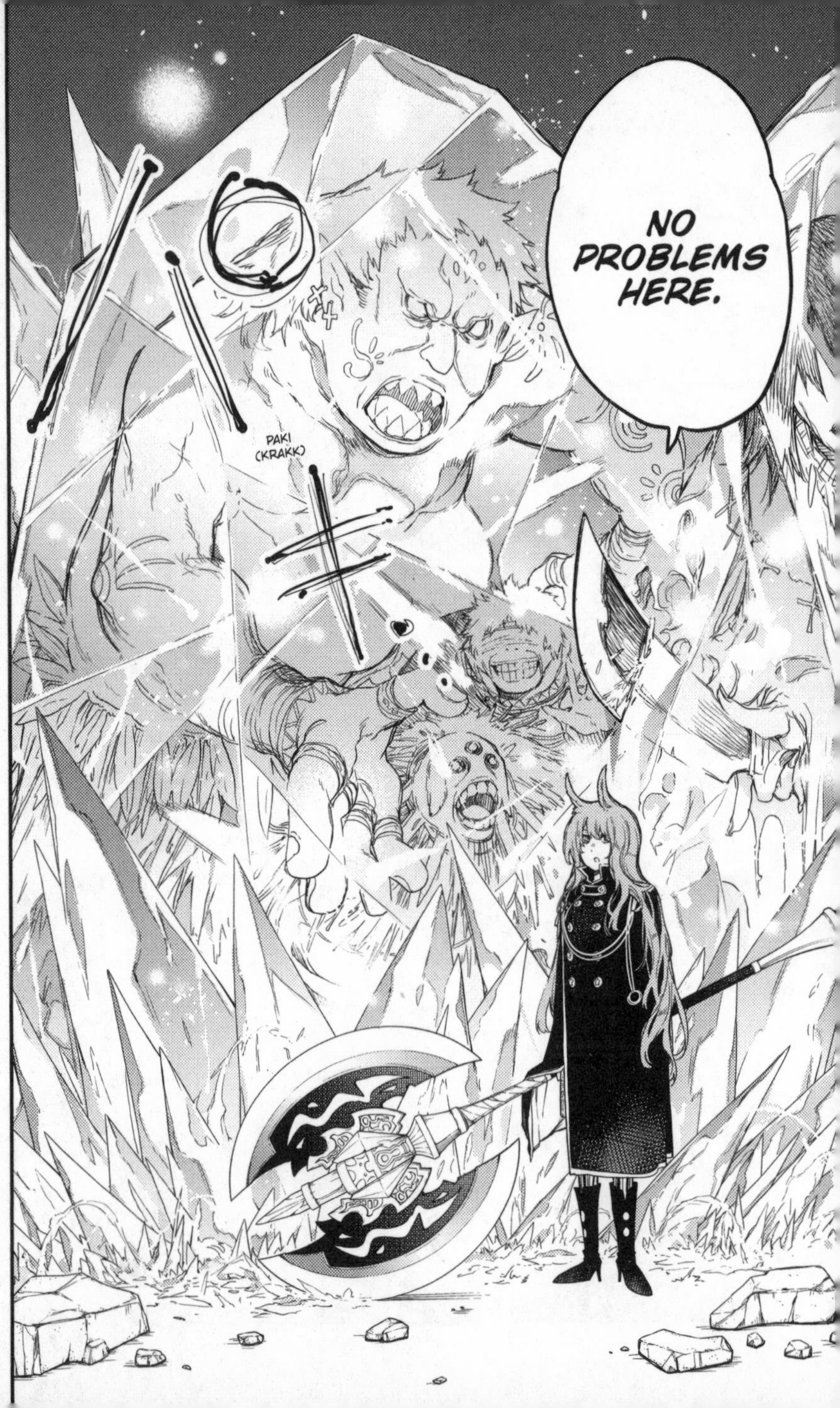
NO PROBLEMS HERE.
PAKI (KRAKK)

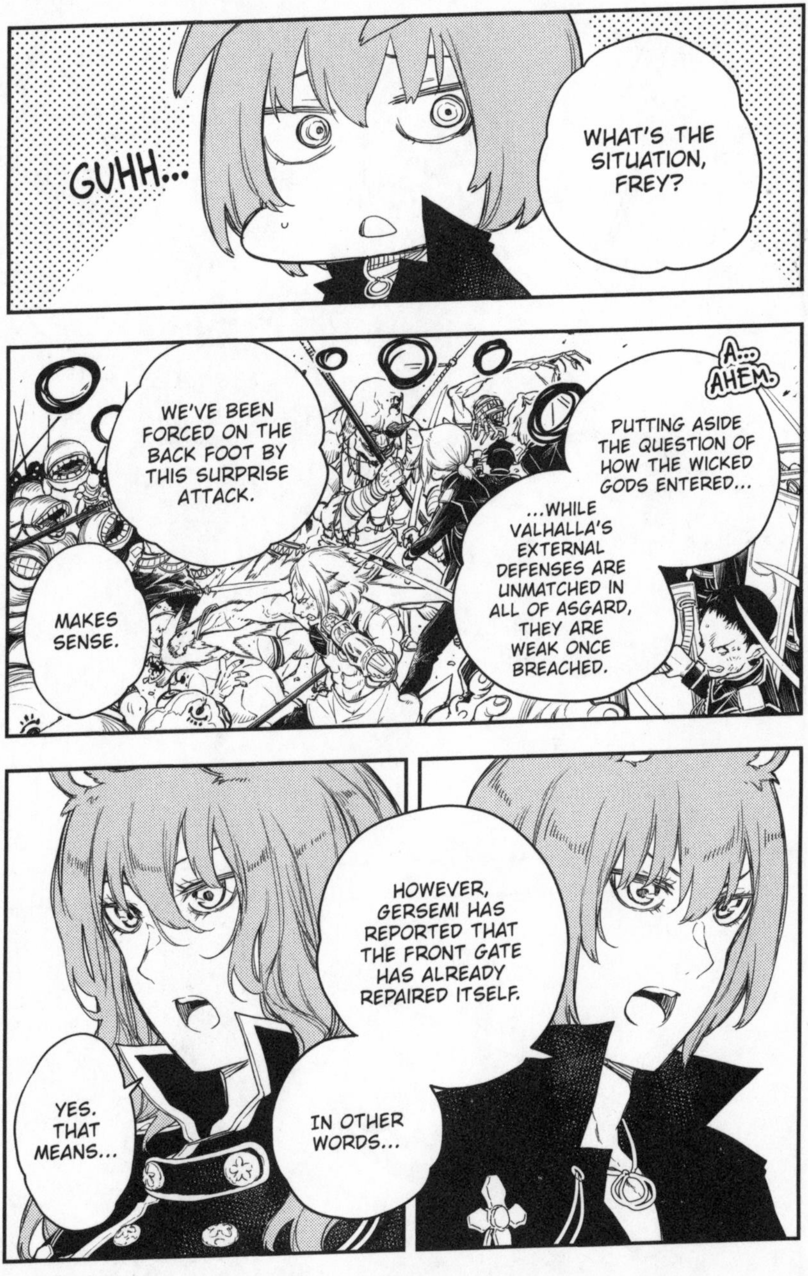
WHAT'S THE SITUATION, FREY?
GUHH...
A... AHEM.
PUTTING ASIDE THE QUESTION OF HOW THE WICKED GODS ENTERED...
...WHILE VALHALLA'S EXTERNAL DEFENSES ARE UNMATCHED IN ALL OF ASGARD, THEY ARE WEAK ONCE BREACHED.
WE'VE BEEN FORCED ON THE BACK FOOT BY THIS SURPRISE ATTACK.
MAKES SENSE.
HOWEVER, GERSEMI HAS REPORTED THAT THE FRONT GATE HAS ALREADY REPAIRED ITSELF.
IN OTHER WORDS...
YES. THAT MEANS...

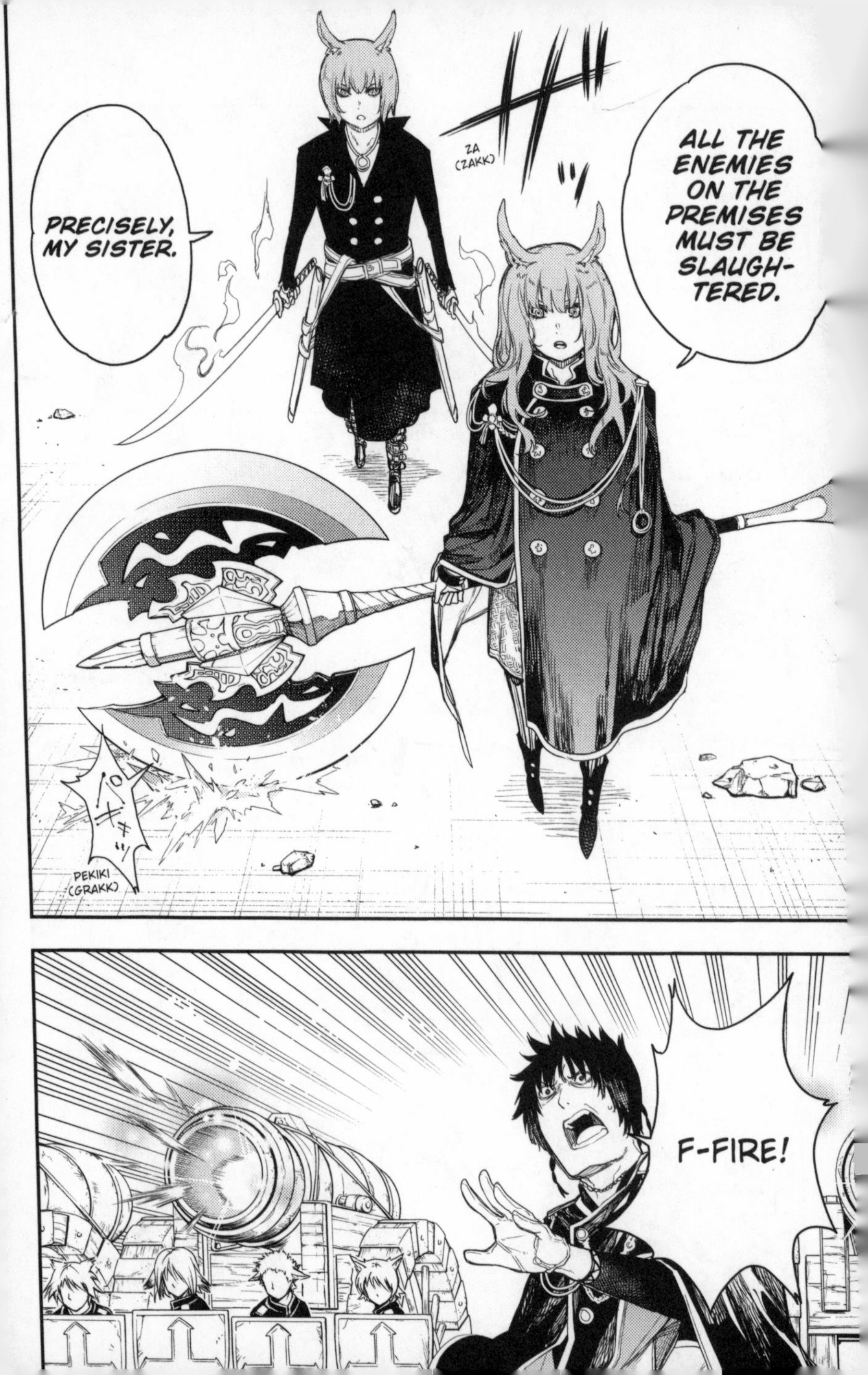
ZA (ZAKK)
ALL THE ENEMIES ON THE PREMISES MUST BE SLAUGH-TERED.
PRECISELY, MY SISTER.
PEKIKI (GRAKK)
F-FIRE!

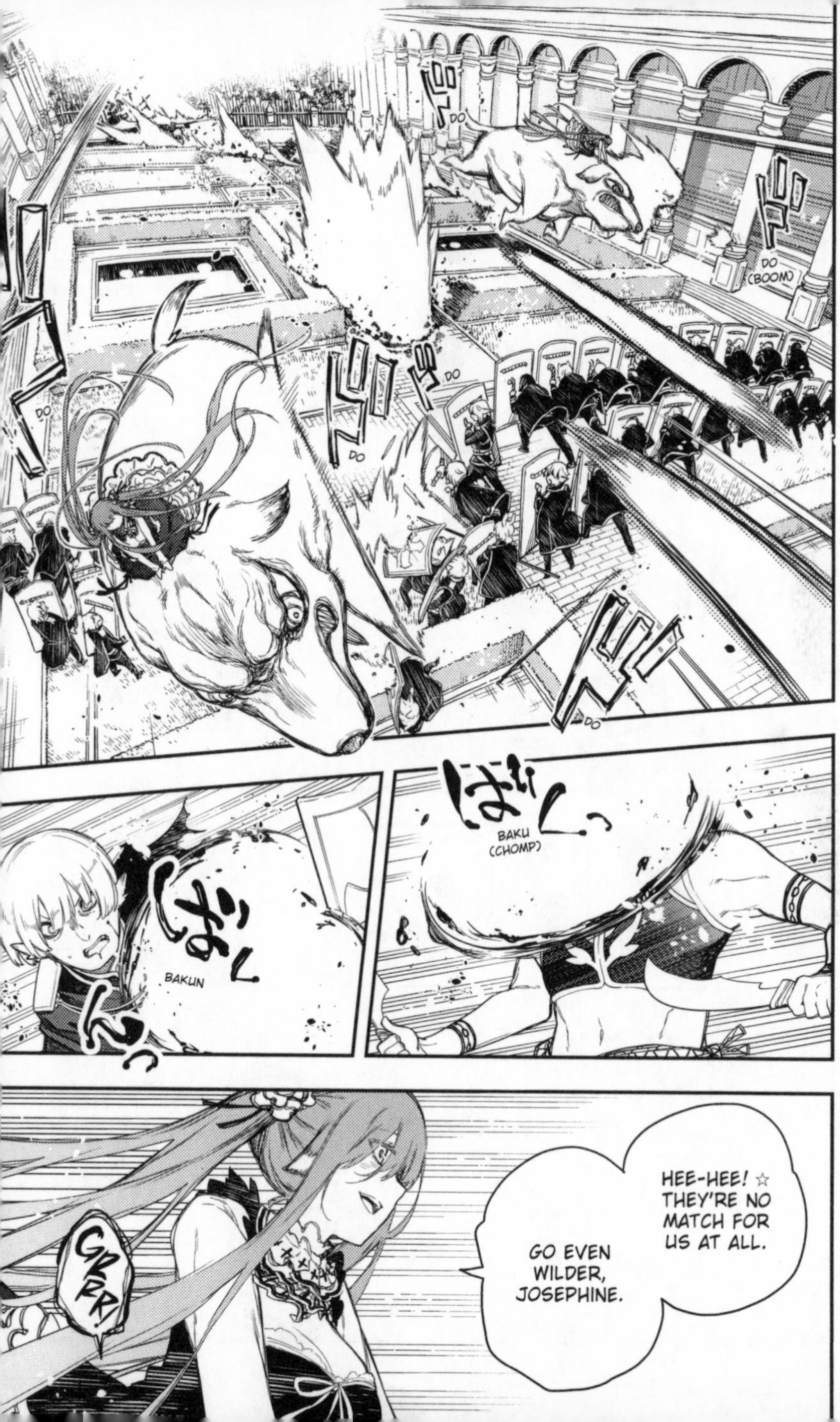
DO (BOOM)
DO
DO
DO
DO
DO
BAKU (CHOMP)
BAKUN
HEE-HEE! ☆ THEY'RE NO MATCH FOR US AT ALL.
GO EVEN WILDER, JOSEPHINE.
GRRR!

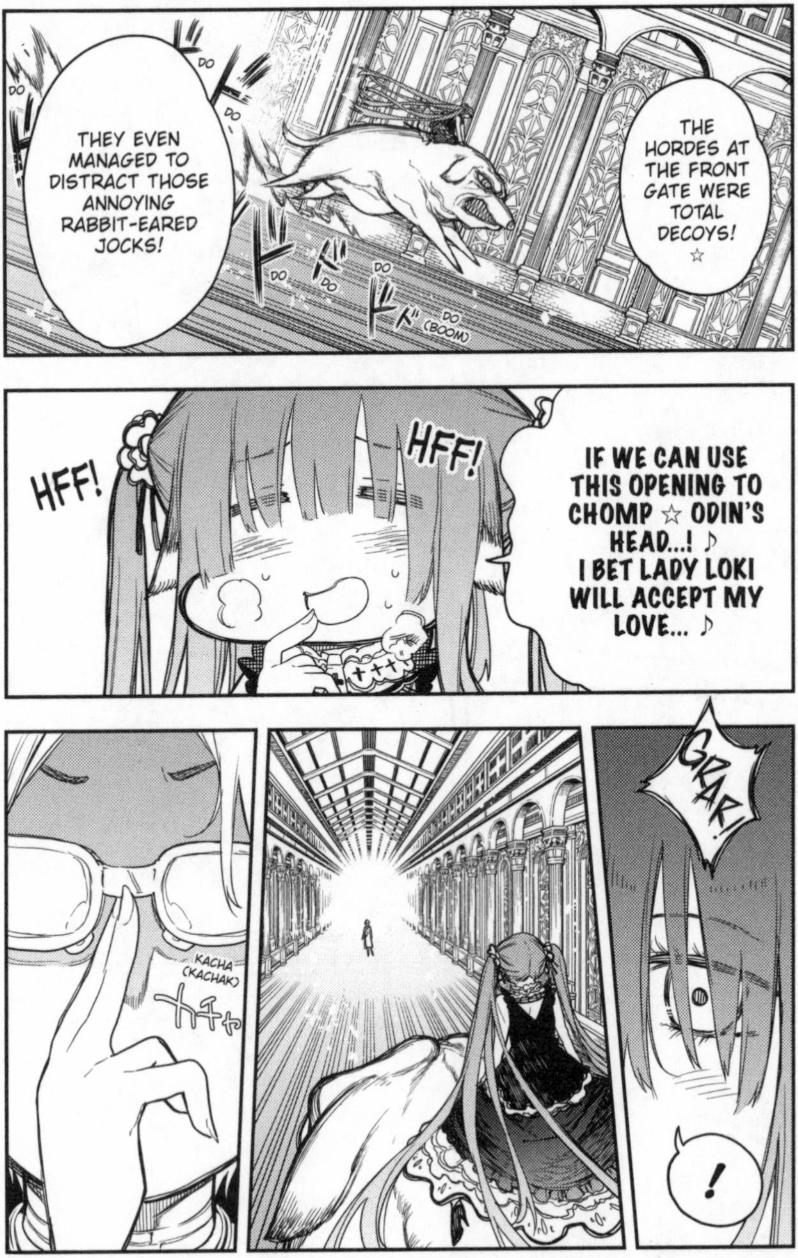
THE HORDES AT THE FRONT GATE WERE TOTAL DECOYS! ☆
THEY EVEN MANAGED TO DISTRACT THOSE ANNOYING RABBIT-EARED JOCKS!
DO DO DO DO DO DO DO DO (BOOM)
IF WE CAN USE THIS OPENING TO CHOMP ☆ ODIN'S HEAD...! ♪ I BET LADY LOKI WILL ACCEPT MY LOVE... ♪
HFF!
HFF!
GRAR!
!
KACHA (KACHAK)

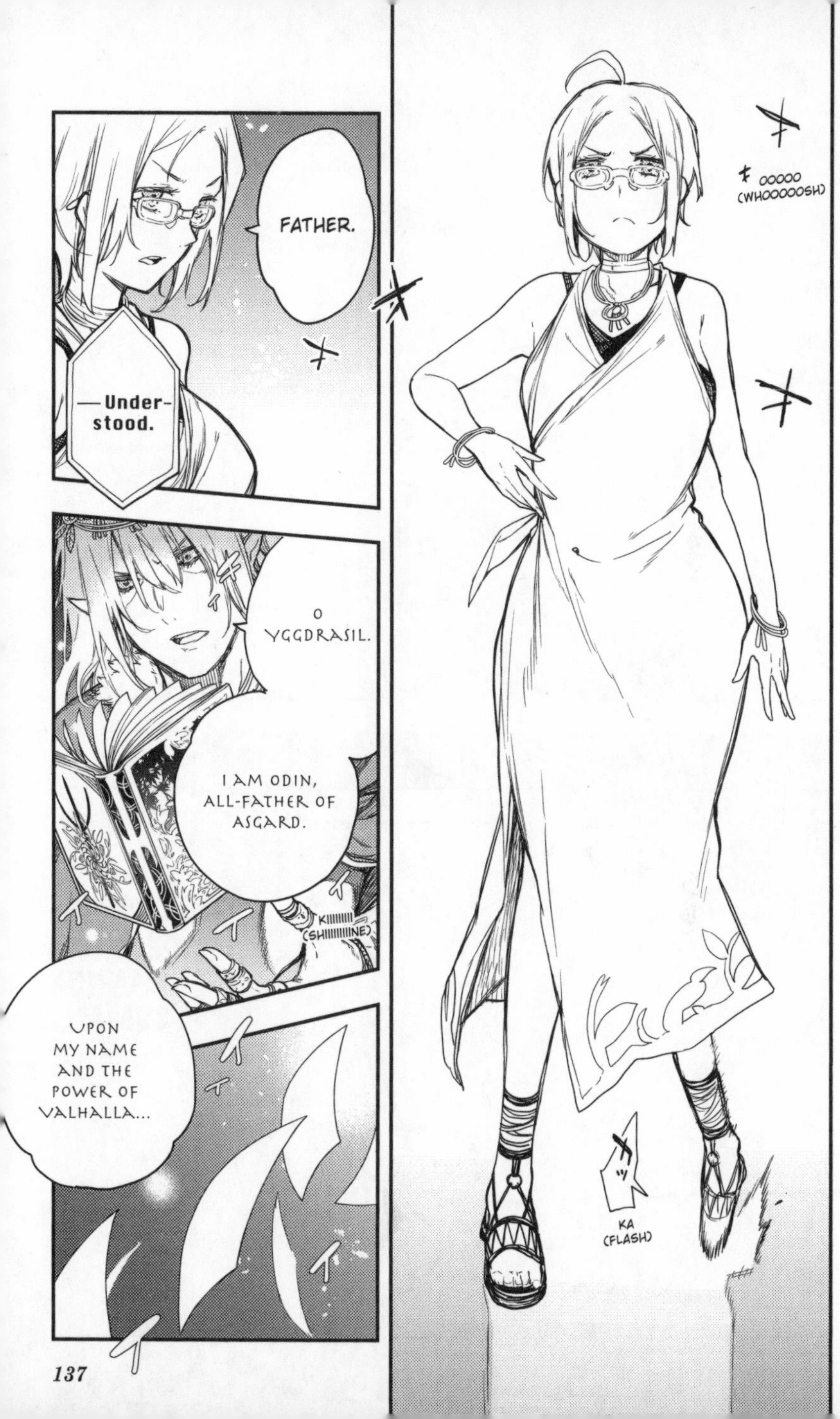
OOOOO (WHOOOOOSH)
KA (FLASH)
FATHER.
—Understood.
O YGGDRASIL.
I AM ODIN, ALL-FATHER OF ASGARD.
KIIIIII (SHIIIIIIINE)
UPON MY NAME AND THE POWER OF VALHALLA...

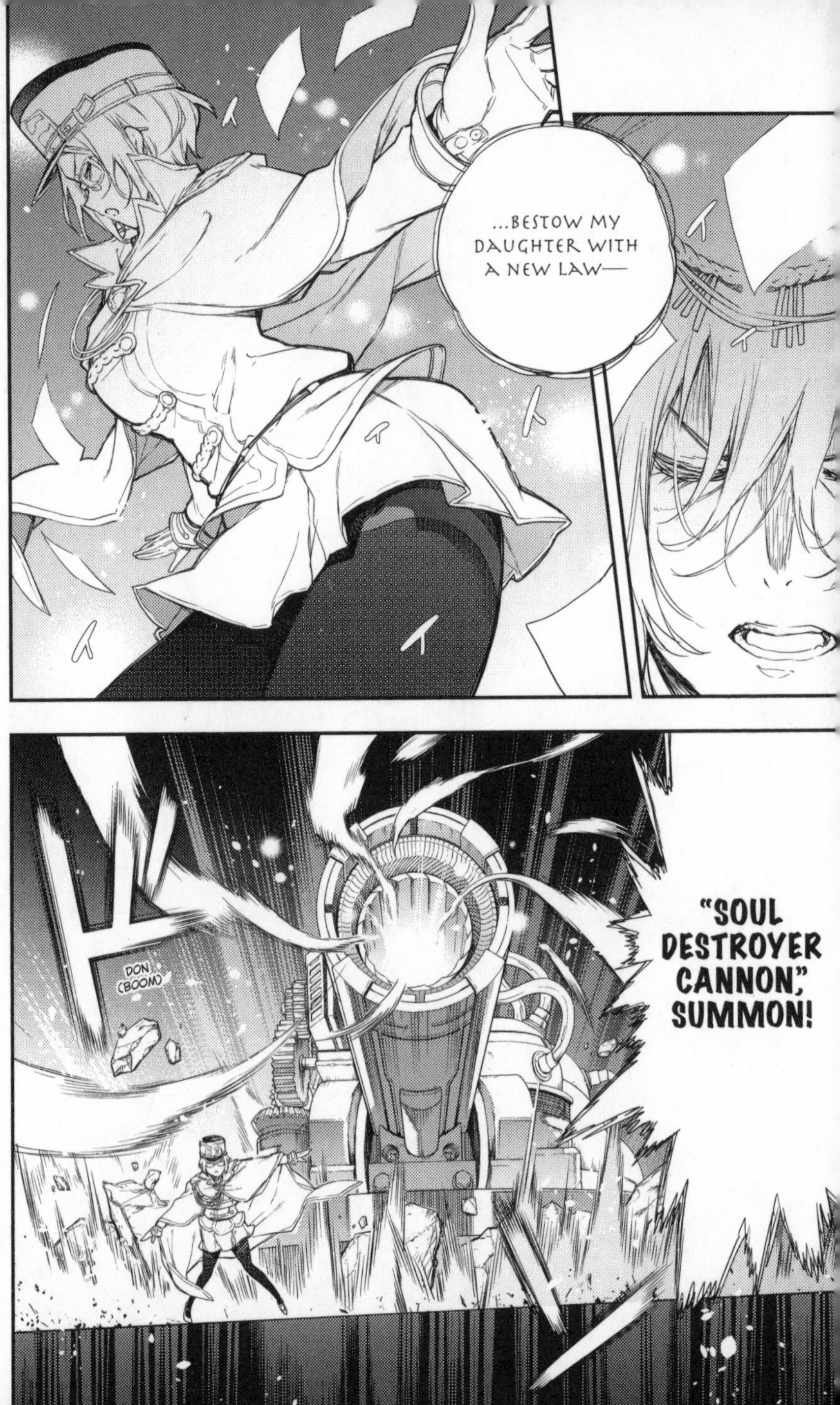
...BESTOW MY DAUGHTER WITH A NEW LAW—
"SOUL DESTROYER CANNON," SUMMON!
DON (BOOM)

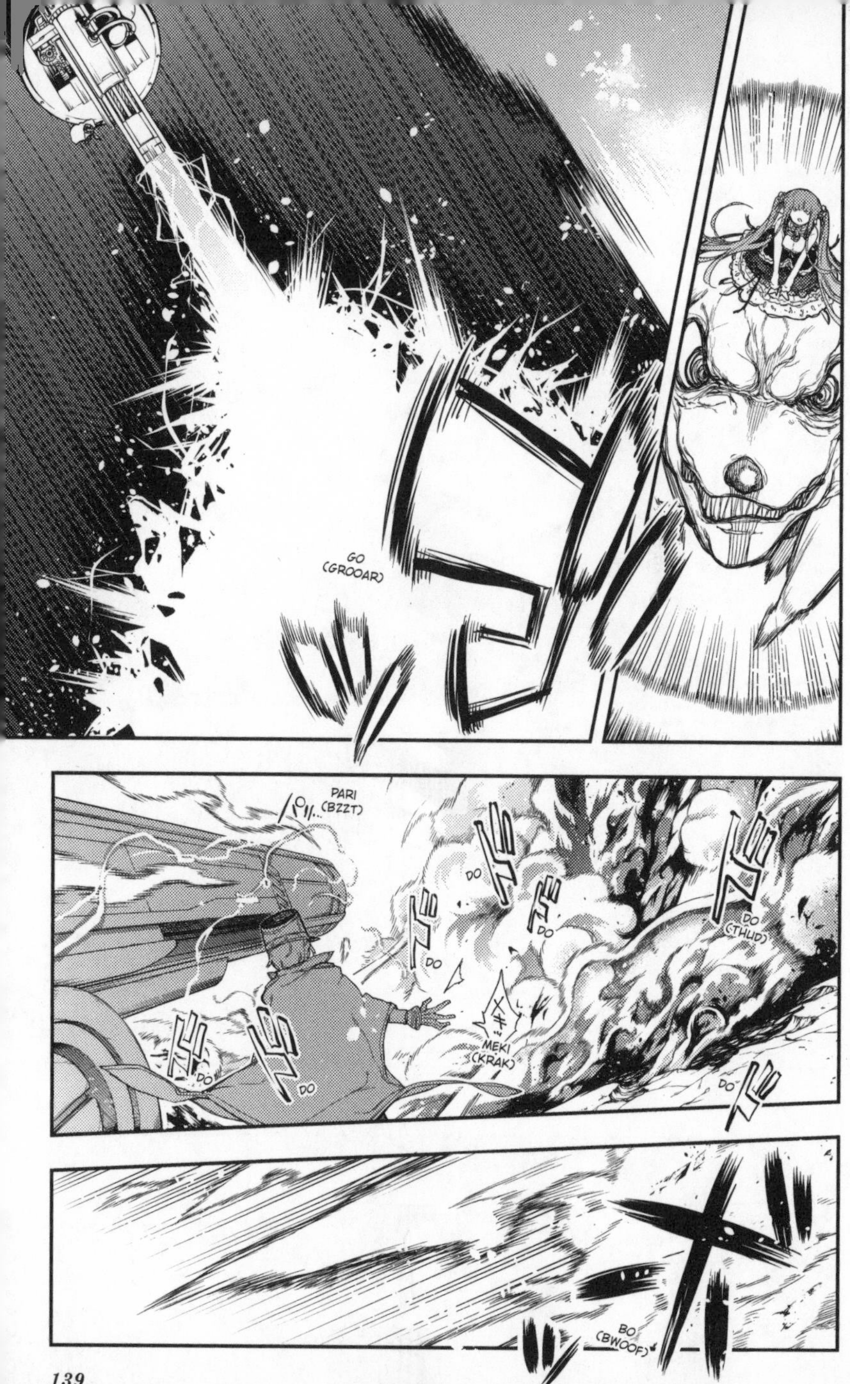
GO (GROOAR)
DO (THUD)
DO
DO
DO
DO
MEKI (KRAK)
PARI (BZZT)
DO
DO
BO (BWOOF)

GOTSUN
(THWAK!)

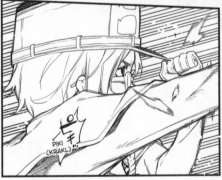

PIKI
(KRAKL)

MISHI
(KREAK)

MEKI
(KRAK)

|||||
(EEEEE)

...FENRIR, THEIR LEADER, HAS BEEN STOPPED IN HER TRACKS BY LADY GERHILDE.

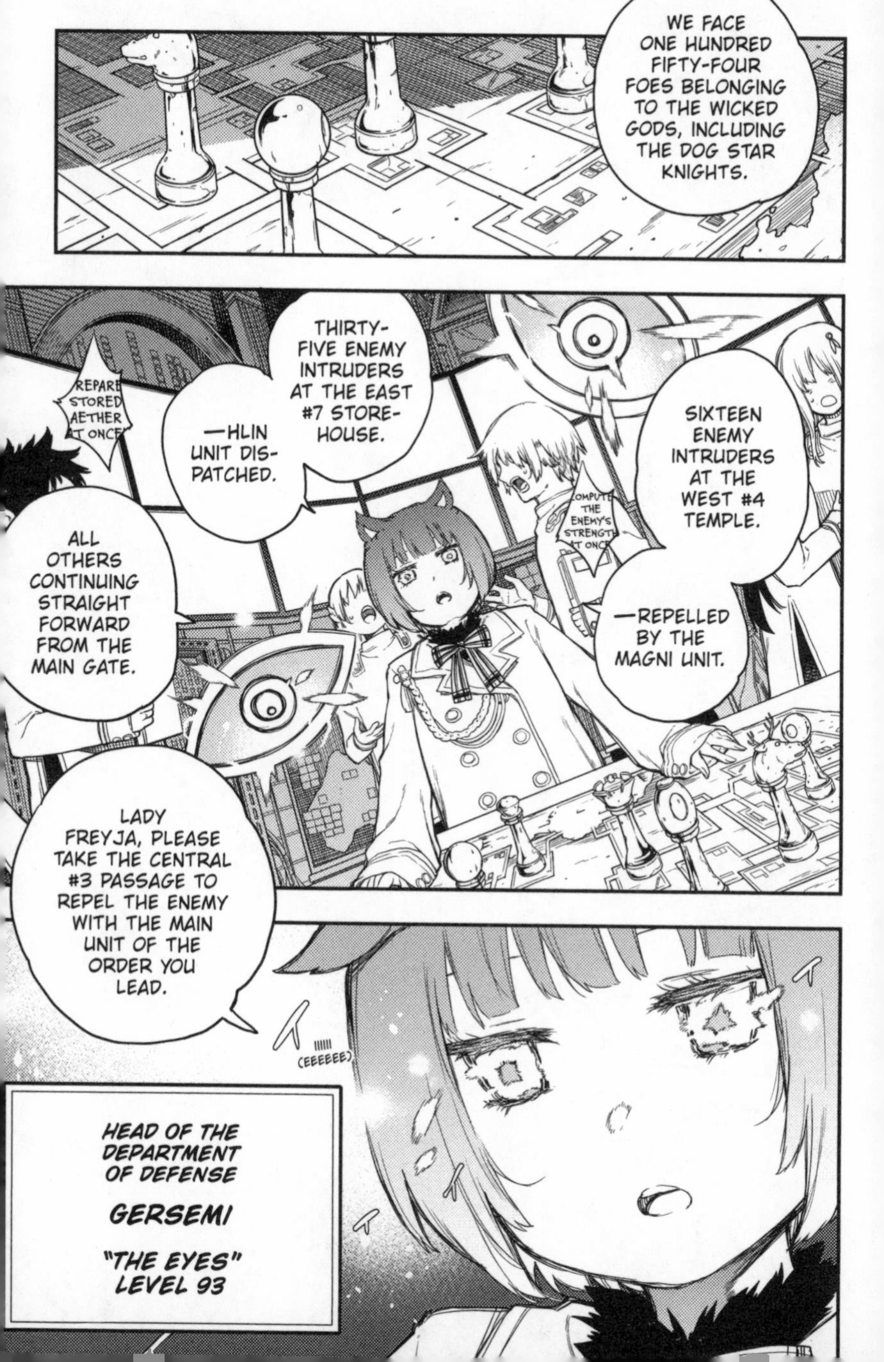
WE FACE ONE HUNDRED FIFTY-FOUR FOES BELONGING TO THE WICKED GODS, INCLUDING THE DOG STAR KNIGHTS.
THIRTY-FIVE ENEMY INTRUDERS AT THE EAST #7 STOREHOUSE.
—HLIN UNIT DISPATCHED.
SIXTEEN ENEMY INTRUDERS AT THE WEST #4 TEMPLE.
—REPELLED BY THE MAGNI UNIT.
COMPUTE THE ENEMY'S STRENGTH AT ONCE
REPARE STORED AETHER AT ONCE
ALL OTHERS CONTINUING STRAIGHT FORWARD FROM THE MAIN GATE.
LADY FREYJA, PLEASE TAKE THE CENTRAL #3 PASSAGE TO REPEL THE ENEMY WITH THE MAIN UNIT OF THE ORDER YOU LEAD.
IIIIII (EEEEEE)
HEAD OF THE DEPARTMENT OF DEFENSE
GERSEMI
"THE EYES" LEVEL 93

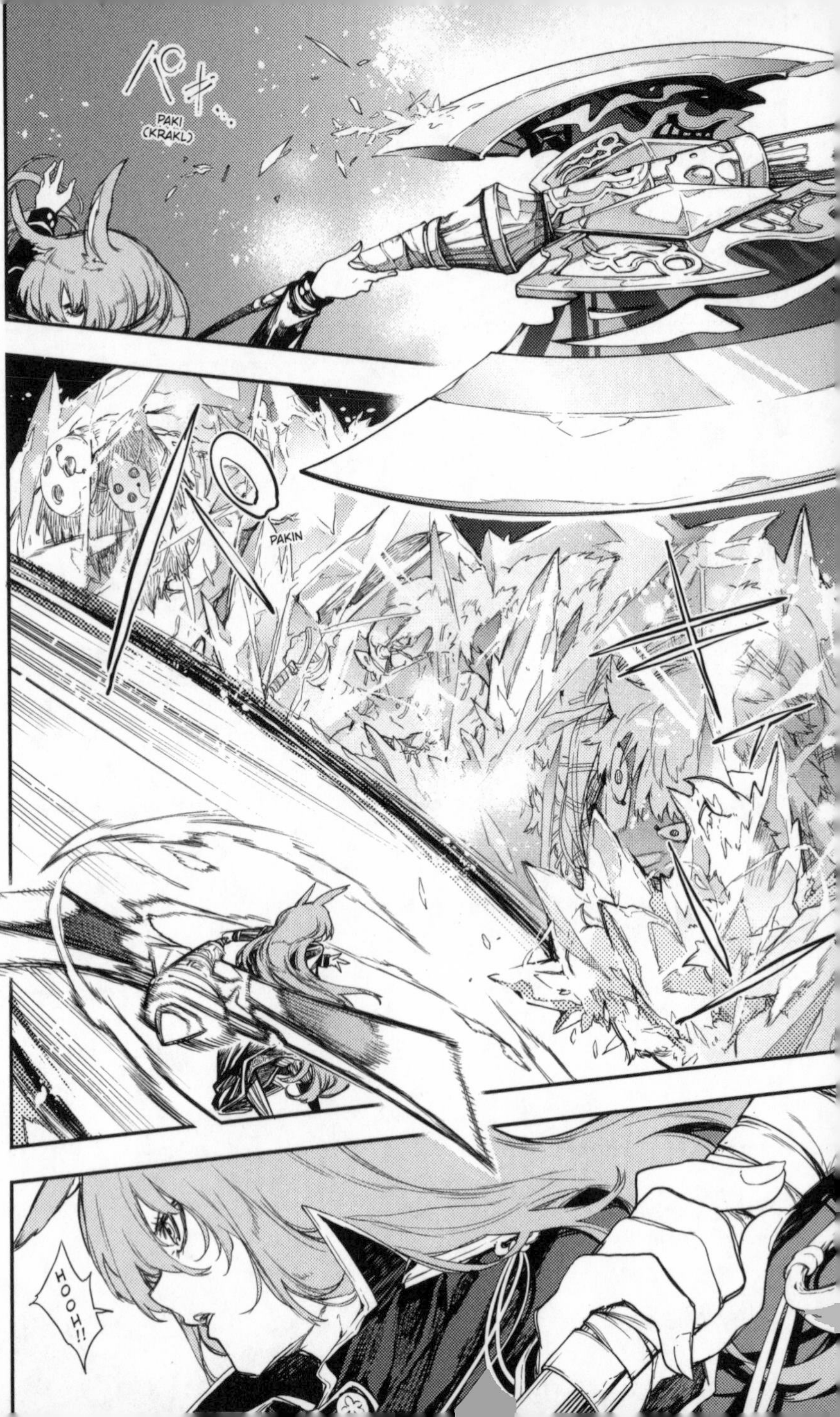
パキ…
PAKI (KRAKL)
PAKIN
HOOOH!!

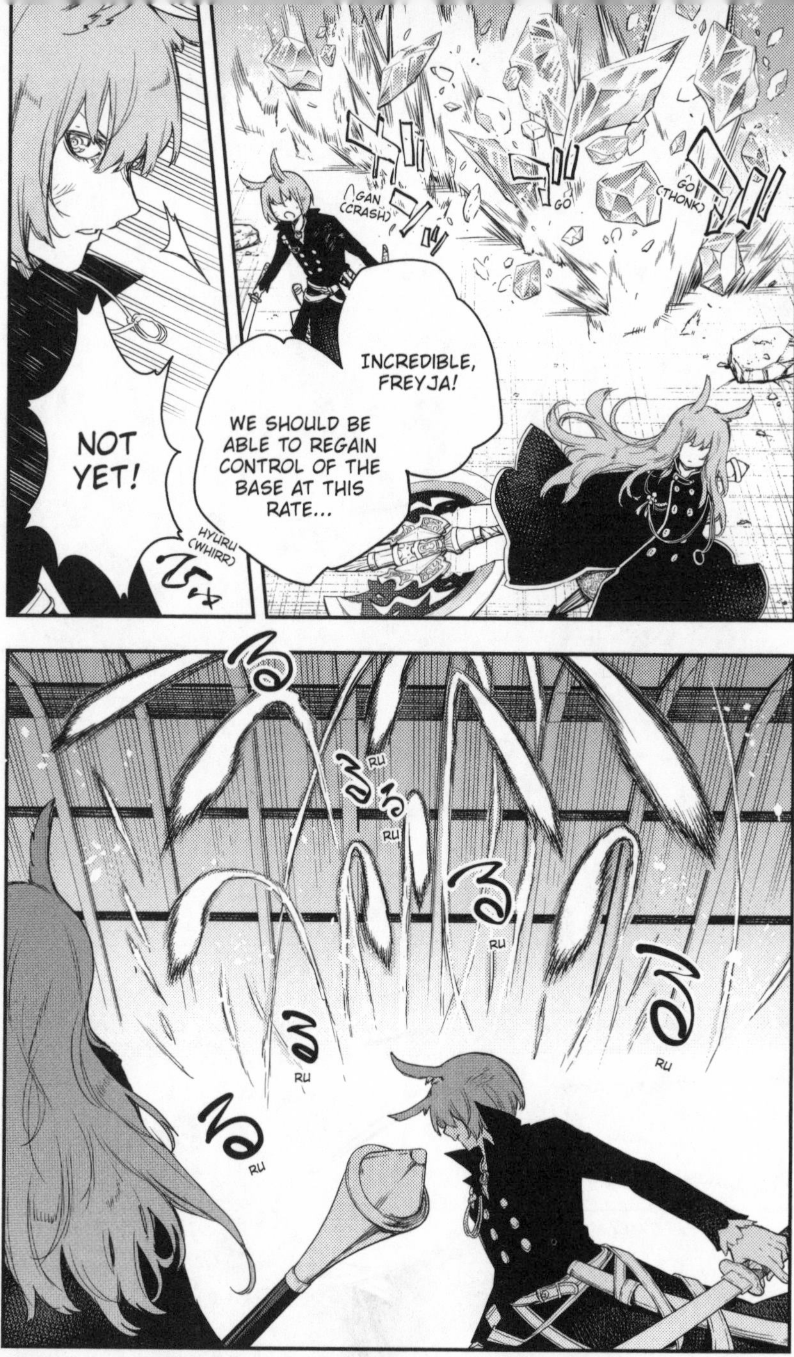
GO (THONK)
GO
GAN (CRASH)
INCREDIBLE, FREYJA!
WE SHOULD BE ABLE TO REGAIN CONTROL OF THE BASE AT THIS RATE...
NOT YET!
HYURU (WHIRR)
RU
RU
RU
RU
RU
RU

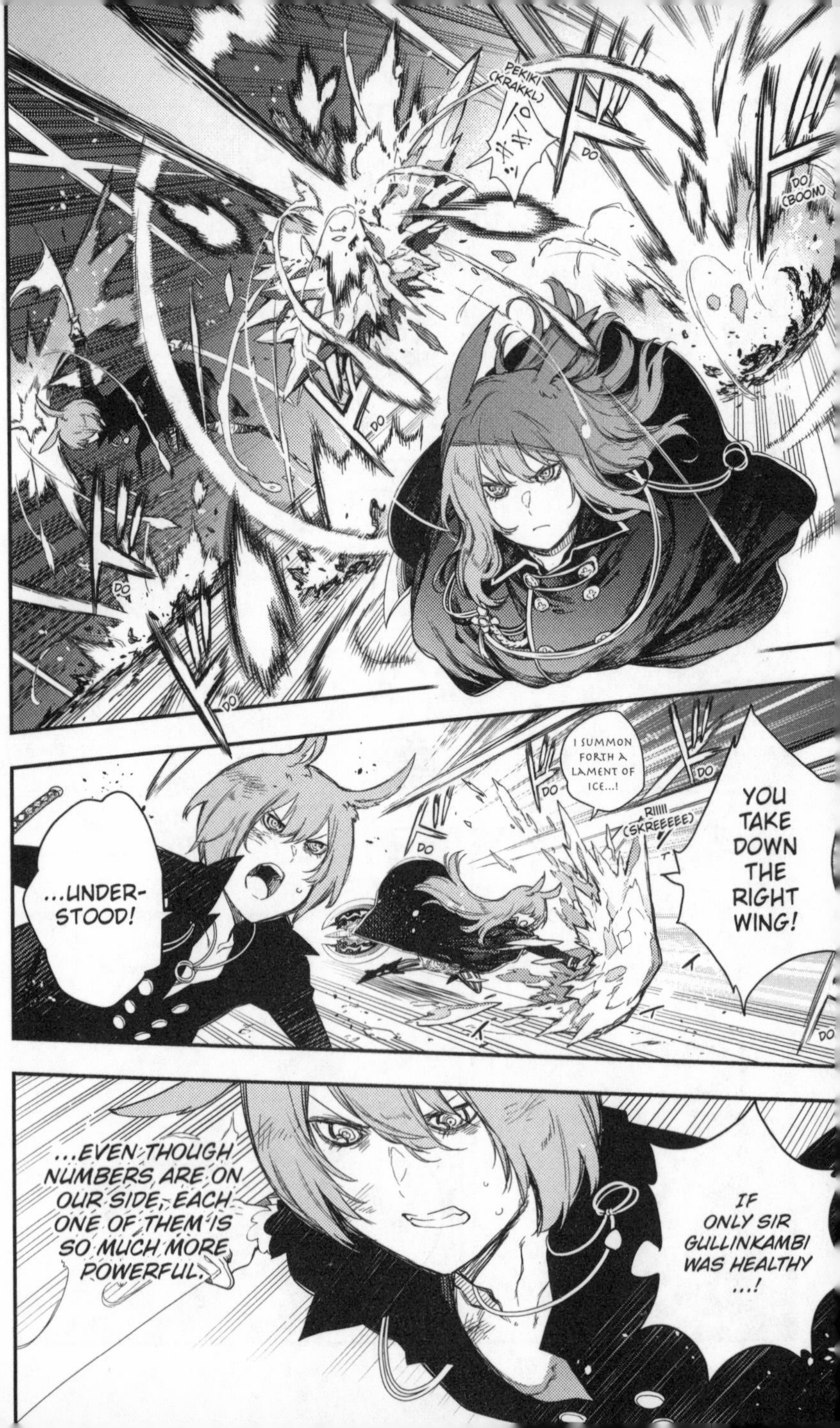
DO (BOOM)
DO
PEKIKI (KRAKKL)
DO
DO
DO
YOU TAKE DOWN THE RIGHT WING!
DO
I SUMMON FORTH A LAMENT OF ICE...!
RIIII (SKREEEEE)
DO
DO
...UNDER-STOOD!
IF ONLY SIR GULLINKAMBI WAS HEALTHY...!
...EVEN THOUGH NUMBERS ARE ON OUR SIDE, EACH ONE OF THEM IS SO MUCH MORE POWERFUL.

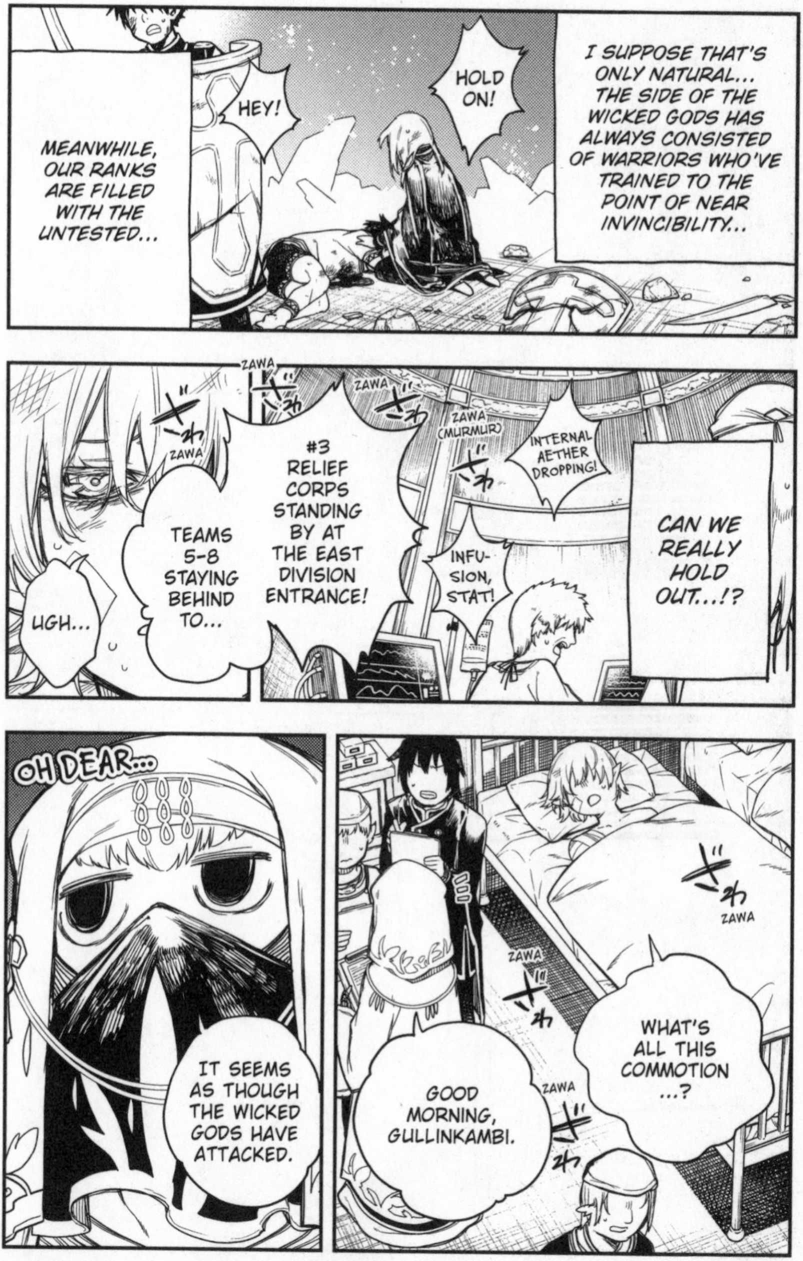
I SUPPOSE THAT'S ONLY NATURAL... THE SIDE OF THE WICKED GODS HAS ALWAYS CONSISTED OF WARRIORS WHO'VE TRAINED TO THE POINT OF NEAR INVINCIBILITY...
HOLD ON!
HEY!
MEANWHILE, OUR RANKS ARE FILLED WITH THE UNTESTED...
CAN WE REALLY HOLD OUT...!?
INTERNAL AETHER DROPPING!
ZAWA (MURMUR)
INFU- SION, STAT!
ZAWA
ZAWA
#3 RELIEF CORPS STANDING BY AT THE EAST DIVISION ENTRANCE!
ZAWA
TEAMS 5-8 STAYING BEHIND TO...
UGH...
ZAWA
WHAT'S ALL THIS COMMOTION ...?
ZAWA
ZAWA
GOOD MORNING, GULLINKAMBI.
OH DEAR...
IT SEEMS AS THOUGH THE WICKED GODS HAVE ATTACKED.

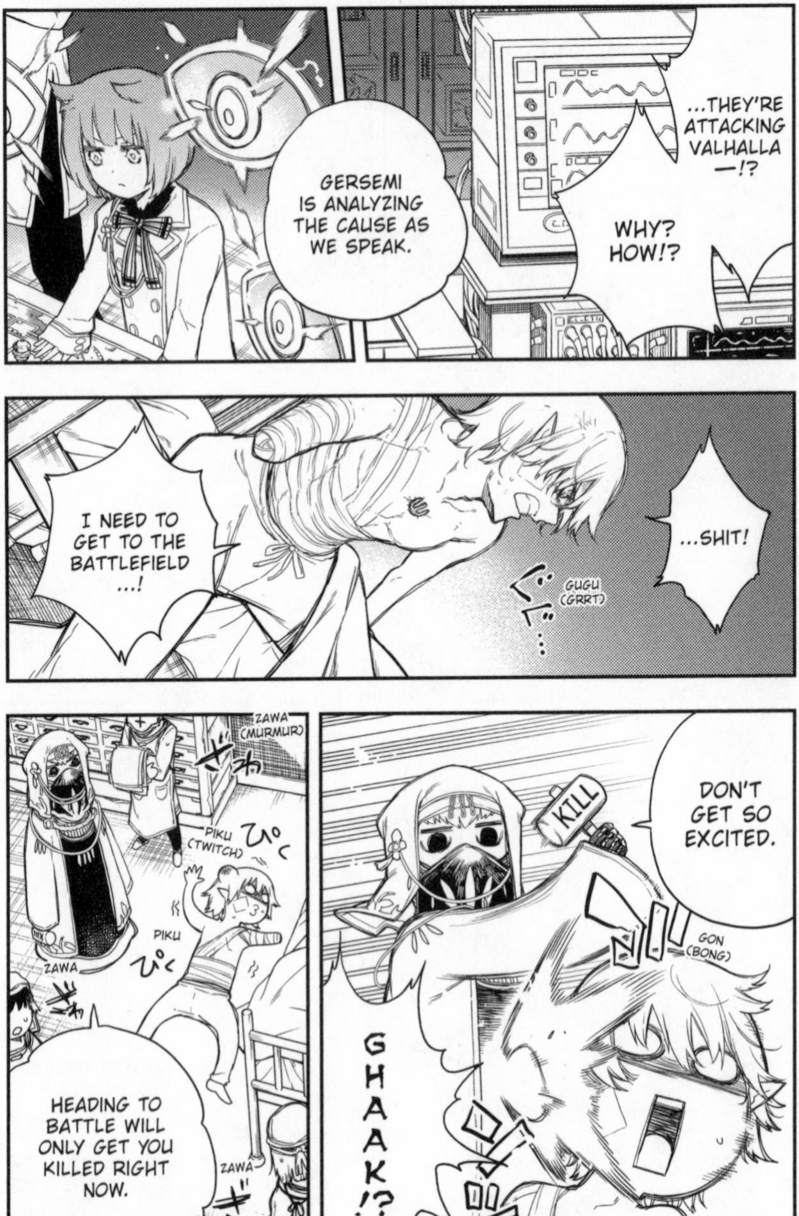
...THEY'RE ATTACKING VALHALLA —!?
WHY? HOW!?
GERSEMI IS ANALYZING THE CAUSE AS WE SPEAK.
...SHIT!
GUGU (GRRT)
I NEED TO GET TO THE BATTLEFIELD ...!
DON'T GET SO EXCITED.
KILL
GON (BONG)
GHAAK!?
ZAWA (MURMUR)
PIKU (TWITCH)
PIKU
ZAWA
HEADING TO BATTLE WILL ONLY GET YOU KILLED RIGHT NOW.
ZAWA

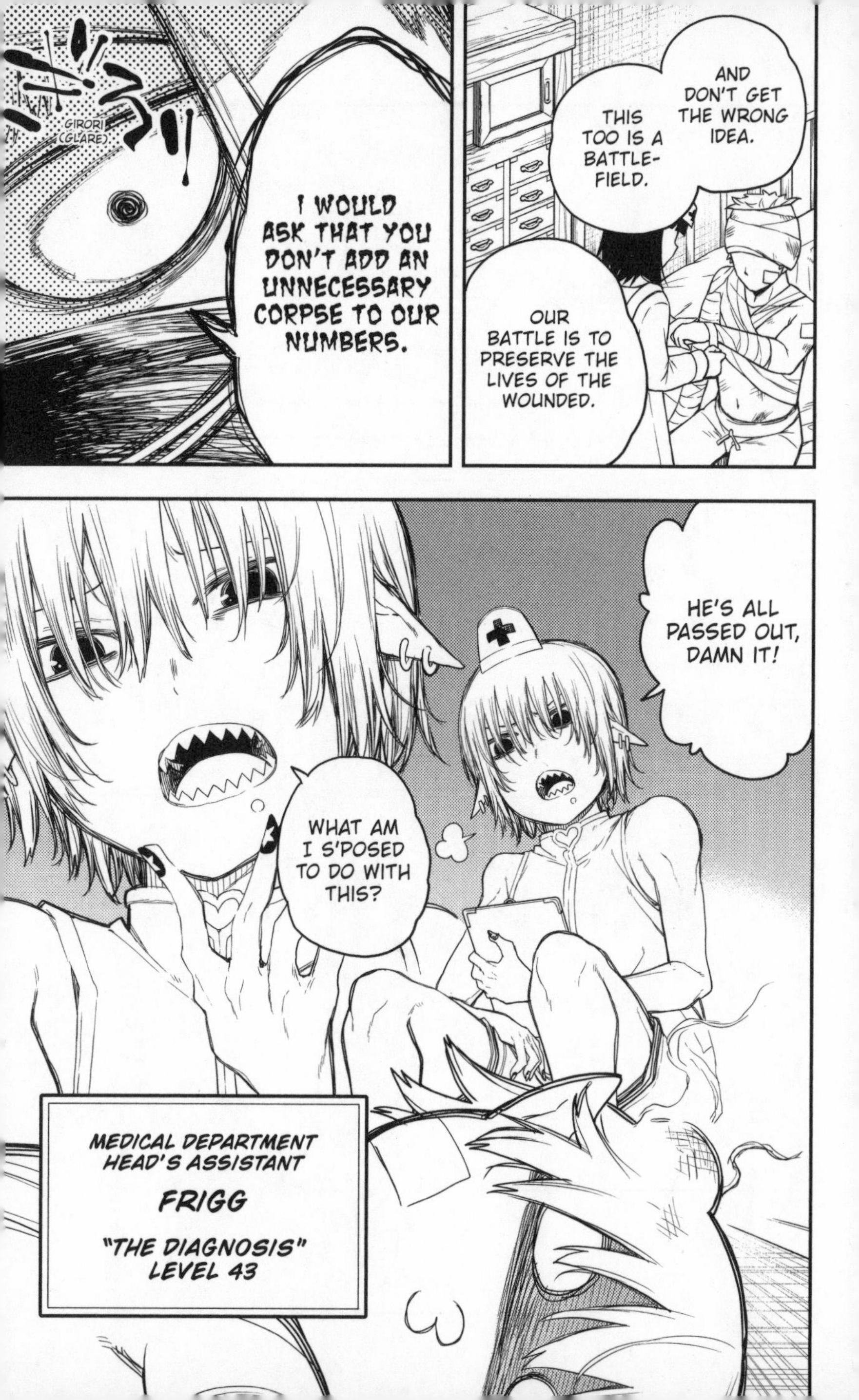
AND DON'T GET THE WRONG IDEA.
THIS TOO IS A BATTLE-FIELD.
OUR BATTLE IS TO PRESERVE THE LIVES OF THE WOUNDED.
GIRORI (GLARE)
I WOULD ASK THAT YOU DON'T ADD AN UNNECESSARY CORPSE TO OUR NUMBERS.
HE'S ALL PASSED OUT, DAMN IT!
WHAT AM I S'POSED TO DO WITH THIS?
MEDICAL DEPARTMENT HEAD'S ASSISTANT
FRIGG
"THE DIAGNOSIS" LEVEL 43

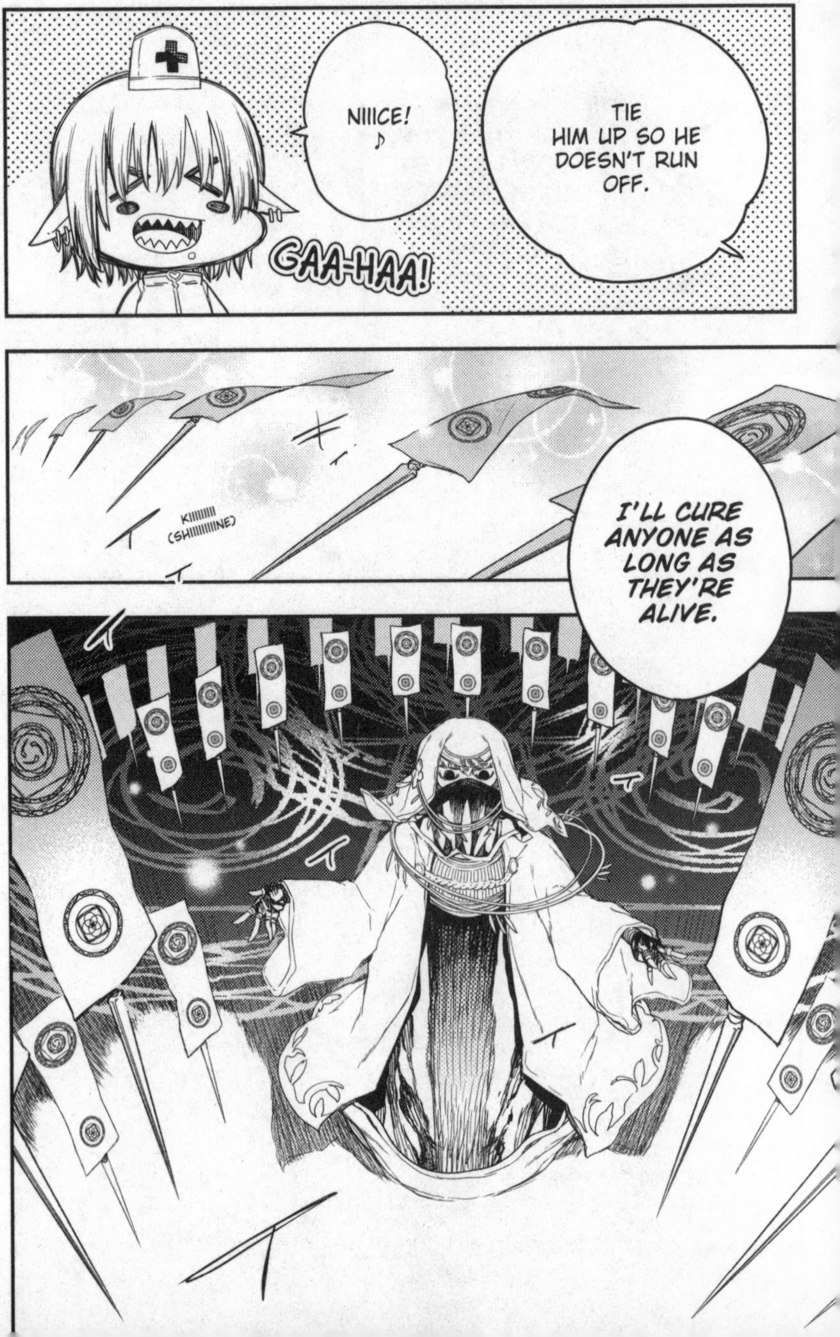
TIE HIM UP SO HE DOESN'T RUN OFF.
NIIICE! ♪
GAA-HAA!
I'LL CURE ANYONE AS LONG AS THEY'RE ALIVE.
KIIIIIIII (SHIIIIIIIINE)

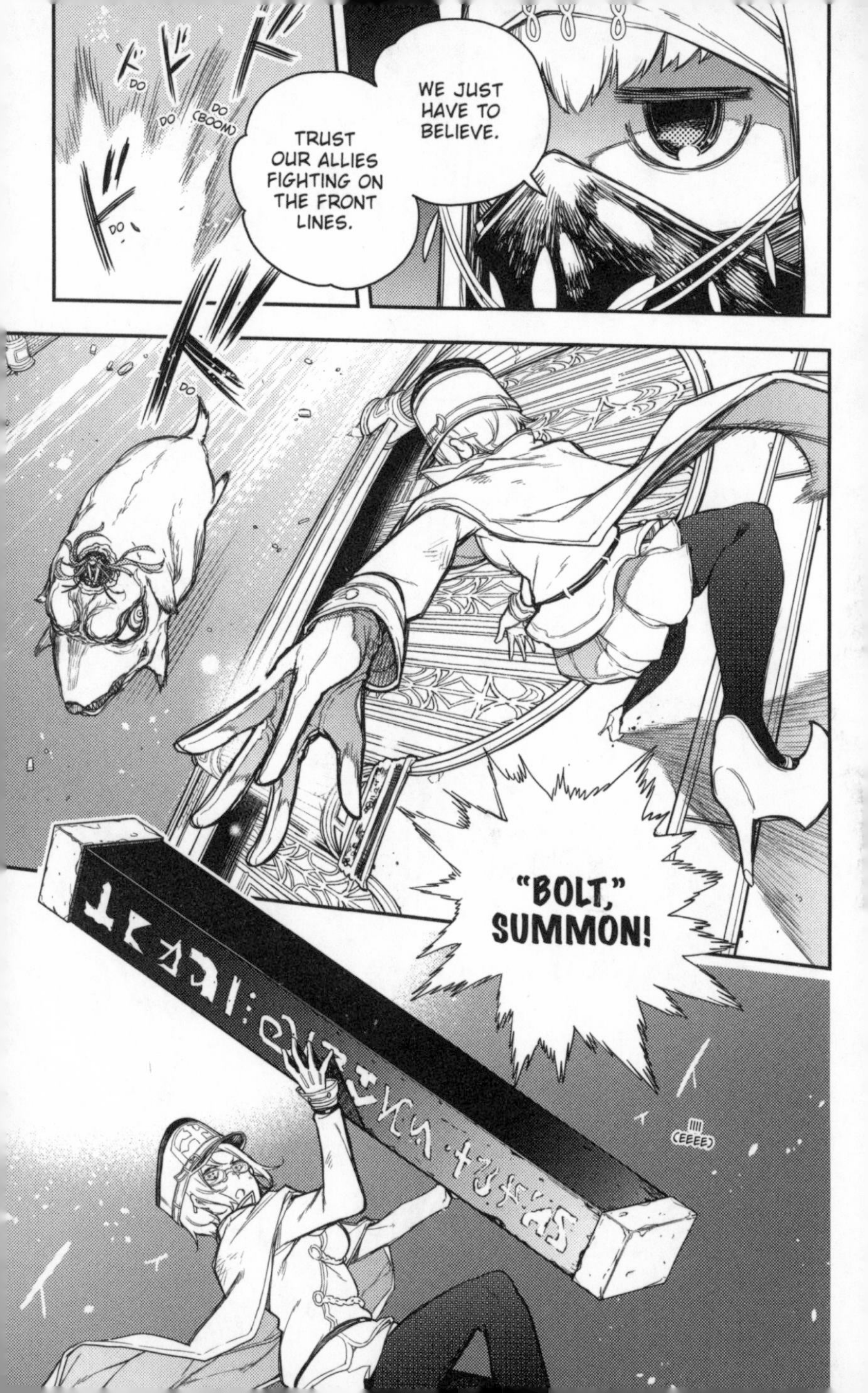
WE JUST HAVE TO BELIEVE.
TRUST OUR ALLIES FIGHTING ON THE FRONT LINES.
DO DO DO (BOOM)
DO
DO
"BOLT," SUMMON!
(EEEE)

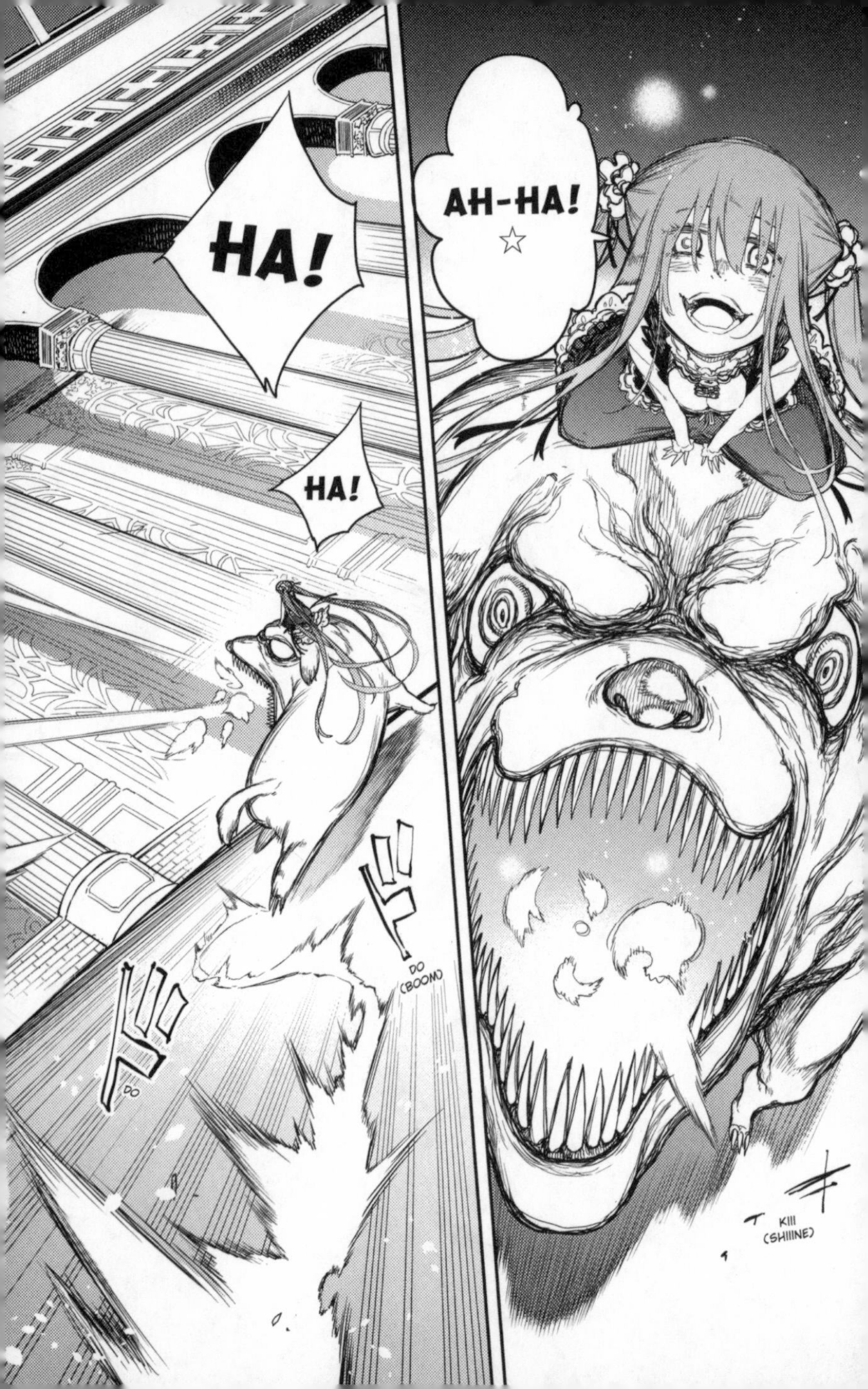
AH-HA! ☆
KIII (SHIIINE)
HA!
HA!
DO (BOOM)
DO

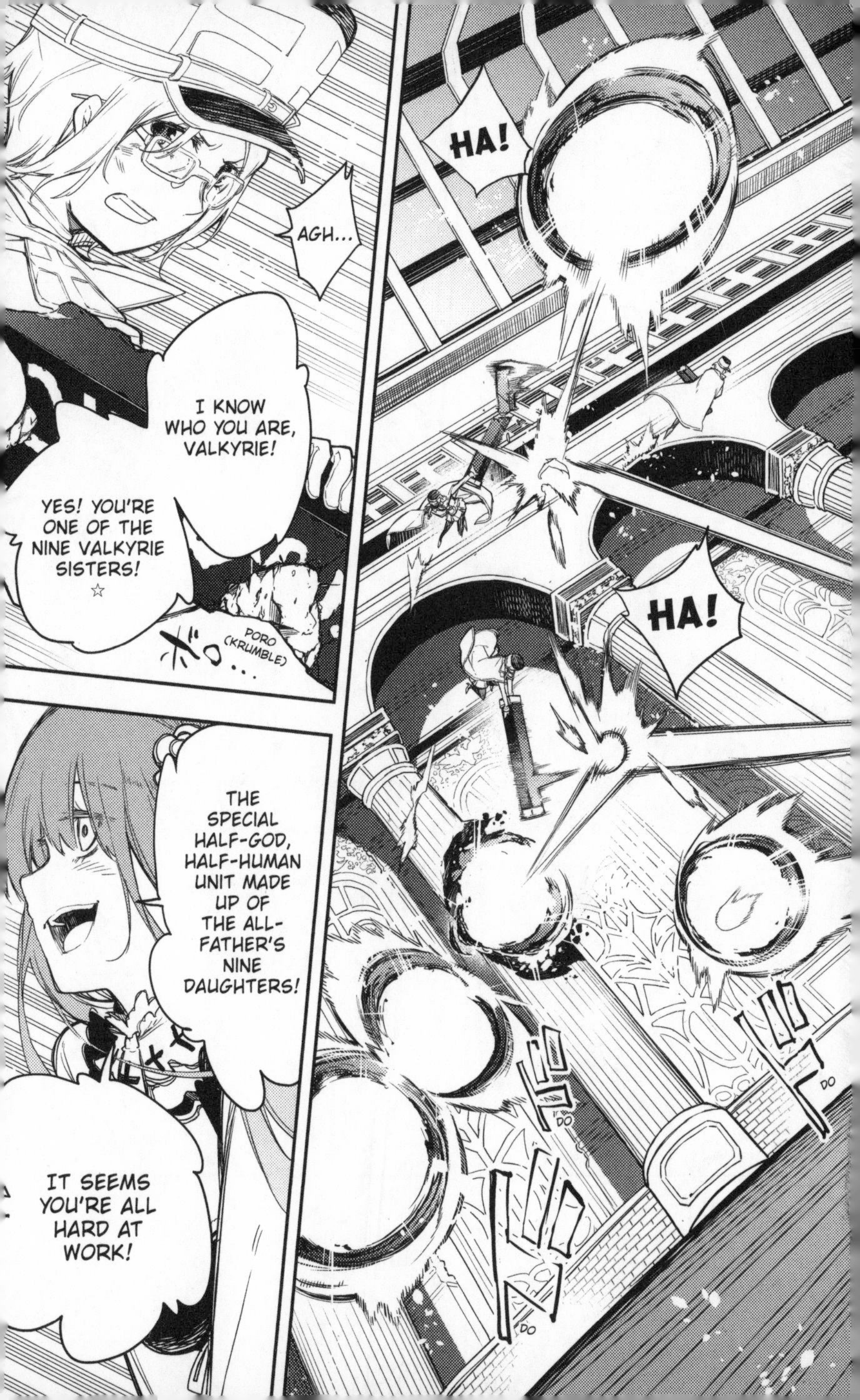
HA!
HA!
DO
DO
DO
AGH...
I KNOW WHO YOU ARE, VALKYRIE!
YES! YOU'RE ONE OF THE NINE VALKYRIE SISTERS! ☆
PORO (KRUMBLE)
THE SPECIAL HALF-GOD, HALF-HUMAN UNIT MADE UP OF THE ALL-FATHER'S NINE DAUGHTERS!
IT SEEMS YOU'RE ALL HARD AT WORK!

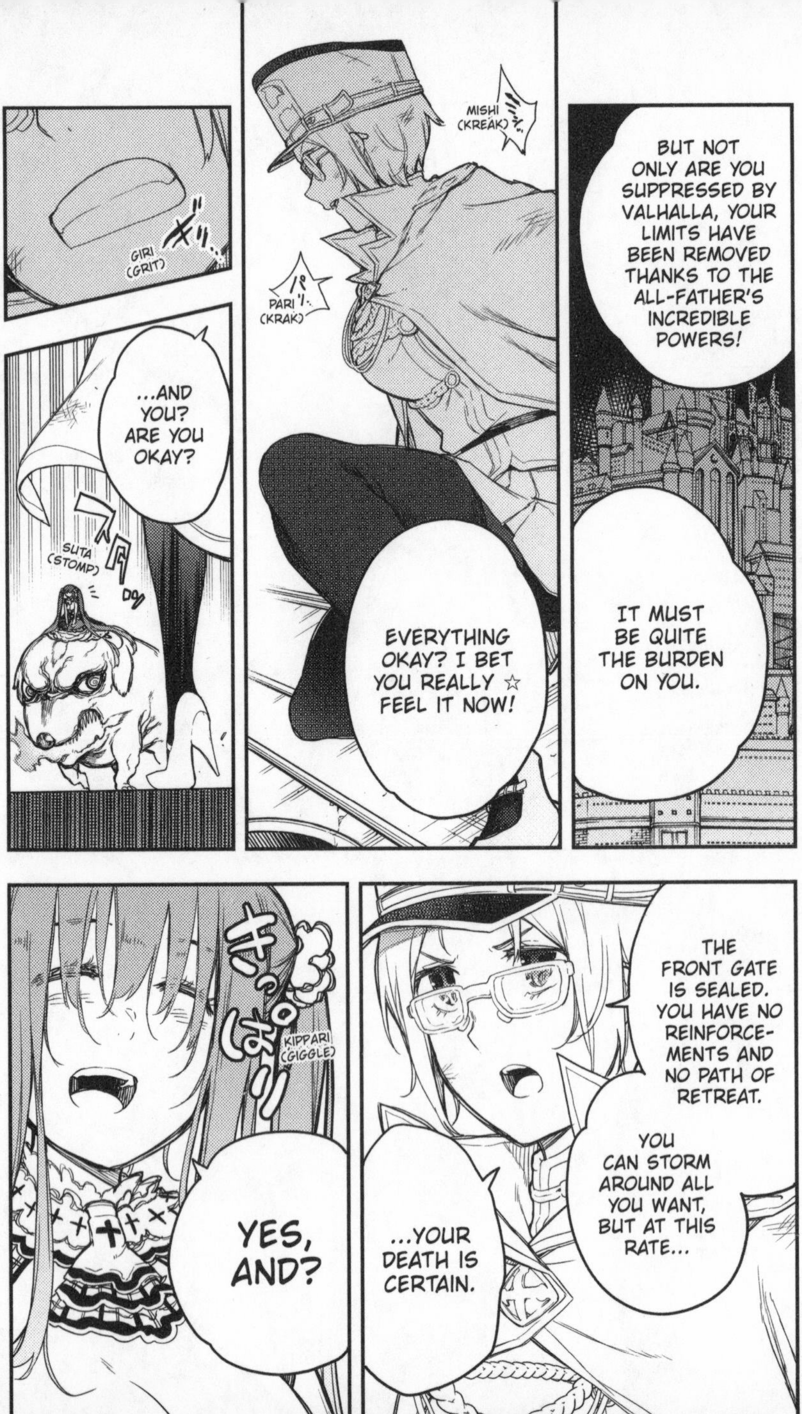
BUT NOT ONLY ARE YOU SUPPRESSED BY VALHALLA, YOUR LIMITS HAVE BEEN REMOVED THANKS TO THE ALL-FATHER'S INCREDIBLE POWERS!
IT MUST BE QUITE THE BURDEN ON YOU.
MISHI (KREAK)
PARI (KRAK)
EVERYTHING OKAY? I BET YOU REALLY ☆ FEEL IT NOW!
GIRI (GRIT)
...AND YOU? ARE YOU OKAY?
SUTA (STOMP)
THE FRONT GATE IS SEALED. YOU HAVE NO REINFORCE-MENTS AND NO PATH OF RETREAT.
YOU CAN STORM AROUND ALL YOU WANT, BUT AT THIS RATE...
...YOUR DEATH IS CERTAIN.
KIPPARI (GIGGLE)
YES, AND?

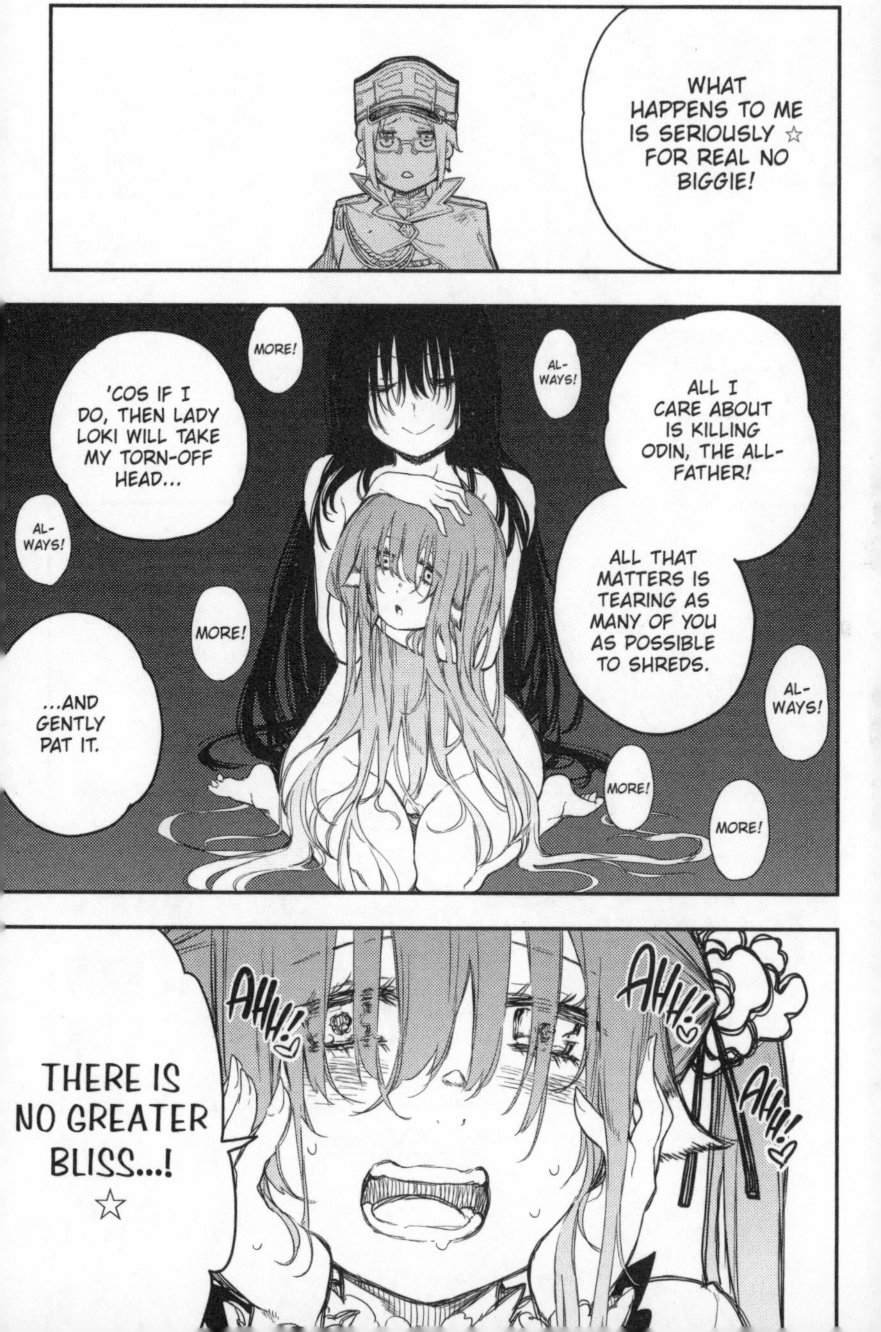
WHAT HAPPENS TO ME IS SERIOUSLY ☆ FOR REAL NO BIGGIE!
ALL I CARE ABOUT IS KILLING ODIN, THE ALL-FATHER!
AL-WAYS!
MORE!
'COS IF I DO, THEN LADY LOKI WILL TAKE MY TORN-OFF HEAD...
ALL THAT MATTERS IS TEARING AS MANY OF YOU AS POSSIBLE TO SHREDS.
AL-WAYS!
MORE!
AL-WAYS!
...AND GENTLY PAT IT.
MORE!
MORE!
AHH!♡
AHH!♡
AHH!♡
THERE IS NO GREATER BLISS...! ☆

PIKU
(TWITCH)

HOW CAN YOU POSSIBLY BE SO DEVOTED TO THIS LOKI WHORE? DISGUSTING.

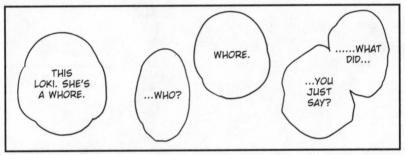

THIS LOKI. SHE'S A WHORE.

...WHO?

WHORE.

......WHAT DID...

...YOU JUST SAY?

DOOON
(BOOOM)

THE WICKED GOD LOKI IS A PIECE-OF-SHIT WHORE! ♪

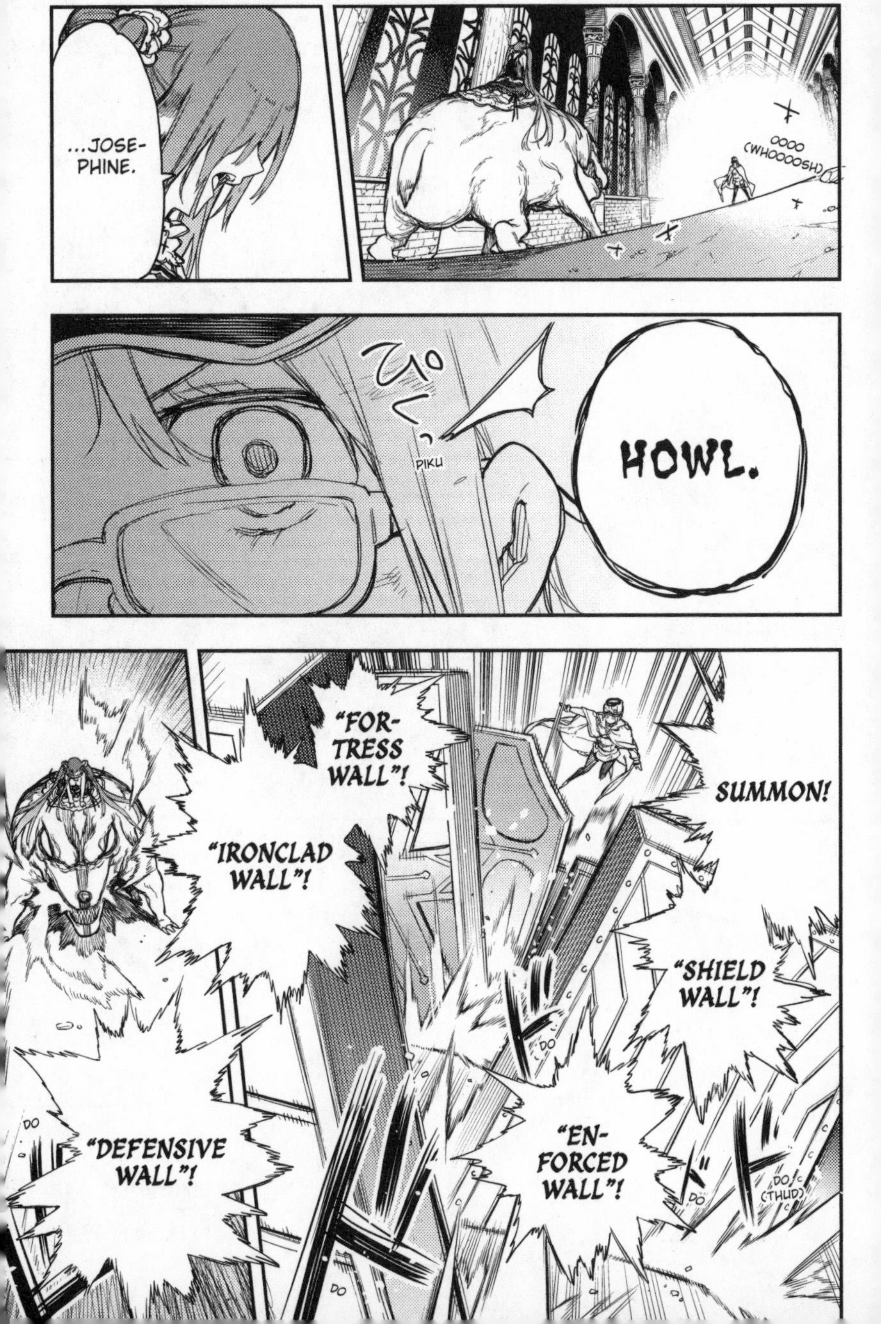
OOOO (WHOOOOSH)
...JOSE-PHINE.
HOWL.
ぴくっ
PIKU
SUMMON!
"FOR-TRESS WALL"!
"IRONCLAD WALL"!
"SHIELD WALL"!
DO
DO (THUD)
DO
"EN-FORCED WALL"!
"DEFENSIVE WALL"!
DO
DO

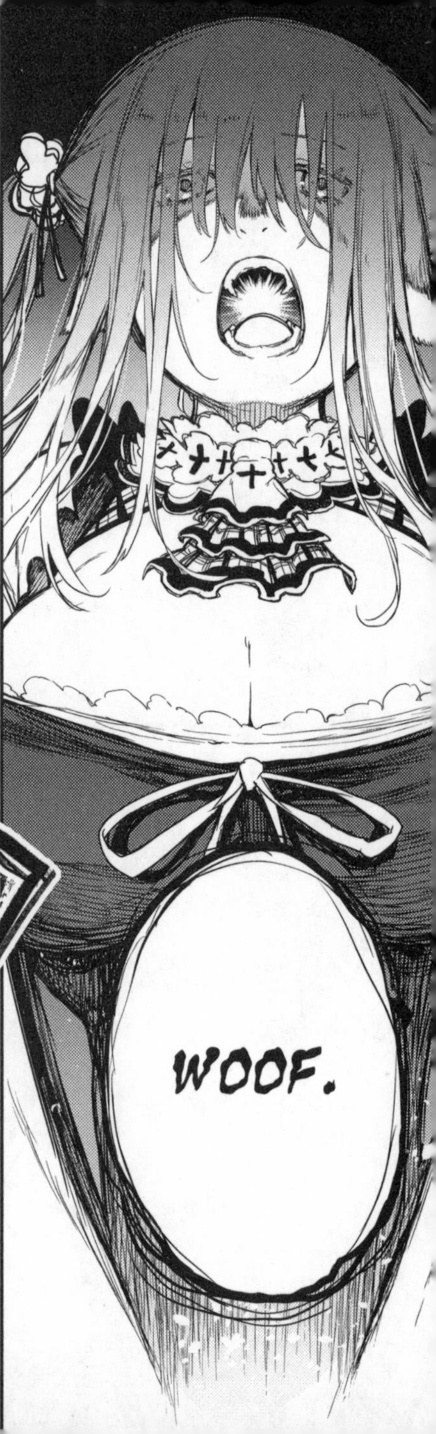
WOOF.
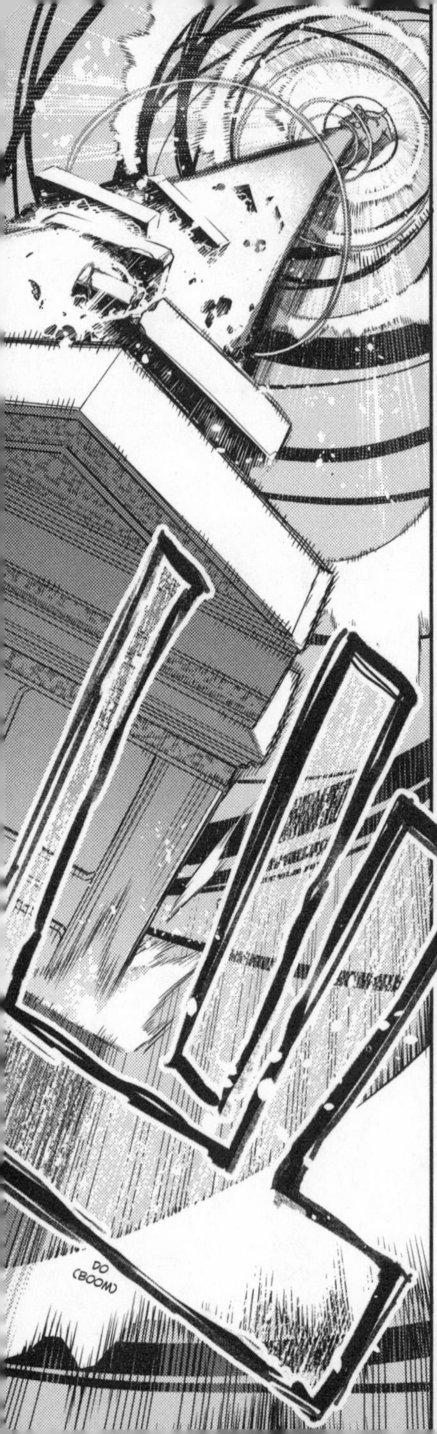
DO
(BOOM)

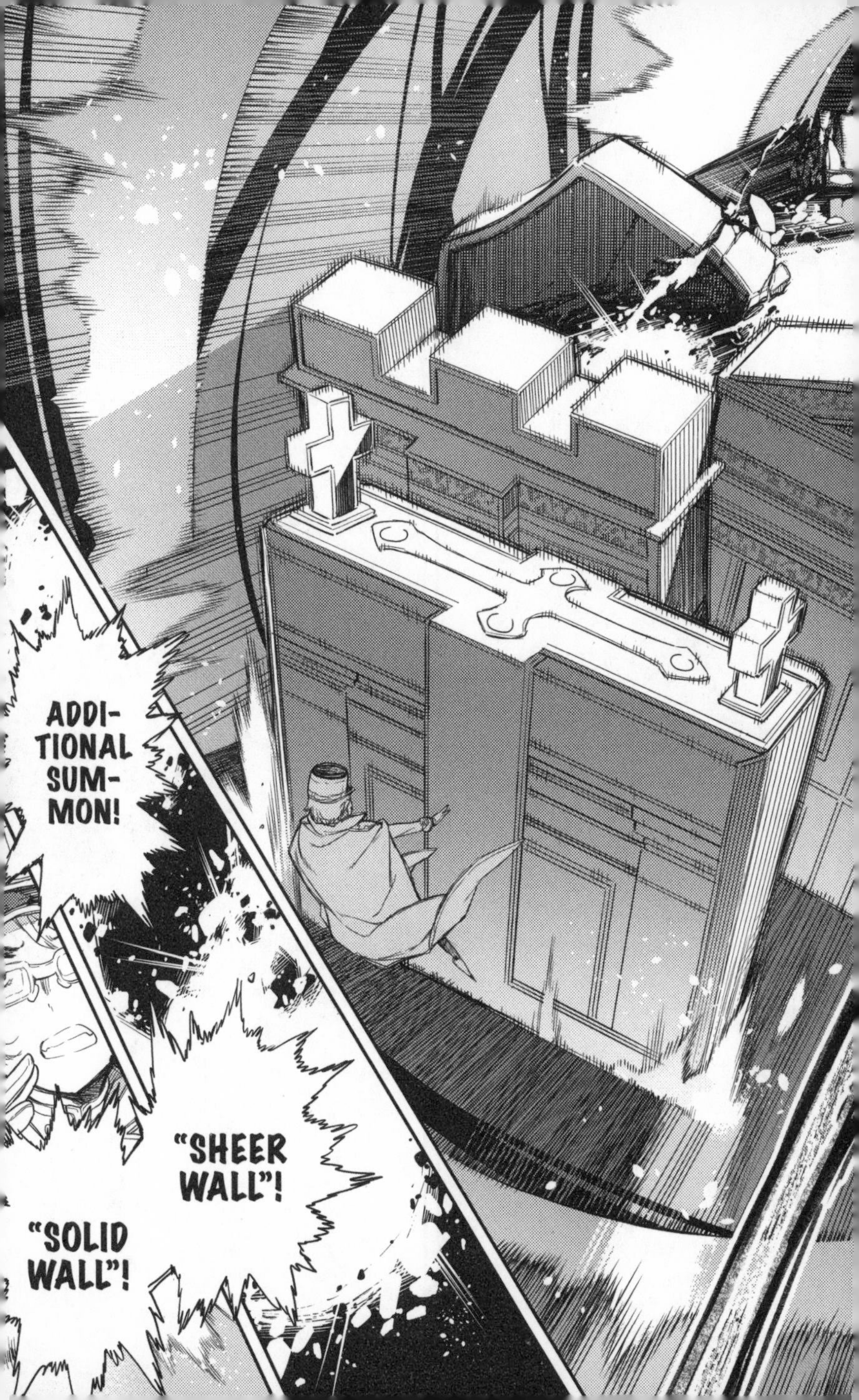
ADDITIONAL SUMMON!
"SHEER WALL"!
"SOLID WALL"!

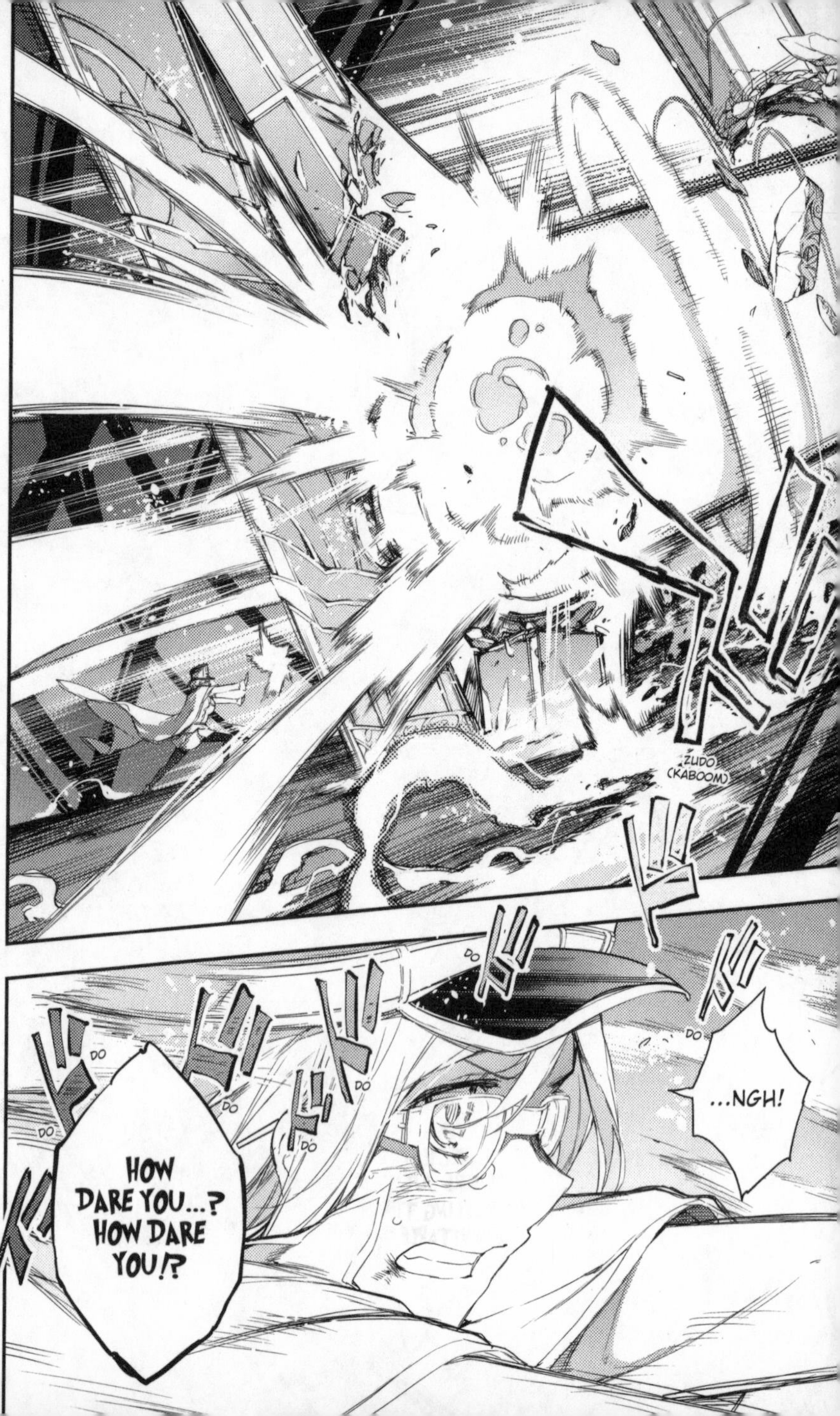
ZUDO
(KABOOM)
DO
DO
...NGH!
DO
DO
DO
DO
DO
HOW DARE YOU...? HOW DARE YOU!?

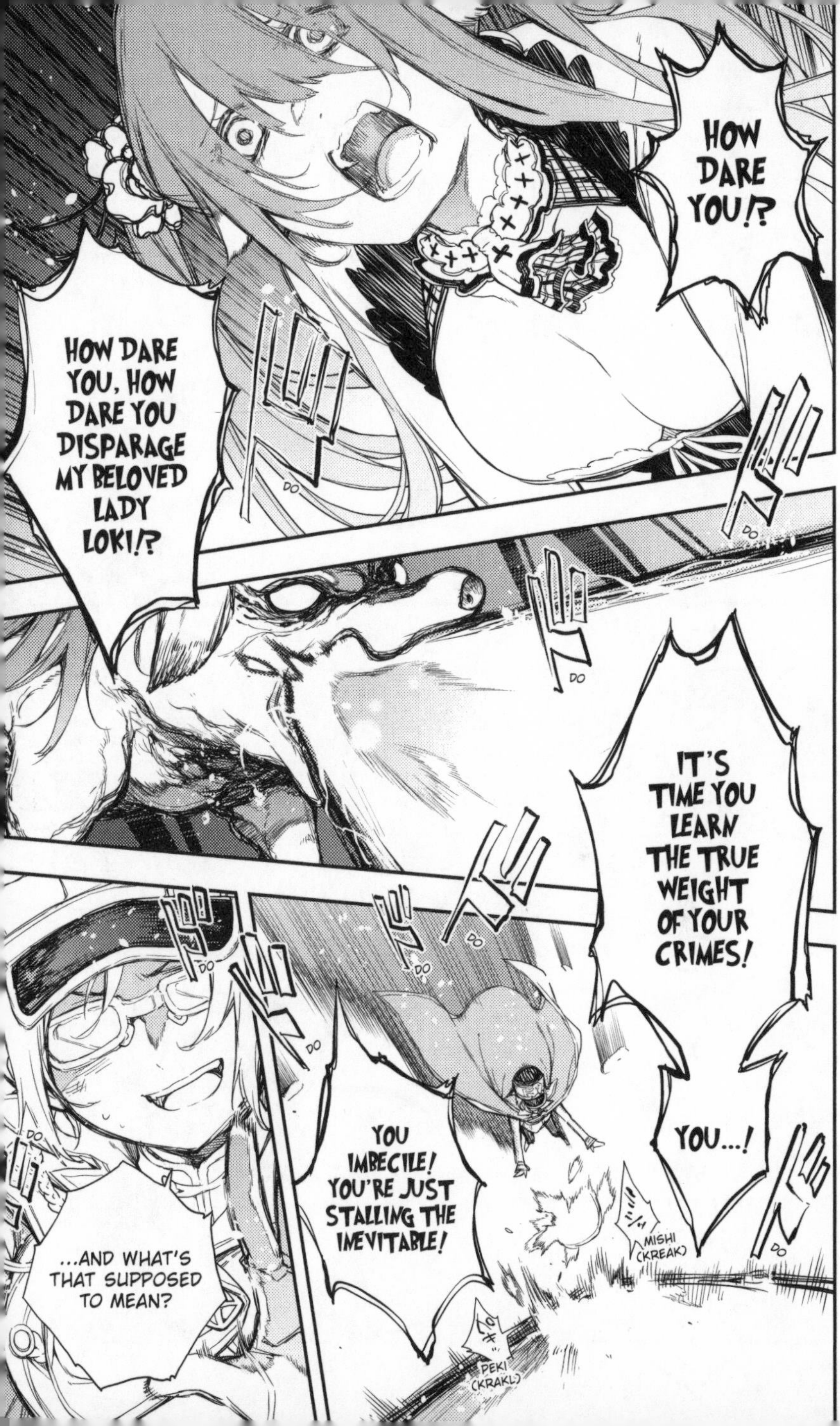
HOW DARE YOU!?
HOW DARE YOU, HOW DARE YOU DISPARAGE MY BELOVED LADY LOKI!?
DO
DO
DO
IT'S TIME YOU LEARN THE TRUE WEIGHT OF YOUR CRIMES!
DO
YOU...!
MISHI (KREAK)
DO
DO
DO
YOU IMBECILE! YOU'RE JUST STALLING THE INEVITABLE!
PEKI (KRAKL)
DO
...AND WHAT'S THAT SUPPOSED TO MEAN?

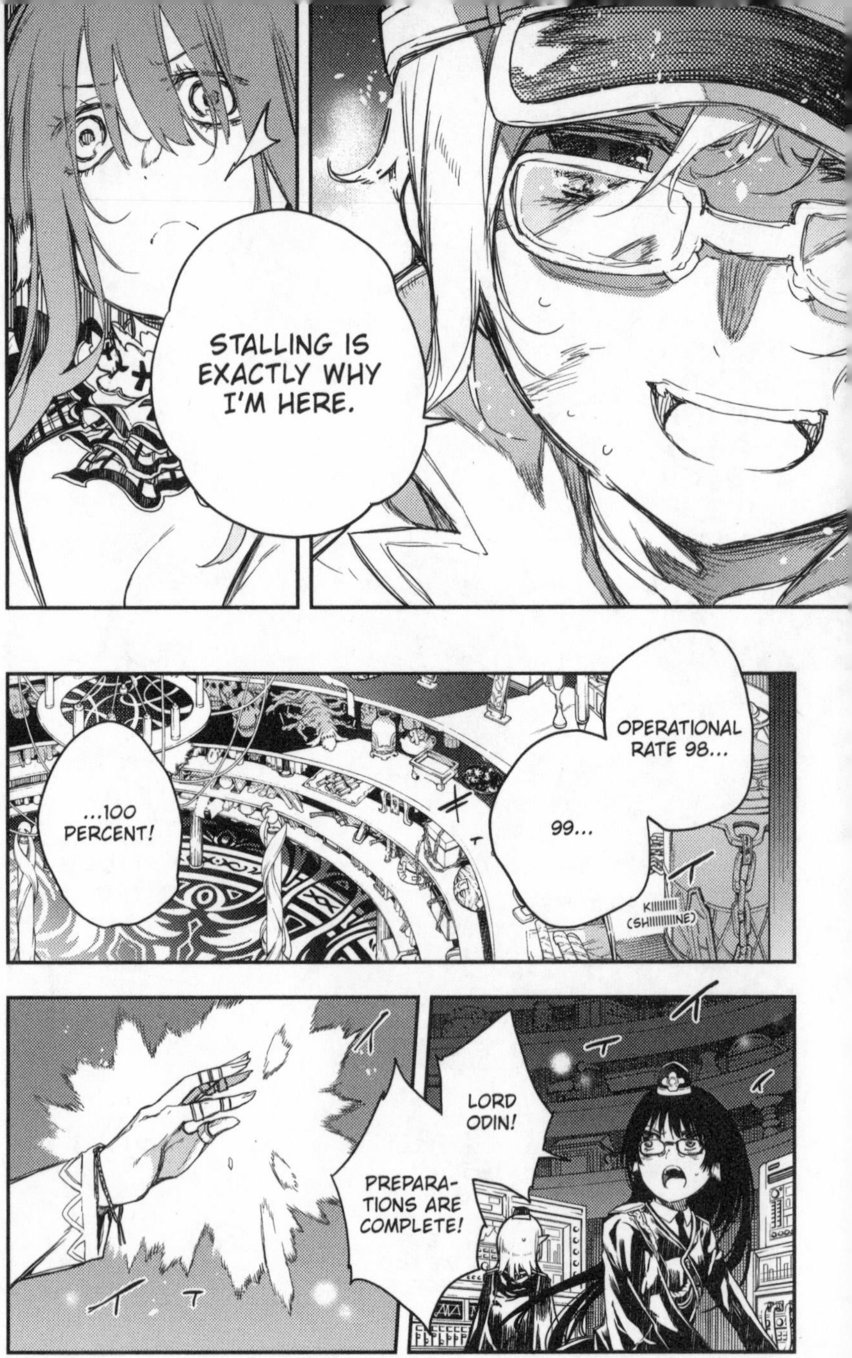
STALLING IS EXACTLY WHY I'M HERE.
OPERATIONAL RATE 98...
99...
KIIIIIII (SHIIIIIIINE)
...100 PERCENT!
LORD ODIN!
PREPARATIONS ARE COMPLETE!

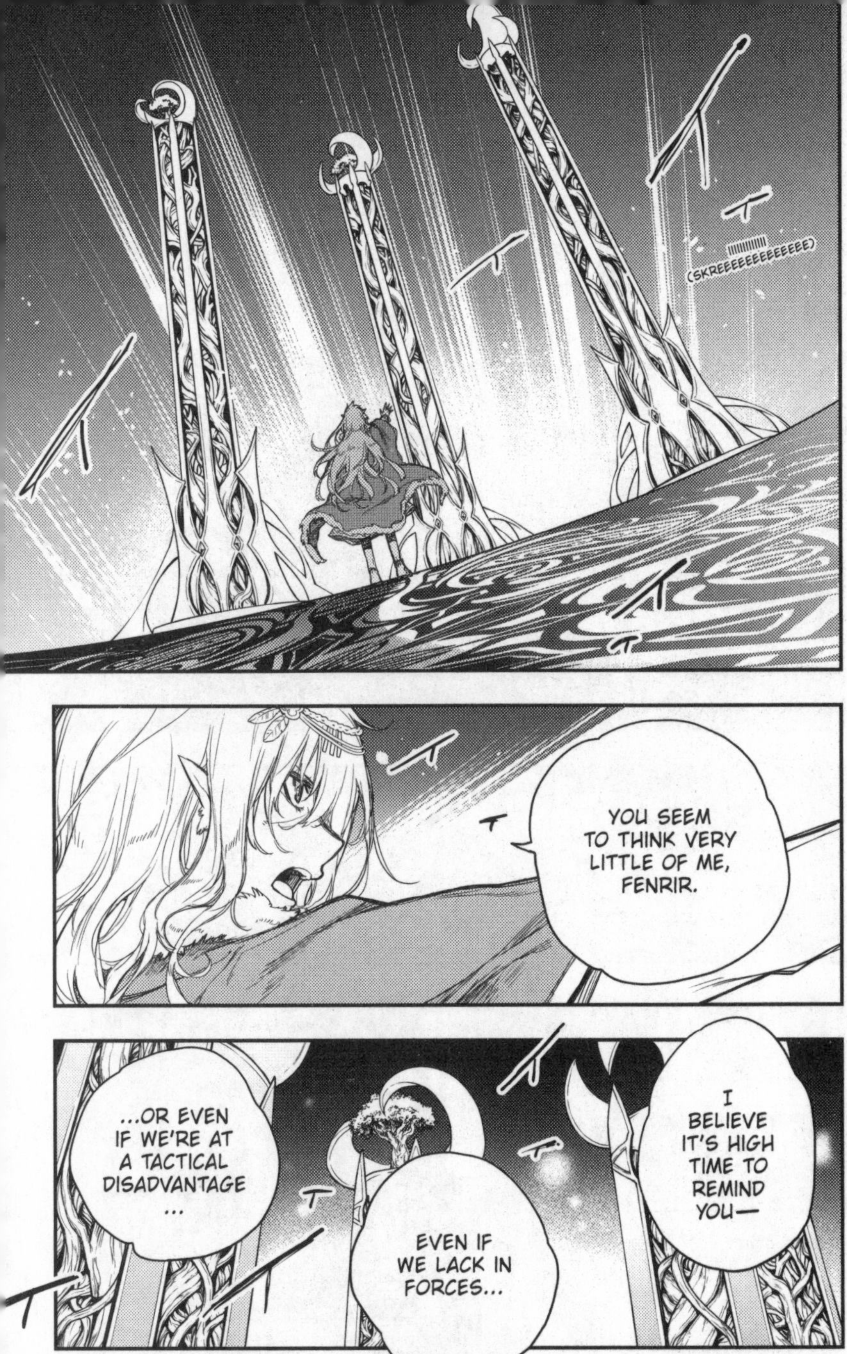
(SKREEEEEEEEEEEEEEE)
YOU SEEM TO THINK VERY LITTLE OF ME, FENRIR.
I BELIEVE IT'S HIGH TIME TO REMIND YOU—
EVEN IF WE LACK IN FORCES...
...OR EVEN IF WE'RE AT A TACTICAL DISADVANTAGE ...

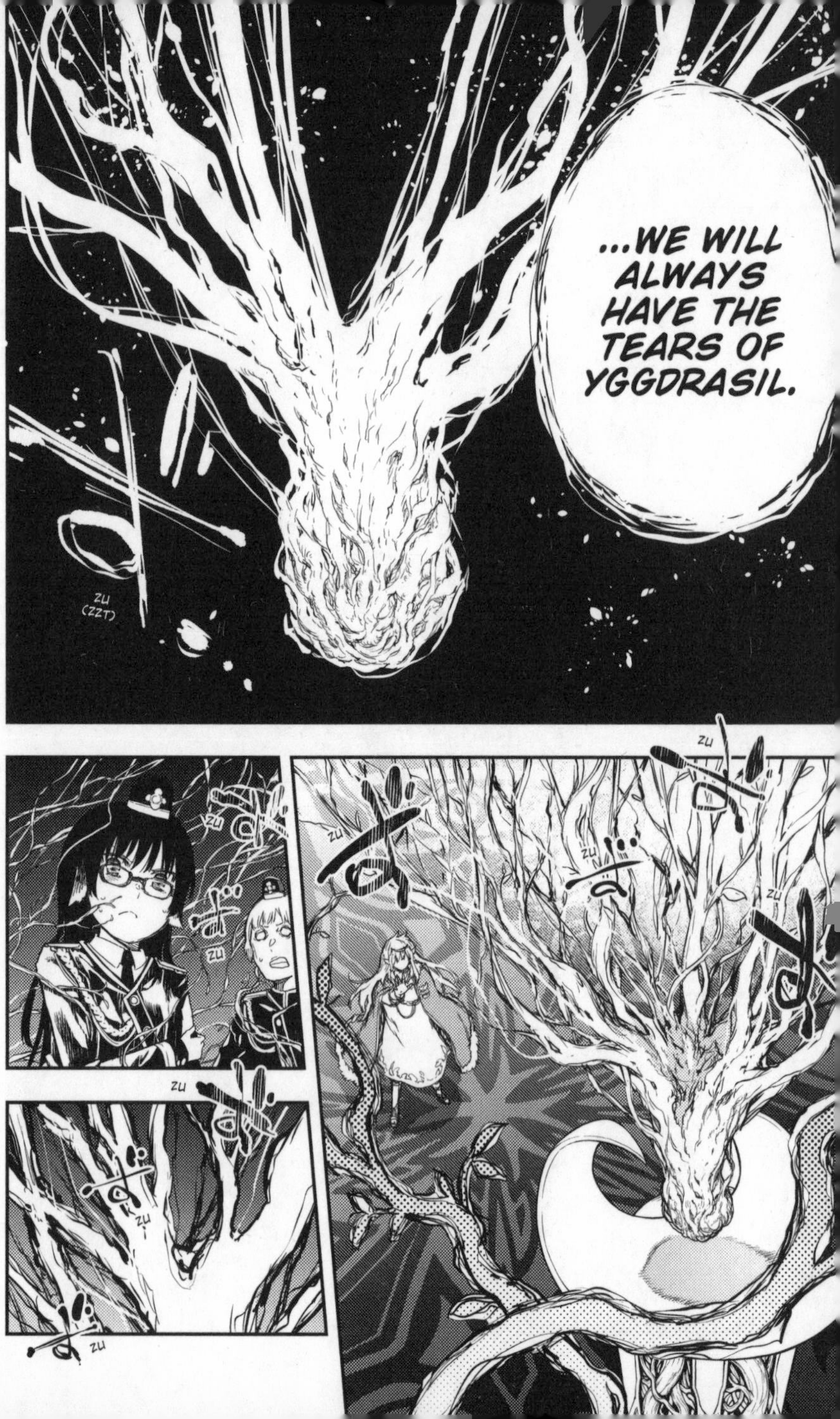
...WE WILL ALWAYS HAVE THE TEARS OF YGGDRASIL.
ZU (ZZT)
ZU
ZU
ZU
ZU
ZU
ZU
ZU
ZU
ZU

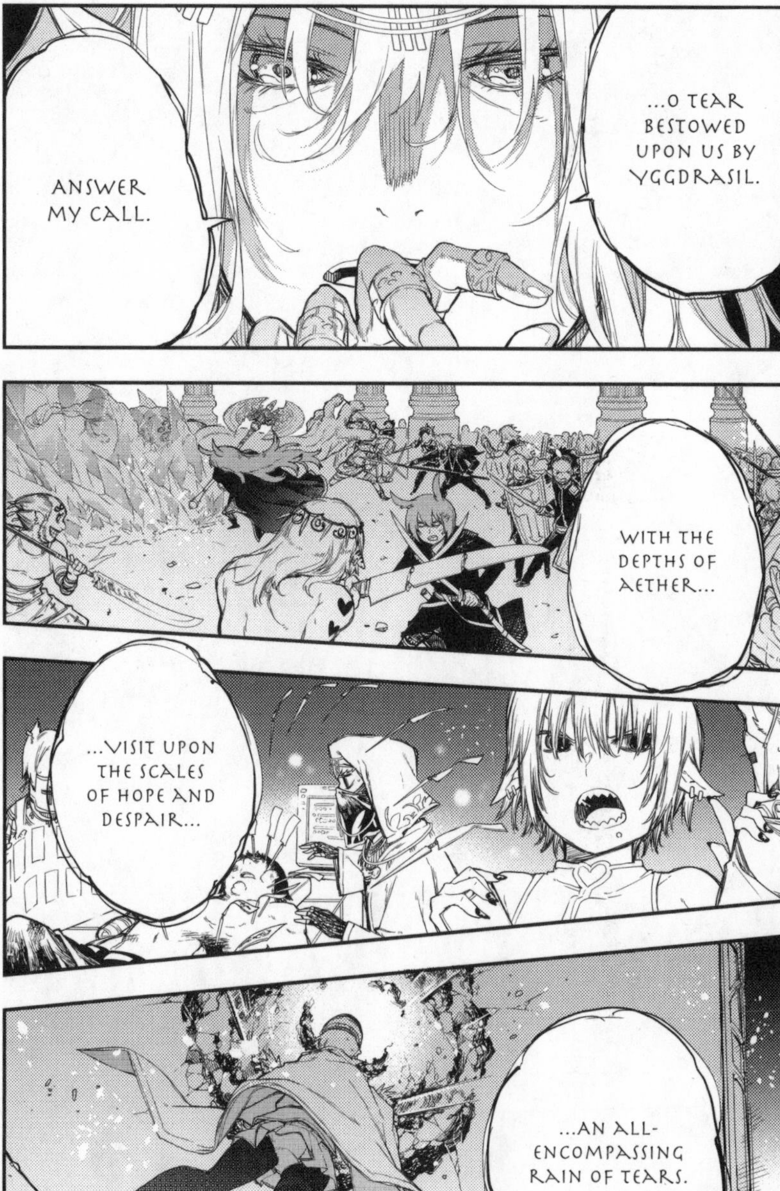
...O TEAR BESTOWED UPON US BY YGGDRASIL.
ANSWER MY CALL.
WITH THE DEPTHS OF AETHER...
...VISIT UPON THE SCALES OF HOPE AND DESPAIR...
...AN ALL-ENCOMPASSING RAIN OF TEARS.

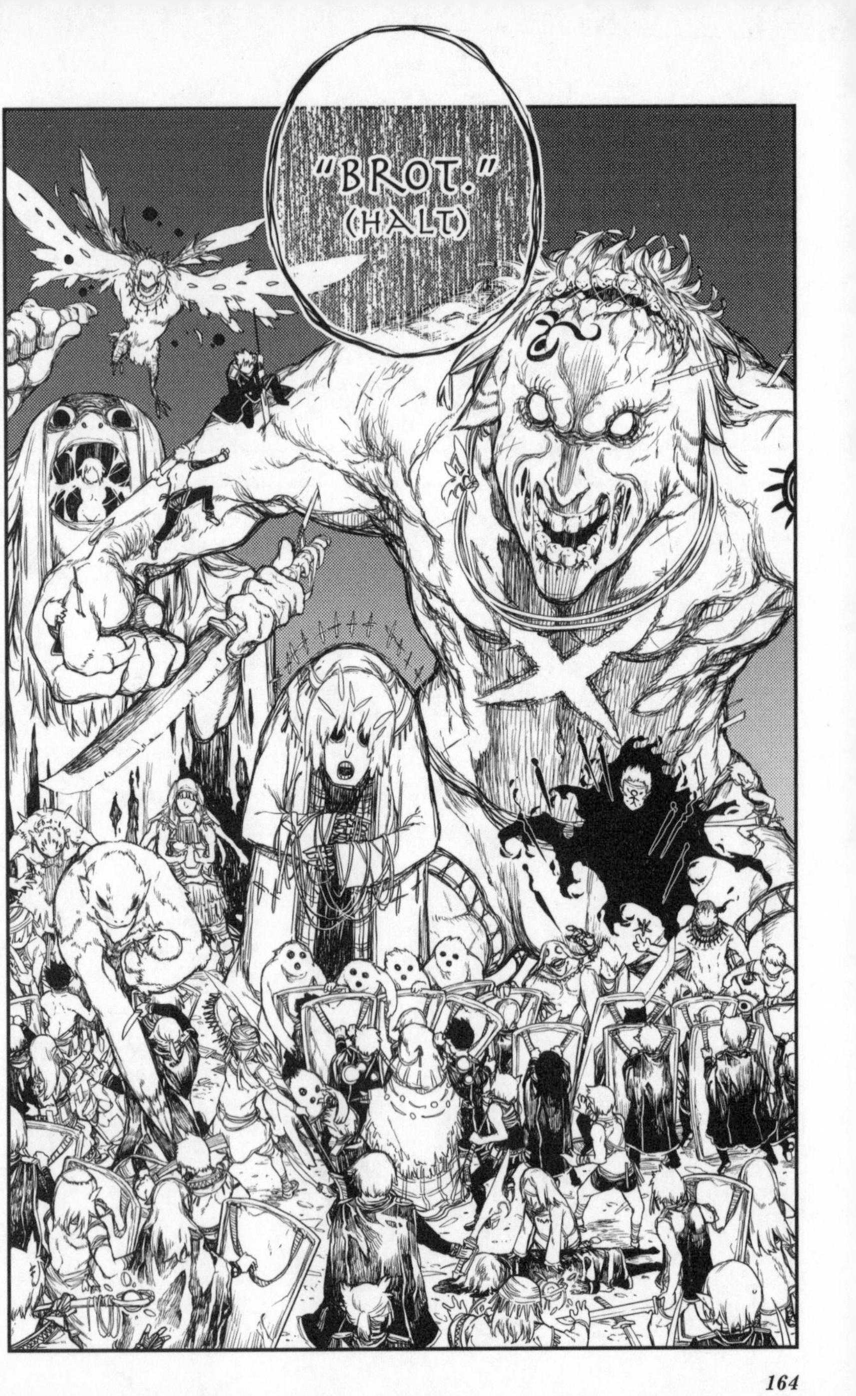
"BROT."
(HALT)

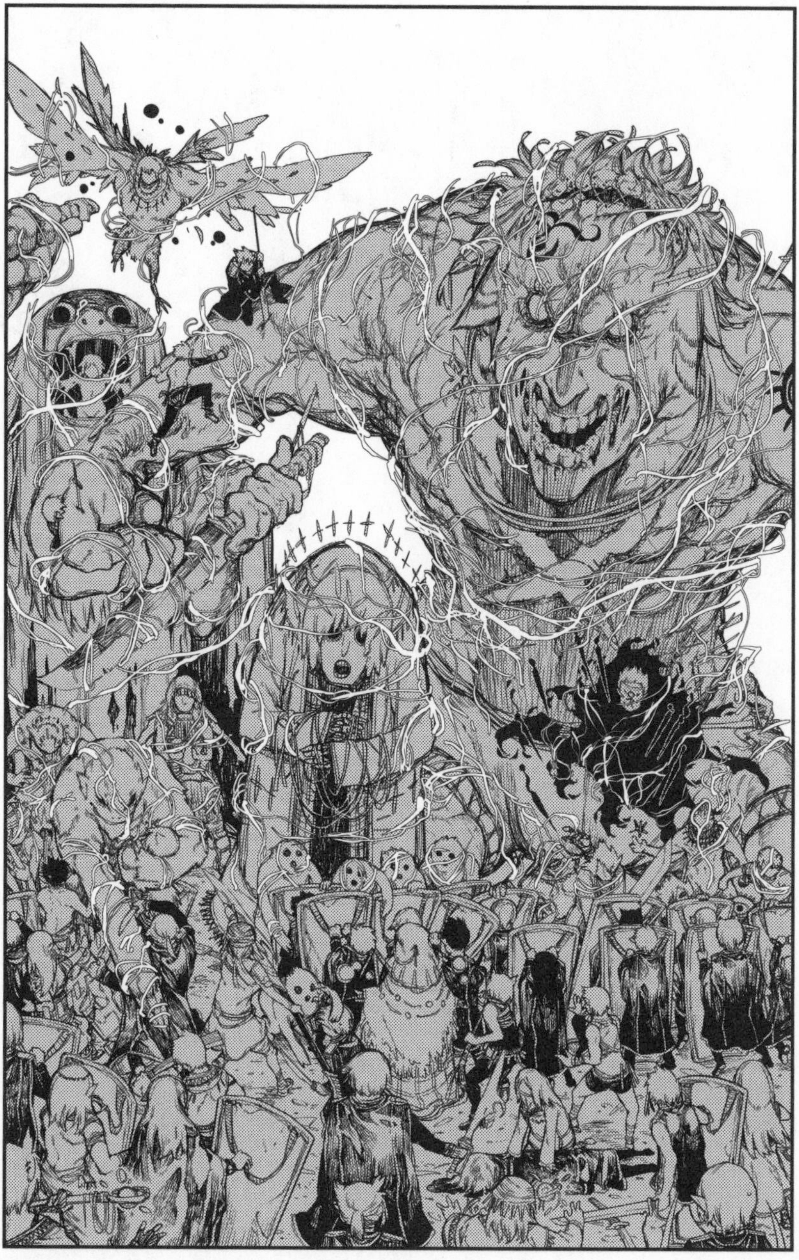

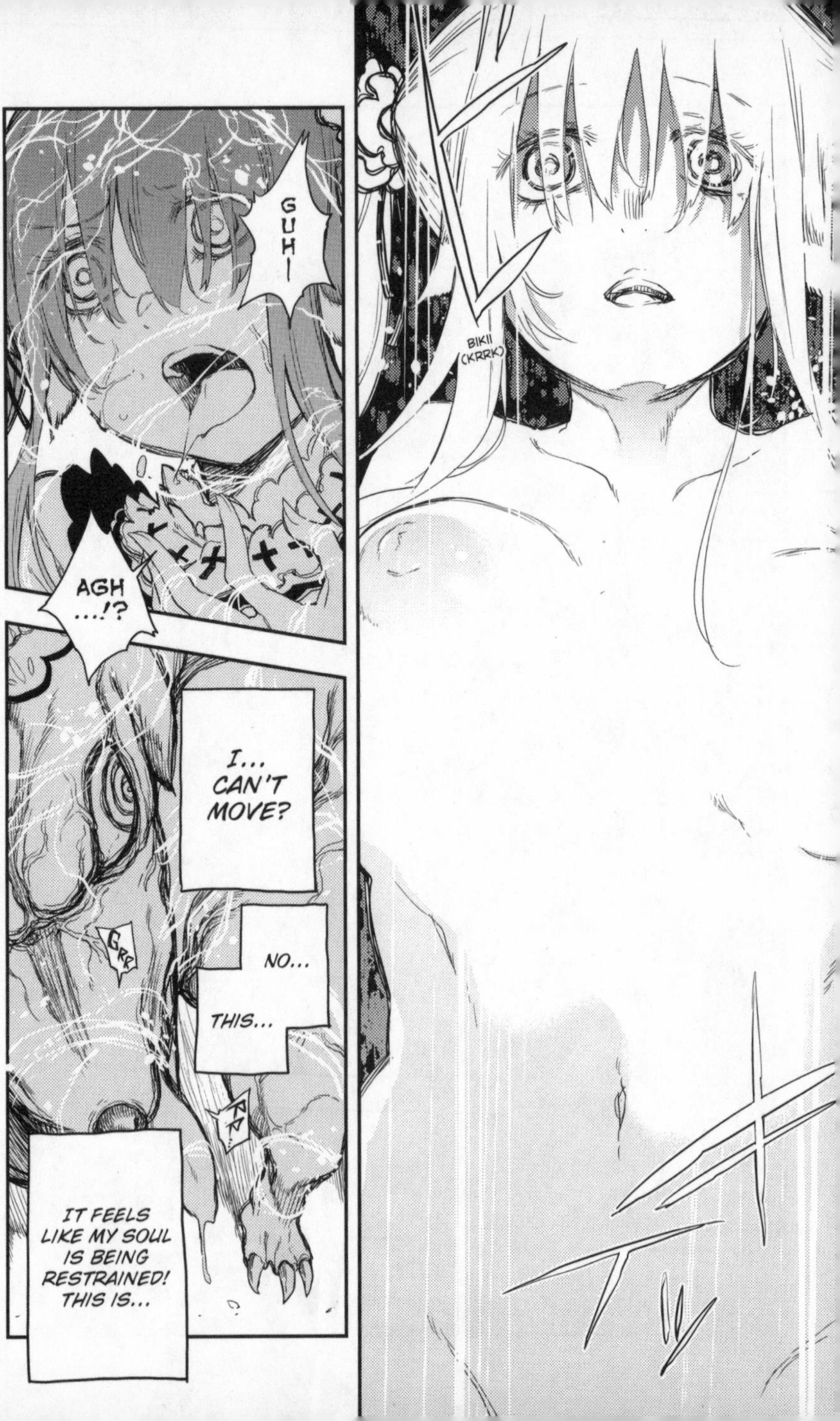
BIKII (KRRK)
GUH!
AGH ...!?
I... CAN'T MOVE?
NO... THIS...
GRR
IT FEELS LIKE MY SOUL IS BEING RESTRAINED! THIS IS...

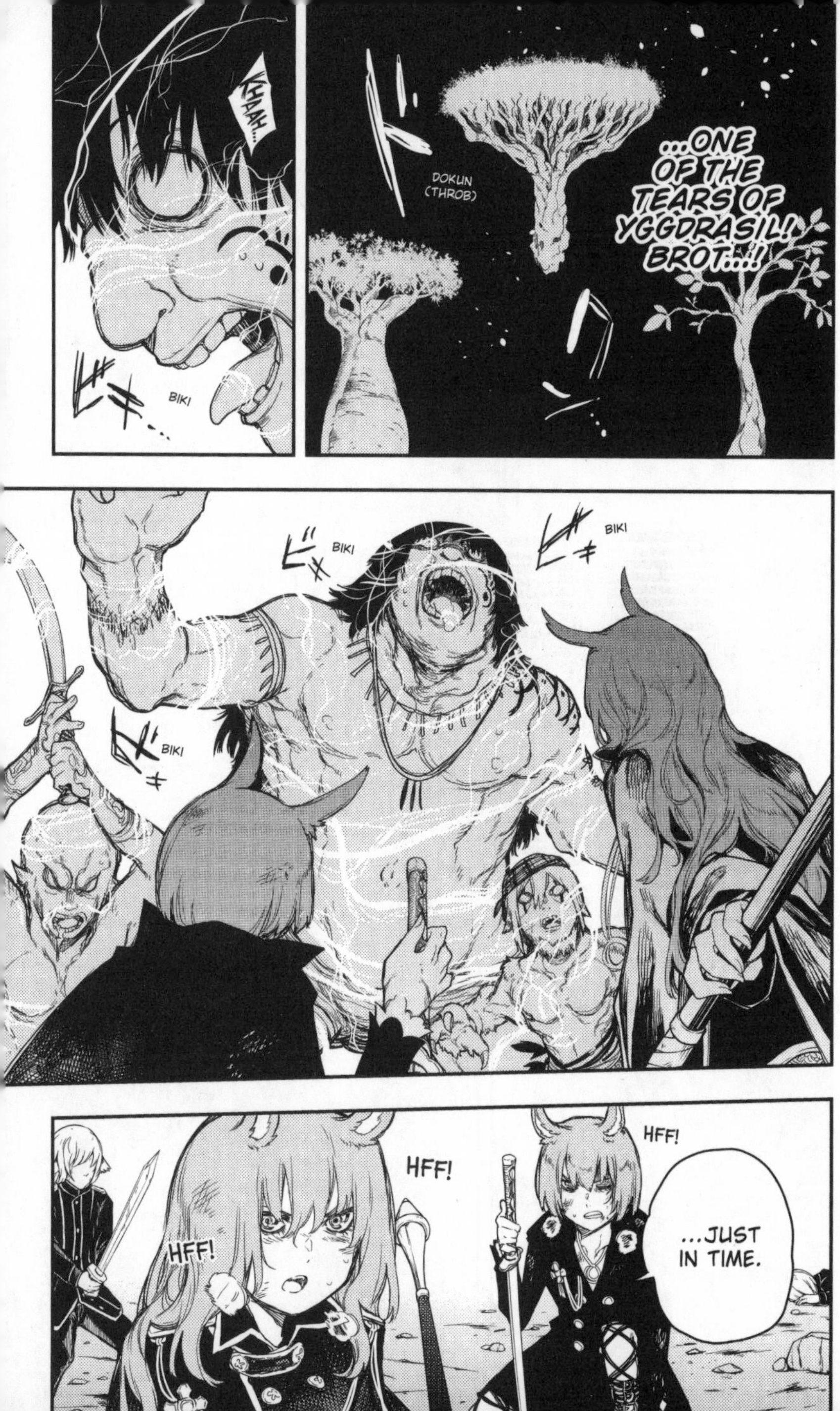
...ONE OF THE TEARS OF YGGDRASIL! BROT...!
DOKUN (THROB)
KHAAH...
BIKI
BIKI
BIKI
BIKI
HFF!
...JUST IN TIME.
HFF!
HFF!

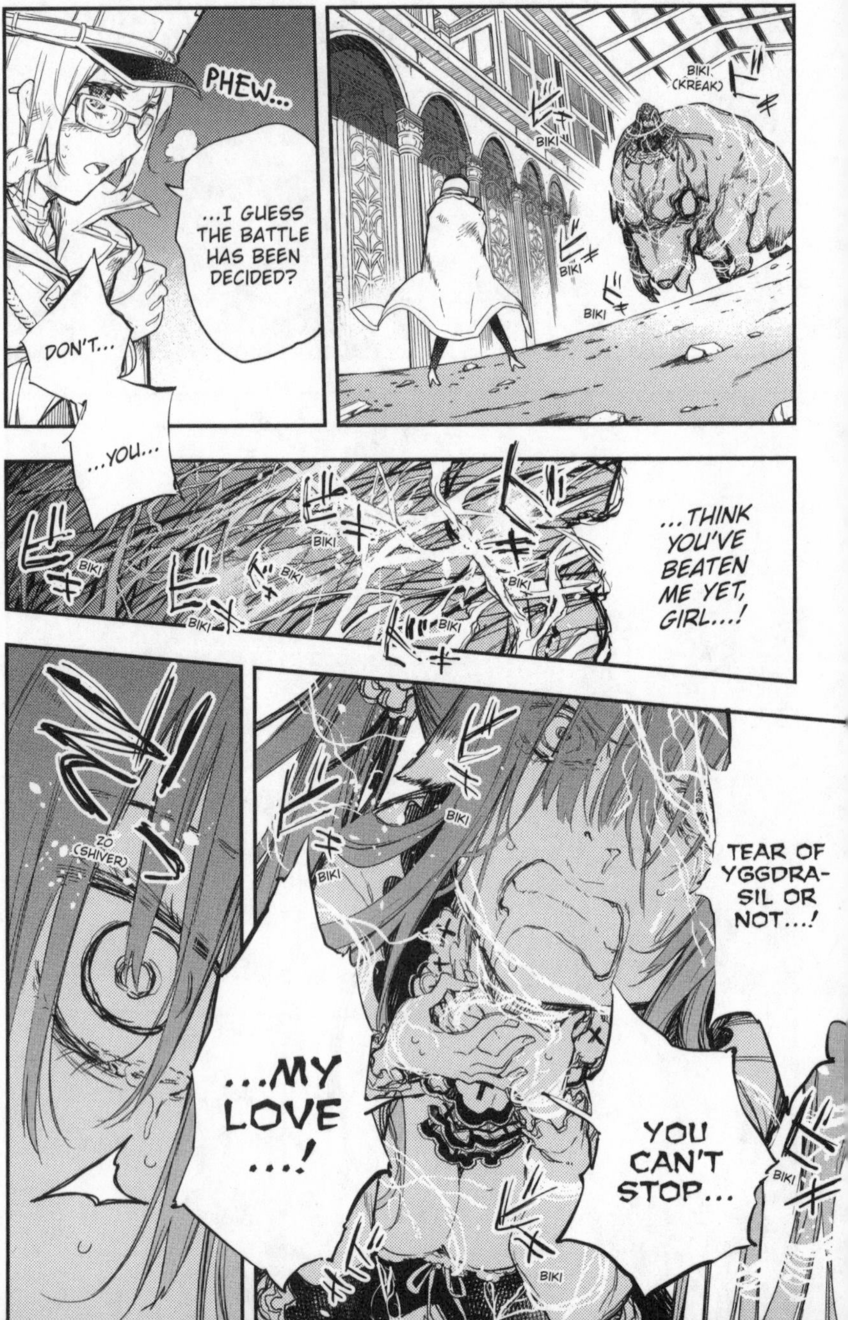
BIKI (KREAK)
BIKI
BIKI
BIKI
PHEW...
...I GUESS THE BATTLE HAS BEEN DECIDED?
DON'T...
...YOU...
...THINK YOU'VE BEATEN ME YET, GIRL...!
BIKI
BIKI
BIKI
BIKI
BIKI
BIKI
TEAR OF YGGDRA-SIL OR NOT...!
BIKI
BIKI
YOU CAN'T STOP...
BIKI
BIKI
...MY LOVE ...!
ZO (SHIVER)

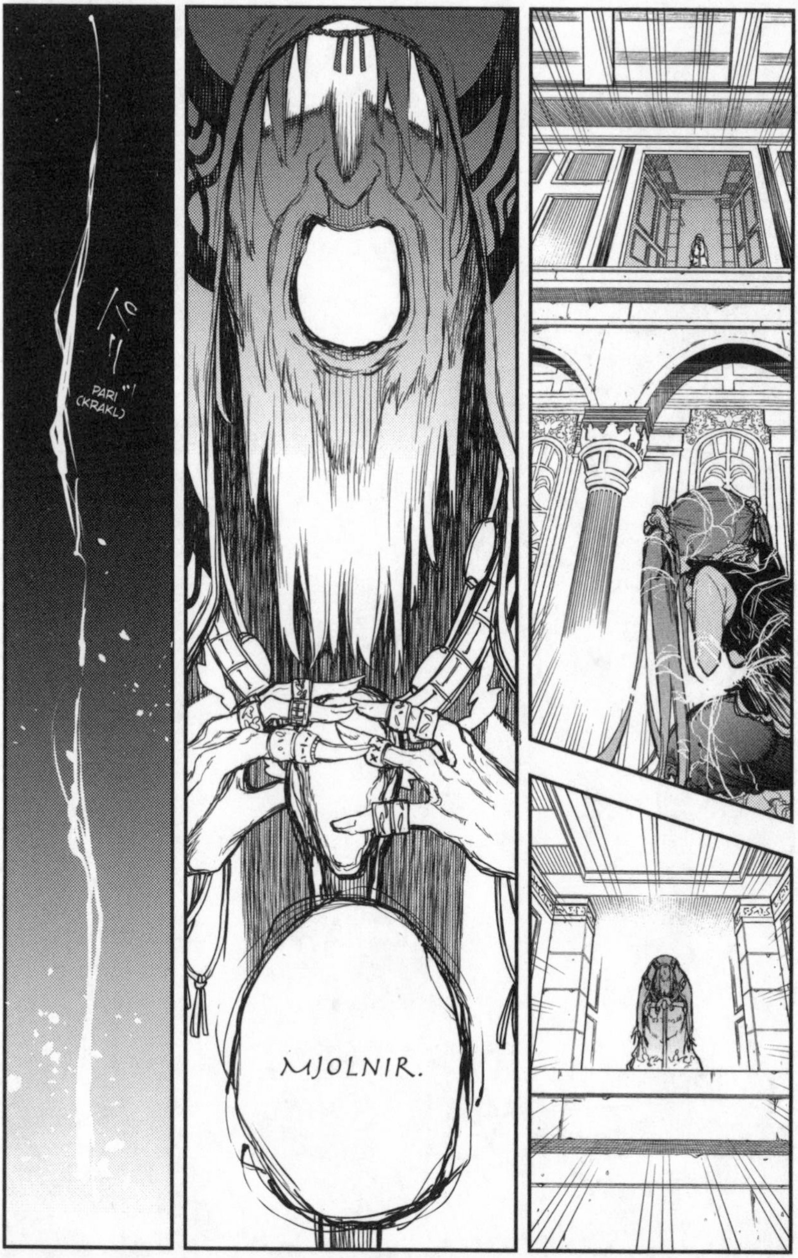
MJOLNIR.
PARI
(KRAKL)

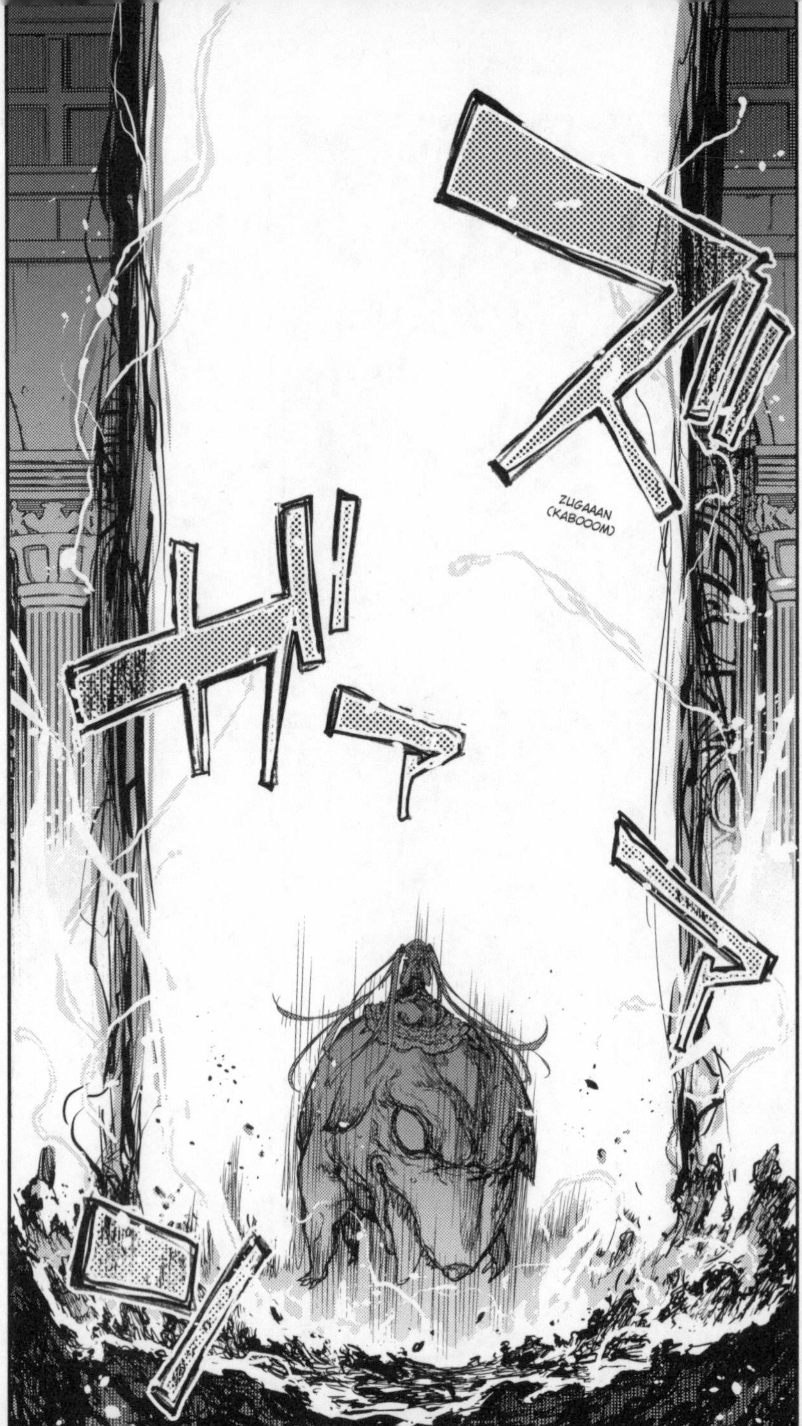
ZUGAAAN
(KABOOOM)

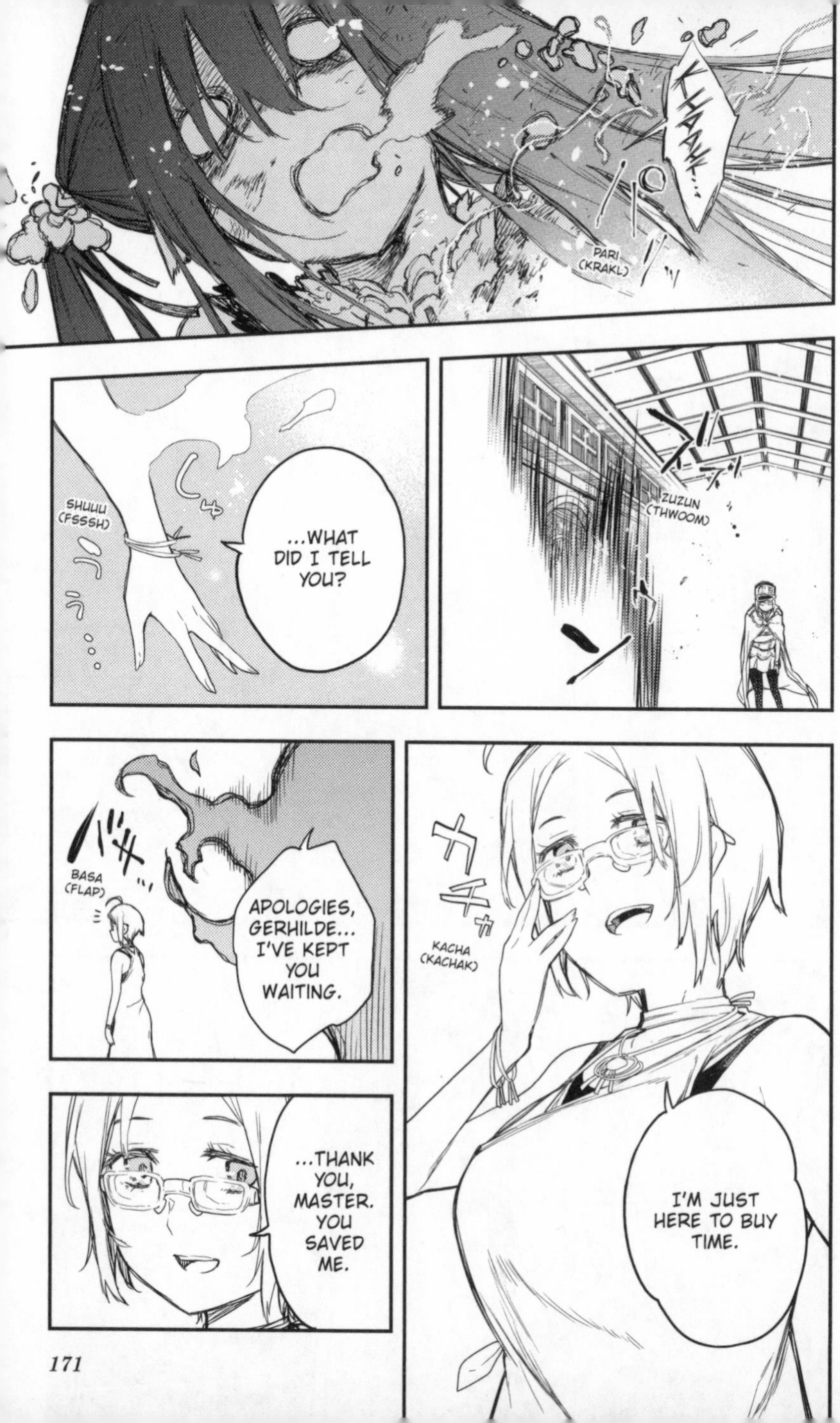
KHAAAK...
PARI (KRAKL)
ZUZUN (THWOOM)
SHUUU (FSSSH)
...WHAT DID I TELL YOU?
KACHA (KACHAK)
I'M JUST HERE TO BUY TIME.
BASA (FLAP)
APOLOGIES, GERHILDE... I'VE KEPT YOU WAITING.
...THANK YOU, MASTER. YOU SAVED ME.

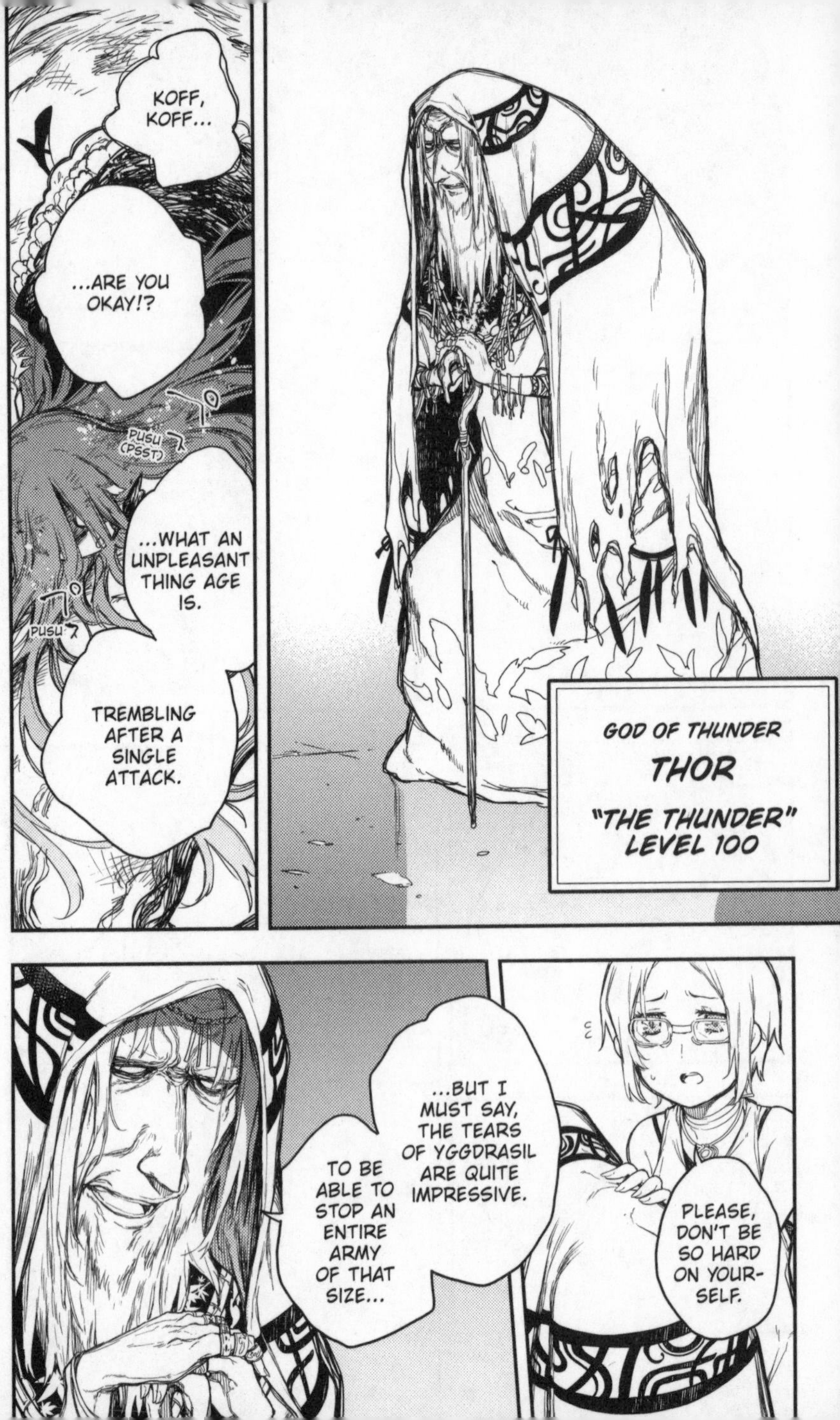
GOD OF THUNDER
THOR
"THE THUNDER"
LEVEL 100
KOFF, KOFF...
...ARE YOU OKAY!?
PUSU (PSST)
...WHAT AN UNPLEASANT THING AGE IS.
PUSU
TREMBLING AFTER A SINGLE ATTACK.
PLEASE, DON'T BE SO HARD ON YOURSELF.
...BUT I MUST SAY, THE TEARS OF YGGDRASIL ARE QUITE IMPRESSIVE.
TO BE ABLE TO STOP AN ENTIRE ARMY OF THAT SIZE...

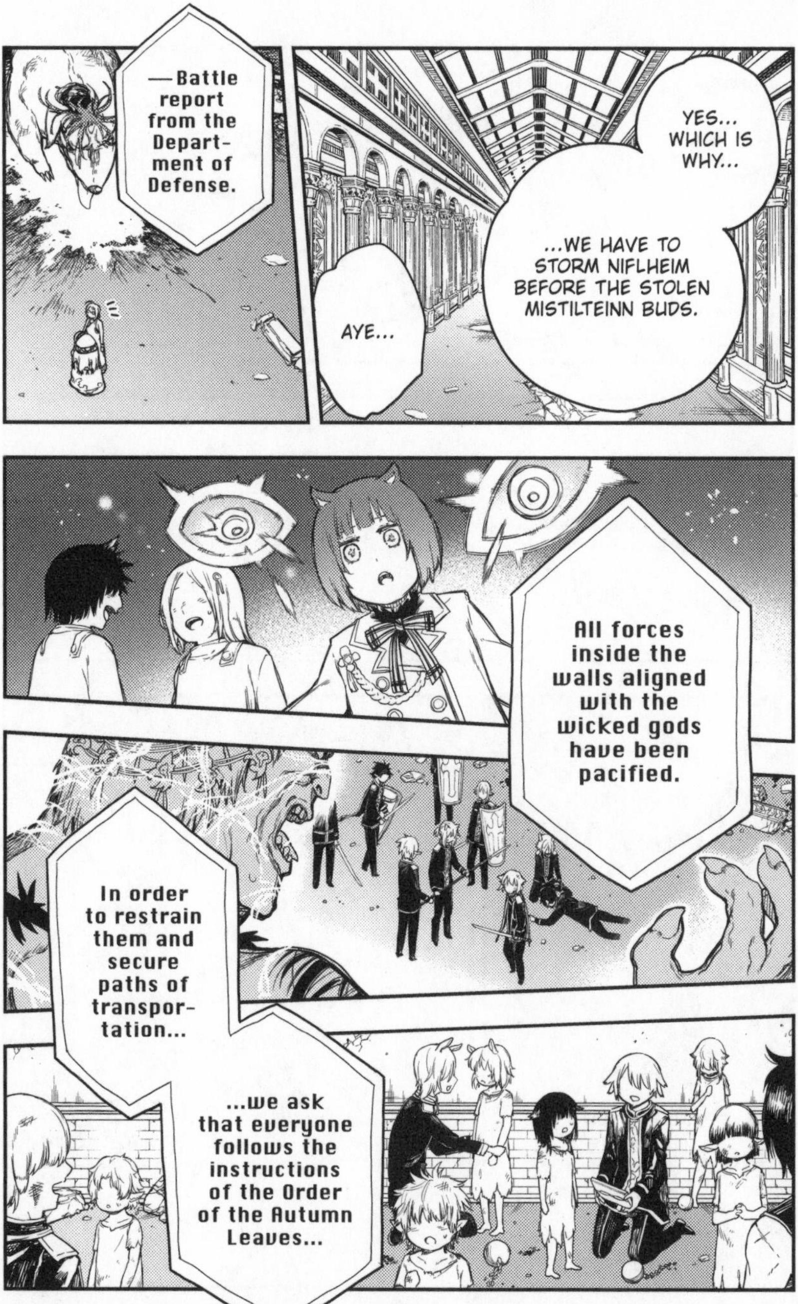
YES... WHICH IS WHY...
...WE HAVE TO STORM NIFLHEIM BEFORE THE STOLEN MISTILTEINN BUDS.
AYE...
—Battle report from the Depart-ment of Defense.
All forces inside the walls aligned with the wicked gods have been pacified.
In order to restrain them and secure paths of transpor-tation...
...we ask that everyone follows the instructions of the Order of the Autumn Leaves...

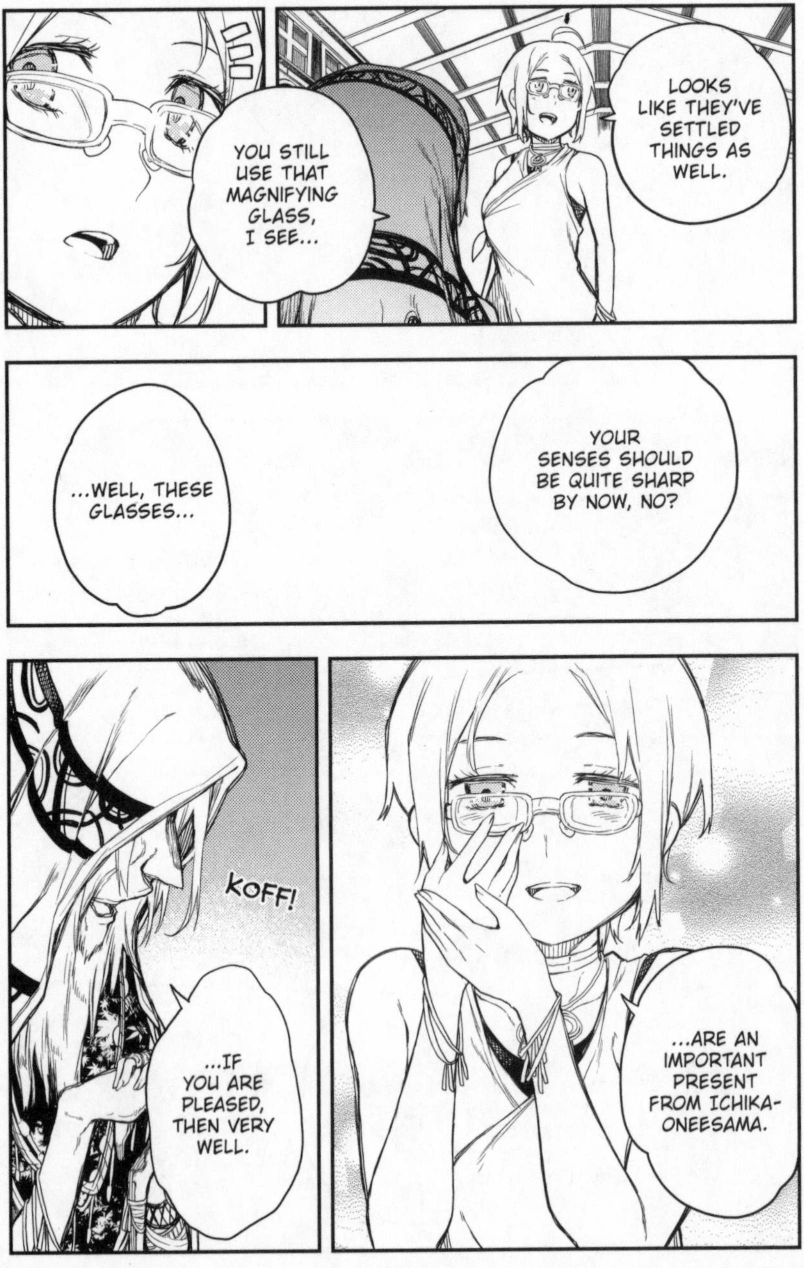
LOOKS LIKE THEY'VE SETTLED THINGS AS WELL.
YOU STILL USE THAT MAGNIFYING GLASS, I SEE...
YOUR SENSES SHOULD BE QUITE SHARP BY NOW, NO?
...WELL, THESE GLASSES...
...ARE AN IMPORTANT PRESENT FROM ICHIKA-ONEESAMA.
KOFF!
...IF YOU ARE PLEASED, THEN VERY WELL.

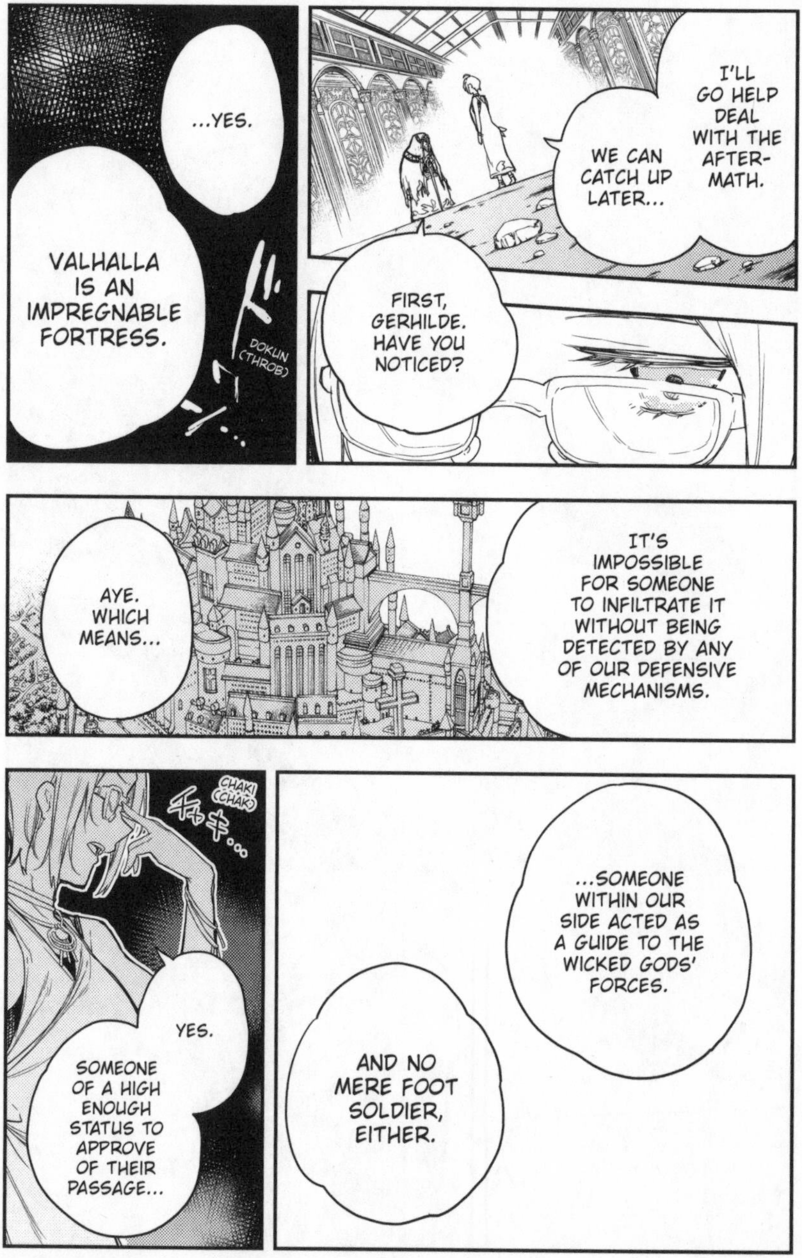
I'LL GO HELP DEAL WITH THE AFTER-MATH.
WE CAN CATCH UP LATER...
FIRST, GERHILDE. HAVE YOU NOTICED?
...YES.
VALHALLA IS AN IMPREGNABLE FORTRESS.
DOKUN (THROB)
IT'S IMPOSSIBLE FOR SOMEONE TO INFILTRATE IT WITHOUT BEING DETECTED BY ANY OF OUR DEFENSIVE MECHANISMS.
AYE. WHICH MEANS...
...SOMEONE WITHIN OUR SIDE ACTED AS A GUIDE TO THE WICKED GODS' FORCES.
AND NO MERE FOOT SOLDIER, EITHER.
CHAKI (CHAK)
YES.
SOMEONE OF A HIGH ENOUGH STATUS TO APPROVE OF THEIR PASSAGE...

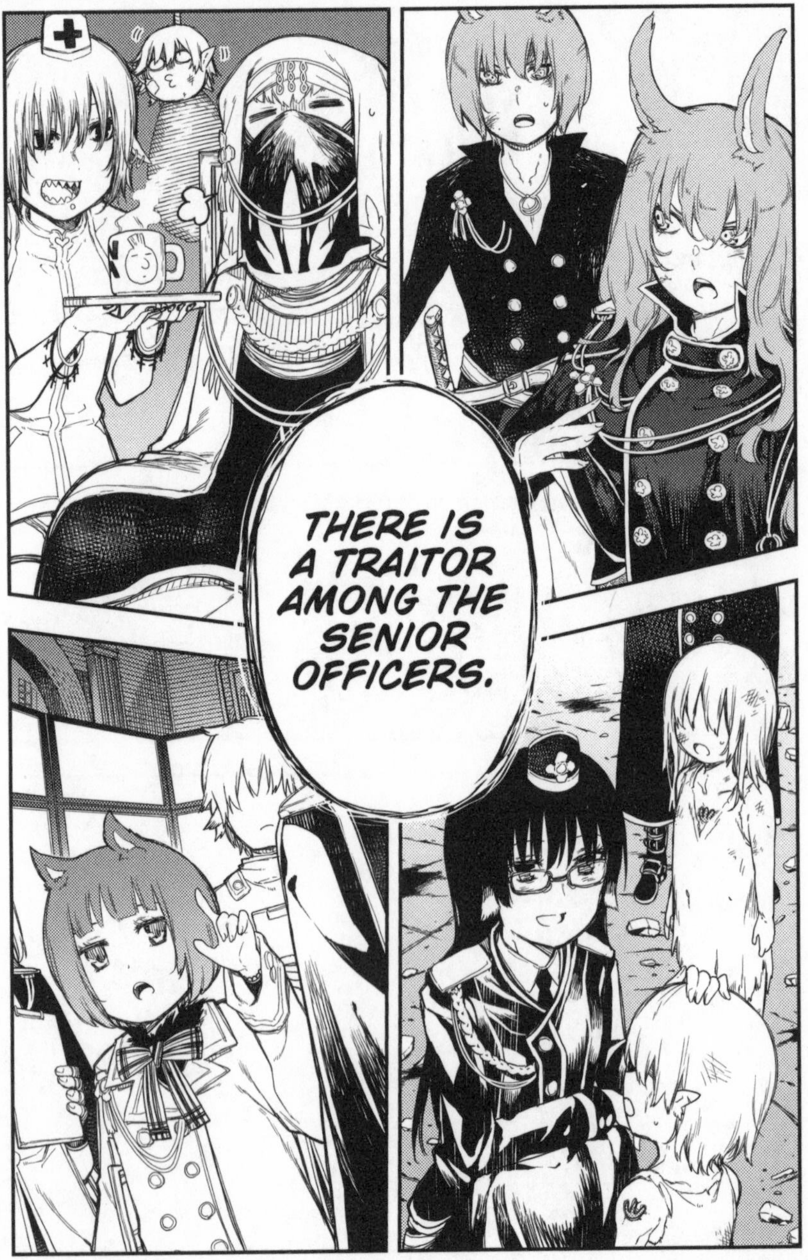
THERE IS A TRAITOR AMONG THE SENIOR OFFICERS.

Val X Love

MEANWHILE, IN MIDGARD (2)

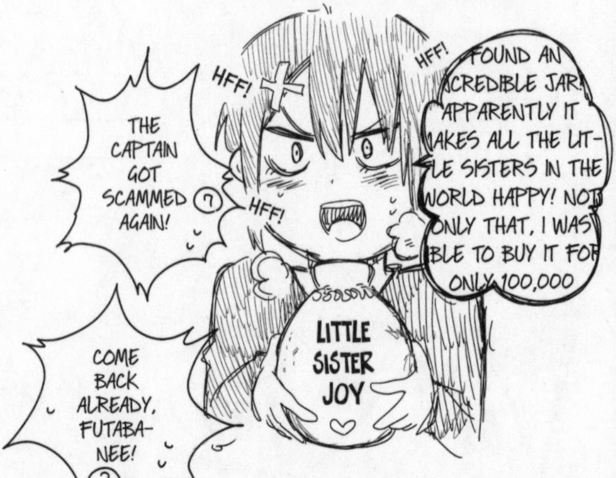
HFF!
FOUND AN CREDIBLE JAR! APPARENTLY IT AKES ALL THE LIT-LE SISTERS IN THE ORLD HAPPY! NOT ONLY THAT, I WAS BLE TO BUY IT FOR ONLY 100,000
HFF!
HFF!
THE CAPTAIN GOT SCAMMED AGAIN! 7
LITTLE SISTER JOY
COME BACK ALREADY, FUTABA-NEE! 3

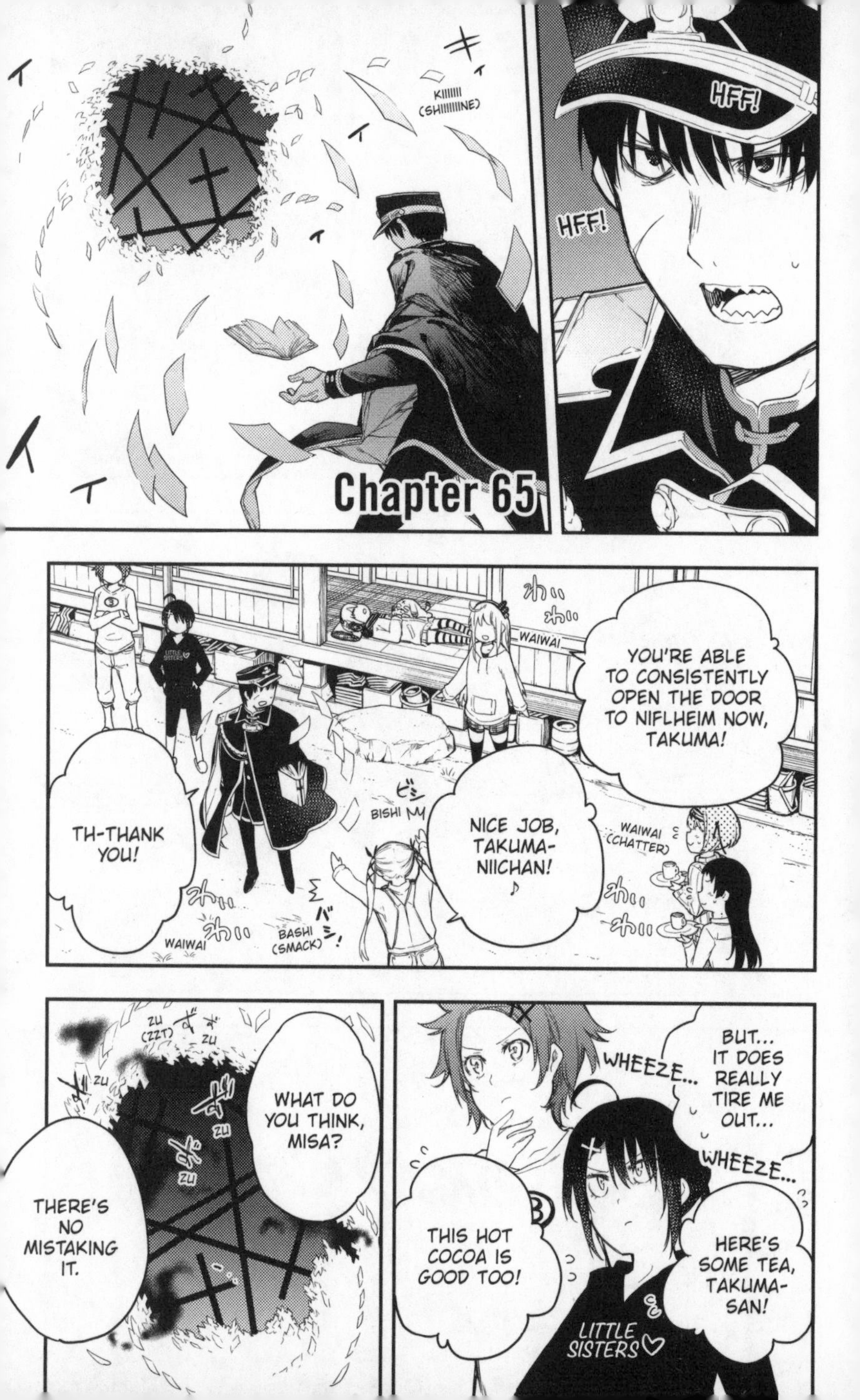
HFF!
HFF!
KIIIIIII (SHIIIIIINE)
Chapter 65
WAIWAI
YOU'RE ABLE TO CONSISTENTLY OPEN THE DOOR TO NIFLHEIM NOW, TAKUMA!
WAIWAI (CHATTER)
NICE JOB, TAKUMA-NIICHAN! ♪
BISHI
TH-THANK YOU!
BASHI (SMACK)
WAIWAI
BUT... IT DOES REALLY TIRE ME OUT...
WHEEZE...
WHEEZE...
HERE'S SOME TEA, TAKUMA-SAN!
THIS HOT COCOA IS GOOD TOO!
LITTLE SISTERS
WHAT DO YOU THINK, MISA?
ZU (ZZT) ZU
ZU
ZU
ZU
THERE'S NO MISTAKING IT.

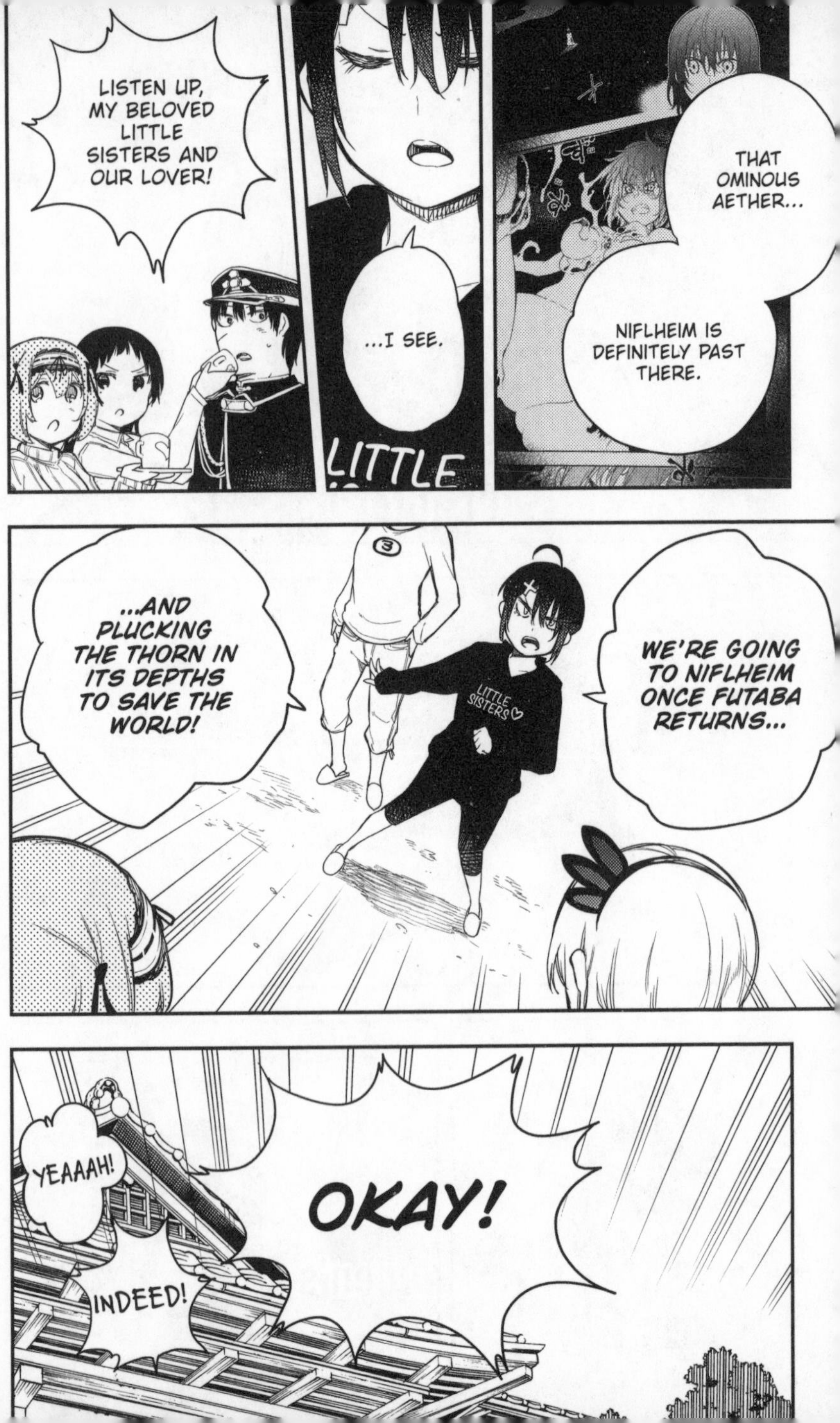
THAT OMINOUS AETHER...
NIFLHEIM IS DEFINITELY PAST THERE.
...I SEE.
LITTLE
LISTEN UP, MY BELOVED LITTLE SISTERS AND OUR LOVER!
WE'RE GOING TO NIFLHEIM ONCE FUTABA RETURNS...
LITTLE SISTERS♡
...AND PLUCKING THE THORN IN ITS DEPTHS TO SAVE THE WORLD!
OKAY!
YEAAAH!
INDEED!

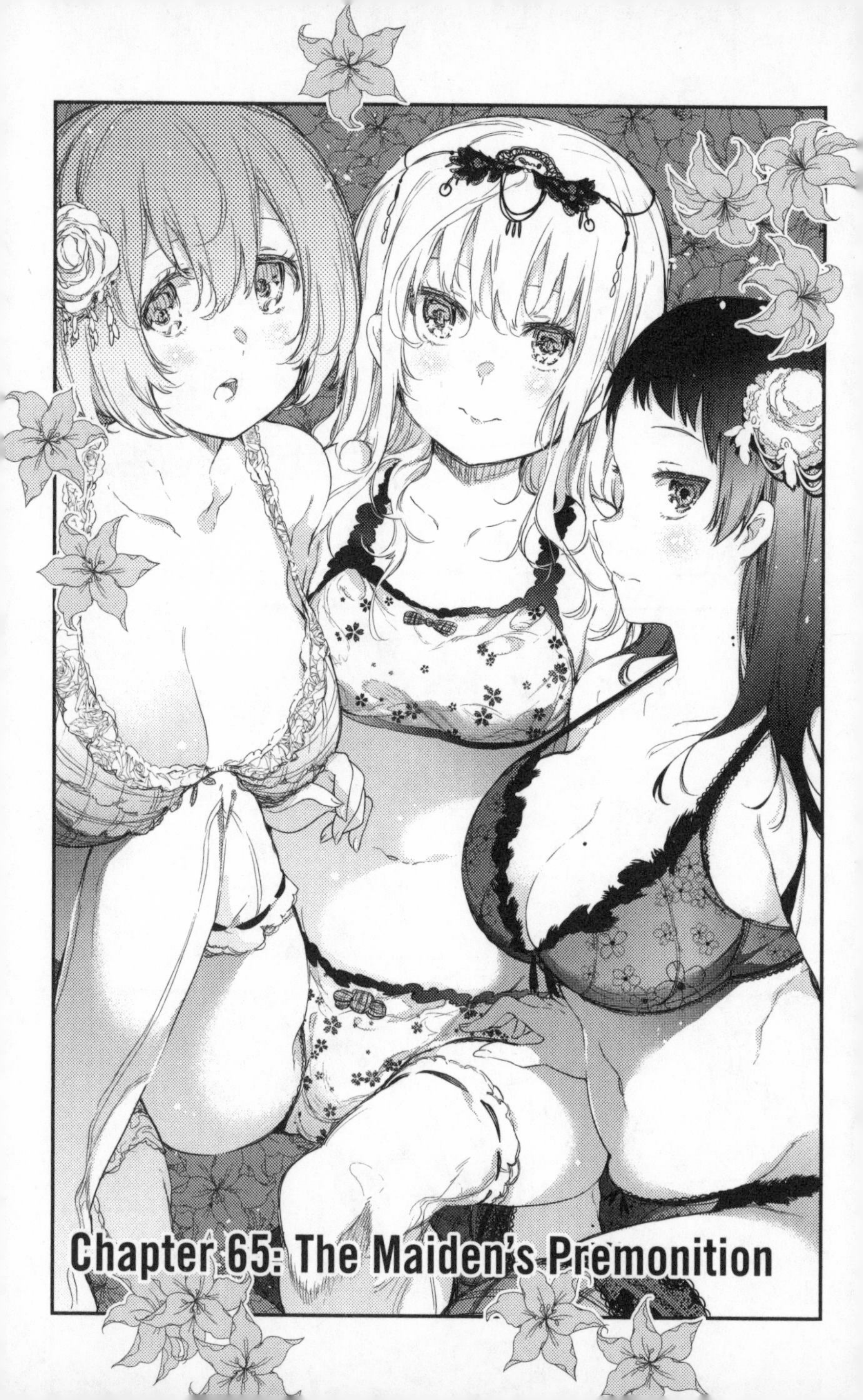

Chapter 65: The Maiden's Premonition

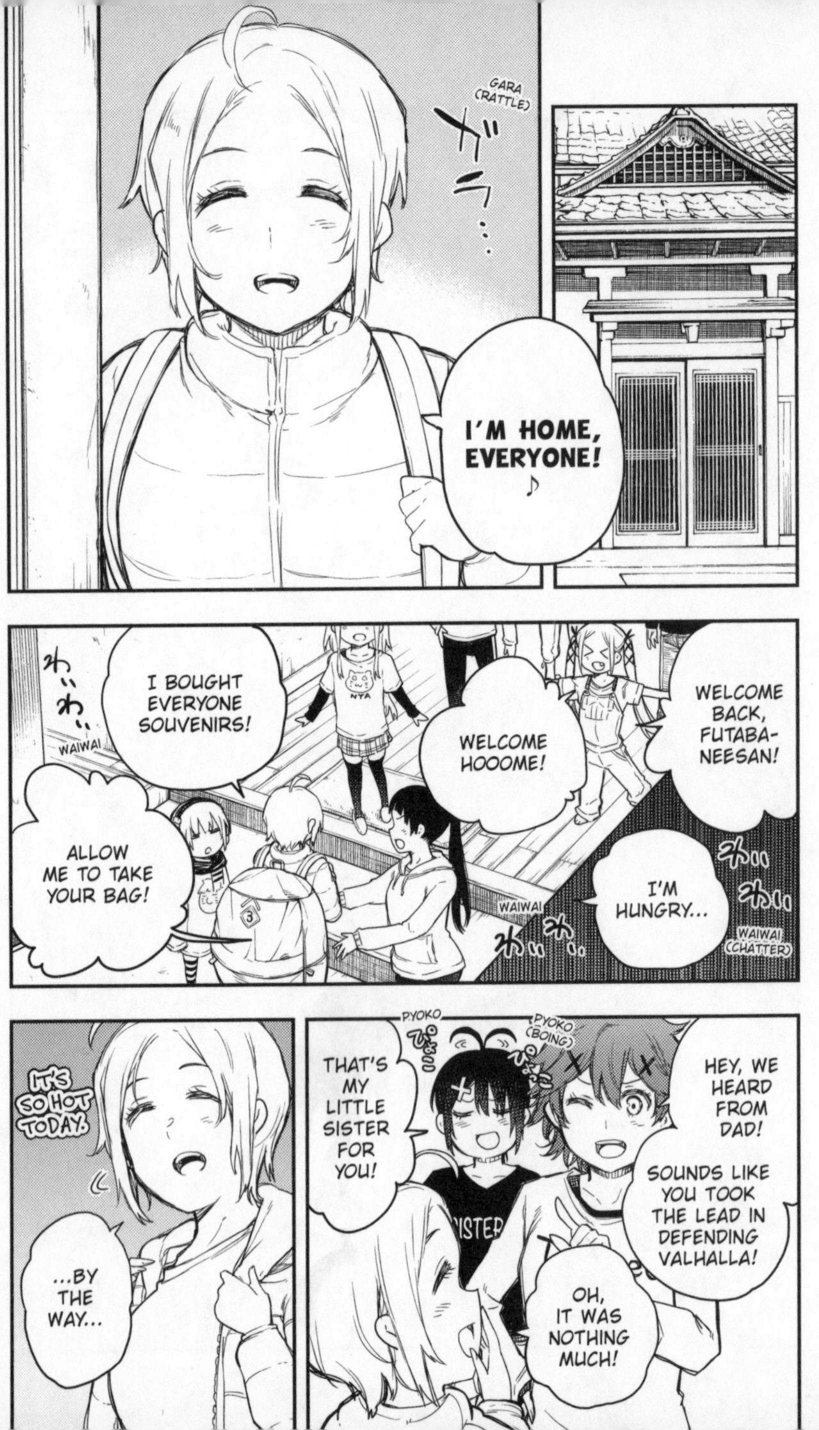
GARA (RATTLE)
I'M HOME, EVERYONE! ♪
WELCOME BACK, FUTABA-NEESAN!
WELCOME HOOOME!
I BOUGHT EVERYONE SOUVENIRS!
WAIWAI
I'M HUNGRY...
WAIWAI (CHATTER)
WAIWAI
ALLOW ME TO TAKE YOUR BAG!
PYOKO (BOING)
HEY, WE HEARD FROM DAD!
PYOKO
THAT'S MY LITTLE SISTER FOR YOU!
SOUNDS LIKE YOU TOOK THE LEAD IN DEFENDING VALHALLA!
OH, IT WAS NOTHING MUCH!
IT'S SO HOT TODAY.
...BY THE WAY...

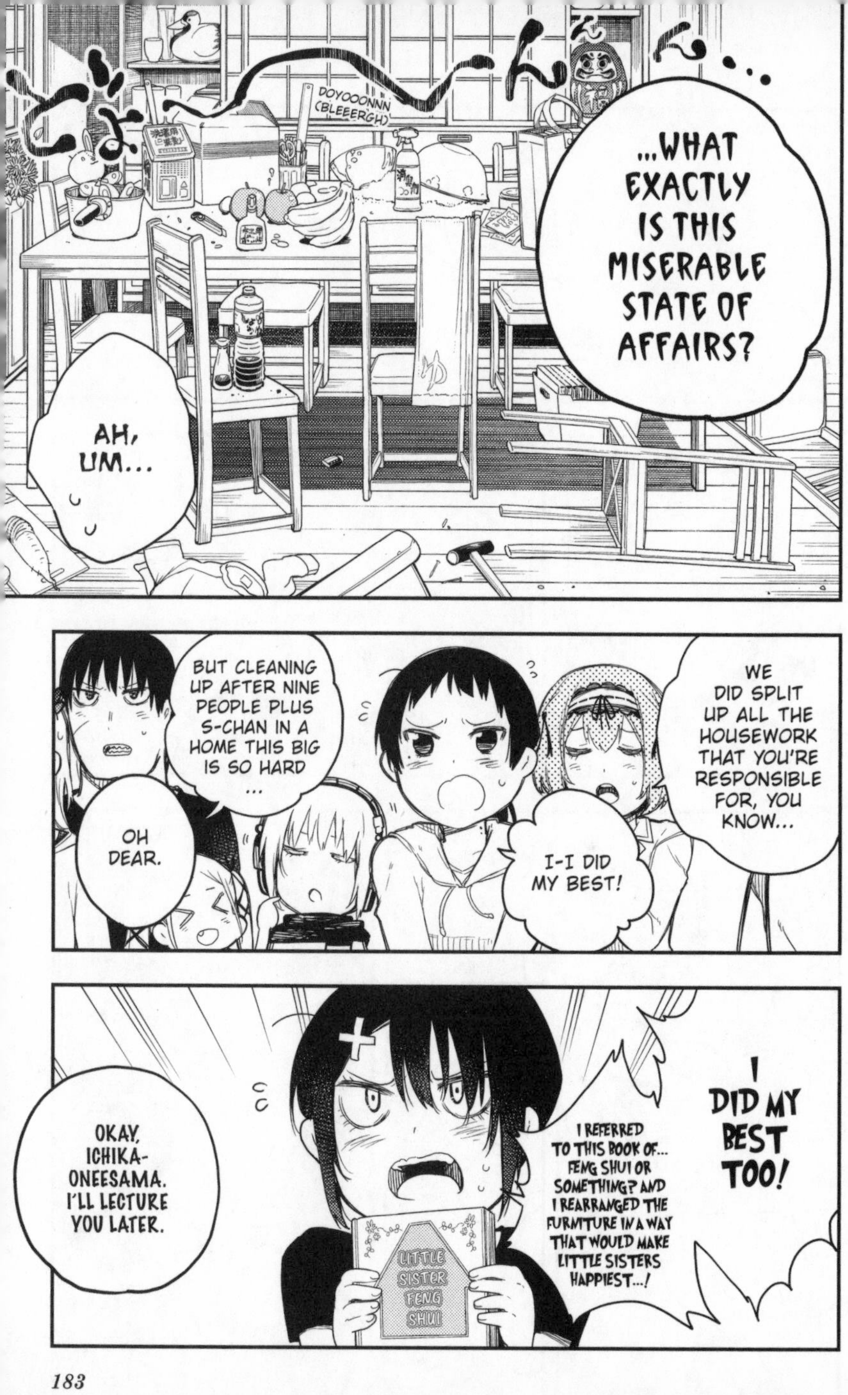
DOYOOONNN (BLEEERGH)
...WHAT EXACTLY IS THIS MISERABLE STATE OF AFFAIRS?
AH, UM...
WE DID SPLIT UP ALL THE HOUSEWORK THAT YOU'RE RESPONSIBLE FOR, YOU KNOW...
I-I DID MY BEST!
BUT CLEANING UP AFTER NINE PEOPLE PLUS S-CHAN IN A HOME THIS BIG IS SO HARD ...
OH DEAR.
I DID MY BEST TOO!
I REFERRED TO THIS BOOK OF... FENG SHUI OR SOMETHING? AND I REARRANGED THE FURNITURE IN A WAY THAT WOULD MAKE LITTLE SISTERS HAPPIEST...!
LITTLE SISTER FENG SHUI
OKAY, ICHIKA-ONEESAMA. I'LL LECTURE YOU LATER.

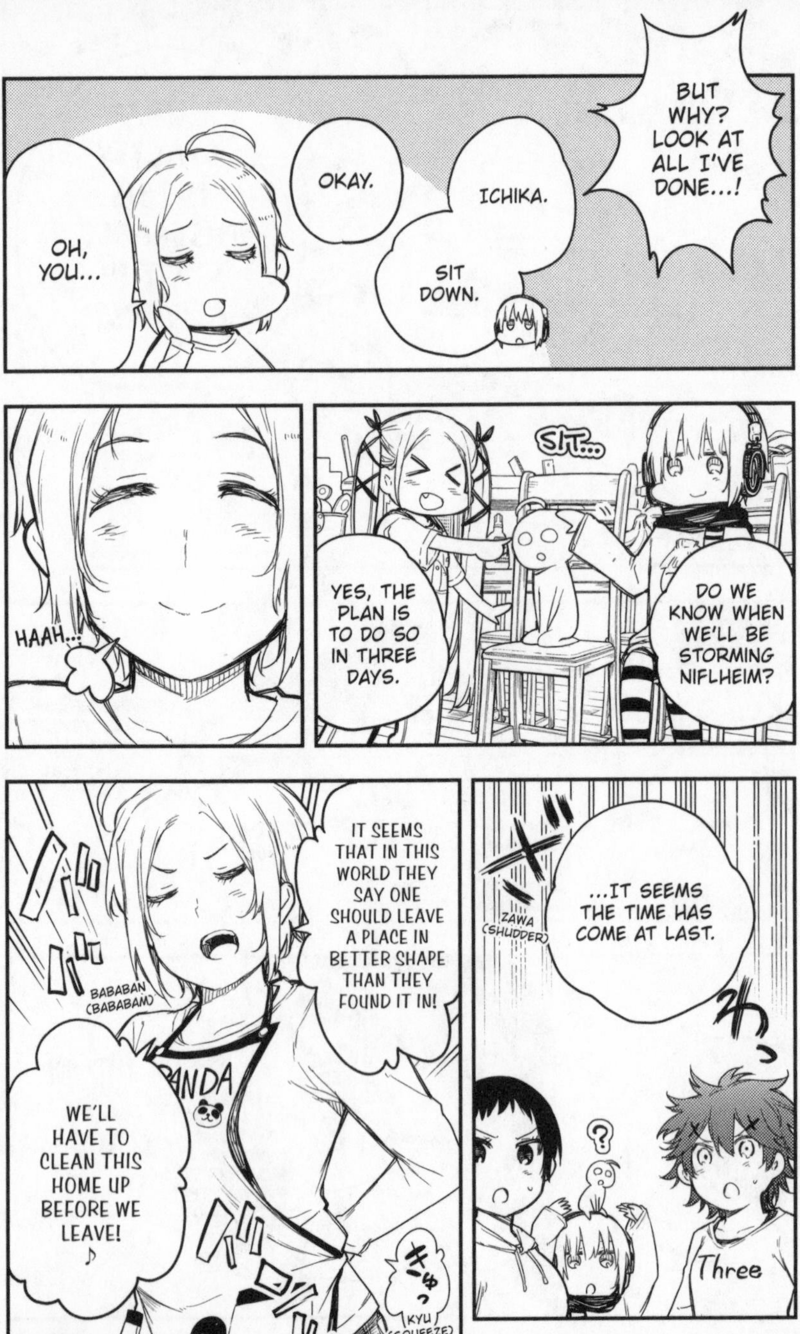
BUT WHY? LOOK AT ALL I'VE DONE...!
ICHIKA.
SIT DOWN.
OKAY.
OH, YOU...
SIT...
DO WE KNOW WHEN WE'LL BE STORMING NIFLHEIM?
YES, THE PLAN IS TO DO SO IN THREE DAYS.
HAAH...
...IT SEEMS THE TIME HAS COME AT LAST.
ZAWA (SHUDDER)
Three
IT SEEMS THAT IN THIS WORLD THEY SAY ONE SHOULD LEAVE A PLACE IN BETTER SHAPE THAN THEY FOUND IT IN!
BABABAN (BABABAM)
PANDA
WE'LL HAVE TO CLEAN THIS HOME UP BEFORE WE LEAVE! ♪
KYU (SQUEEZE)

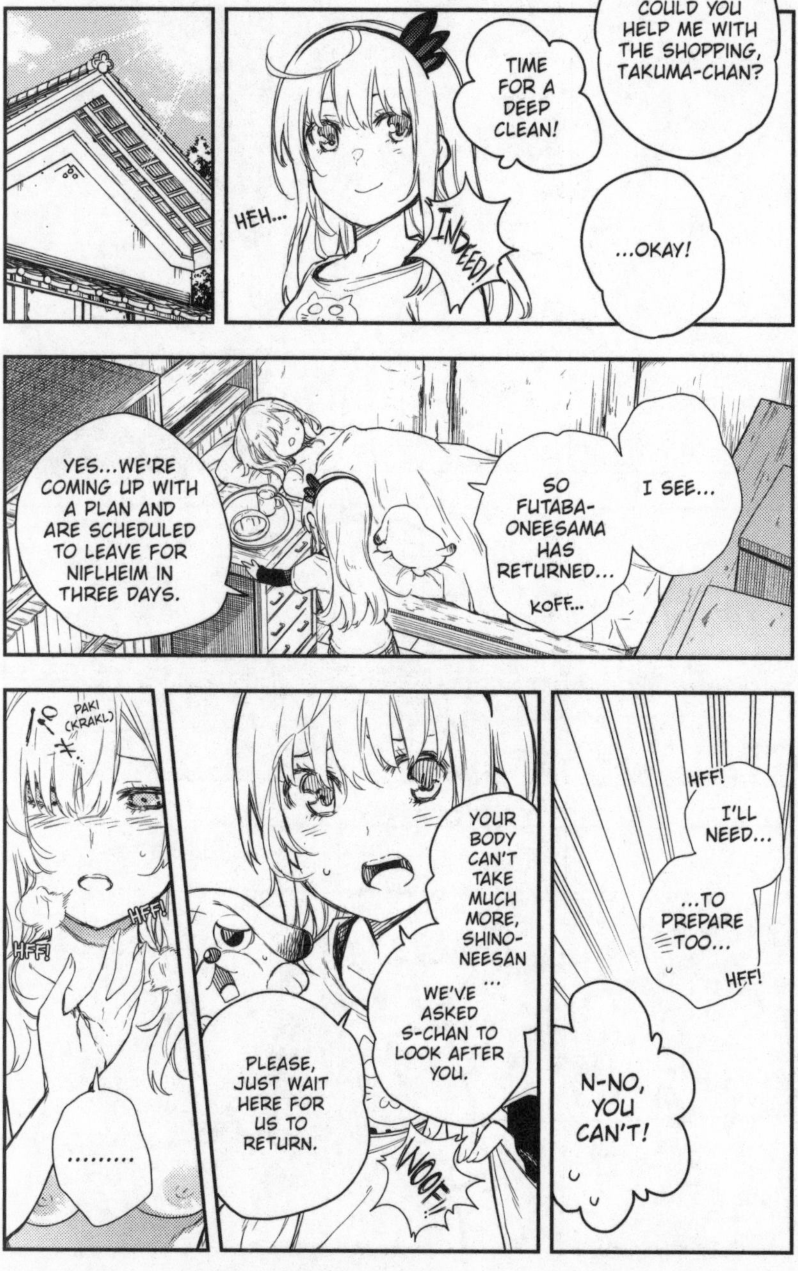
COULD YOU HELP ME WITH THE SHOPPING, TAKUMA-CHAN?
TIME FOR A DEEP CLEAN!
...OKAY!
INDEED!
HEH...
I SEE...
SO FUTABA-ONEESAMA HAS RETURNED... KOFF...
YES...WE'RE COMING UP WITH A PLAN AND ARE SCHEDULED TO LEAVE FOR NIFLHEIM IN THREE DAYS.
HFF! I'LL NEED...
...TO PREPARE TOO... HFF!
N-NO, YOU CAN'T!
YOUR BODY CAN'T TAKE MUCH MORE, SHINO-NEESAN...
WE'VE ASKED S-CHAN TO LOOK AFTER YOU.
PLEASE, JUST WAIT HERE FOR US TO RETURN.
WOOF!!
PAKI (KRAKL)
HFF!
HFF!
....

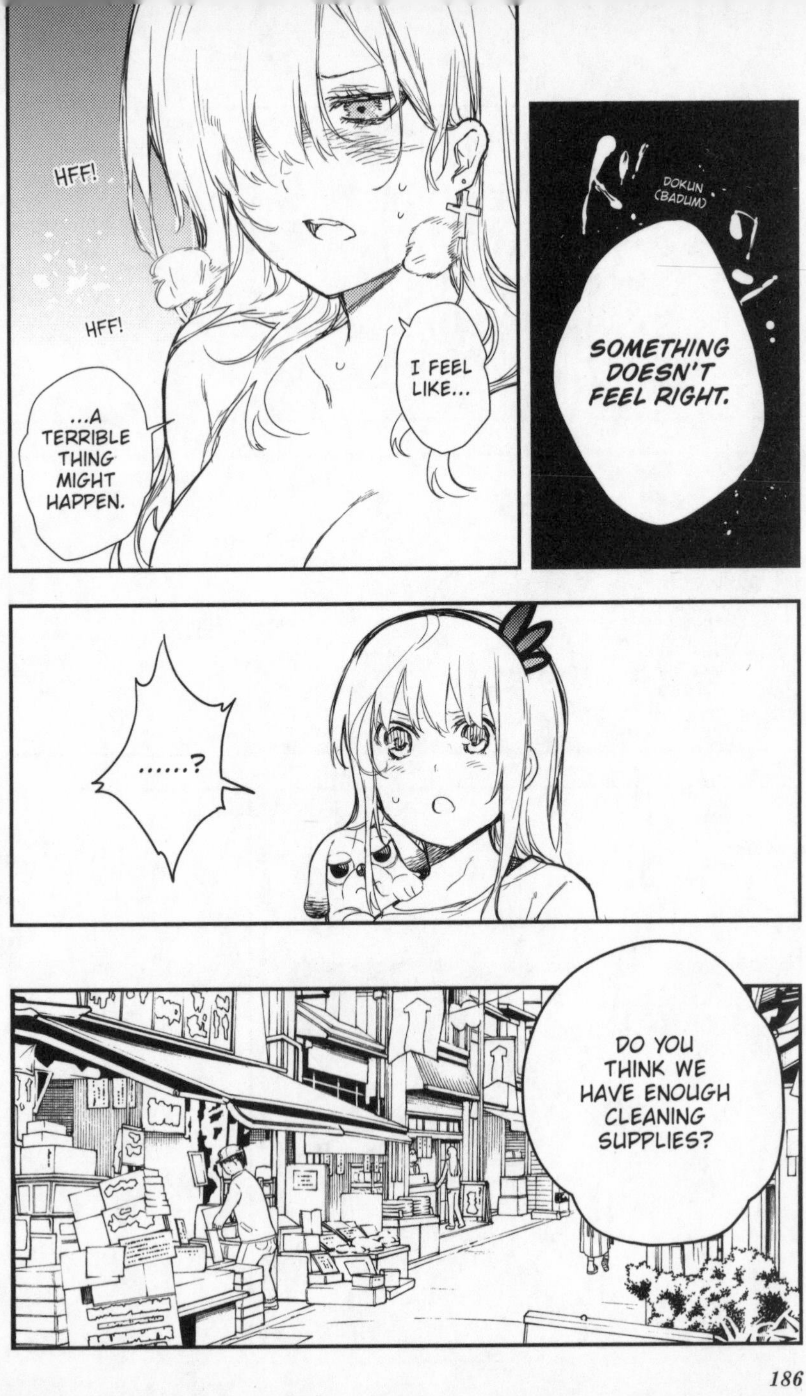
DOKUN (BADUM)
SOMETHING DOESN'T FEEL RIGHT.
HFF!
HFF!
I FEEL LIKE...
...A TERRIBLE THING MIGHT HAPPEN.
......?
DO YOU THINK WE HAVE ENOUGH CLEANING SUPPLIES?

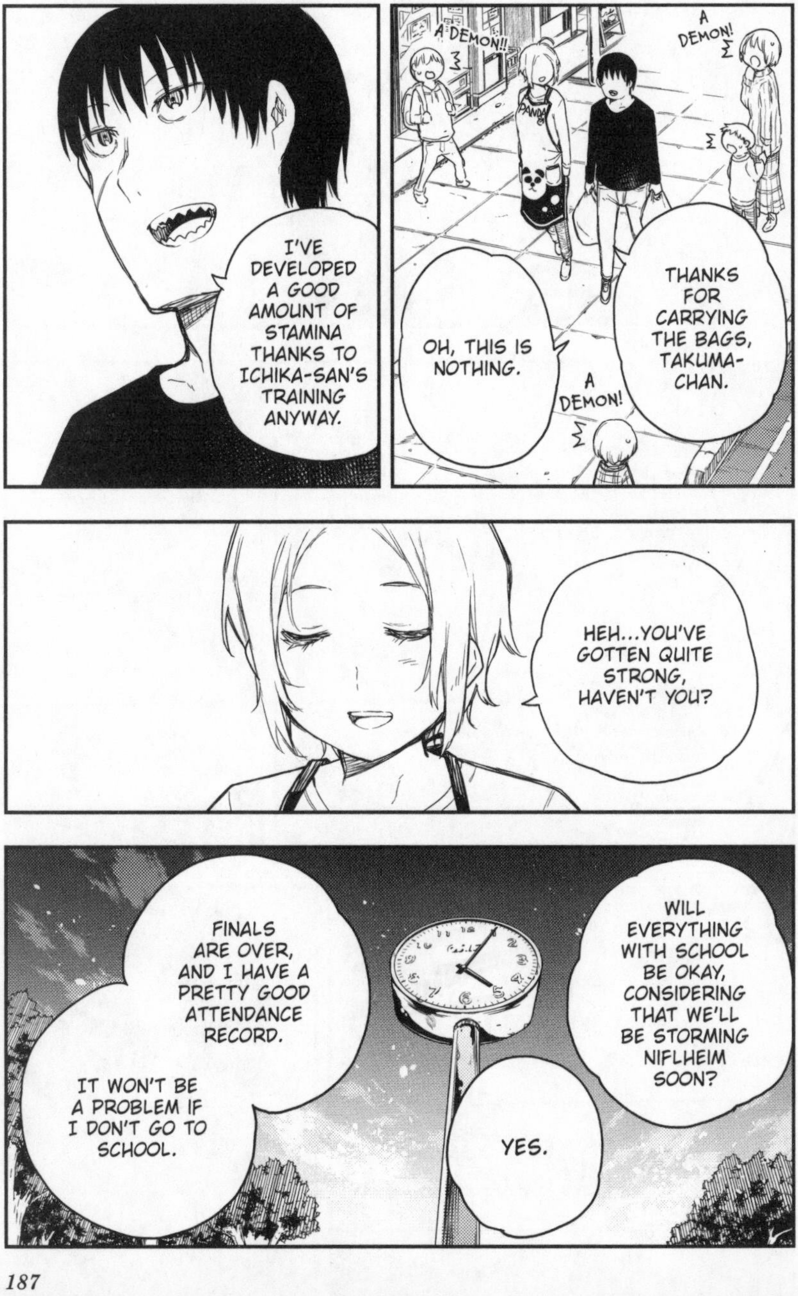
A DEMON!
A DEMON!!
THANKS FOR CARRYING THE BAGS, TAKUMA-CHAN.
OH, THIS IS NOTHING.
A DEMON!
I'VE DEVELOPED A GOOD AMOUNT OF STAMINA THANKS TO ICHIKA-SAN'S TRAINING ANYWAY.
HEH...YOU'VE GOTTEN QUITE STRONG, HAVEN'T YOU?
WILL EVERYTHING WITH SCHOOL BE OKAY, CONSIDERING THAT WE'LL BE STORMING NIFLHEIM SOON?
YES.
FINALS ARE OVER, AND I HAVE A PRETTY GOOD ATTENDANCE RECORD.
IT WON'T BE A PROBLEM IF I DON'T GO TO SCHOOL.

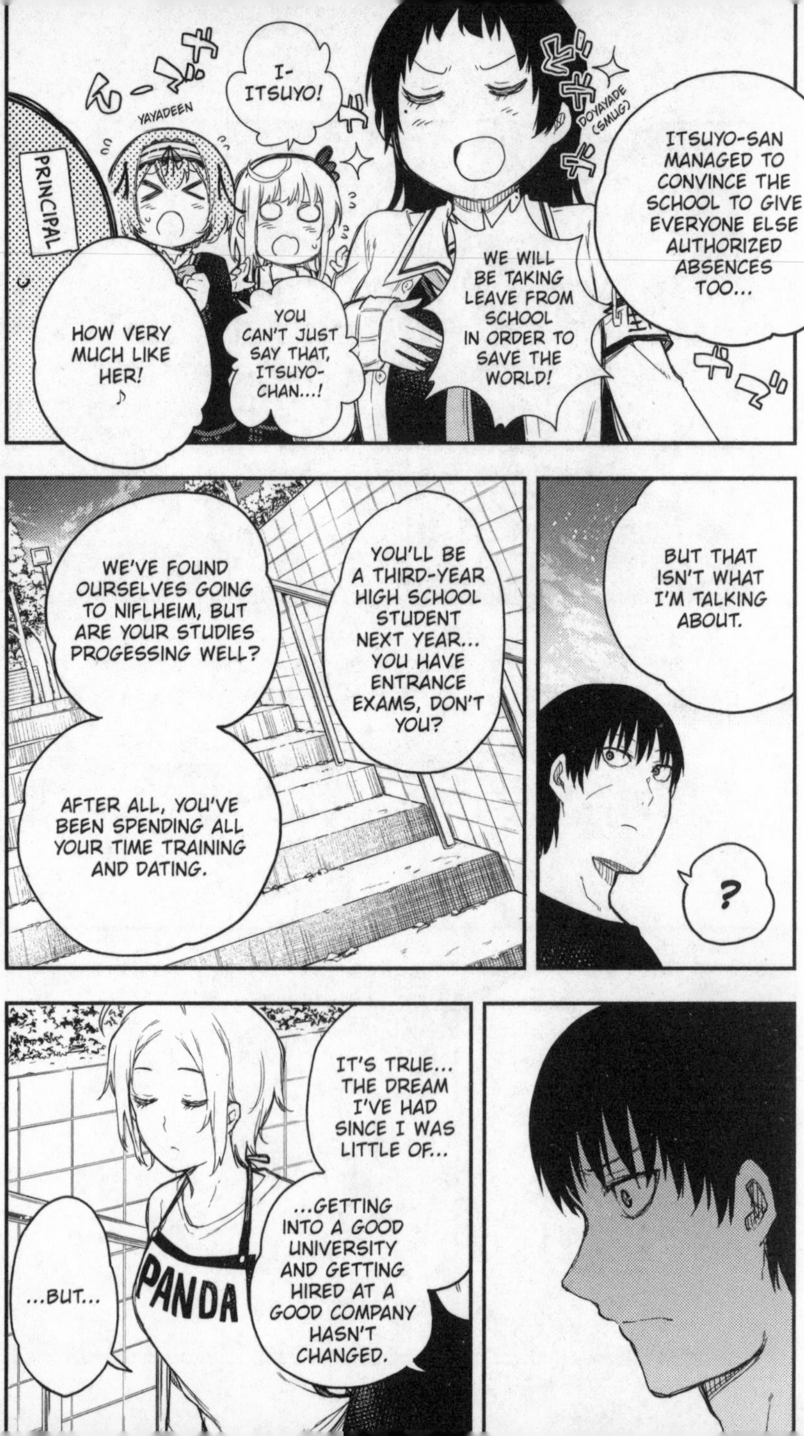
DOYAYADE (SMUG)
ITSUYO-SAN MANAGED TO CONVINCE THE SCHOOL TO GIVE EVERYONE ELSE AUTHORIZED ABSENCES TOO...
WE WILL BE TAKING LEAVE FROM SCHOOL IN ORDER TO SAVE THE WORLD!
I- ITSUYO!
YAYADEEN
YOU CAN'T JUST SAY THAT, ITSUYO-CHAN...!
PRINCIPAL
HOW VERY MUCH LIKE HER! ♪
BUT THAT ISN'T WHAT I'M TALKING ABOUT.
?
YOU'LL BE A THIRD-YEAR HIGH SCHOOL STUDENT NEXT YEAR... YOU HAVE ENTRANCE EXAMS, DON'T YOU?
WE'VE FOUND OURSELVES GOING TO NIFLHEIM, BUT ARE YOUR STUDIES PROGESSING WELL?
AFTER ALL, YOU'VE BEEN SPENDING ALL YOUR TIME TRAINING AND DATING.
IT'S TRUE... THE DREAM I'VE HAD SINCE I WAS LITTLE OF...
...GETTING INTO A GOOD UNIVERSITY AND GETTING HIRED AT A GOOD COMPANY HASN'T CHANGED.
PANDA
...BUT...

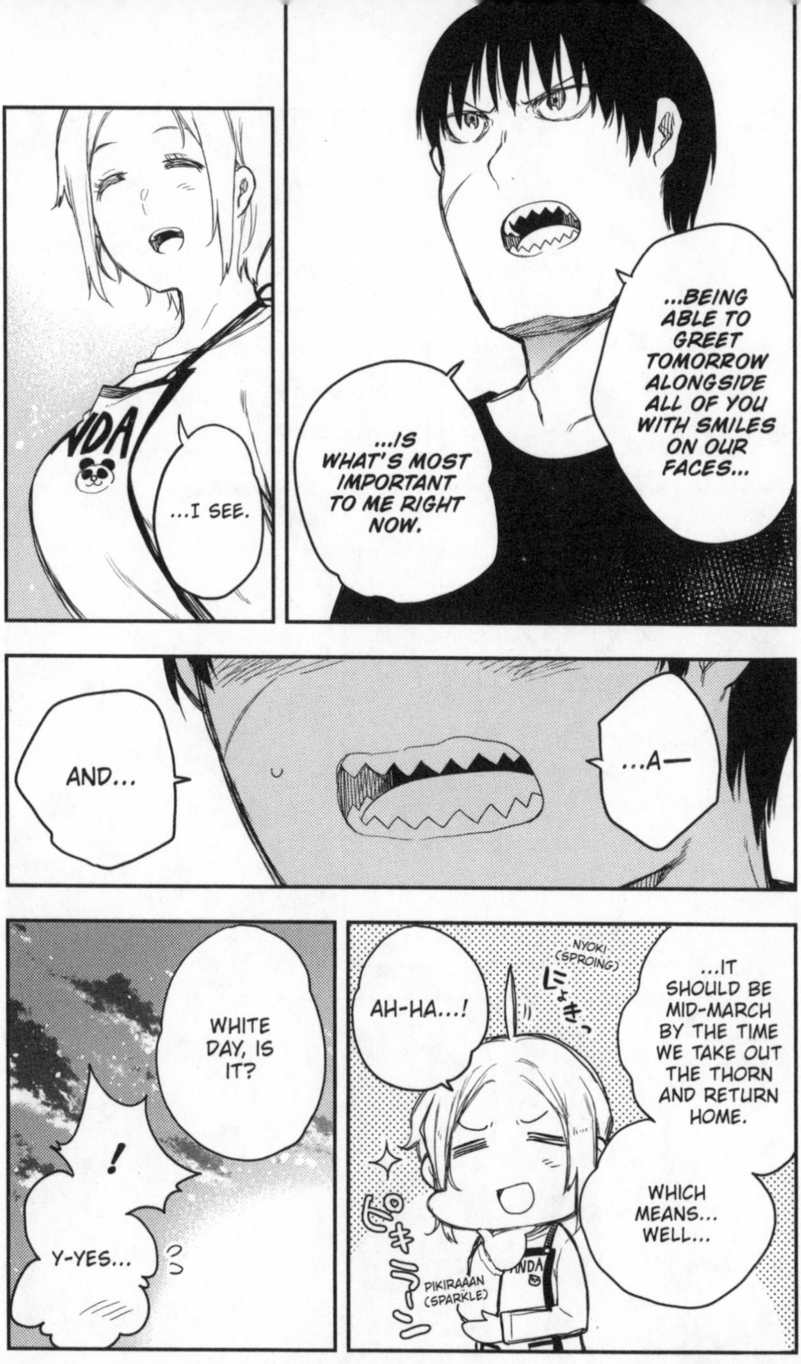
...BEING ABLE TO GREET TOMORROW ALONGSIDE ALL OF YOU WITH SMILES ON OUR FACES...
...IS WHAT'S MOST IMPORTANT TO ME RIGHT NOW.
...I SEE.
...A—
AND...
...IT SHOULD BE MID-MARCH BY THE TIME WE TAKE OUT THE THORN AND RETURN HOME.
NYOKI (SPROING)
AH-HA...!
WHICH MEANS... WELL...
PIKIRAAAN (SPARKLE)
WHITE DAY, IS IT?
!
Y-YES...

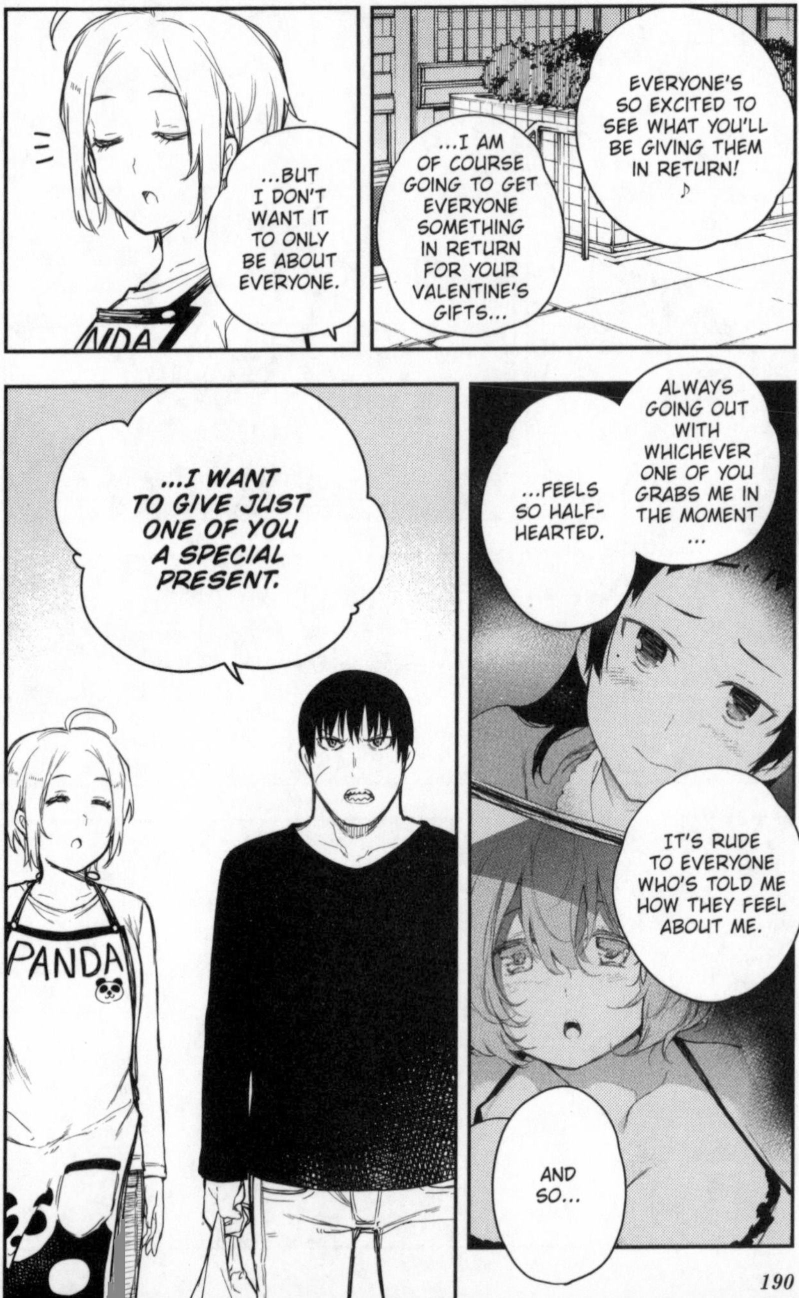
EVERYONE'S SO EXCITED TO SEE WHAT YOU'LL BE GIVING THEM IN RETURN! ♪
...I AM OF COURSE GOING TO GET EVERYONE SOMETHING IN RETURN FOR YOUR VALENTINE'S GIFTS...
...BUT I DON'T WANT IT TO ONLY BE ABOUT EVERYONE.
ALWAYS GOING OUT WITH WHICHEVER ONE OF YOU GRABS ME IN THE MOMENT ...
...FEELS SO HALF-HEARTED.
IT'S RUDE TO EVERYONE WHO'S TOLD ME HOW THEY FEEL ABOUT ME.
AND SO...
...I WANT TO GIVE JUST ONE OF YOU A SPECIAL PRESENT.
PANDA

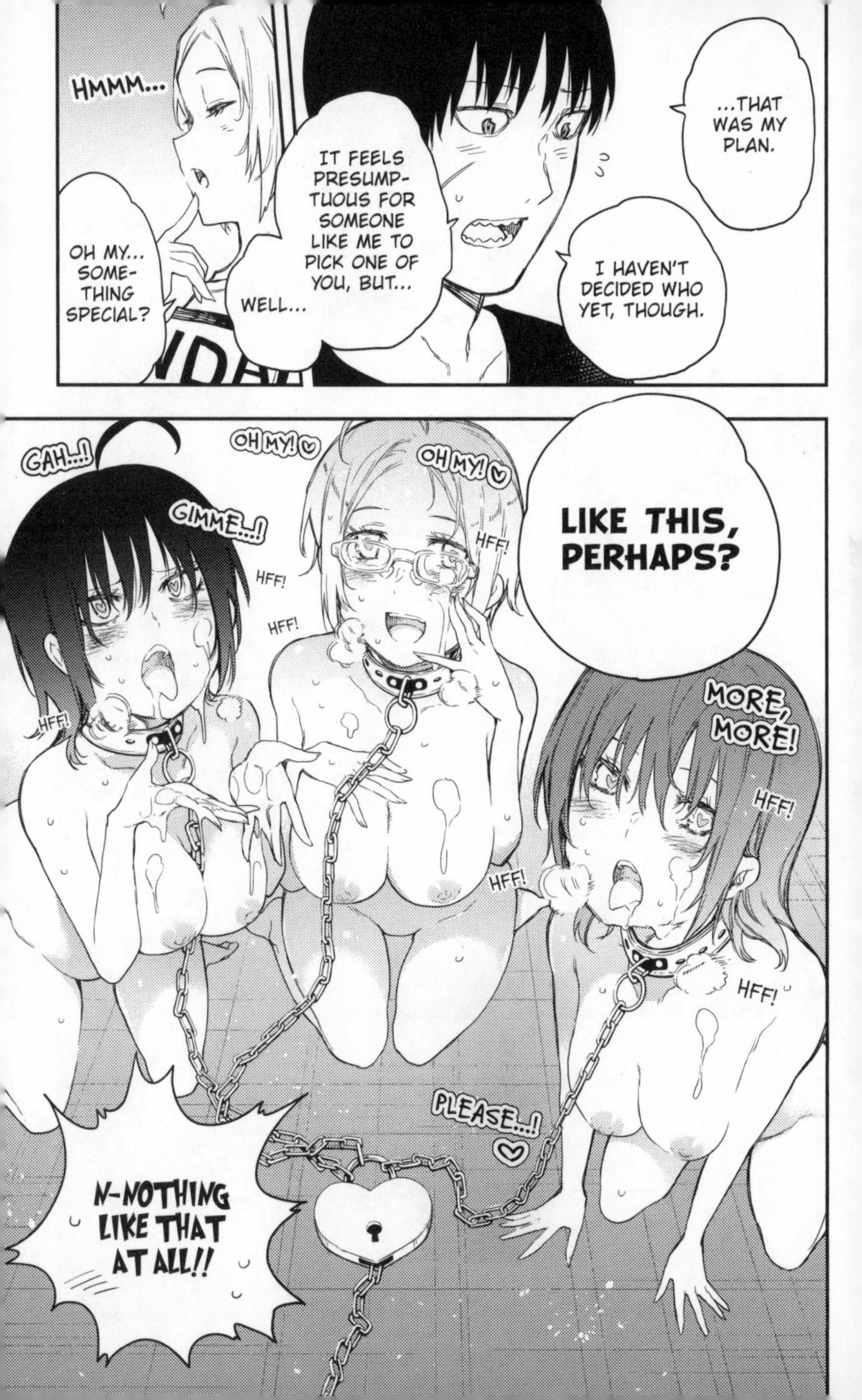
...THAT WAS MY PLAN.
I HAVEN'T DECIDED WHO YET, THOUGH.
IT FEELS PRESUMPTUOUS FOR SOMEONE LIKE ME TO PICK ONE OF YOU, BUT...
WELL...
HMMM...
OH MY... SOMETHING SPECIAL?
LIKE THIS, PERHAPS?
MORE, MORE!
HFF!
HFF!
HFF!
OH MY! ♡
HFF!
OH MY! ♡
GIMME...!
HFF!
HFF!
GAH...!
HFF!
PLEASE...! ♡
N-NOTHING LIKE THAT AT ALL!!

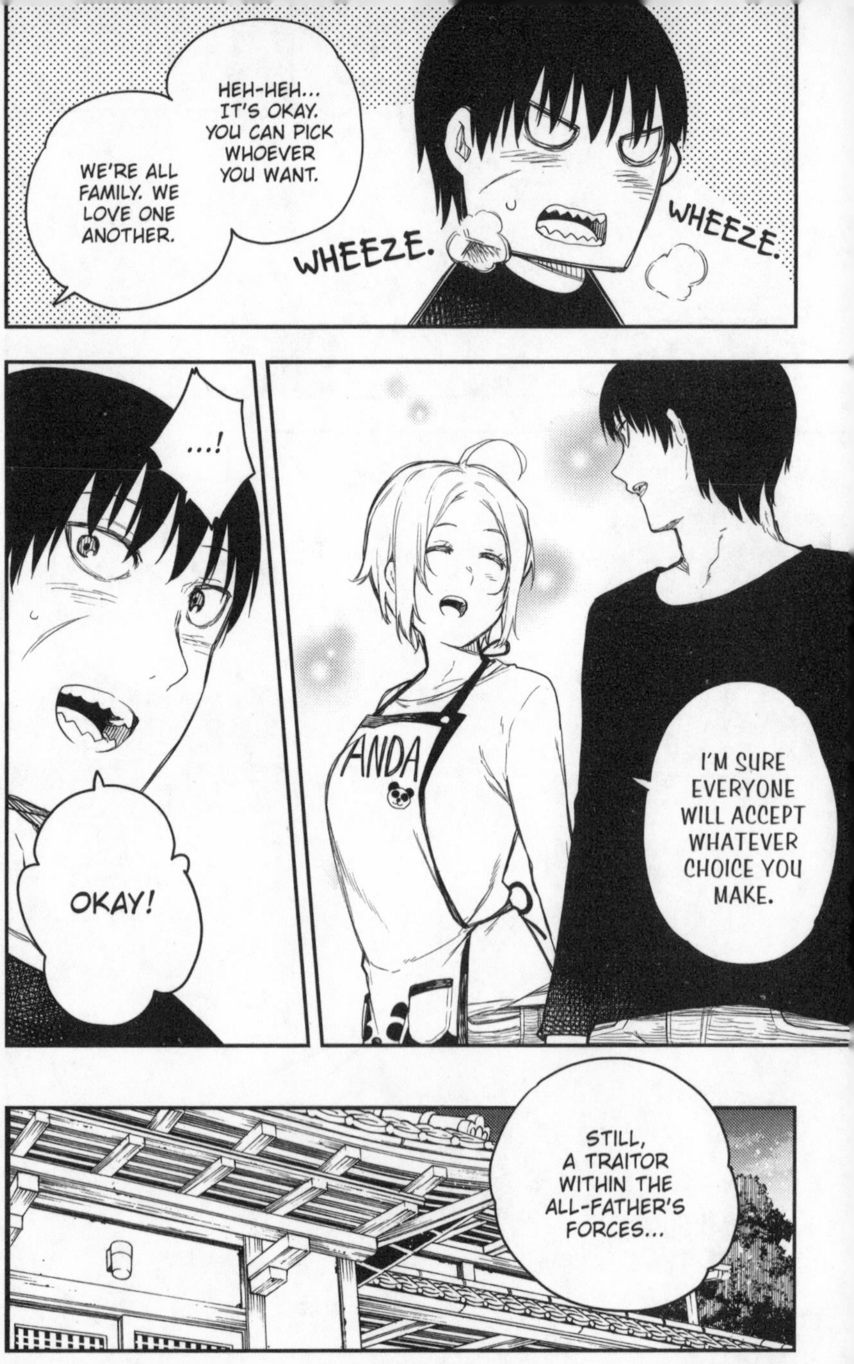
HEH-HEH... IT'S OKAY. YOU CAN PICK WHOEVER YOU WANT.
WE'RE ALL FAMILY. WE LOVE ONE ANOTHER.
WHEEZE.
WHEEZE.
I'M SURE EVERYONE WILL ACCEPT WHATEVER CHOICE YOU MAKE.
...!
OKAY!
STILL, A TRAITOR WITHIN THE ALL-FATHER'S FORCES...

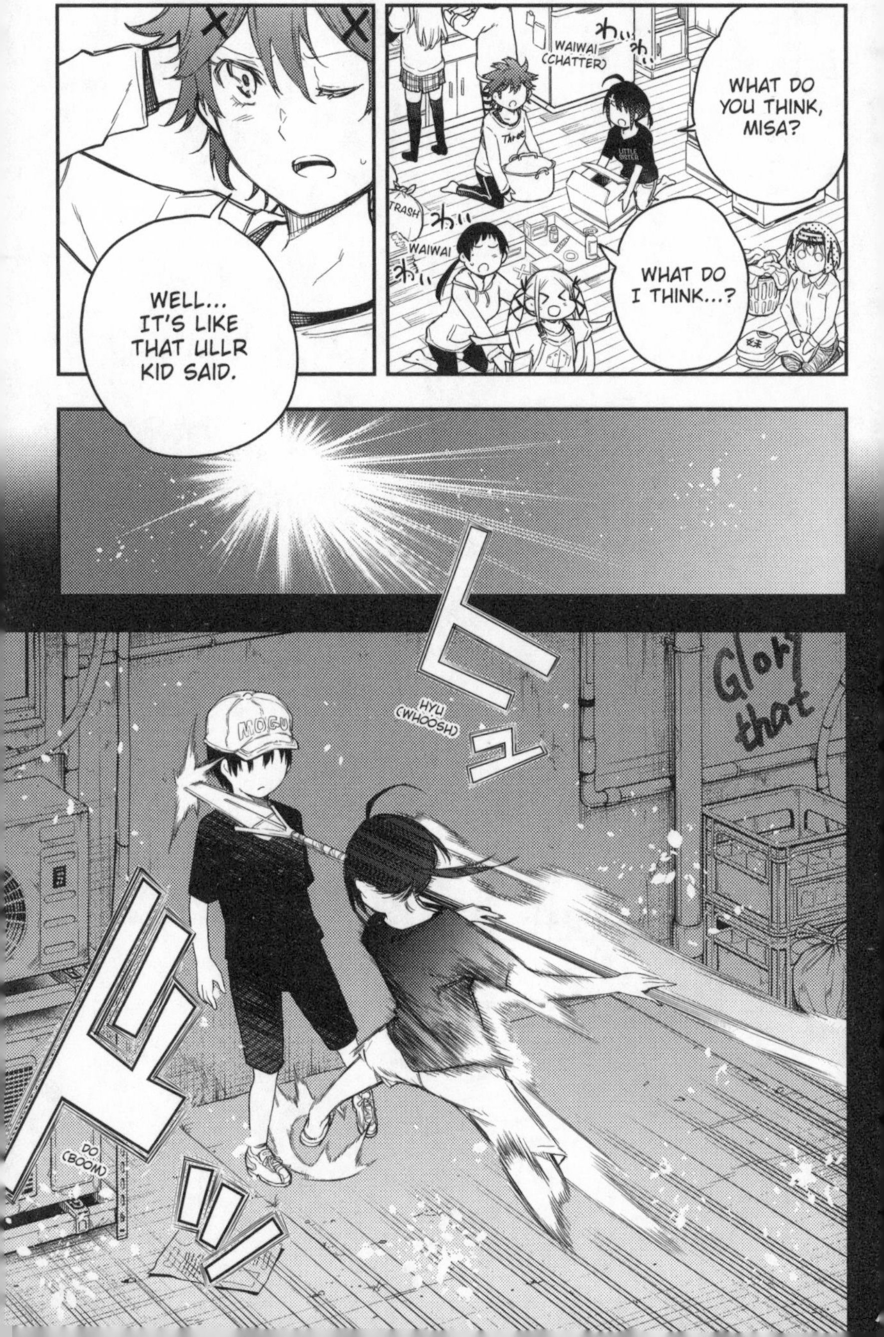
WHAT DO YOU THINK, MISA?
WAIWAI (CHATTER)
Three
LITTLE SISTER
TRASH
WAIWAI
WHAT DO I THINK...?
WELL... IT'S LIKE THAT ULLR KID SAID.
HYU (WHOOSH)
MOGU
DO (BOOM)

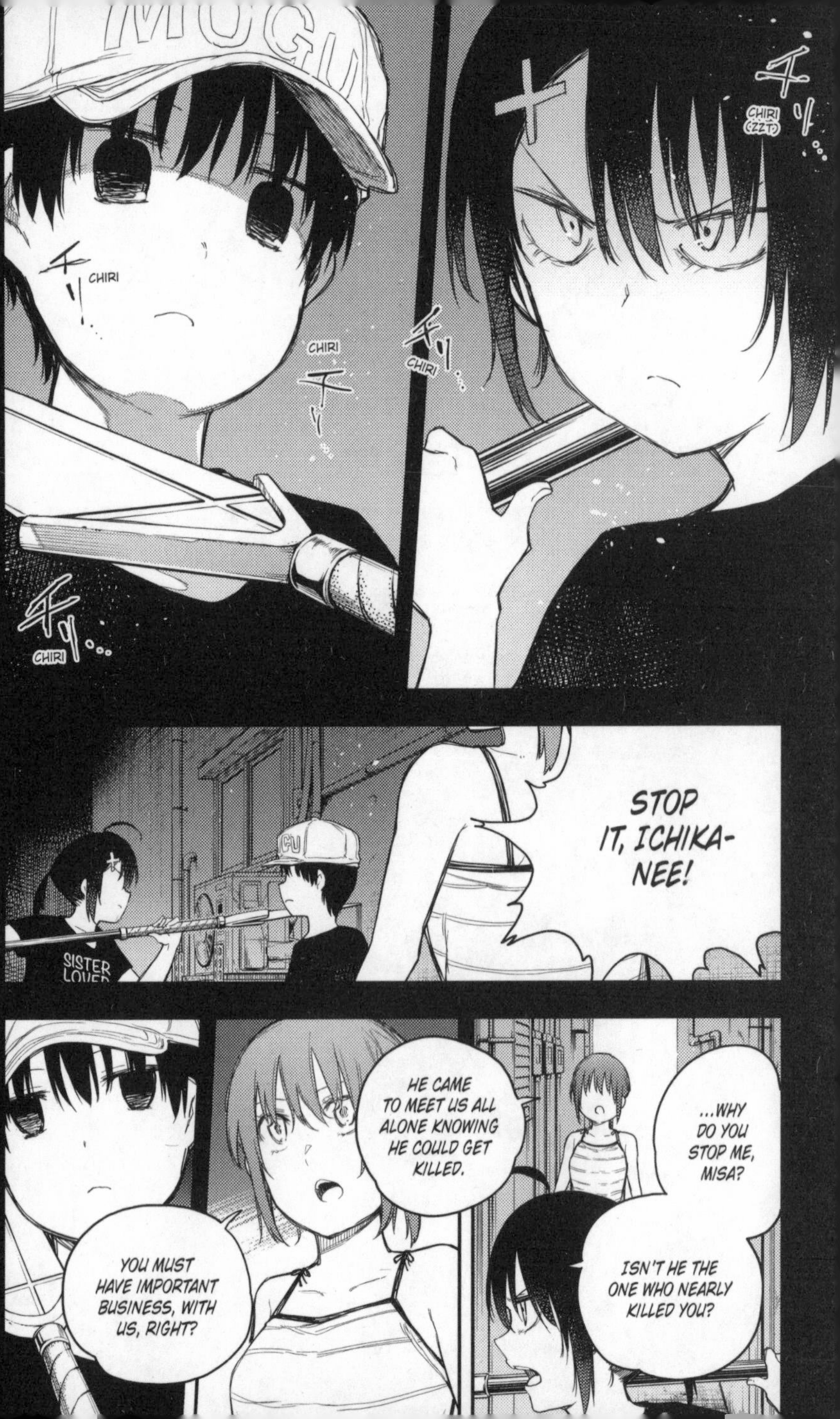
CHIRI (ZZT)
CHIRI
CHIRI
CHIRI
CHIRI
STOP IT, ICHIKA-NEE!
SISTER
...WHY DO YOU STOP ME, MISA?
ISN'T HE THE ONE WHO NEARLY KILLED YOU?
HE CAME TO MEET US ALL ALONE KNOWING HE COULD GET KILLED.
YOU MUST HAVE IMPORTANT BUSINESS, WITH US, RIGHT?

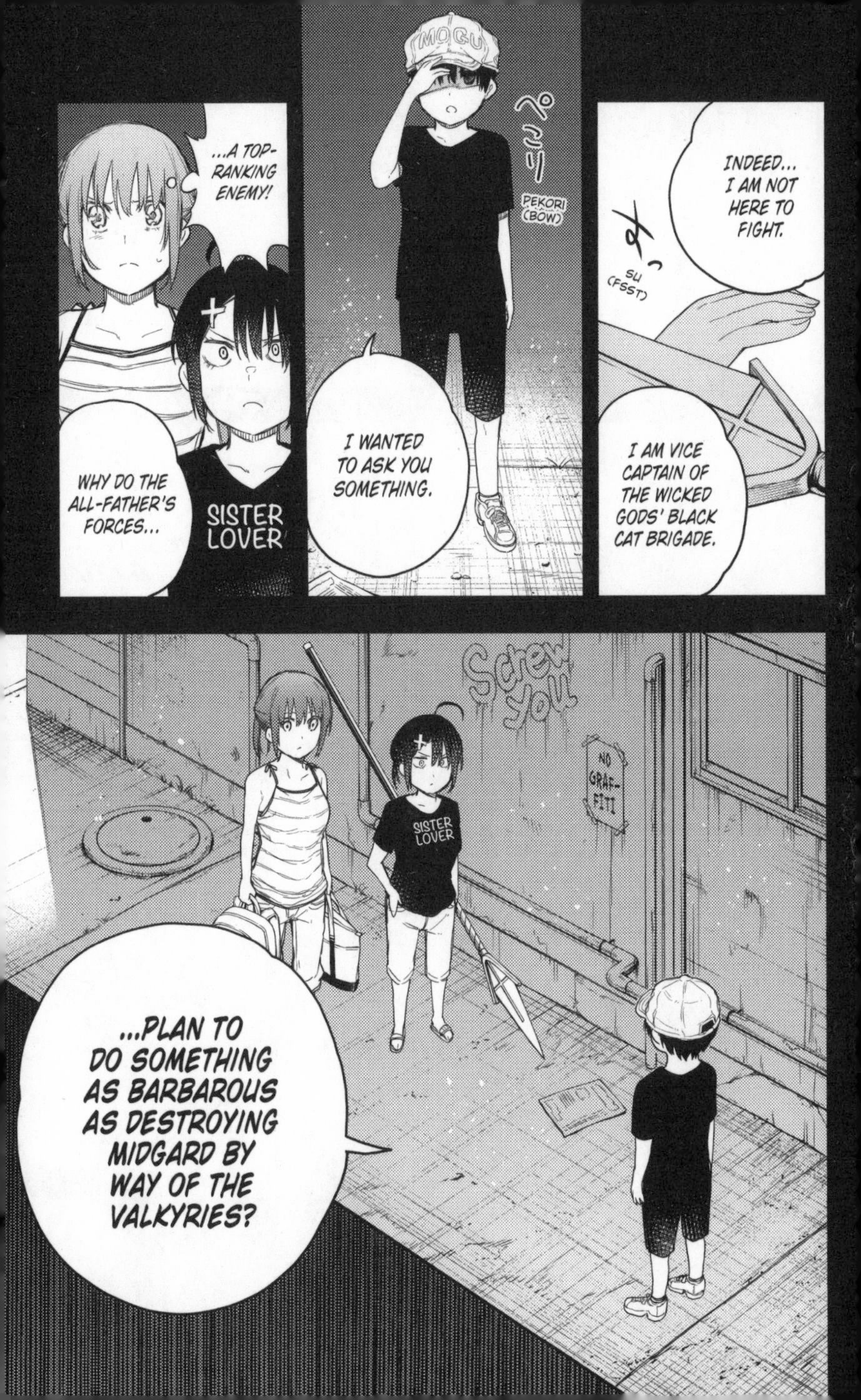
INDEED... I AM NOT HERE TO FIGHT.
す
SU (FSST)
I AM VICE CAPTAIN OF THE WICKED GODS' BLACK CAT BRIGADE.
MOGU
ぺこり
PEKORI (BOW)
I WANTED TO ASK YOU SOMETHING.
...A TOP-RANKING ENEMY!
SISTER LOVER
WHY DO THE ALL-FATHER'S FORCES...
Screw you
NO GRAFFITI
SISTER LOVER
...PLAN TO DO SOMETHING AS BARBAROUS AS DESTROYING MIDGARD BY WAY OF THE VALKYRIES?

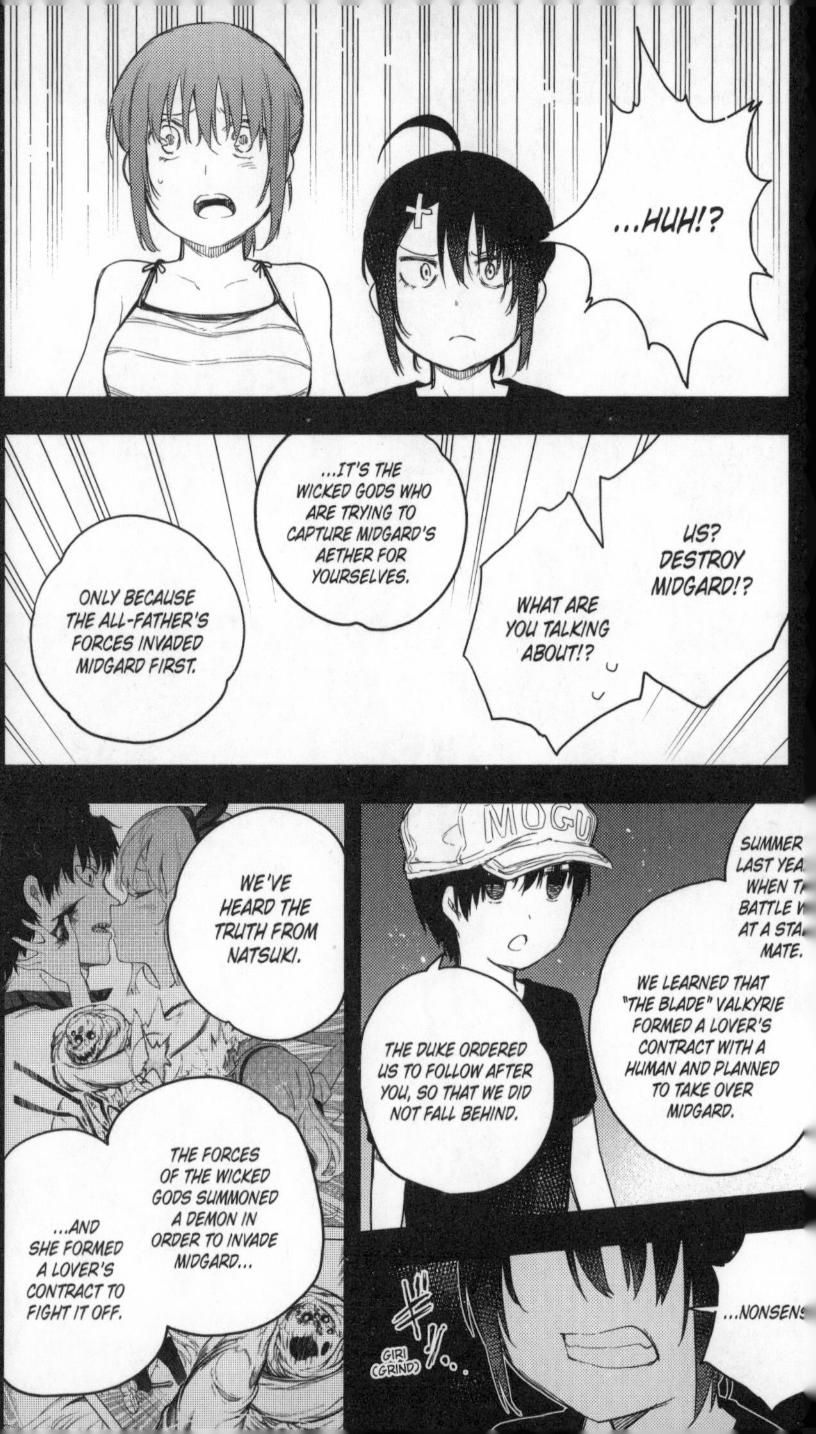
...HUH!?
US? DESTROY MIDGARD!?
WHAT ARE YOU TALKING ABOUT!?
...IT'S THE WICKED GODS WHO ARE TRYING TO CAPTURE MIDGARD'S AETHER FOR YOURSELVES.
ONLY BECAUSE THE ALL-FATHER'S FORCES INVADED MIDGARD FIRST.
SUMMER LAST YEA WHEN T BATTLE W AT A STA MATE.
WE LEARNED THAT "THE BLADE" VALKYRIE FORMED A LOVER'S CONTRACT WITH A HUMAN AND PLANNED TO TAKE OVER MIDGARD.
THE DUKE ORDERED US TO FOLLOW AFTER YOU, SO THAT WE DID NOT FALL BEHIND.
...NONSENS
GIRI (GRIND)
WE'VE HEARD THE TRUTH FROM NATSUKI.
THE FORCES OF THE WICKED GODS SUMMONED A DEMON IN ORDER TO INVADE MIDGARD...
...AND SHE FORMED A LOVER'S CONTRACT TO FIGHT IT OFF.

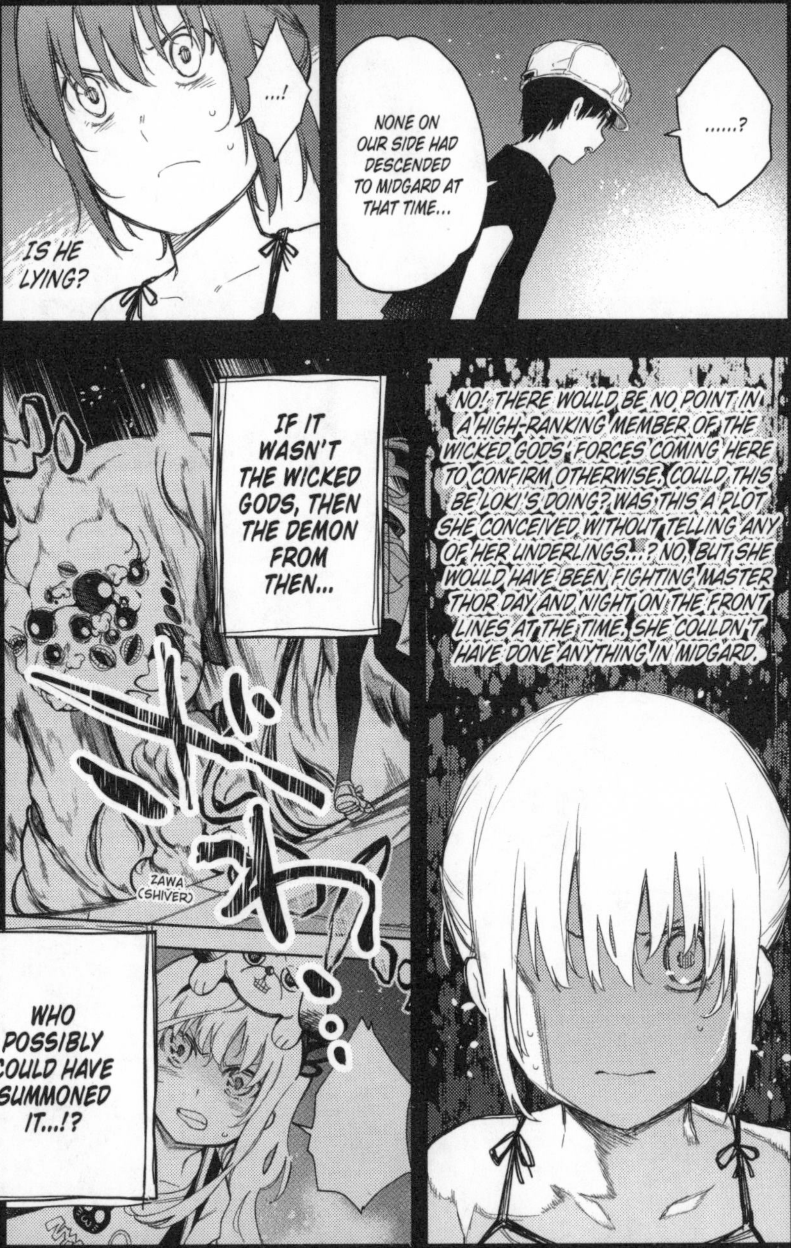
......?
NONE ON OUR SIDE HAD DESCENDED TO MIDGARD AT THAT TIME...
...!
IS HE LYING?
NO! THERE WOULD BE NO POINT IN A HIGH-RANKING MEMBER OF THE WICKED GODS' FORCES COMING HERE TO CONFIRM OTHERWISE. COULD THIS BE LOKI'S DOING? WAS THIS A PLOT SHE CONCEIVED WITHOUT TELLING ANY OF HER UNDERLINGS...? NO, BUT SHE WOULD HAVE BEEN FIGHTING MASTER THOR DAY AND NIGHT ON THE FRONT LINES AT THE TIME. SHE COULDN'T HAVE DONE ANYTHING IN MIDGARD.
IF IT WASN'T THE WICKED GODS, THEN THE DEMON FROM THEN...
ZAWA (SHIVER)
WHO POSSIBLY COULD HAVE SUMMONED IT...!?

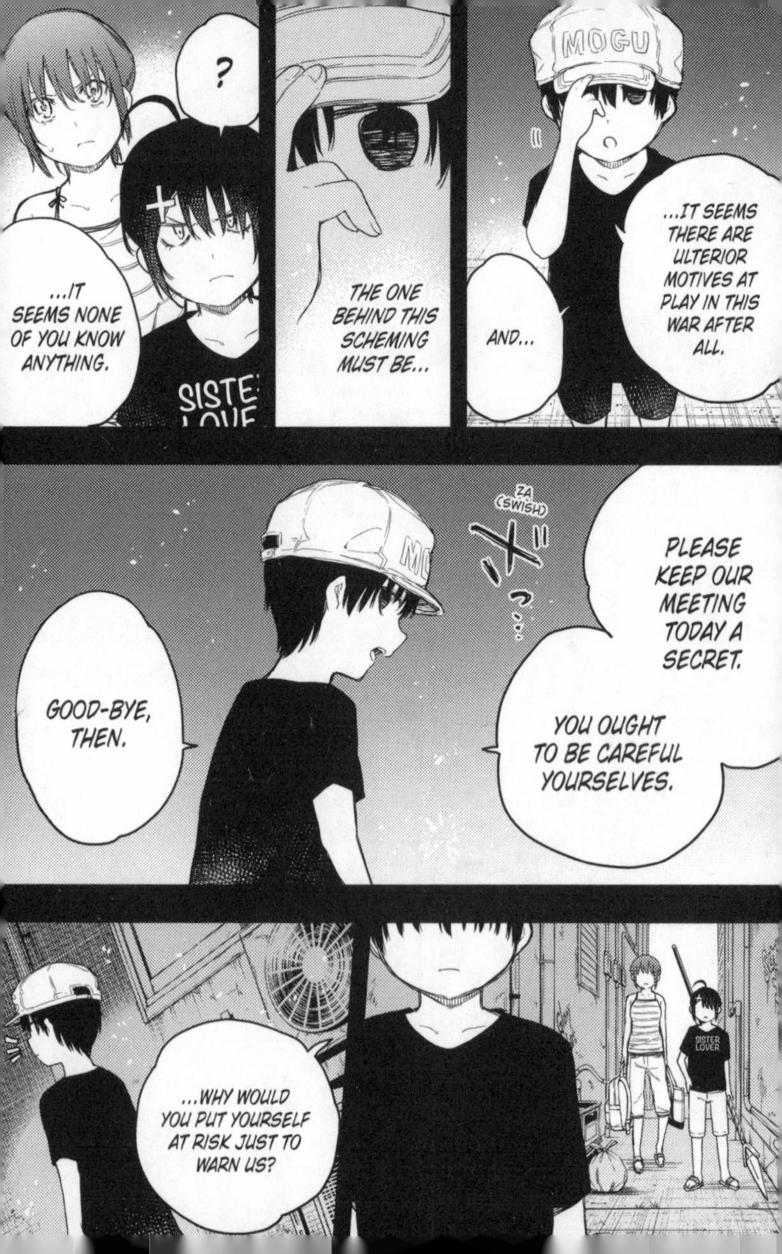
MOGU
...IT SEEMS THERE ARE ULTERIOR MOTIVES AT PLAY IN THIS WAR AFTER ALL.
AND...
THE ONE BEHIND THIS SCHEMING MUST BE...
?
...IT SEEMS NONE OF YOU KNOW ANYTHING.
PLEASE KEEP OUR MEETING TODAY A SECRET.
YOU OUGHT TO BE CAREFUL YOURSELVES.
ZA (SWISH)
GOOD-BYE, THEN.
SISTER LOVER
...WHY WOULD YOU PUT YOURSELF AT RISK JUST TO WARN US?

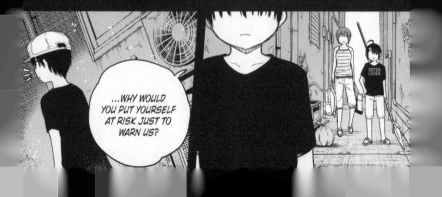

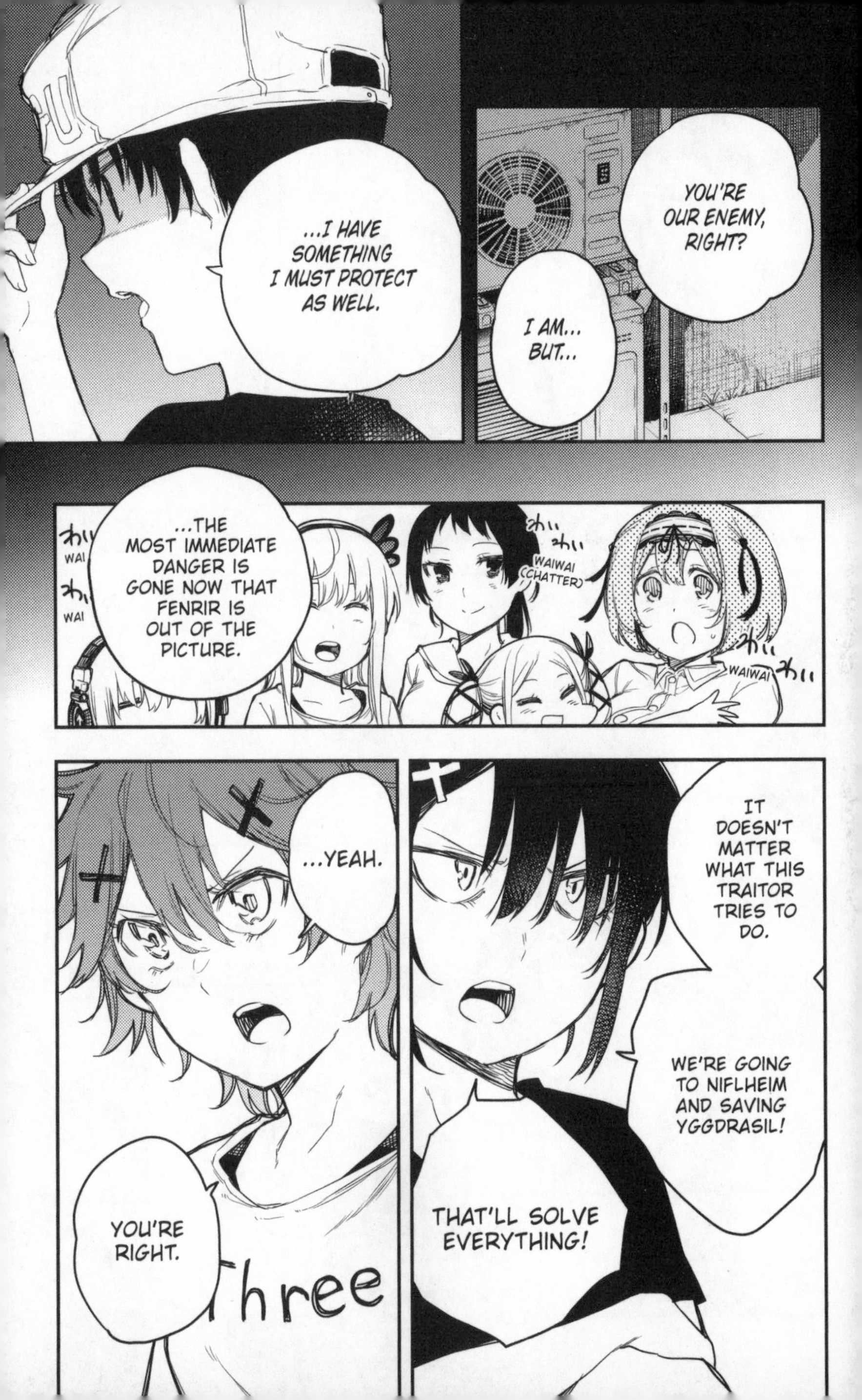
YOU'RE OUR ENEMY, RIGHT?
I AM... BUT...
...I HAVE SOMETHING I MUST PROTECT AS WELL.
わい わい
WAIWAI (CHATTER)
わい
WAIWAI
わい
...THE MOST IMMEDIATE DANGER IS GONE NOW THAT FENRIR IS OUT OF THE PICTURE.
わい
WAI
わい
WAI
IT DOESN'T MATTER WHAT THIS TRAITOR TRIES TO DO.
WE'RE GOING TO NIFLHEIM AND SAVING YGGDRASIL!
THAT'LL SOLVE EVERYTHING!
...YEAH.
YOU'RE RIGHT.
Three

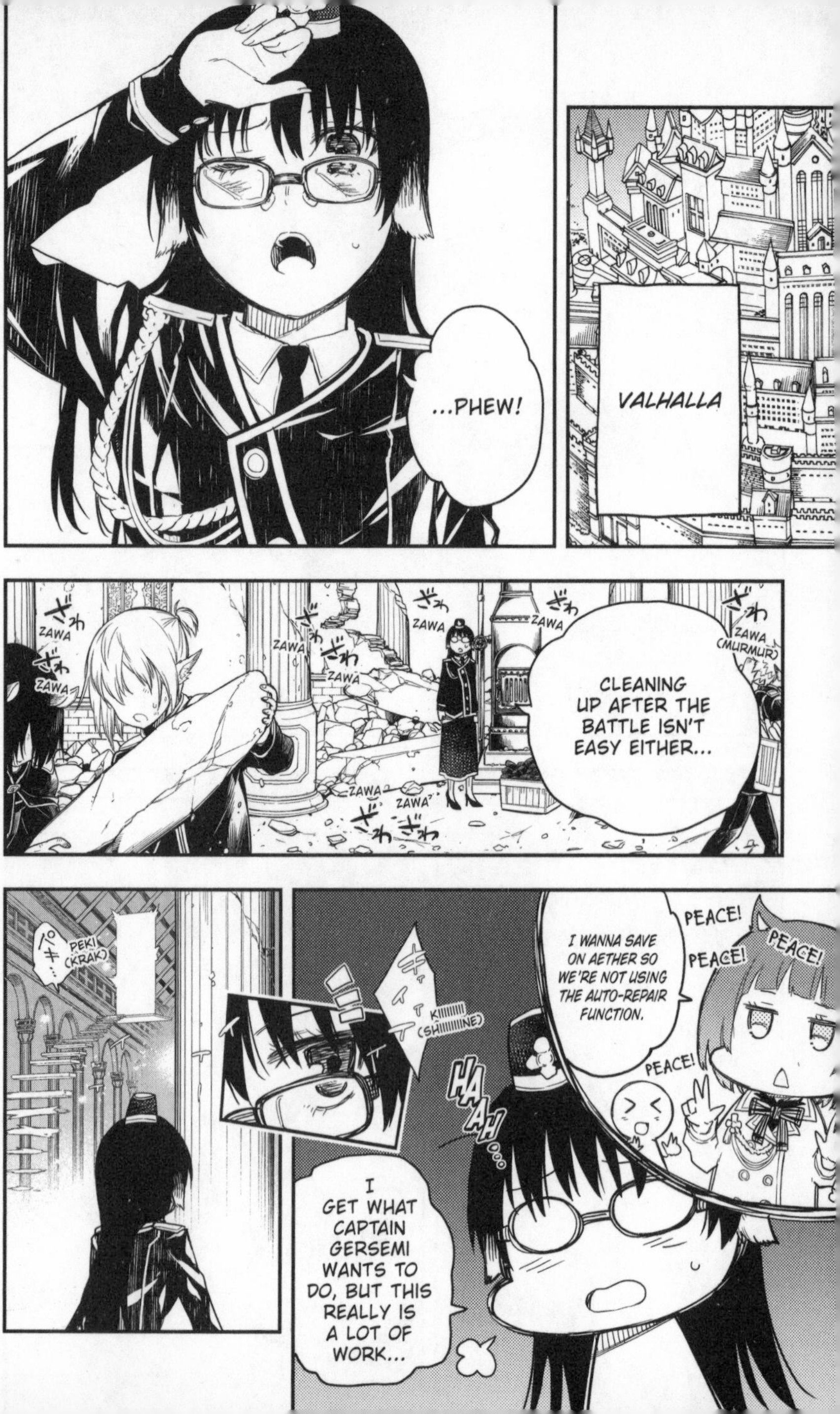

VALHALLA
...PHEW!
ざわ
ZAWA (MURMUR)
ざわ
ZAWA
ざわ
ZAWA
CLEANING UP AFTER THE BATTLE ISN'T EASY EITHER...
ざわ
ZAWA
ざわ
ZAWA
ざわ
ZAWA
ざわ
ZAWA
ざわ
ZAWA
ZAWA
ZAWA
ざわ ざわ
PEACE!
PEACE!
I WANNA SAVE ON AETHER SO WE'RE NOT USING THE AUTO-REPAIR FUNCTION.
PEACE!
PEACE!
KIIIIIIII (SHIIIIIIINE)
HAAH...
I GET WHAT CAPTAIN GERSEMI WANTS TO DO, BUT THIS REALLY IS A LOT OF WORK...
パキ...
PEKI (KRAK)

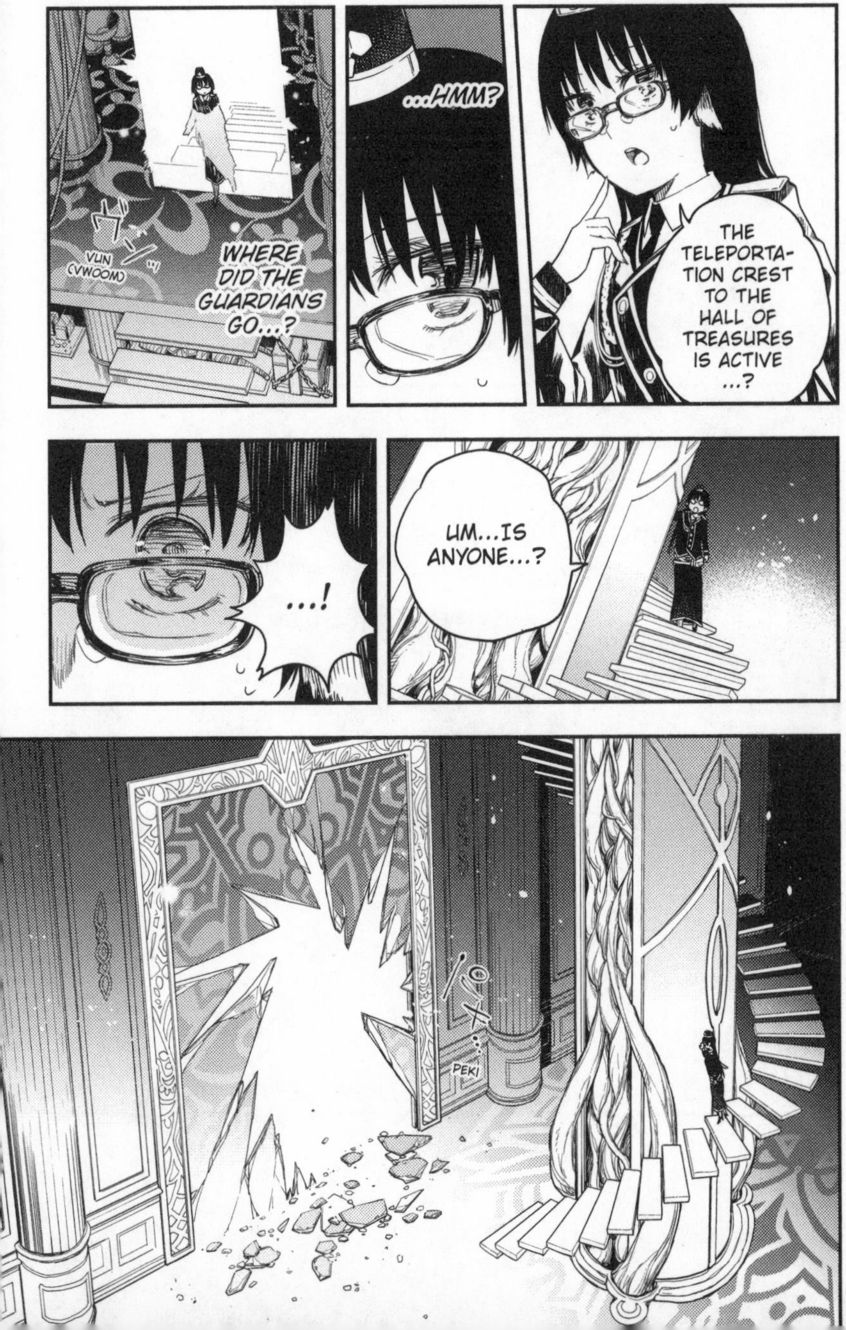
THE TELEPORTATION CREST TO THE HALL OF TREASURES IS ACTIVE ...?
...HMM?
WHERE DID THE GUARDIANS GO...?
VUN (VWOOM)
UM...IS ANYONE...?
...!
PEKI

AH!

NO —!!

THE BARRIER'S BEEN BROKEN!?

WHY!?

DA

DA

DA (THUD)

DA

DA

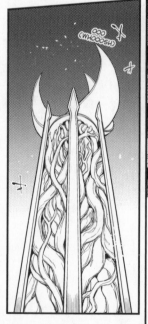

OOO (WHOOOSH)

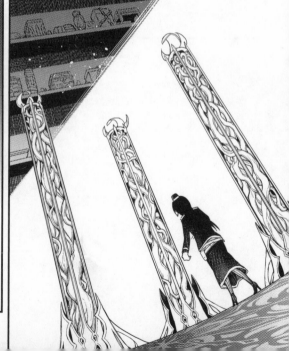

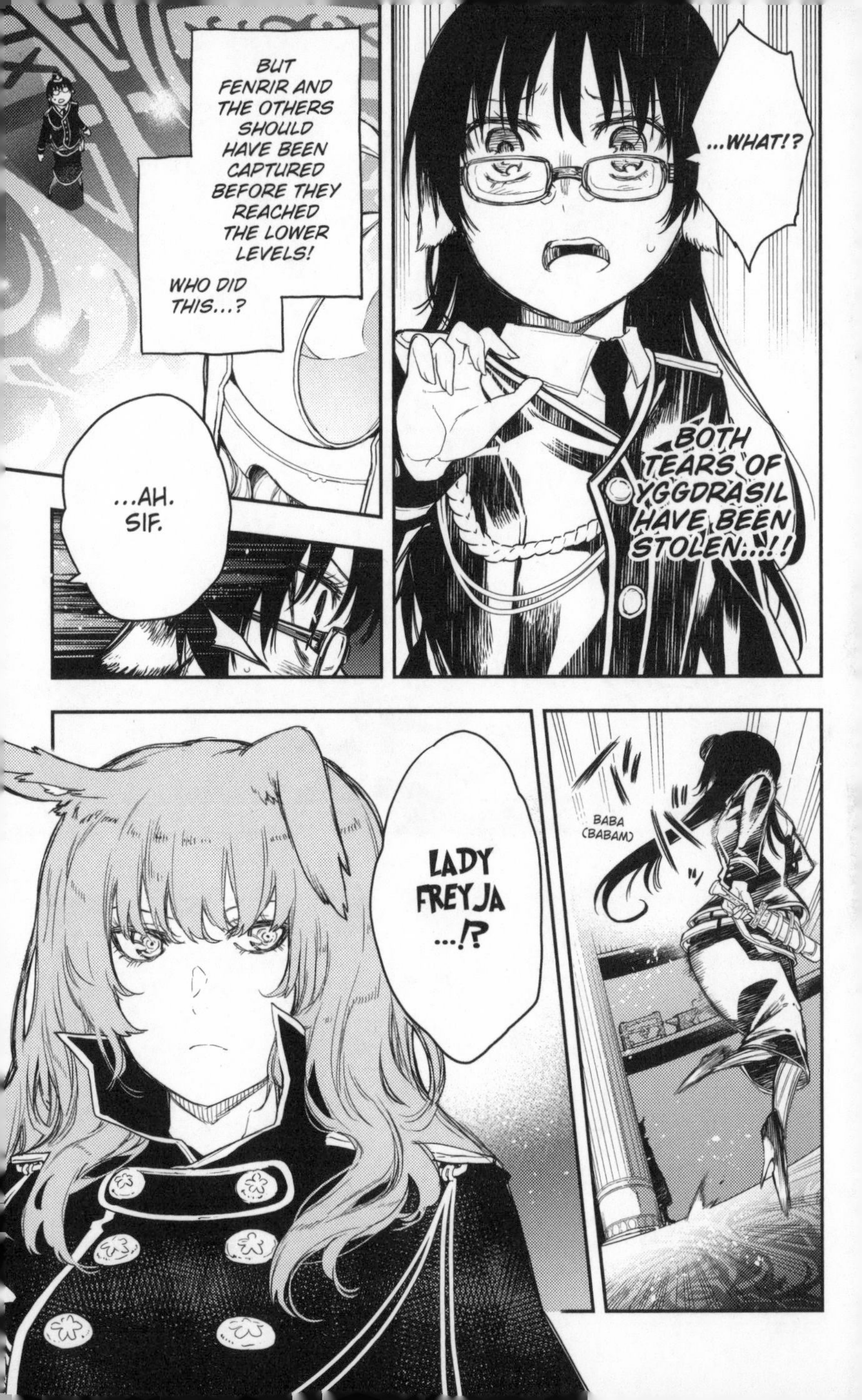
...WHAT!?
BOTH TEARS OF YGGDRASIL HAVE BEEN STOLEN...!!
BUT FENRIR AND THE OTHERS SHOULD HAVE BEEN CAPTURED BEFORE THEY REACHED THE LOWER LEVELS!
WHO DID THIS...?
...AH. SIF.
BABA (BABAM)
LADY FREYJA ...!?

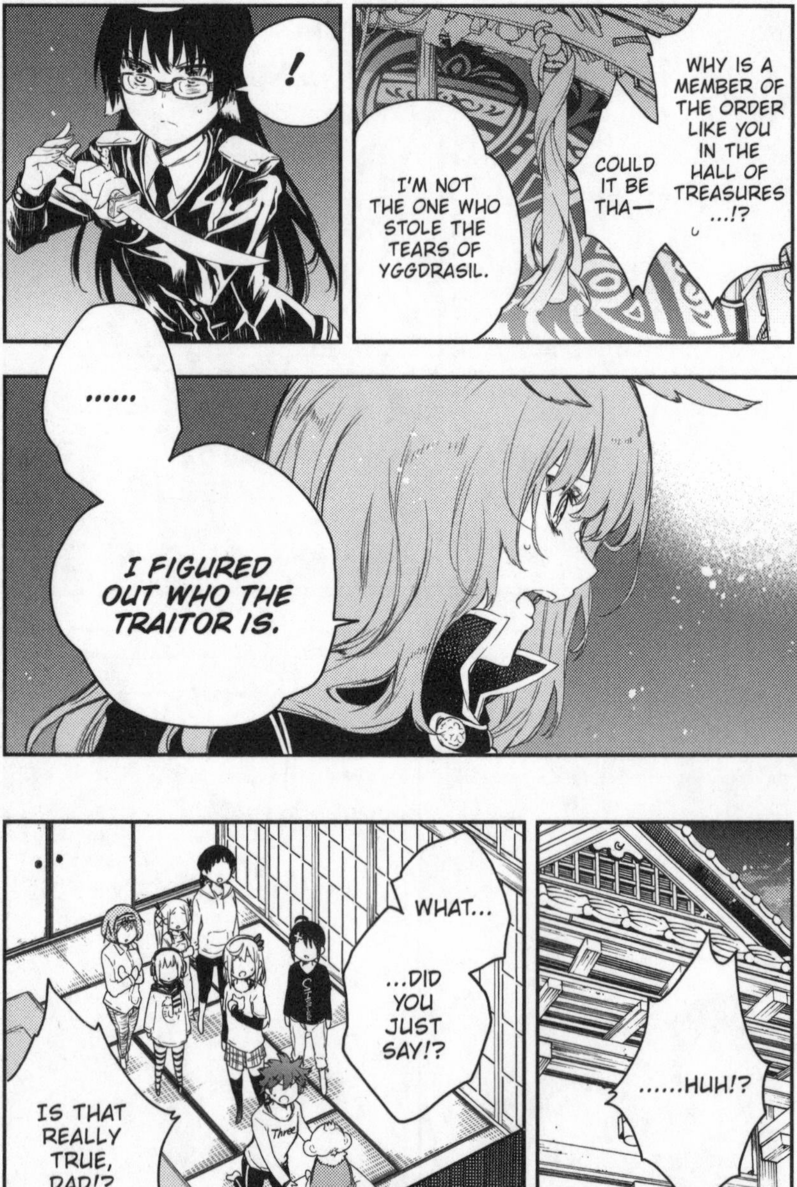
WHY IS A MEMBER OF THE ORDER LIKE YOU IN THE HALL OF TREASURES ...!?
COULD IT BE THA—
I'M NOT THE ONE WHO STOLE THE TEARS OF YGGDRASIL.
!
......
I FIGURED OUT WHO THE TRAITOR IS.
......HUH!?
WHAT...
...DID YOU JUST SAY!?
IS THAT REALLY TRUE, DAD!?

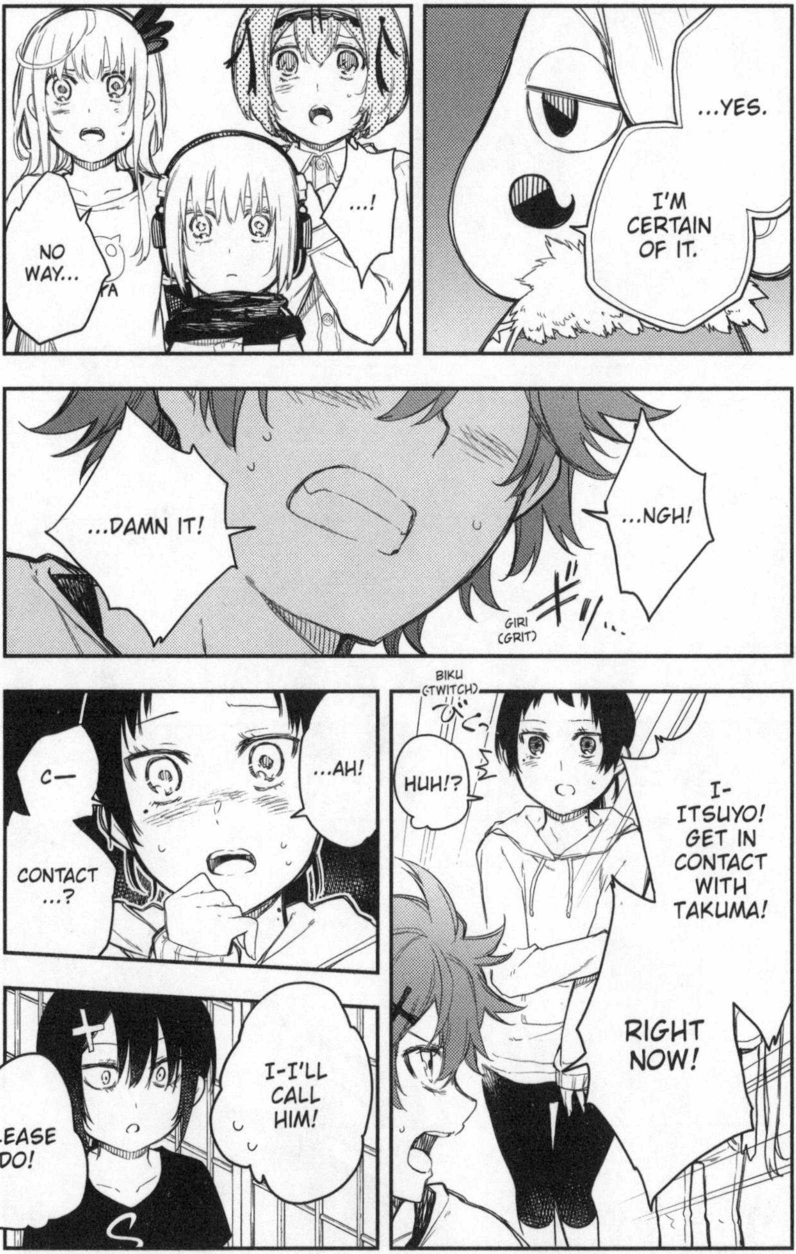
...YES.
I'M CERTAIN OF IT.
...!
NO WAY...
...NGH!
GIRI (GRIT)
...DAMN IT!
BIKU (TWITCH)
I- ITSUYO! GET IN CONTACT WITH TAKUMA!
HUH!?
RIGHT NOW!
...AH!
C—
CONTACT ...?
I-I'LL CALL HIM!
PLEASE DO!

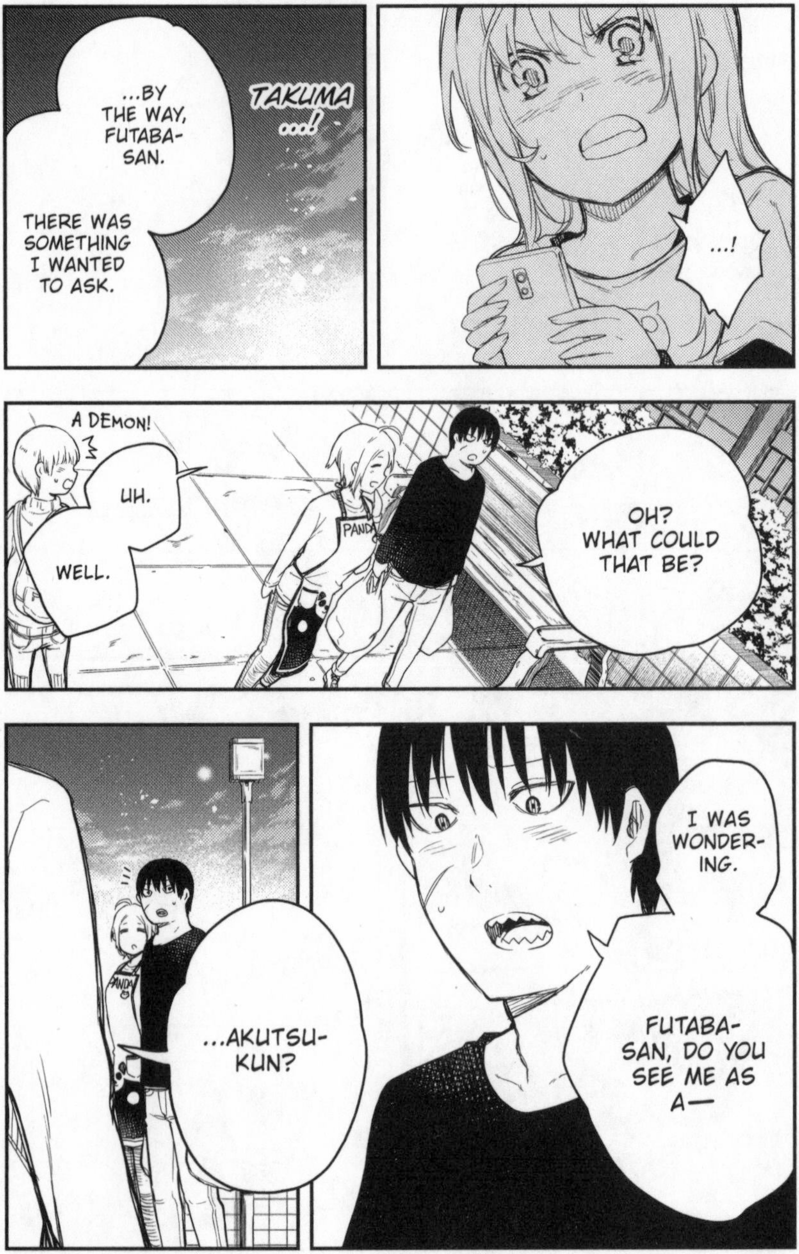
...!
TAKUMA ...!
...BY THE WAY, FUTABA-SAN.
THERE WAS SOMETHING I WANTED TO ASK.
OH? WHAT COULD THAT BE?
UH.
WELL.
A DEMON!
I WAS WONDER-ING.
FUTABA-SAN, DO YOU SEE ME AS A—
...AKUTSU-KUN?

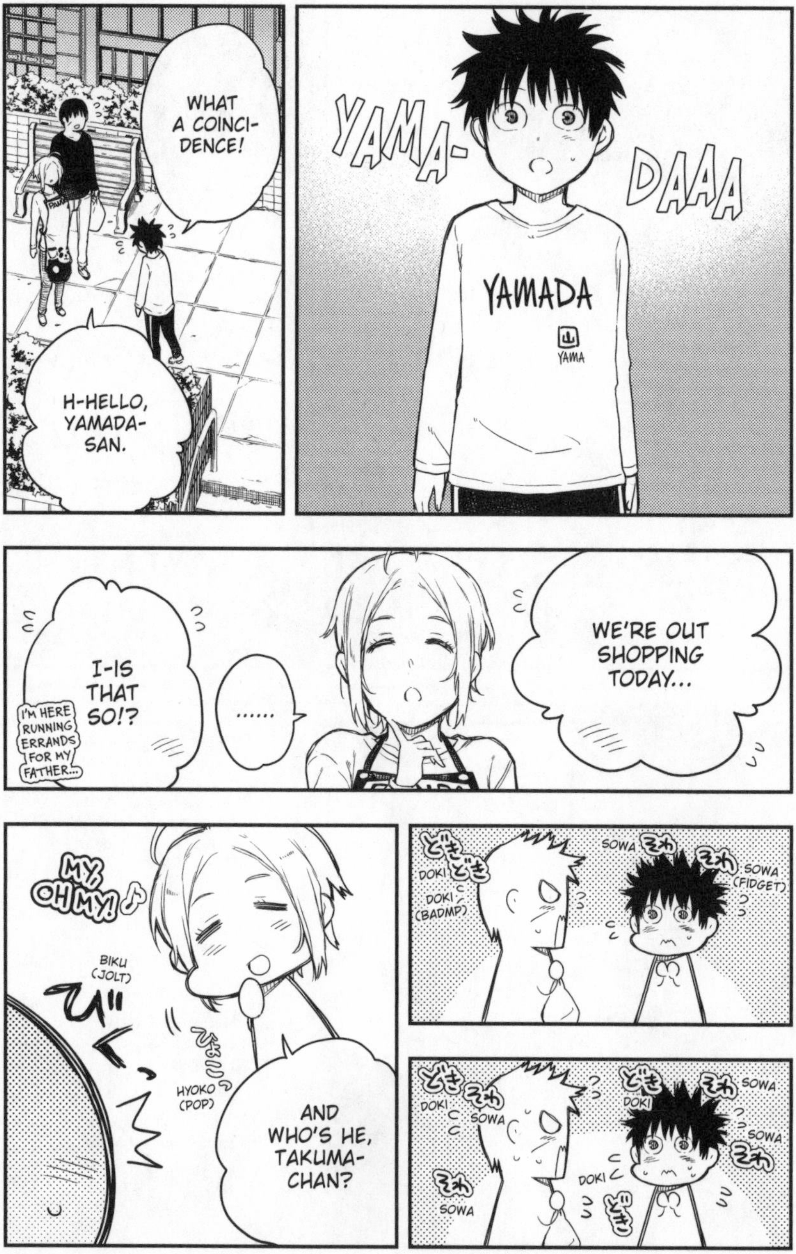
YAMA-DAAA
YAMADA
YAMA
WHAT A COINCIDENCE!
H-HELLO, YAMADA-SAN.
WE'RE OUT SHOPPING TODAY...
......
I-IS THAT SO!?
I'M HERE RUNNING ERRANDS FOR MY FATHER...
SOWA そわ そわ SOWA (FIDGET)
どきどき DOKI DOKI (BADMP)
SOWA そわ どき DOKI SOWA そわ
どき DOKI そわ SOWA
そわ SOWA どき DOKI
MY, OH MY!♪
BIKU (JOLT) びくっ
ひょこ HYOKO (POP)
AND WHO'S HE, TAKUMA-CHAN?

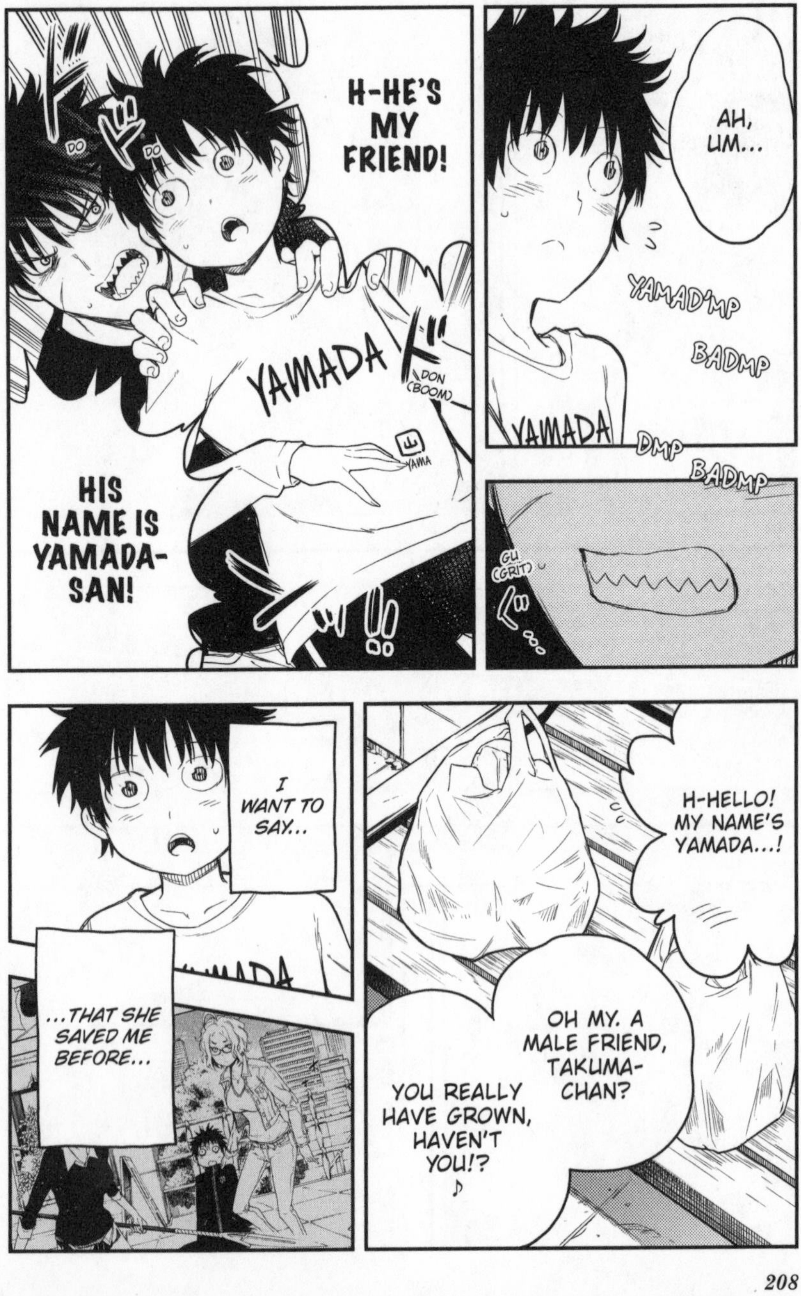

AH, UM...
YAMAD'MP
BADMP
YAMADA
DMP
BADMP
GU (GRIT)
H-HE'S MY FRIEND!
DO
DO
YAMADA
DON (BOOM)
YAMA
HIS NAME IS YAMADA-SAN!
H-HELLO! MY NAME'S YAMADA...!
OH MY. A MALE FRIEND, TAKUMA-CHAN?
YOU REALLY HAVE GROWN, HAVEN'T YOU!? ♪
I WANT TO SAY...
...THAT SHE SAVED ME BEFORE...

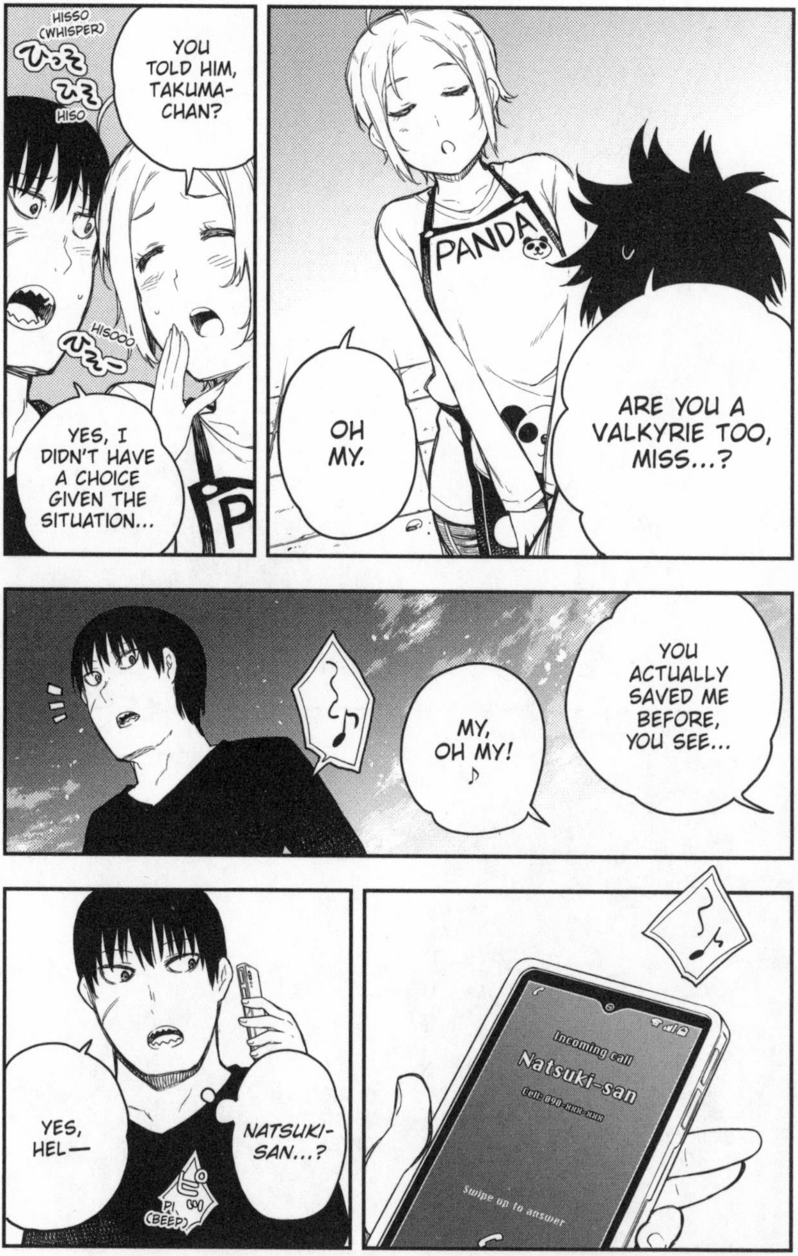
ARE YOU A VALKYRIE TOO, MISS...?
OH MY.
HISSO (WHISPER)
ひっそ
ひそ
HISO
YOU TOLD HIM, TAKUMA-CHAN?
HISOOO
ひそー
YES, I DIDN'T HAVE A CHOICE GIVEN THE SITUATION...
YOU ACTUALLY SAVED ME BEFORE, YOU SEE...
MY, OH MY! ♪
Incoming call
Natsuki-san
Swipe up to answer
NATSUKI-SAN...?
YES, HEL—
PI (BEEP)

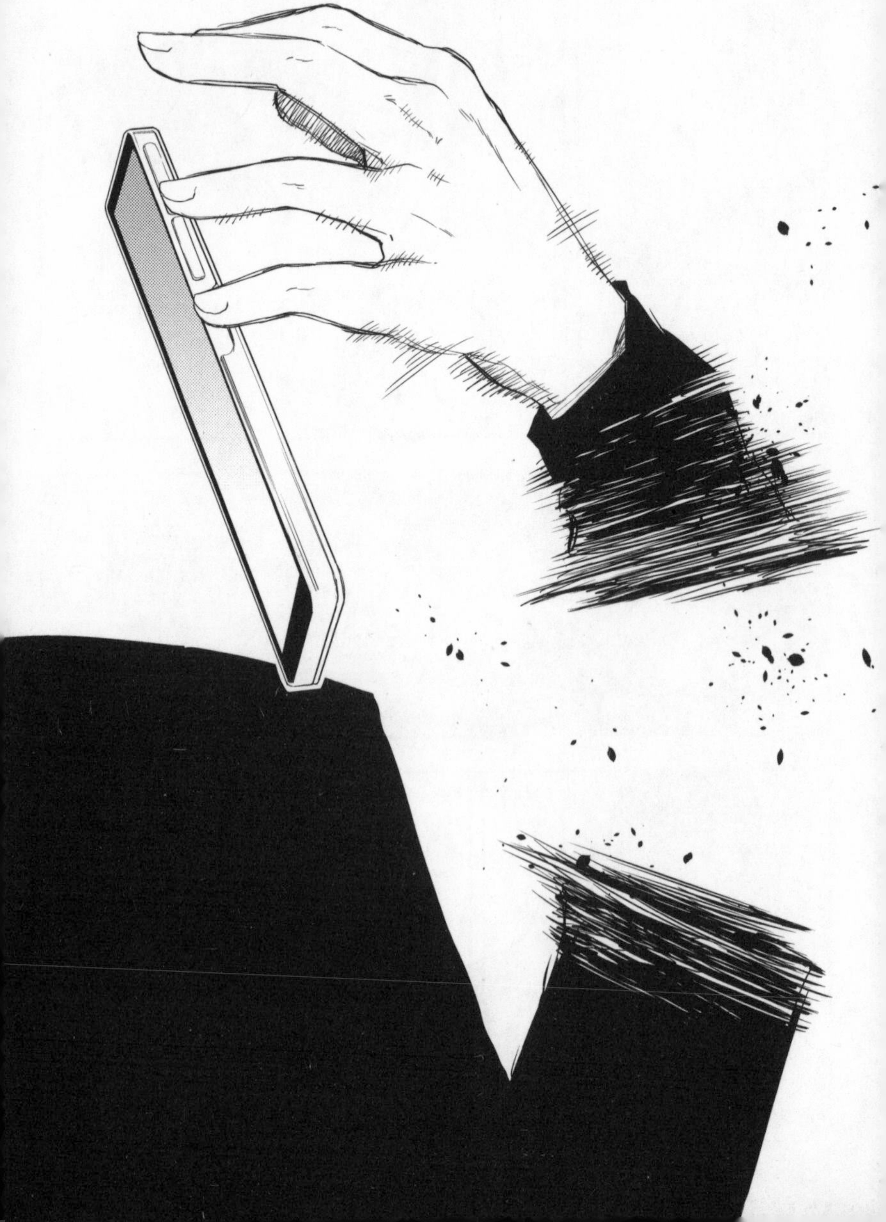

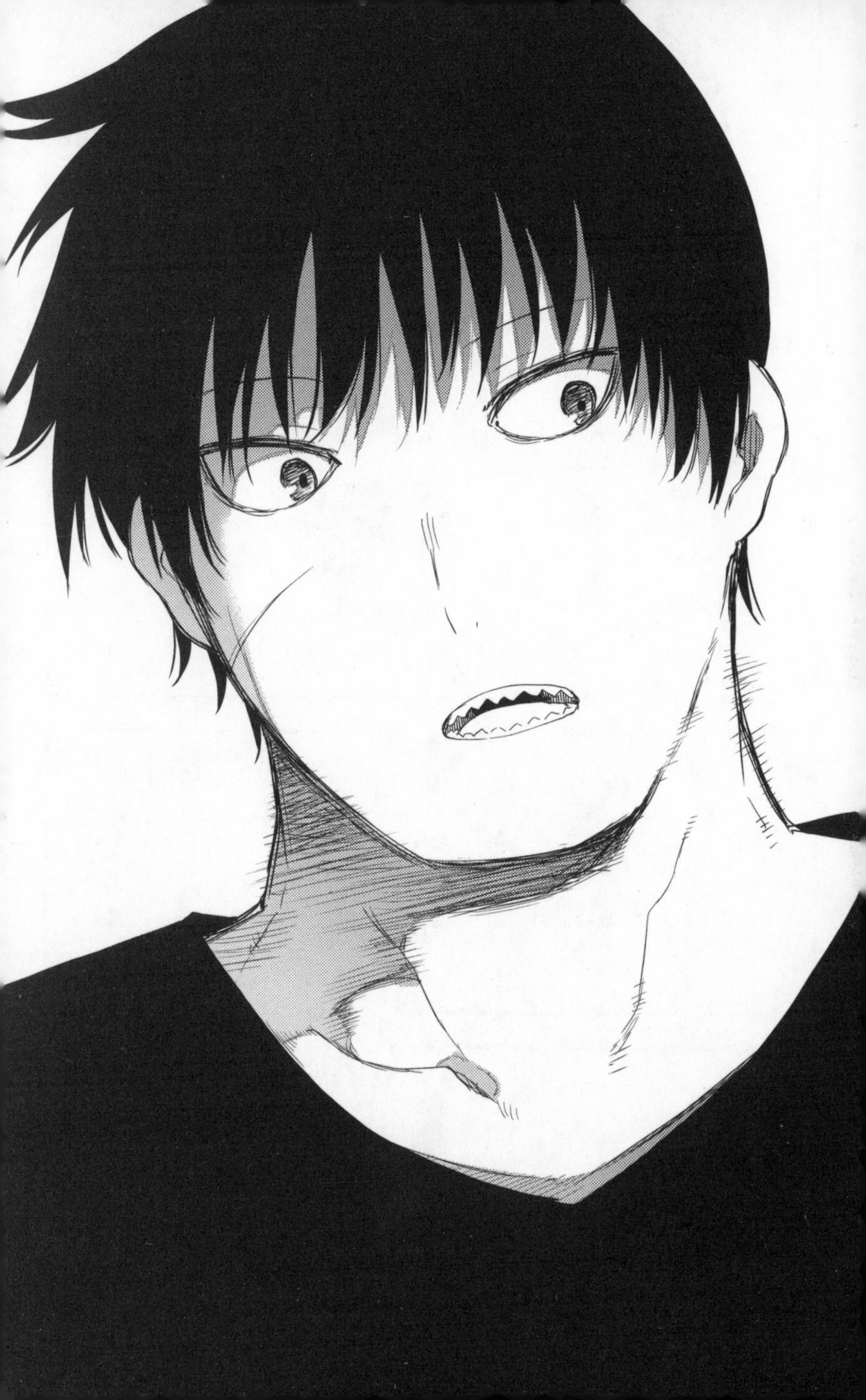

HUH?

......

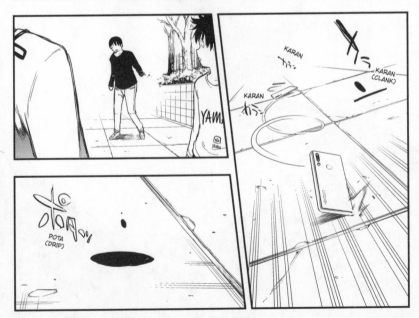

KARAN

KARAN
(CLANK)

KARAN

POTA
(DRIP)

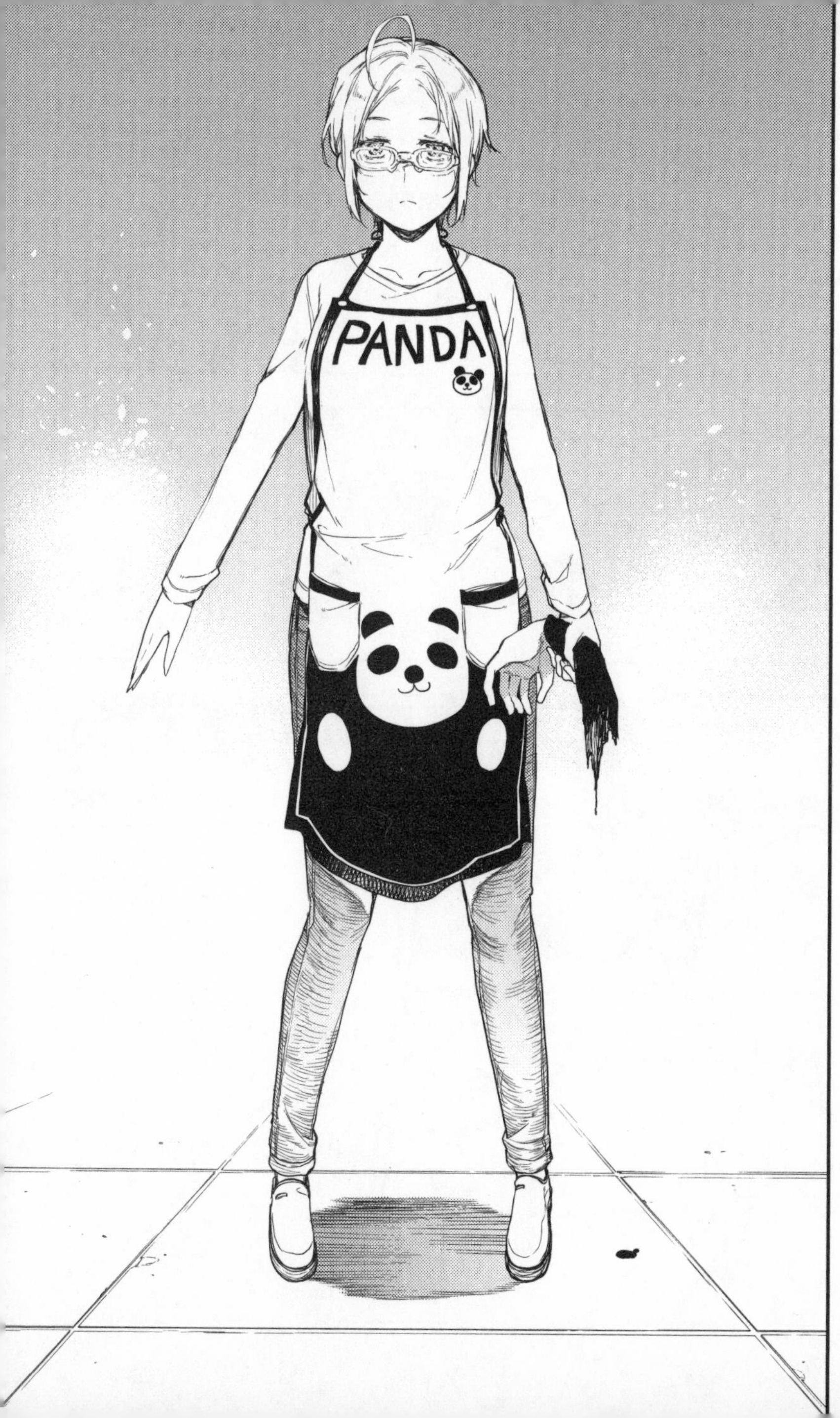
PANDA

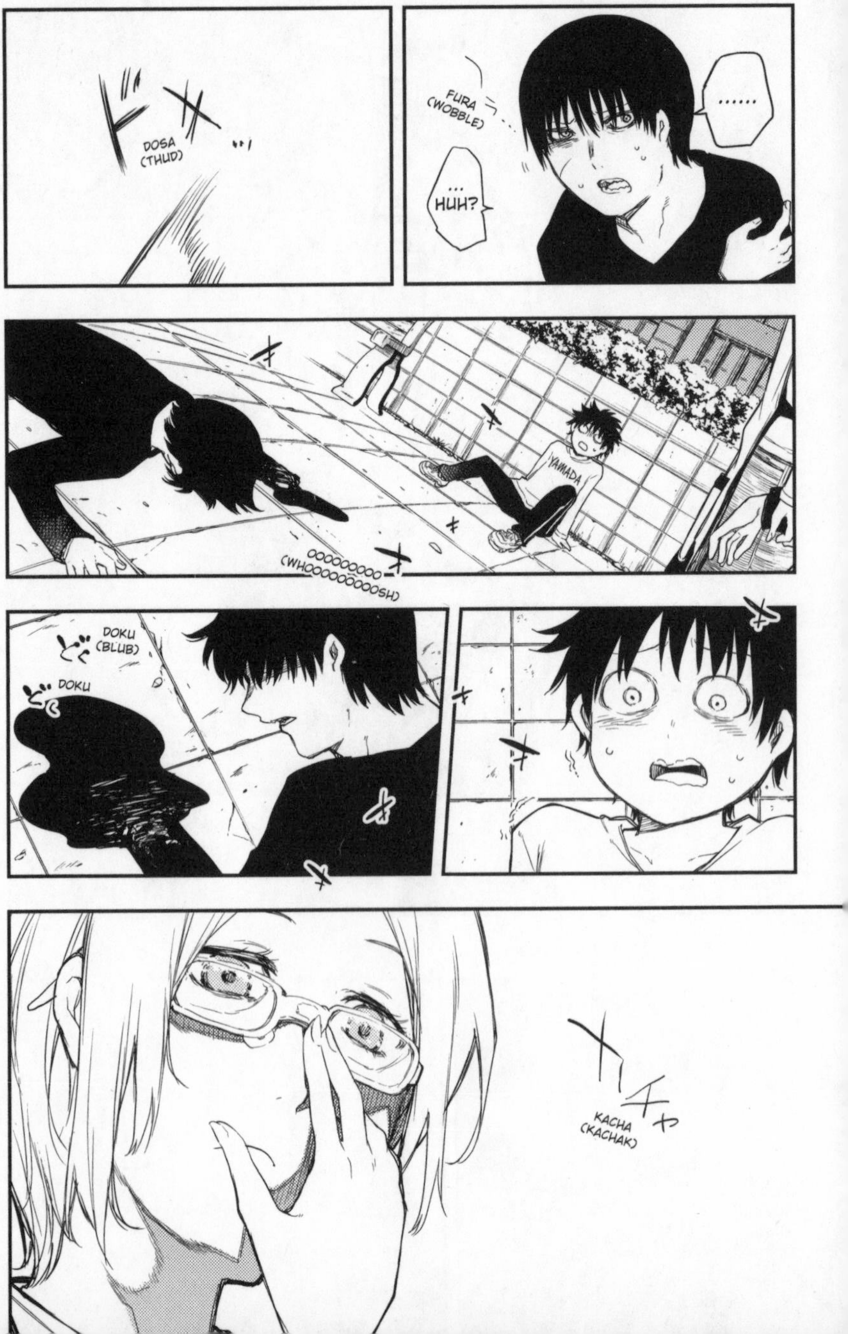
......
FURA (WOBBLE)
... HUH?
DOSA (THUD)
OOOOOOOOO (WHOOOOOOOOOSH)
DOKU (BLUB)
DOKU
KACHA (KACHAK)

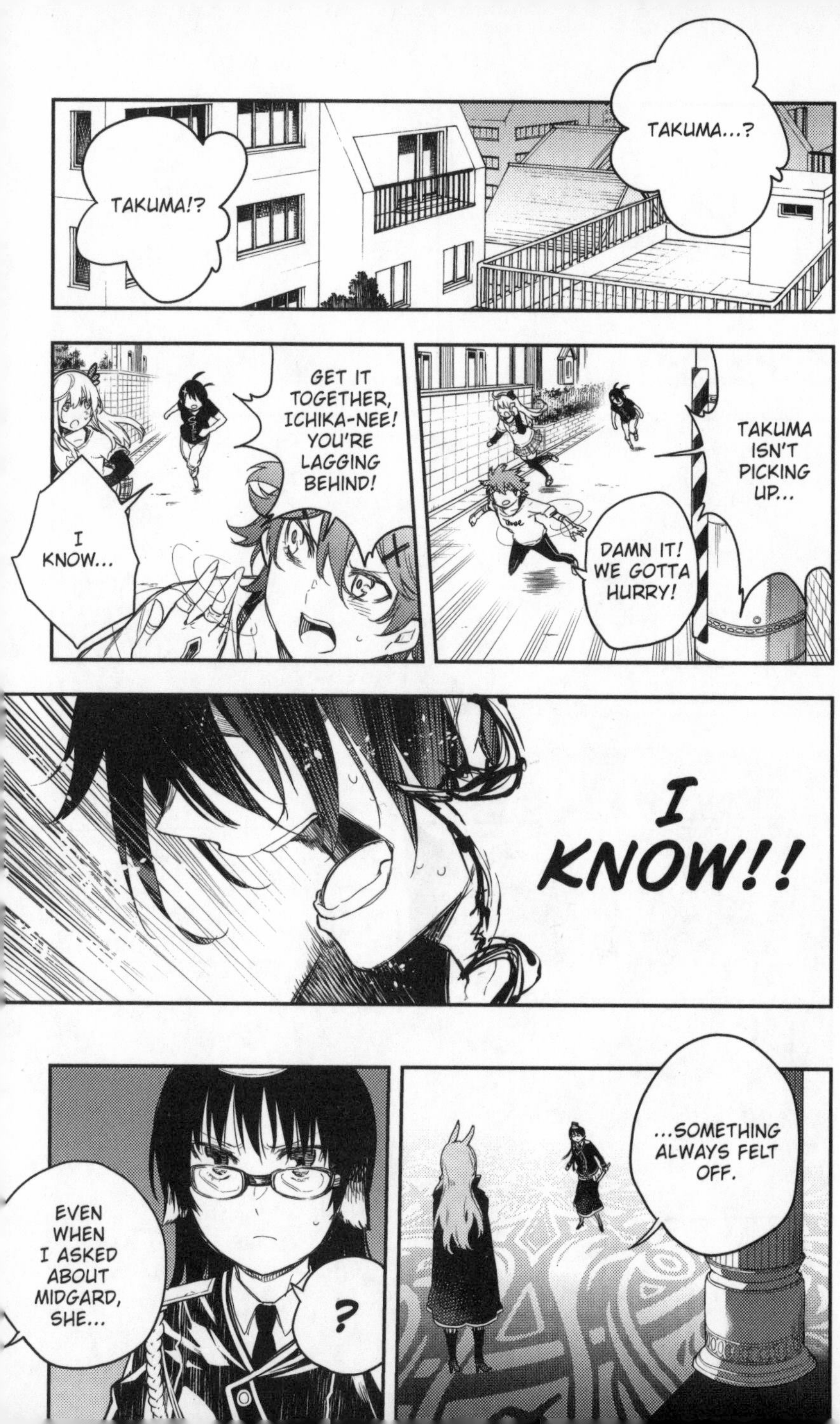
TAKUMA...?
TAKUMA!?
TAKUMA ISN'T PICKING UP...
DAMN IT! WE GOTTA HURRY!
GET IT TOGETHER, ICHIKA-NEE! YOU'RE LAGGING BEHIND!
I KNOW...
I KNOW!!
...SOMETHING ALWAYS FELT OFF.
EVEN WHEN I ASKED ABOUT MIDGARD, SHE...
?

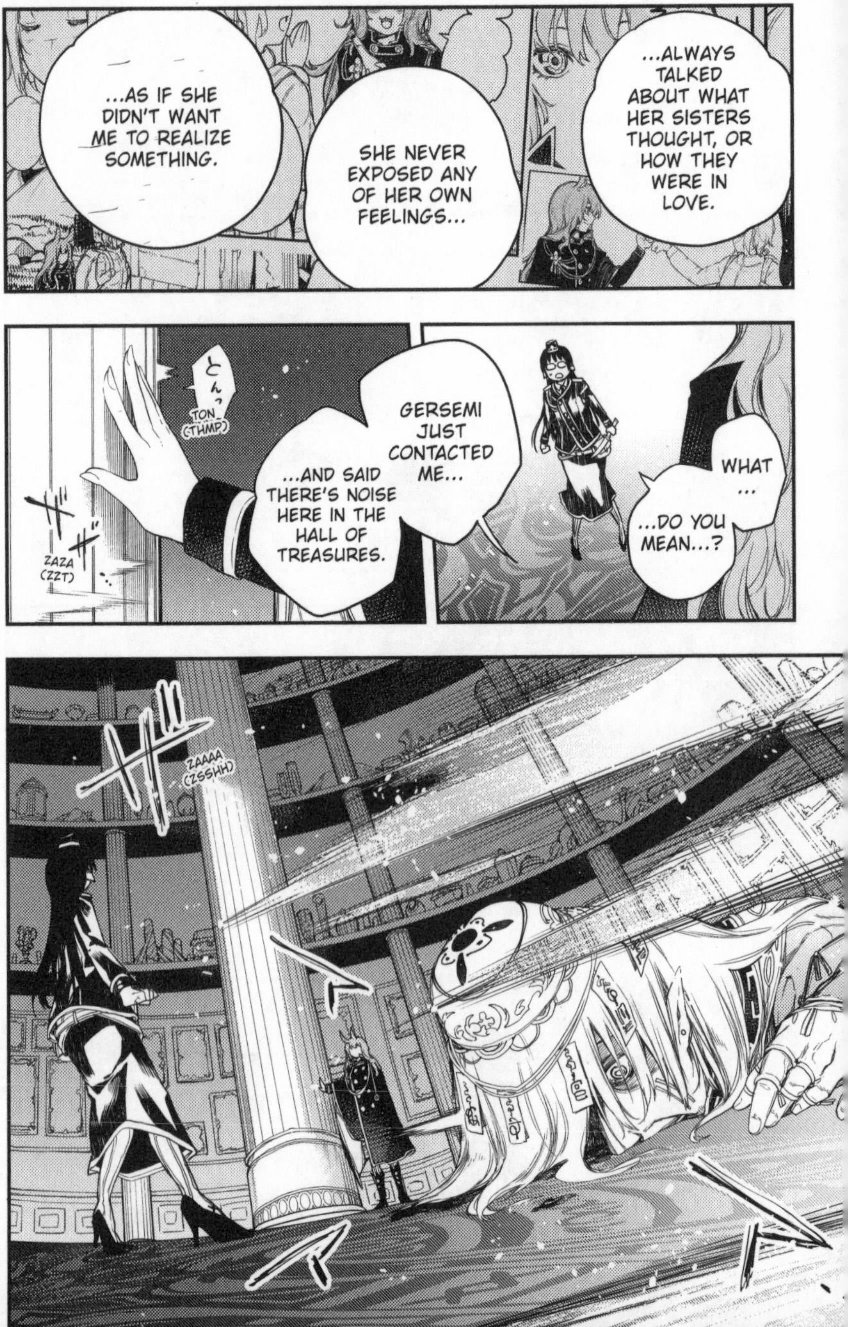
...ALWAYS TALKED ABOUT WHAT HER SISTERS THOUGHT, OR HOW THEY WERE IN LOVE.
SHE NEVER EXPOSED ANY OF HER OWN FEELINGS...
...AS IF SHE DIDN'T WANT ME TO REALIZE SOMETHING.
WHAT ...
...DO YOU MEAN...?
GERSEMI JUST CONTACTED ME...
...AND SAID THERE'S NOISE HERE IN THE HALL OF TREASURES.
とんっ
TON (THMP)
ZAZA (ZZT)
ZAAAA (ZSSHH)

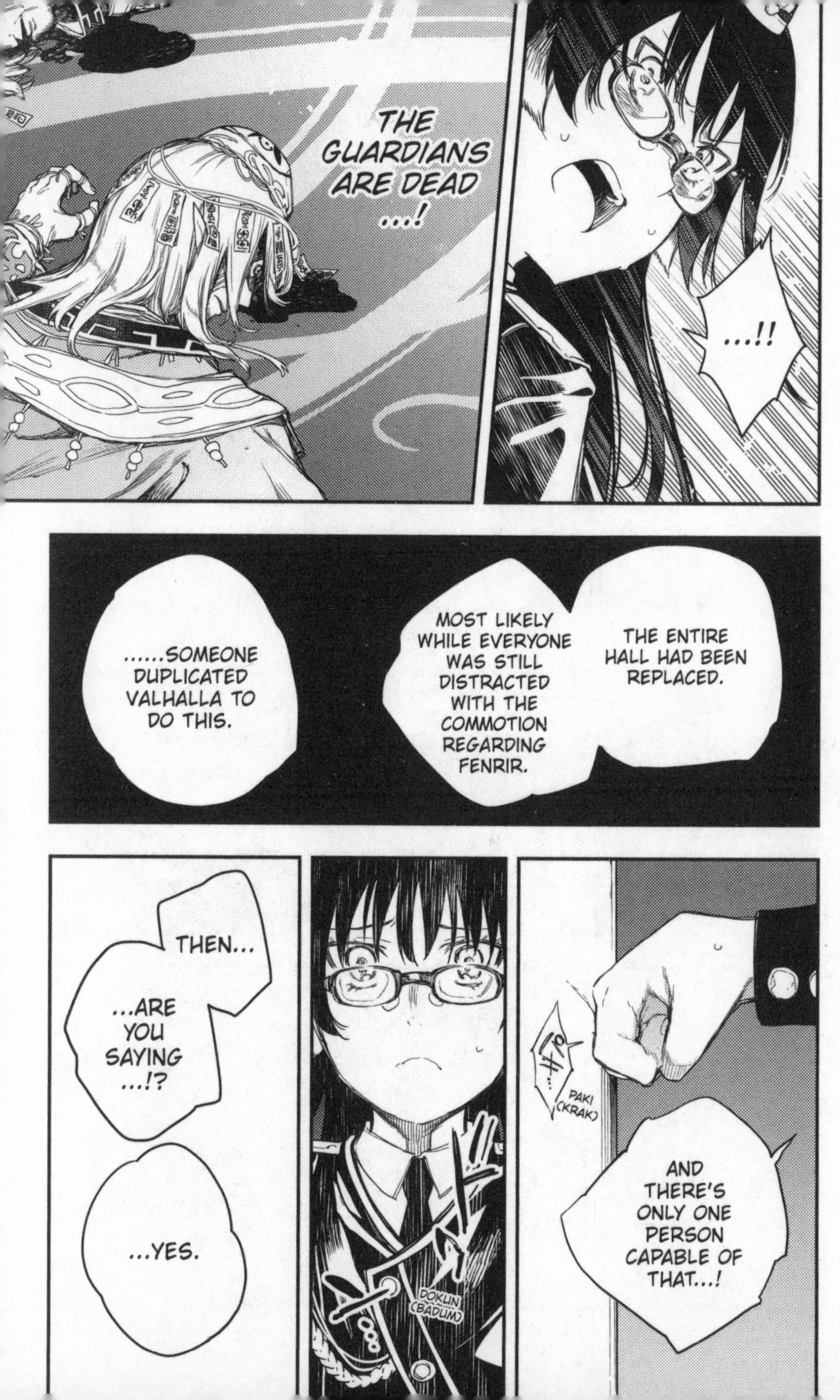
...!!
THE GUARDIANS ARE DEAD ...!
THE ENTIRE HALL HAD BEEN REPLACED.
MOST LIKELY WHILE EVERYONE WAS STILL DISTRACTED WITH THE COMMOTION REGARDING FENRIR.
......SOMEONE DUPLICATED VALHALLA TO DO THIS.
PAKI (KRAK)
AND THERE'S ONLY ONE PERSON CAPABLE OF THAT...!
DOKUN (BADUM)
THEN...
...ARE YOU SAYING ...!?
...YES.

GERHILDE
IS THE
TRAITOR.

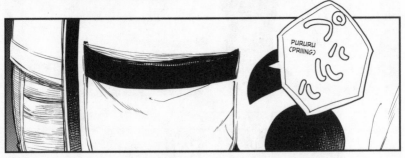

PURURU
(PRIIING)

YES...?

PURURU

RURURU

PI
(BEEP)

PURURURURU

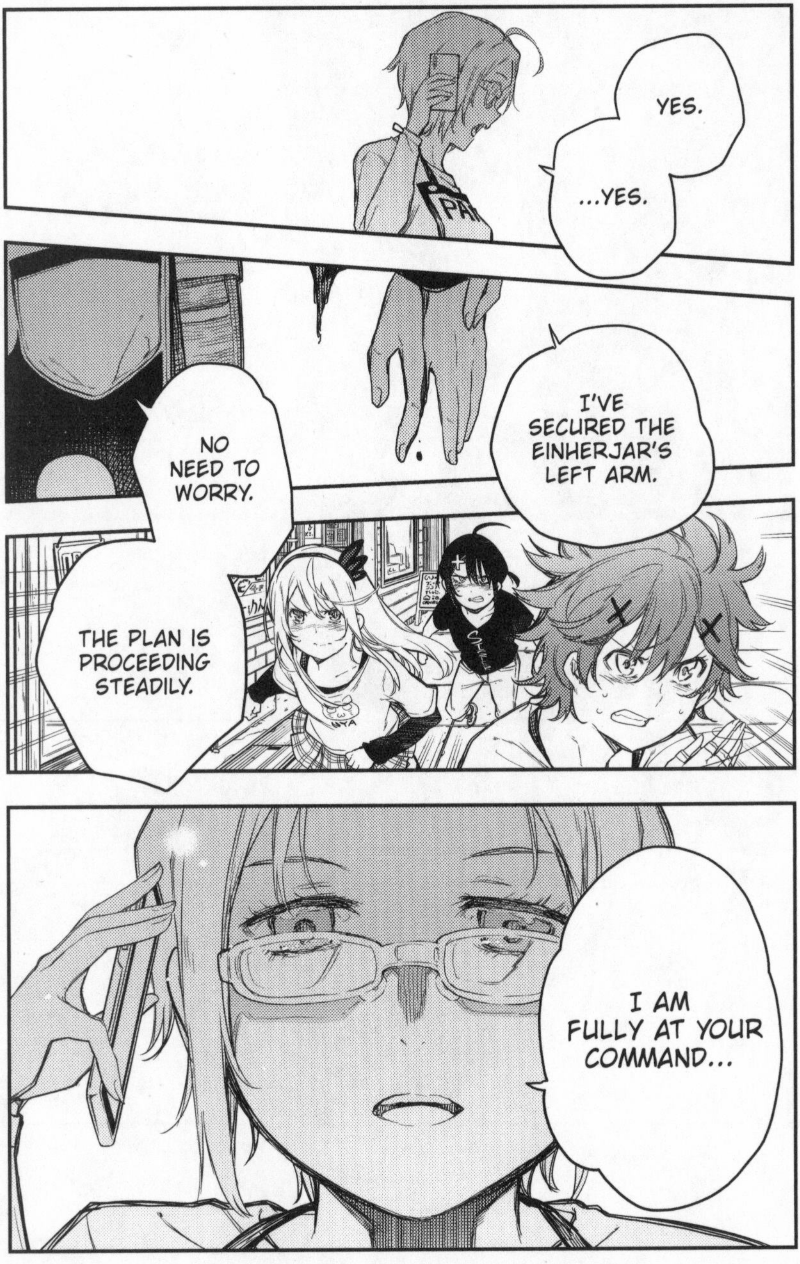
YES.
...YES.
I'VE SECURED THE EINHERJAR'S LEFT ARM.
NO NEED TO WORRY.
THE PLAN IS PROCEEDING STEADILY.
I AM FULLY AT YOUR COMMAND...

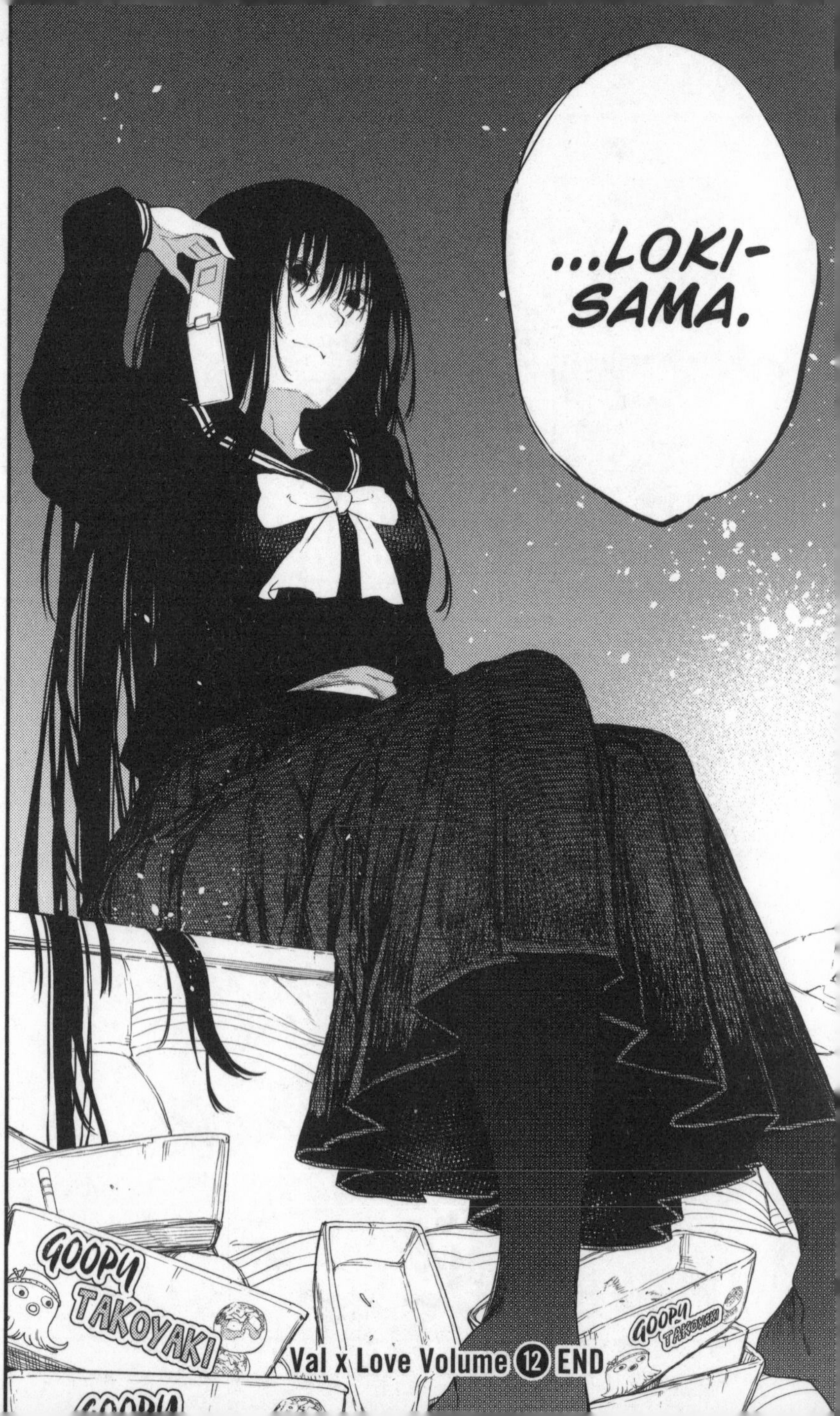
...LOKI-SAMA.
GOOPY TAKOYAKI
GOOPY TAKOYAKI
Val x Love Volume 12 END

Val X Löve

BONUS MANGA

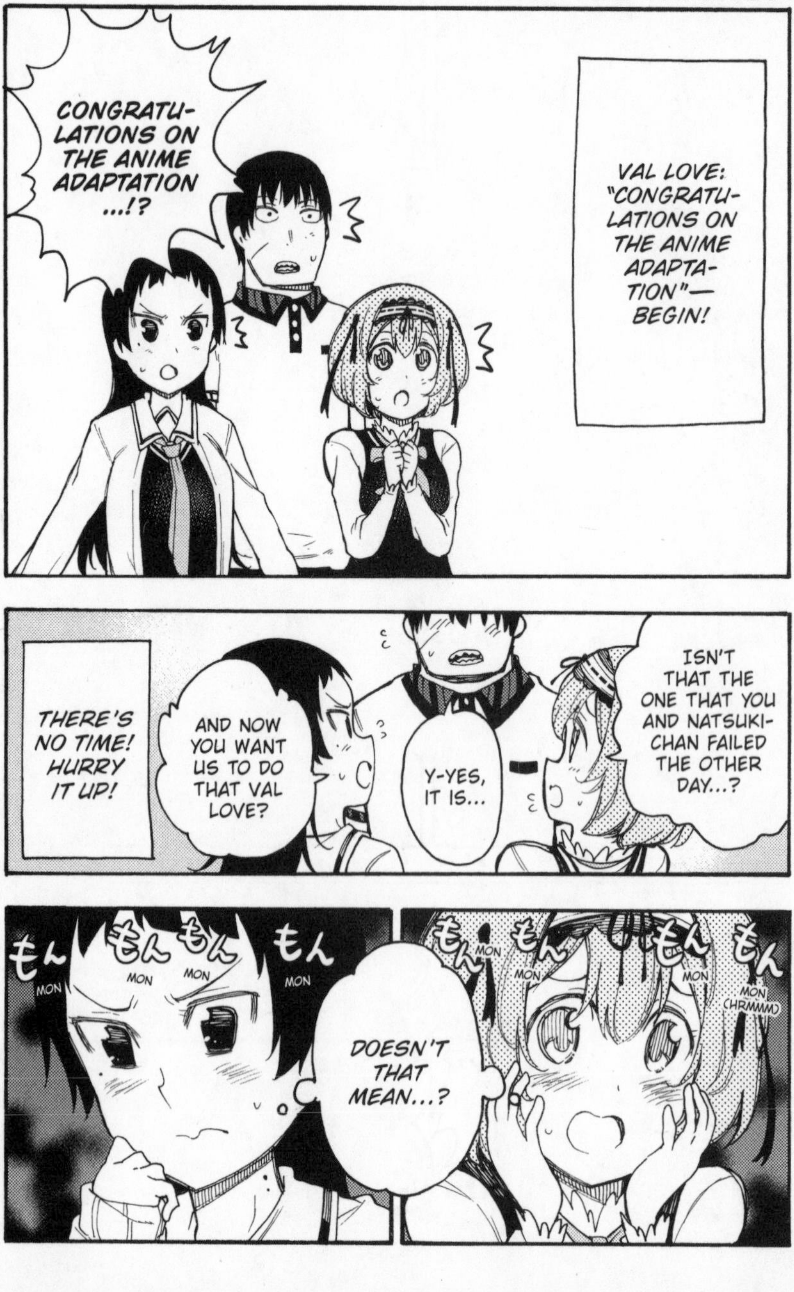

VAL LOVE: "CONGRATULATIONS ON THE ANIME ADAPTATION"—BEGIN!
CONGRATULATIONS ON THE ANIME ADAPTATION ...!?
ISN'T THAT THE ONE THAT YOU AND NATSUKI-CHAN FAILED THE OTHER DAY...?
Y-YES, IT IS...
AND NOW YOU WANT US TO DO THAT VAL LOVE?
THERE'S NO TIME! HURRY IT UP!
もん もん もん もん
MON MON MON MON (HRMMM)
もん もん もん もん
MON MON MON MON
DOESN'T THAT MEAN...?

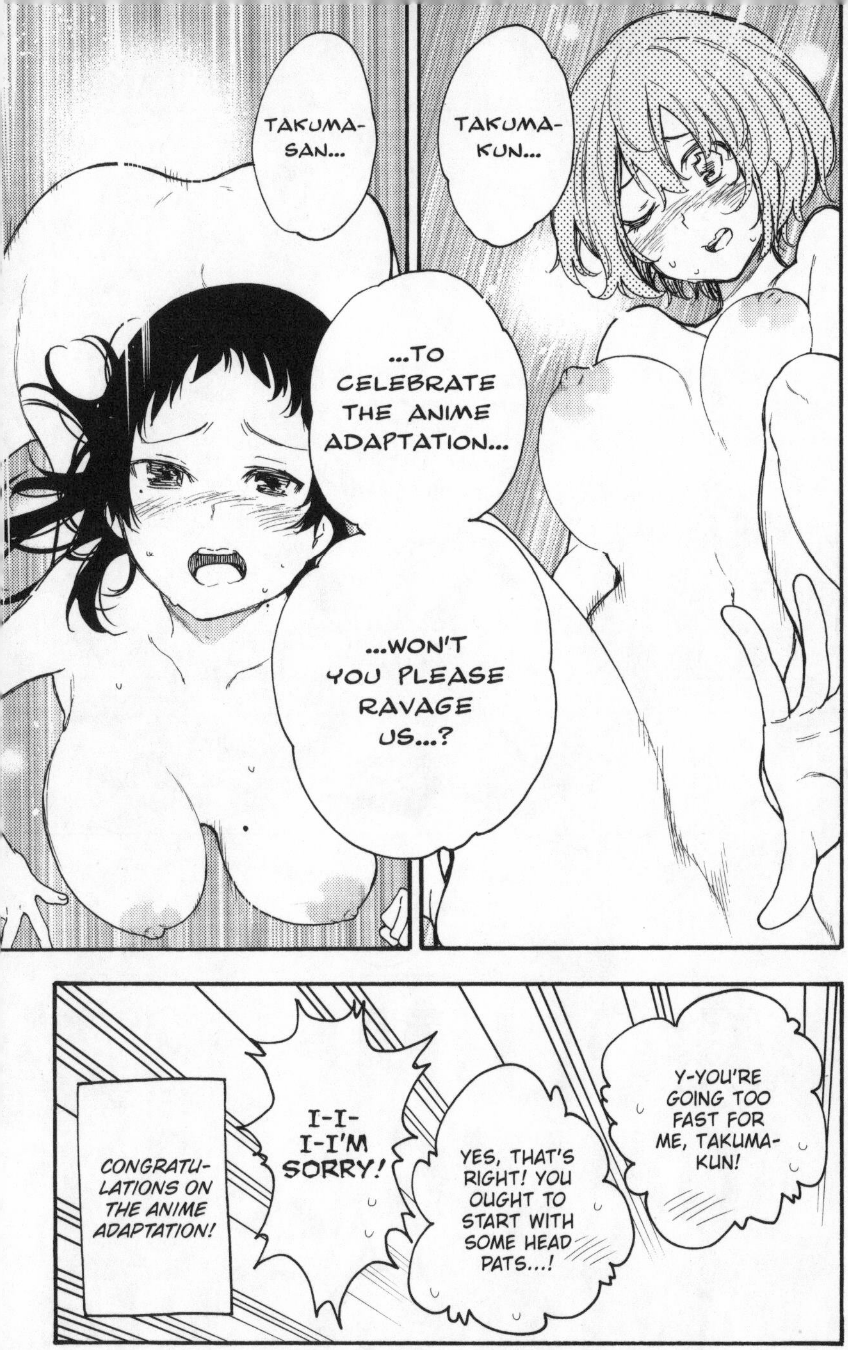
TAKUMA-KUN...
TAKUMA-SAN...
...TO CELEBRATE THE ANIME ADAPTATION...
...WON'T YOU PLEASE RAVAGE US...?
Y-YOU'RE GOING TOO FAST FOR ME, TAKUMA-KUN!
YES, THAT'S RIGHT! YOU OUGHT TO START WITH SOME HEAD PATS...!
I-I-I-I'M SORRY!
CONGRATULATIONS ON THE ANIME ADAPTATION!

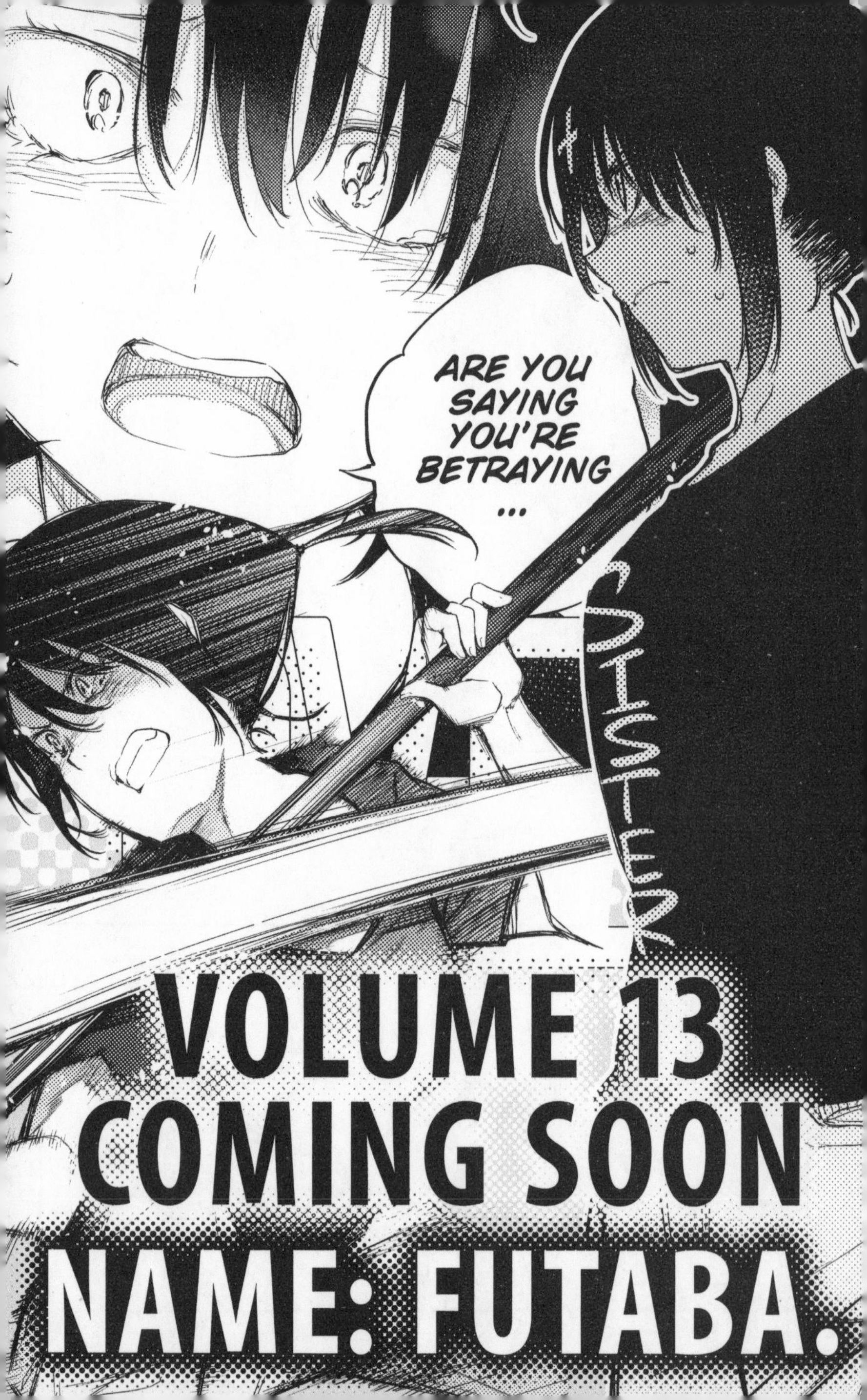
ARE YOU SAYING YOU'RE BETRAYING ...
SISTER
VOLUME 13 COMING SOON
NAME: FUTABA.